THE BIBLE ENCYCLOPEDIA

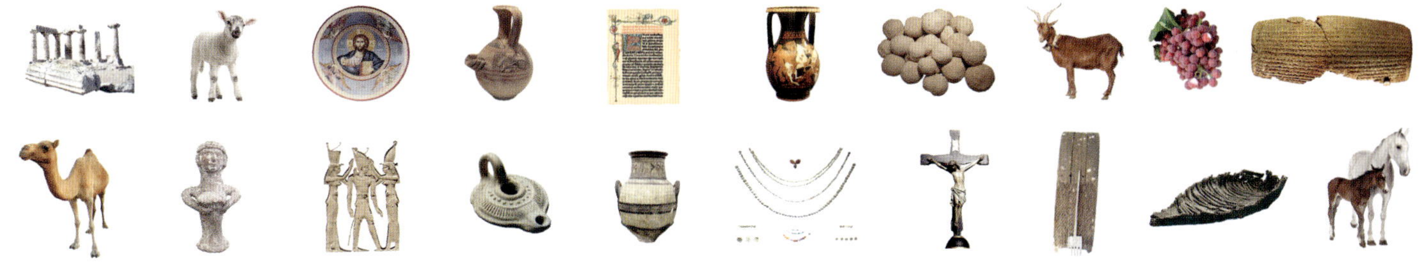

THE BIBLE ENCYCLOPEDIA

MIKE BEAUMONT

LION

SECOND EDITION

First published in Great Britain in 2012 as *The Lion Bible Encyclopedia*
Lion Books
Part of the SPCK Group, Studio 101, The Record Hall, 16–16A Baldwin's Gardens, London EC1N 7RJ
spckpublishing.co.uk

Second edition published 2026

EU GPSR Authorised Representative
LOGOS EUROPE, 9 rue Nicolas Poussin, 17000, LA ROCHELLE, France
E-mail: contact@logoseurope.eu

British Library Cataloguing-in-Publication Data
A catalogue record for this book is available from the British Library

ISBN 978-1-91759-605-3

10 9 8 7 6 5 4 3 2 1

First printed in China by Dream Colour (Hong Kong) Printing Ltd

Produced on paper from sustainable sources

Contents

Introduction 10

Part 1: The Making of the Bible

The Library Book
Many Books, One Story 12

The Old Testament
The Story Begins 14

The Deuterocanonical Books
The Apocrypha 16

The New Testament
The Story Continues 18

The Bible and History
Can We Trust the Bible? 20

Part 2: The Story of the Bible

Beginnings
Looking into the Mists of Time 22

Patriarchs
A Family Begins 24

Exodus
The Great Escape 26

Promised Land
Home at Last 28

Israel's First Kings
Right Request, Wrong Reason 30

A Kingdom Divided
The Results of Folly 32

Assyria and Israel's End
Judgment Day 34

Babylon and Judah's End
The Impossible Happens 36

Exile and Return
Making Sense of Disaster 38

Between the Two Testaments
The Silent Years 40

The Life of Jesus
The Promised Messiah 42

The Birth of the Church
Fired Up for Mission 44

The Growth of the Church
To the Ends of the Earth 46

Part 3: The Land of the Bible

The Ancient Near East
The Setting of the Bible's Story 48

The Land of Canaan
A Land Flowing with Milk and Honey 50

The Holy Land
A Home for God's People 52

Plants, Flowers and Spices
Not Even Solomon… 54

Trees and Shrubs
Pleasing to the Eye, Good for Food 56

Domestic and Working Animals
Gifts of God 58

Wildlife
"God Made the Wild Animals" 60

Part 4: The Nations of the Bible

Mesopotamia
Land of the Rivers 62

The Egyptians
The Power of a River 64

The Hittites
People of the North 66

The Canaanites
A Snare to Israel 68

The Philistines
The Sea People 70

The Assyrians
The Rod of God's Anger 72

The Babylonians
The Pride Before the Fall 74

The Persians
Agents of God 76

The Greeks
A Challenge and a Gift 78

The Romans
From City to Empire 80

Other People Groups
"The Nations" 82

Part 5: Life in the Bible

(A) Family Life

The Family
The Gift of the Relational God 84

Marriage
Two Becoming One 86

Children
A Heritage from the LORD 88

Education
Knowledge and Wisdom 90

Homes
The Heart of Jewish Life 92

Sanitation, Water, and Lighting
Holy Living 94

Daily Life
Give Us Today Our Daily Bread 96

Food and Drink
The Father's Provision 98

Clothing and Cosmetics
The Gift of God 100

(B) Social Life

Villages, Towns, and Cities
Community Life 102

Farming
Living from the Land 104

Fishing
Fishermen and Fishers of Men 106

Crafts and Skills
Gifts of the Creative God 108

Trade and Commerce
Buying and Selling 110

Travel
Journeys in Life 112

Money
Blessing or Snare? 114

Weights and Measures
The Importance of Honesty 116

Government and Justice
Acting Justly, Loving Mercy 118

Writing and Language
Tools of Communication 120

Leisure and Sport
Finding Refreshment 122

Health and Healing
Searching for Wholeness 124

Slavery
Serving Another 126

Warfare
Swords and Ploughshares 128

Part 6: Religion in the Bible

God
The One LORD 130

Covenant
God's Contract 132

The Law
God's Gift to Israel 134

Jewish Identity Markers
Externals and Internals 136

Jewish Festivals and Holy Days
Celebrating God's Goodness 138

Worship
Honouring God 140

Prayer
Talking to God 142

The Supernatural
The World Beyond 144

Places of Worship
The God Who Cannot be Contained 146

Sacrifices and Priests
Renewing Relationship 148

Prophecy and Prophets
Bringing God's Word 150

Groups and Sects
A Divided People 152

Jerusalem
The Holy City 154

Life's Big Questions
Finding God in Life's Challenges 156

The Christian Faith
Following Jesus 158

Death, Burial, and Beyond
Life's End 160

Part 7: The Focus of the Bible–Jesus

The Gospels
Four Accounts, One Story 162

His Coming
The God Who Breaks In 164

His Birth and Childhood
The Real Christmas Story 166

His Launch
The Work Begins 168

His Teaching
Words that Worked 170

His Parables
Mysteries of the Kingdom 172

His Miracles
Demonstrating the Kingdom 174

His Ethics and Lifestyle
Being Good, Doing Good 176

His New Community
Life Together with Jesus 178

His Conflicts
Encountering Opposition 180

His Final Week
Approaching the Goal 182

His Death and Resurrection
God's Ransom 184

His Commission and Ascension
Time to Leave 186

His Gift of the Spirit
God's Empowering Presence 188

His Message
Ongoing Truth 190

His Followers
God's New People 192

His Return
Hope for the Future 194

Index and Fast Fact Finder 196

Introduction

At the heart of the city where I spent most of my working life, Oxford, stands Carfax Tower, where the four main roads of this medieval city meet. The tower was once part of St Martin's Church, demolished in 1896 to ease congestion. While famous with tourists for its delightful figures that strike bells on the quarter-hour, few know its deeper significance. For it was here, in 1528, that Bibles were first burned in Britain. Thomas Garrett, a bookseller secretly peddling Tyndale's Bible, an early translation of the Bible into English, was caught by the authorities, who opposed the Bible in the vernacular. His Bibles were taken to Carfax and burned on the wood he was made to carry there.

This story sums up the Bible's history. Some have loved it, risking everything to share it with others; some have hated it, destroying it and those who love it. Clearly something about this book produces strong reactions. My own journey with it started with my grandfather. One of my earliest memories is of him sitting at the table with his big black Bible as the rest of us went to bed. While fascinated by this, I didn't understand what he was doing at the time, for it was only many years later that the Bible became special to me, too. I was eighteen years old when I first encountered the message of Jesus in any meaningful way. An invitation to a local church youth club led to my starting to attend church (though more for the girls than for God, it has to be confessed!), and gradually the Bible started to make sense. I became a follower of Jesus and have continued to be so ever since.

One of the things I am grateful for is that I always ended up around Christians who, like my grandfather, loved the Bible – youth leaders at the youth club, members of my university Christian Union, lecturers at seminary who could critique it yet were passionate about it – and it is from them that I "caught" something: that this book, properly understood, is the most exciting and helpful book in the world. Of course, some bits aren't easy to understand at first: its thematic rather than chronological arrangement doesn't make grasping its story straightforward; its setting in a worldview so different from ours can be challenging. But the more I dug into its background, the more it made sense of life. So this *Encyclopedia* is written in the hope that it may help the reader to make a bit more sense of the Bible for themselves too by setting the Bible's story in the context of its time and showing the flow of its story, as it steadily reveals what it claims to be God's plan for sorting out the mess the human race has got itself into.

While I have tried to use simple language wherever possible to help newcomers to the Bible, there is an inevitable need at times to use technical words, but these are explained in the Fast Fact Finder, which also serves as an index. I also provide Bible references to direct readers to the source documents (indispensable for people wanting to study anything seriously), where they can see both what was said and where and how it was said. The seven clear sections, along with the Index, will help you find your way around, and a "Faith idea" links each article with some aspect of the Christian faith today.

It is my hope that, just as the Bible moved for me many years ago from being a distant book that others loved to one I loved myself, this *Encyclopedia* might help the reader make a similar journey in some way. I have not assumed all readers will share my Christian faith; but I have assumed you're interested in knowing more about Christianity and its textbook or you wouldn't be reading this book. For both newcomers and old hands, I trust that it will help the Bible to come alive for you in new ways as it still continues to do for me.

Mike Beaumont
Teesside, UK

The Library Book

Many Books, One Story

Something that often surprises newcomers to the Bible is that it isn't *a* book but *a library of books* – written by many authors over a period of around 2,000 years. In the light of that, what is surprising about it is the consistency of its message. For through all its books comes *one* story, Christians believe: God's love for people and his commitment to fixing them and their world.

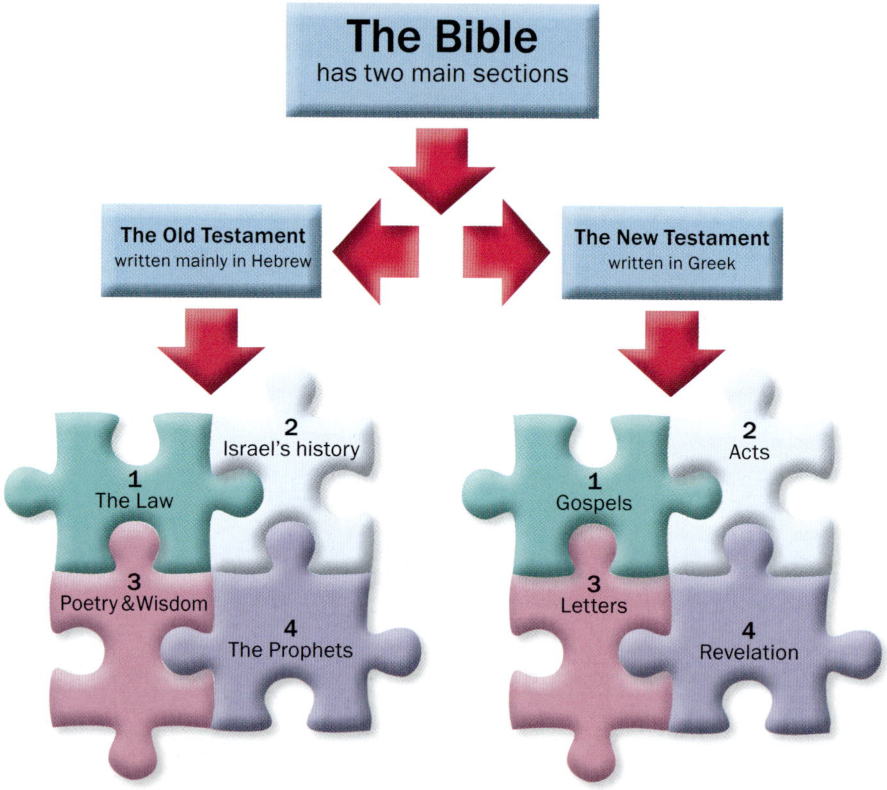

What is the Bible?

The Bible is divided into two unequal halves: the longer **Old Testament**, describing the history of the Jewish nation, and the shorter **New Testament**, telling of Jesus and the church he gave birth to. Yet both halves are part of the *same* story, Christians believe. The diagram above shows how the various parts of that story fit together.

The Bible as literature

The Bible's books cannot all be read in the same way. While Christians believe it is God's inspired word, they also recognize it has a human aspect, reflected in the *style* of the writers (for God didn't obliterate their character and personality) and in the *genre* (literary category) they used. So we find history, laws, poetry, wisdom, parables, prophecy, letters – just like in any library; but instead of being on different shelves, they're all in the one book. Just as we wouldn't read a poetry book as if it were history, nor should we do that when reading the Bible. If we do, we'll read into the text what was never meant to be there.

The Bible as history

The Bible is not a series of ad-hoc philosophical principles or religious sayings but *a story revealed through history*. This means we cannot read it "flat", picking random passages to suit our purpose. Get the flow of the history, and you get the sense of the message.

The Bible as truth

For Christians, the Bible is much more than literature or history, however: it is God's word, God's truth, his own revelation of his character and purposes, reinforced by Jesus, who said, "Your Word is truth" (John 17:17). While the idea of universal "truth" seems quaint to many nowadays, the Bible claims to both *bring* and *be* God's truth and invites us to test it for ourselves.

Bible

The word "Bible" comes from the Greek and Latin word *biblia* ("books"), which in turn comes from Byblos, the Phoenician city where parchment for scrolls was manufactured and exported.

The canon

The Jewish list of thirty-nine Old Testament books was finalized some time after Jerusalem's destruction (AD 70), using the tests of *antiquity* (did it agree with the Torah, the most authoritative and foundational of books?) and *authenticity* (did it have prophetic associations?), and this list or "canon" ("measuring rod" in Greek) was adopted by the early

See also
The Deuterocanonical Books pp. 16–17
The Old Testament pp. 14–15
The New Testament pp. 18–19

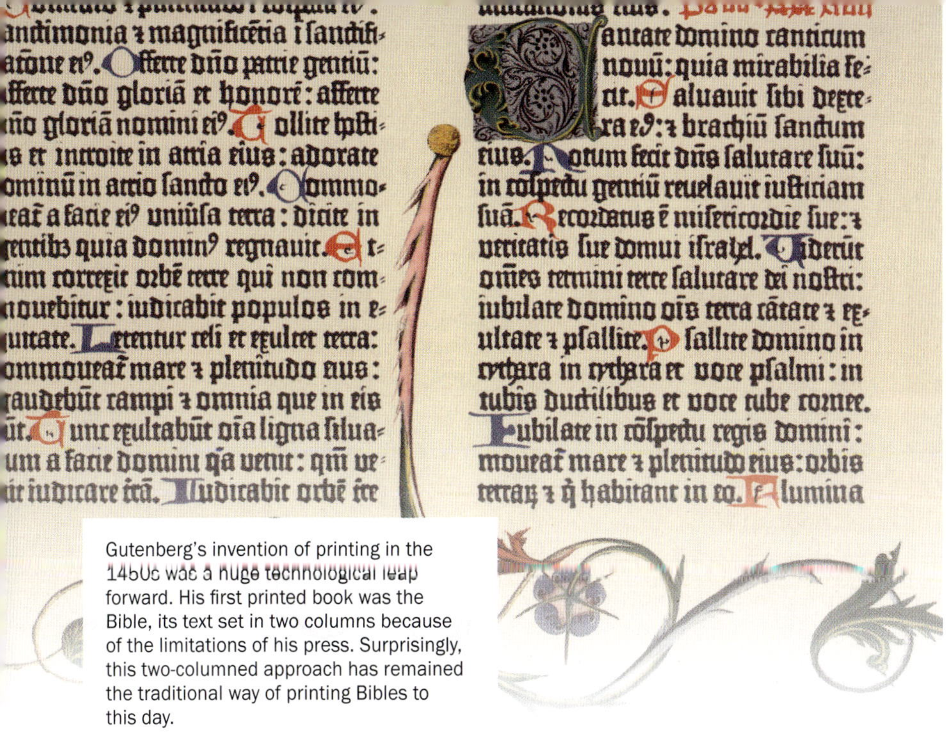

Gutenberg's invention of printing in the 1450s was a huge technological leap forward. His first printed book was the Bible, its text set in two columns because of the limitations of his press. Surprisingly, this two-columned approach has remained the traditional way of printing Bibles to this day.

church. The New Testament's twenty-seven books were determined along similar guidelines: *apostolicity* (was it written by or associated with an apostle?), *orthodoxy* (was it in line with the church's understanding of Jesus?), and *catholicity* (was it aimed at the church at large?). In addition some other inter-testamental Jewish writings slowly came to be accepted by some parts of the church. These "Deuterocanonical" books are interspersed with the main text in Roman Catholic and Eastern Orthodox Bibles but are either omitted or inserted between the Old and New Testaments in Protestant Bibles.

Bible languages

By the middle of the second decade of the twenty-first century, 3,756 languages had at least part of the Bible. Of these, 756 had a complete Bible, 1,726 had the New Testament, and 1,274 at least a portion. This still leaves around 3,640 living languages that do not even have one book of the Bible, but AI (artificial intelligence) is helping translators to rapidly speed up their work.

Chapters and verses

To help us find our way around, Bible books are divided into chapters and verses, like this:

Name of the book (preceded by 1 or 2 if the book has two halves or if two letters went to the same church)

Chapter
Verse
John 3:16

These chapters and verses weren't in the original Hebrew and Greek texts but were added later – the chapters in 1205 by Stephen Langton, Archbishop of Canterbury, and the verses in 1551 by Robert Estienne, a Parisian printer and scholar. While chapters and verses are useful for finding our way around, they can also be a hindrance, as they sometimes hinder the flow of an argument. So when reading the Bible, it's important to remember that they weren't there in the original.

Why is the Bible important?

Jews became known as "the people of the book". But why was that book so important to them? Because when God made his covenant with them at Sinai, he gave them a gift, his word – initially, the Ten Commandments (Exodus 20:1–17) and the "Book of the Covenant" (20:22 – 23:19). They therefore left Sinai as his newly constituted people with two things: *God's presence* (symbolized by cloud and fire) and *God's word* (showing them how to live). The first Christians experienced a similar thing, as the risen Jesus gave them the same two gifts: *God's presence* through the Holy Spirit (John 20:21–22) and *God's word*, initially taking them to the Old Testament Scriptures, showing how they pointed to him (Luke 24:25–27), and later guiding them to write the New Testament.

For Christians *God's presence* and *God's word* remain central to how God works, speaks, and guides, which is why the Bible is so central to their faith.

Faith idea: God's word

For Christians, the Bible is God's word, his revelation to us, rather than our attempt to search for him. As such, it is seen as inspired and authoritative, the only true guide for life, with the same Holy Spirit who caused it to be written helping people today to understand it, just as Jesus promised (John 16:13).

The Bible's books were originally handwritten on scrolls of parchment, papyrus, or leather. But scrolls were awkward and by the second century AD were being replaced by the "codex", an early form of book with folded and stitched pages. This one is the Aleppo Codex.

The Old Testament

The Story Begins

After its opening eleven chapters covering the origins of everything (creation, life, civilization, sin) the Old Testament moves on to tell the story of the beginnings of Israel, through whom God would redeem not just that nation, but the whole world. But this part of the Bible is important not just to Jews, but also to Christians, for it forms the background to why Jesus came.

The Torah

"The Torah was revealed from heaven. This implies our belief that the whole of the Torah found in our hands this day is the Torah that was handed down by Moses, and that it is all of divine origin."
(Maimonides, twelfth-century Jewish scholar)

Content

While the Jewish and Christian Scriptures are essentially the same, they are categorized differently.

Christian categorization:

- **The Law:** Genesis–Deuteronomy (often called "The Pentateuch")
- **History:** Joshua–Esther
- **Poetry and Wisdom:** Job–Song of Songs
- **The Prophets:** Isaiah–Malachi

Jewish categorization:

- **Torah** ("Teaching, Guidance"): Genesis, Exodus, Leviticus, Numbers, Deuteronomy
- **Nevi'im** ("Prophets"): "Former Prophets" (Joshua, Judges, 1 & 2 Samuel, 1 & 2 Kings) and "Latter Prophets" (Isaiah, Jeremiah, Ezekiel, and "the twelve" or "Minor Prophets")
- **Ketuv'im** ("Writings"): Psalms, Proverbs, Job, Song of Songs, Ruth, Lamentations, Ecclesiastes, Esther, Daniel, Ezra, Nehemiah, 1 & 2 Chronicles

Jews do not use the term "Old Testament" because to them their "testament" ("covenant") is not "old" but still valid. Instead, taking the first letters of the three sections of Scripture (T-N-K), they use the word "Tanak" for their Scriptures.

Jews give priority to the Torah over other parts of Scripture because it is seen as direct revelation from God, whereas other books were given "indirectly". Some even think the Torah existed eternally in heaven before God gave it; others see it simply as a collection of traditions over a long period.

Compilation

The Old Testament's books cover Israel's history from around 2150 BC to 440 BC, or right up to New Testament times if one includes the Deuterocanonicals. There is also a prologue of "pre-history" going back into the mists of time. But while written over a long period, these books were collected together at key stages in Israel's history.

The writings of Moses (the first five books) were passed on to Joshua, becoming known as "The Book of the Law [of Moses]" (Joshua 1:8; 8:30), the foundation of God's word. In the days of the early monarchy, when Israel was reflecting back on its journey and God's faithfulness to his promises, their early history (Joshua–Samuel) was probably added, based on earlier source materials.

In 586 BC, having failed to learn the lessons of its northern neighbour, Israel, which had been destroyed by Assyria in 722 BC, Judah fell to the new rising superpower, Babylon, to where it was exiled. Here they questioned what had caused their expulsion from the Promised Land

A Jewish scribe. Great care has always been taken to ensure accuracy and strict rules are followed, such as counting the number of words and letters on each page and forbidding copying from memory. If the copyist made a mistake, the whole sheet of parchment was destroyed; if he made three mistakes on a page, the entire manuscript was destroyed and he had to start again – incentive enough to ensure you copied accurately.

See also
The Deuterocanonical Books pp. 16–17
Ezra p. 39
The Library Book pp. 12–13

The Leningrad Codex

The Leningrad Codex (AD 1008), the oldest complete Hebrew Bible in existence and one of the best examples of "the Masoretic Text". Working in the seventh to eleventh centuries AD, the Masoretes ("Transmitters") sought to preserve the pronunciation of the ancient Hebrew text that had no vowels and was no longer a spoken language. They developed a system of "vowel points", little marks written above and below the consonants to aid reading. They were careful copyists, adding notes in the margins to highlight unusual words so that later copyists did not think an error had been made. The Masoretic Text remains the authoritative Hebrew text of the Jewish Bible.

A Jewish boy at his "Bar Mitzvah" ("Son of the Commandment") ceremony when, now aged thirteen, he is deemed to be an adult and is allowed to read from the Tanak publicly for the first time. A silver pointer is used to follow the ancient Hebrew script, which is written from right to left.

and, as they surveyed their history, they came to a simple conclusion: disobedience to God and his word. And so it was at this time that the next stage of their history (Samuel–Kings) was written up from earlier source documents (e.g. 1 Kings 11:41; 14:19, 29), seeking to highlight this understanding.

As Babylon's power gave way to Persia's, its very different policies allowed Judah to return home. It was at this time, according to Jewish tradition, that Ezra arranged and collected all the books of the Hebrew Bible as we have them today.

Translation

After the exile, many Jews lost their ability to speak Hebrew, the language of the Tanak (apart from some small sections which are written in Aramaic). By Roman times, there were more Jews in Alexandria, Egypt, than in Jerusalem, which prompted scholars there to translate the Scriptures into Greek, the world language of the day. Their translation became known as **the Septuagint**, named after the seventy scholars who reputedly worked on it, and this became the main Bible of most Jews by New Testament times.

It was the Septuagint (sometimes referred to by the Roman numerals LXX) that gave the Old Testament books the order they have today and that included other writings ("Deuterocanonical writings") that weren't among the original thirty-nine books. While most Protestant Bibles, which are based on the original Hebrew text rather than the Septuagint, do not contain these additional books, they are accepted by the Roman Catholic and Eastern Orthodox churches and are interspersed within the Old Testament text.

Further translations followed – into Latin (**the Vulgate**, translated by St Jerome), Syriac (**the Peshitta**), and Egyptian (**Coptic**). These ancient translations, carefully undertaken, can often help scholars interpret the Bible's Hebrew text in their translation work today.

Faith idea: Promise

The Old Testament's story is built around God's promise to Abraham to give him a family through which every nation would be blessed (Genesis 12:2–3). This theme recurs constantly, as God's faithfulness to his promise is highlighted by the Old Testament writers again and again. It is also foundational to the New Testament, where Jesus is seen as the fulfiller of that promise and every other promise that flows from it.

The Deuterocanonical Books

The Apocrypha

As well as the thirty-nine Old Testament books and twenty-seven New Testament books accepted by all Christians, some parts of the church accept other books as part of their Bible, called the Deuterocanonical Books or Apocrypha.

History

The Deuterocanonicals are Jewish texts written between 300 BC and the late first century AD. While never seen as Scripture by the Jews, they were nevertheless esteemed highly by them and were included in the Septuagint, the Greek translation of the Hebrew Scriptures. Since most early Christians were Gentiles who spoke Greek, the Septuagint inevitably became their "Bible", which is how the Deuterocanonicals came into the church.

With the Temple's destruction (AD 70) and Christianity's rapid growth threatening Judaism's survival, the Jews closed their "canon" of Scripture, rejecting the Septuagint's additional books, thus declaring, "The Christian Bible is false." However, Christian acceptance of these books continued to be widespread, though not universal.

In the fourth century AD Jerome was commissioned to produce a definitive Latin translation of the Bible, which became known as the Vulgate. Convinced only the Hebrew text was authoritative, Jerome excluded the Deuterocanonicals; but his view did not prevail, and the Western Catholic Church soon added them (in Latin), recognizing this expanded collection as canonical Scripture.

In the sixteenth century the Protestant reformers, eager to return to the Bible's original Hebrew text, again excluded them – though Luther included them in his German translation, but in a separate section after the Old Testament. The Roman Catholic Church reaffirmed them as Scripture at the Council of Trent (1546), and soon afterwards they were named "Deuterocanonicals", from the Greek *deuteros*, meaning second – though second in time rather than importance.

The Eastern Orthodox Church has always seen the Deuterocanonicals as part of Scripture. However, most Protestants reject them as Scripture, while increasingly seeing their value for insights into Jewish beliefs in the inter-testamental period.

Apocrypha

This title was given to the Deuterocanonicals by Jerome. Greek for "hidden", it is unclear why he chose this word, as there was nothing hidden about these books.

Books accepted by the Roman Catholic and Eastern Orthodox Church	Additional books accepted by the Eastern Orthodox Church
Tobit	1 Esdras
Judith	The Prayer of Manasseh
Additions to Esther	Psalm 151
Wisdom of Solomon	3 Maccabees
Ecclesiasticus (or The Wisdom of Jesus ben Sira)	4 Maccabees
Baruch	
The Letter of Jeremiah	**In the Vulgate appendix**
Additions to Daniel	2 Esdras
1 Maccabees	
2 Maccabees	
The Protestant Old Testament excludes all these books.	

Content

Tobit (c. 200–180 BC)
Tobit, a pious Jew exiled in Assyria, having become blind and impoverished, sends his son Tobias to recover a debt. Tobias encounters an angel who leads him to a relative, Sarah, who has been tormented by demons. A miraculous fish enables Tobias to overcome the demons, freeing her to marry him and to heal his father's blindness, showing the righteous are ultimately rewarded.

Judith (c.150–100 BC)
A pious widow uses her feminine charms to save her town from Assyrian attack by killing their general and then exhorting the men to crush the enemy. Despite confused historical references, its purpose was to strengthen faith in God.

Additions to Esther (second century BC)
Six passages added to give a more religious tone to a book renowned for not mentioning God, showing that piety lay behind the Jews' deliverance.

Wisdom of Solomon (c.100–50 BC)
Presented as Solomon's own testimony, this poem seeks to stir a love for wisdom as it reflects on wisdom and man's destiny, the origin and nature of wisdom, and wisdom in Israel's history.

See also
Between the Two Testaments pp. 40–41
The Canon p. 12
The Septuagint p. 15

Illuminated manuscript of 1 Maccabees 1 from the Gutenberg (or 42 line) Bible.

Additions to Daniel (second century BC)
Three passages added to Daniel: (1) *The Prayer of Azariah and the Song of the Three Jews*, recording prayers of the three men thrown into the fiery furnace; (2) *Susanna*, who is spared from false charges of adultery through Daniel's wisdom; (3) *Bel and the Dragon*, in which Daniel exposes the falseness of two Babylonian gods.

1 & 2 Maccabees (c. 100 BC)
Record of the second-century BC Jewish revolt against Antiochus IV Epiphanes, who wanted to destroy Judaism, showing how faithful Jews fought to preserve their faith. The same events are recalled in 2 Maccabees, but from a theological perspective.

Ecclesiasticus (Hebrew c. 175 BC; Greek c. 130 BC)
Originally called The Wisdom of Jesus ben Sira but renamed Ecclesiasticus in the Vulgate, these wise sayings are undergirded by respect for the Jewish Law and veneration of Israel's great heroes.

Baruch (c. mid-second century BC)
Purportedly written in exile by Baruch, Jeremiah's scribe, this work calls Israel back to faithfulness to God in the hope of restoration. It spoke to the needs of second-century BC Jews, who by now felt permanently exiled.

Letter of Jeremiah (third century BC)
Written as a letter from Jeremiah to the Jews in exile in Babylon, it urges them not to worship idols, which are ridiculed. It is sometimes printed as chapter 6 of Baruch.

1 Esdras (c. 150–100 BC)
A compilation of events from passages in 2 Chronicles, Ezra, and Nehemiah recounting Judah's history from Josiah to Ezra, it claims Zerubbabel's wise answer in a debate led to his being sent to Jerusalem to rebuild it.

Prayer of Manasseh (first century BC)
Purportedly the prayer of the repentant King Manasseh when he was briefly exiled to Babylon.

Psalm 151 (date uncertain)
A psalm attributed to David, reflecting on God's call and his victory over Goliath.

3 Maccabees (first century BC)
Linked with 1 & 2 Maccabees only by its theme of resisting Gentile rulers who impose Greek traditions, this book recalls God's deliverance of Jews living in late third-century BC Egypt through prayer and obedience, themes crucial to the author's first-century BC readers.

4 Maccabees (date uncertain)
Philosophical discussion on the power of pious reason over passions and suffering.

2 Esdras (late first century AD)
Written as Ezra's reflections on the Temple's destruction (586 BC) and the theological problems this provoked, its true audience was Jews troubled by its destruction by Rome in AD 70.

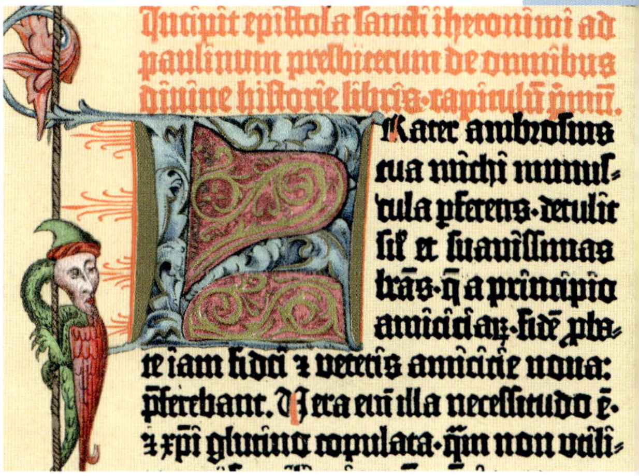

Part of the preface to Luke's Gospel in the Gutenberg Bible, which references other books not included in the Canon but which it says are still valuable to read.

Faith idea: Encouragement

The Deuterocanonicals contain many encouraging stories, some overtly fictional, some historical, as well as much helpful wisdom, to help God's people keep going in difficult times. The Bible speaks highly of the value of encouragement, frequently urging believers to receive God's encouragement and also to encourage one another.

The New Testament

The Story Continues

Like the Old Testament, the New Testament is a collection of books, twenty-seven in all, telling the story of Jesus, his new "covenant" or "testament" (Luke 22:20), and his first followers. It is important to remember that the New Testament isn't a separate story from the Old Testament but rather, from its authors' viewpoint, the continuation and fulfilment of it. In fact, many things in the New Testament cannot be fully understood apart from the Old Testament.

This icon depicts Athanasius, Bishop of Alexandria, who wrote a letter in AD 367 containing the present list of twenty-seven New Testament books, declaring they alone were accepted by the church, thus clarifying the canon (accepted list) of New Testament books.

The first Christians' Bible

Since Christianity had its roots in Judaism, the Christians' first Bible was the Hebrew Scriptures, but particularly its Greek translation, the Septuagint. Jesus held these Scriptures in high esteem and, while ruthlessly challenging current interpretations of them, never undermined them, but rather said he had come to fulfil them (Matthew 5:17–18). That fulfilment, his followers saw, came about through his death and resurrection. Suddenly they understood that the Old Testament's rituals, sacrifices, and stories were preparations and "shadows" (Hebrews 10:1) of what Jesus had come to do. So this only increased their love of what became known by Christians as "the Old Testament".

It seems unlikely, therefore, that when the apostles wrote their Gospels and letters they thought they were writing Scripture. Yet slowly, the truth dawned on them. Hence, Peter wrote of Paul's letters that they "contain some things that are hard to understand, which ignorant and unstable people distort, *as they do the other Scriptures*" (2 Peter 3:16), suggesting that Peter was starting to see there was something "Scripture-like" in what Paul was writing. The penny was beginning to drop. The New Testament was taking shape.

Content

The New Testament has four main types of writing:

- **Gospels** (Matthew, Mark, Luke, John): Accounts of the life, teaching, death, and resurrection of Jesus.
- **Acts**: The story of the first Christians, revealing struggles as well as successes.
- **Letters** (Romans, 1 & 2 Corinthians, Galatians, Ephesians, Philippians, Colossians, 1 & 2 Thessalonians, 1 & 2 Timothy, Titus, Philemon, Hebrews, James, 1 & 2 Peter, 1, 2, & 3 John, Jude): Written to churches and leaders, explaining the faith, applying it to life, and addressing problems. Paul wrote thirteen of these twenty-one letters.

See also
The Canon p. 12
The Gospels pp. 162–63
The Septuagint p. 15

- **Revelation**: A glimpse behind the scenes to reassure persecuted Christians and to help them to see life from God's perspective.

The creation of the New Testament

The message of Jesus was originally passed on orally – not as difficult or dubious as that might sound, for not only was memorization a key way of learning, it was also the main way of transmitting information in those days. Moreover, Jesus' style and structure made it easy for people to remember his teaching – read, for example, the Beatitudes (Matthew 5:3–11).

Eventually, these sayings and stories were written down, perhaps to help with teaching, and were used by the Gospel writers. Luke, for example, knew that "many have undertaken to draw up an account of the things that have been fulfilled among us" (Luke 1:1) and said that his account (since he was not an eyewitness) was based on having "carefully investigated everything from the beginning" (Luke 1:3).

However, prior to the writing of the Gospels, and within just twenty years of the resurrection, church leaders had already been writing letters to churches to explain the Christian faith and apply it to the varied situations in which the recipients found themselves. While these letters initially had localized objectives, their usefulness for the whole church was quickly grasped, and collections of letters were being circulated by the end of the first century AD.

By the beginning of the second century AD, almost all our present New Testament books were widely used and highly valued. Some (Hebrews, Revelation, 2 Peter, 2 & 3 John) took longer to be accepted. But increasingly all were accepted as "Scripture", on a par with the Old Testament. So when the Council of Carthage published its list of twenty-seven New Testament books in AD 397, it was simply confirming what had become obvious.

Excluded writings

The fact that the early church was serious about which books went into the canon is reflected in those that were left out. For example, The Didache (Greek for "teaching"), written at the turn of the first century, was quoted by many early writers and was much loved. It gave guidance on life in the Christian community, teaching on baptism, the Eucharist, fasting, and the Lord's Prayer, with many similarities to Matthew's Gospel. Yet while loving it, the church excluded it from the canon of Scripture. Another was The First Letter of Clement, written at the end of the first century AD and read in churches just like Paul's letters. But again, the church felt it did not meet the requirements of the canon.

The Gospel of Thomas, dating from the middle of the second century AD, was a mixture of ad-hoc sayings of Jesus (some of which may have been genuine) and later Gnostic ideas. But some of its teachings, such as women only being able to enter God's kingdom by becoming men, were so far removed from the picture of Jesus in the four Gospels that it was quickly rejected and eventually disappeared, only to be rediscovered at the end of the nineteenth century.

It is this sort of selectivity that shows that the early church gave much thought to determining which books should and should not be included in the canon.

The fourth-century Codex Sinaiticus, the earliest complete copy of the New Testament. The text is in *koinē* ("common") Greek, a simplified version of Greek that was used across the eastern Mediterranean. Written over 1,600 years ago, it contains the complete New Testament and is the oldest complete early copy in existence.

Faith idea: Fulfilment

Christians believe the Bible shows that God never leaves things half-done. If he starts something, he finishes it; if he promises something, he fulfils it. The New Testament shows the fulfilment of God's promises in the Old Testament through the coming of his Son, Jesus, who brought into reality the promises made to Abraham in a way no one could ever have imagined.

The Bible and History

Can We Trust the Bible?

An accusation that Christians often face is that the Bible cannot be trusted; that, at best, it is unreliable history, at worst, old fables of no relevance for today. So, can the Bible be trusted? For those open to examining the evidence, Christians believe the answer is a resounding "yes".

Historical reliability

Because Christianity is rooted in history, we can check it against external evidence that continually confirms the Bible's story, as this chart shows. Indeed, no archaeological discovery has so far disproved the Bible.

External evidence

- The Temple of Amun in Thebes lists cities of Judah and Israel attacked by Shishak in 926 BC, a campaign noted in 1 Kings 14:25–28.
- The Assyrian "Black Obelisk" records Shalmaneser III's triumph over Jehu, mentioned in the Bible.
- Tiglath-Pileser III's annals record his invasion of Israel, which the Bible describes (2 Kings 15:19–20) but using his alternative name, Pul.
- Assyrian inscriptions record Sennacherib's siege of Jerusalem in 701 BC, though not the embarrassing outcome recorded in 2 Kings 18:17 - 19:37.

Contemporary customs

Customs described in non-Israelite sources show that the Old Testament's portrayal of life is utterly realistic. For example:

- Countless documents show that patriarchal names match those of their period.
- A man's liberty to father a child by his wife's maid if his wife were barren is attested in the Babylonian Code of Hammurabi.
- Joseph was sold as a slave for 20 shekels, the right price according to contemporary trade tablets.
- Solomon's marriage to an Egyptian princess, impossible by Egyptian tradition two or three centuries earlier, was a real possibility when Egypt was much weaker.

Archaeological discoveries

- References to camels in Genesis, once thought anachronistic, have been confirmed by references to them in the third millennium BC in Turkmenistan and Afghanistan, and in Syria and Palestine at the beginning of the second millennium BC.
- Excavations at Shechem revealed a gate system containing the temple of Baal, destroyed by Abimelech (Judges 9:46–49).
- A relief in Sennacherib's palace shows the siege of Lachish (710 BC). The site was excavated in the 1930s, revealing evidence of this siege.
- David's capture of Jerusalem by climbing up the watershaft was once thought fanciful until the shaft was discovered.

Internal accuracy

Luke was a careful historian, as external evidence confirms:

- He uses precise titles correctly, such as tetrarch, proconsul, praetor, lector.
- He describes the rulers of Thessalonica as "politarchs", recently confirmed as accurate, even if unique.
- His claim that people returned home for censuses, once rejected, has been confirmed as accurate.
- His description of Lysanias as Tetrarch of Abilene, once rejected, was confirmed by the discovery of an inscription.
- One prominent archaeologist, having examined Luke's references to thirty-two countries, fifty-four cities, and nine islands, found he never made a single mistake in any of his details.

Below: A relief from Sennacherib's palace in Nineveh showing his siege of Lachish, referred to in 2 Kings 18.

See also
Archaeology pp. 48–49
Qumran pp. 152–53
Scribes pp. 14–15

Evidence for Jesus

While most evidence for Jesus inevitably comes from the Gospels and earlier oral traditions recorded in some of the New Testament letters (e.g. 1 Corinthians 15:3–8), evidence from non-Christian sources at least confirms his existence.

Jewish sources:

- *Josephus* (c. AD 37–100), former Jewish governor of Galilee who became a Roman historian, mentions Jesus in two works, noting his teaching, miracles, crucifixion, and claims of resurrection.
- In the *Talmud* the rabbis hoped they "did not have a son or disciple who taught heresy like Jesus the Nazarene".
- *Sanhedrin* notes that "on the eve of Passover they hanged Jesus the Nazarene... [who] practised magic and led Israel astray".

Non-Jewish sources:

- *Mara ben Serapion*, Syrian philosopher, c. AD 73: "What advantage did the Jews gain from executing their wise king? It was just after that their kingdom was abolished... Nor did the wise king die for good; he lived on in the teaching which he had given."
- *Tacitus*, Roman historian, c. AD 110: "Christus, from whom the name Christian had its origin, suffered the extreme penalty during the reign of Tiberius at the hands of one of our procurators, Pontius Pilatus, and a most mischievous superstition, thus checked for the moment, again broke out not only in Judea, the first source of the evil, but even in Rome."

Such external evidence points, at the very least, to the existence of the historical Jesus.

This chart shows how there is far more, and far earlier, evidence for Jesus' life than for any other event of ancient history. The figures only cover New Testament manuscripts in Greek; add early copies in Syriac, Latin, Coptic, and Aramaic, and the number comes to around 24,000.

	Date of original document	Date of oldest surviving copy	Time gap	Number of ancient copies
Thucydides *History of the Peloponnesian War*	430–400 BC	AD 900	1,300 years	8
Caesar *Gallic Wars*	52–51 BC	AD 850	900 years	10
Tacitus *Histories*	AD 104–109	AD 800	700 years	2
Matthew, Mark, Luke, John *The Four Gospels*	AD 65–90	AD 350 (whole) AD 200 (much) AD 125 (fragment)	260–285 years 110–135 years 35 years	c. 2,350 (Gospels) c. 5,500 (New Testament)

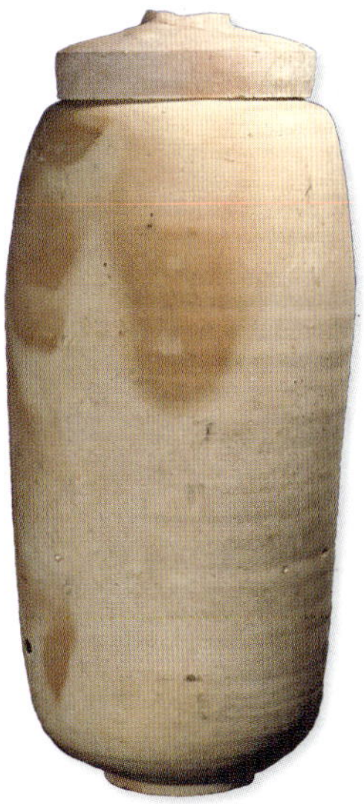

One of the jars discovered in 1947 at Qumran near the Dead Sea, containing the Dead Sea Scrolls. Some 800 manuscripts were found, containing parts of every Old Testament book except Esther. The discovery meant that scholars suddenly had texts of Scripture 1,000 years older than the oldest documents they currently had, which only dated from the seventh century AD; now they had manuscripts which dated from the third century BC. Careful comparison showed that, apart from spelling variants that were inevitable over such a long period, the earlier texts were almost identical to the more recent ones. In other words, the copyists had done their job well, proof that the Old Testament that we have today is as its authors first wrote it centuries ago.

Faith idea: Trust

While God invites people to trust him, this trust isn't "blind faith", Christians would say. It is built on human experience of him in the past (hence the Bible's frequent calls to remember what he has done) and on the testing of his reality and promises in the present ("Taste and see that the Lord is good", Psalm 34:8). God isn't afraid of people examining the evidence, Christians believe, because he knows it will hold up.

Beginnings

Looking into the Mists of Time

In the beginning, the Bible says, there was nothing – except God. Eternally existent, he alone created matter and shaped it into the cosmos. The concern of Genesis isn't *how*, but *why* he did it. This question, fundamental to human existence, self-knowledge, and development, is addressed in the Bible's first eleven chapters, revealing a worldview that guides the rest of the Bible's story.

The Cupola of Creation, St Mark's Basilica, Venice, dating from c. 1230 and depicting the creation of the world.

Creation

"In the beginning God created the heavens and the earth" (Genesis 1:1). With these majestic words, Genesis (meaning "origins" or "beginnings") unfolds the mystery of creation, giving us two parallel accounts, the first (1:1 – 2:3) focusing on the Creator and his creation, the second (2:4–25) on humanity as the crown of that creation. On the first three days (the Hebrew word for day, *yom*, was used both literally and metaphorically), God *forms* the earth (1:3–13); on the second three days, he *fills* it (1:14–30). Each day's work is "good"; but everything together is "very good" (1:31). Then, on day seven, God "rests" (2:2–3) – the word comes from the Hebrew for "sabbath", the Jewish rest day, thereby showing us the divine pattern for life: six days of work, followed by one day of rest.

Foundational teachings

Genesis 1 reveals foundational biblical teachings about life's three key players:

- **God** – eternal; unique; all-powerful; personal; relational.
- **Mankind** – in God's image; complete only as male and female; more than an animal; given work as God's gift.
- **Creation** – good not evil; designed not accidental; to be cared for by people on God's behalf.

Sin

If Genesis 1 and 2 explain the good in the world, Genesis 3 explains the bad. Free will (the ability to choose) was essential if humankind was to be in God's image. Sadly, on the first occasion Adam and Eve used it, they responded to the serpent's lies, rather than trusting God. Suddenly they felt exposed and afraid, and experienced the judgment God had warned them of. Expelled from the Garden of Eden, they were thrust into the world to fend for themselves. It is this loss of God's intimate presence through sin that Christians know as "the fall". Not until Revelation do we find again the tree of life they lost (Revelation 22:2).

Part of a seventh-century BC copy of *Enuma Elish.*

Human development

These chapters record how the human race steadily deteriorated as it repeated Adam and Eve's sin of ignoring God and pleasing self. Yet, humanity was still in God's image. That is why, in Genesis 6–9, we see humanity at its best – developing farming (4:2b; 9:20), family life (4:17–18), music (4:21), technology (4:22), construction (11:4) – and at its worst – Cain's murder of Abel (4:1–16), polygamy (4:19), revenge (4:23–24), and corruption and violence (6:5–12). Sadly, the worst side prevailed.

The Sumerian Kings List (late third millennium BC) records that kings before the flood lived extraordinarily long lives, just as Genesis 5 notes. While the numbers are probably symbolic (common in ancient literature), both reflect an understanding that there was a time when humans lived much longer, before sin had its full effect on them.

See also
Mesopotamia pp. 62–63
New Creation pp. 194–95
Sabbath p. 138

The flood

Human corruption became so extensive, the Bible records, that God decided to start again, sending a flood to destroy everyone and everything (Genesis 6:1–7) – everyone except the godly Noah and his family. Torrential rains fell and underground waters erupted for forty days, flooding the earth (perhaps the result of the end of an ice age). But God had told Noah to build an "ark" – a huge, three-decked floating box – into which he had gathered his family and pairs of all animal life (6:11 – 7:24), where they remained for 150 days until the waters receded and the ark grounded on Mount Ararat in modern Turkey. The new beginning was marked by God's "covenant" with Noah, sealed with the sign of the rainbow, that the seasons would henceforth be consistent (8:22) and the earth would never again be flooded in that way (9:1–17).

Ancient Mesopotamian stories

Many ancient Mesopotamian stories, from the early second millennium BC, parallel those in the early chapters of Genesis:

- ***Enuma Elish*** (see image on the left) recounts on seven stone tablets the story of creation in which the god Marduk kills the monster Tiamat, creating everything from her body.
- ***The Atraharsis Epic*** depicts creation and early human history, including the flood that occurred because the gods, who had created people to relieve them of work, got annoyed with their noise and so destroyed them.
- ***The Gilgamesh Epic*** recounts adventures of Gilgamesh, ruler of Uruk, including his meeting Utnapishtim, the flood's only survivor.

While there are obvious links between these stories and Genesis, which seem to reflect a common memory of primeval events, there are also huge contrasts: for example, Genesis has no battle between gods, simply one God who lovingly creates everything from nothing and makes mankind, not to serve him, but to know him; and God sends the flood, not out of irritation, but because his holiness could not bear the increasing wickedness of humanity any longer.

The Tower of Babel

The Tower of Babel in Shinar (southern Iraq) was almost certainly a ziggurat, like this one, with a square base, sloping stepped sides and a stairway leading to a shrine at the top – a stairway to heaven. However, God confused both the builders' plans and their language, scattering them across the world because of their pride. Unable to communicate, the project ground to a halt and the city was named "Babel" (later, Babylon), meaning "confusion".

The nations

"The Table of Nations" (Genesis 10) lists the development of nations from the writer's middle-eastern viewpoint. It is a map-in-words of the Old Testament world, listing its inhabitants as descendants of Noah's three sons: Shem, ancestor of the Semitic peoples of the Near East; Ham, ancestor of the Hamitic peoples of Africa; and Japheth, ancestor of the Indo-European peoples. Since seventy nations are listed (a multiple of seven, the number of perfection, and ten, the number of completeness), it was probably meant to symbolize absolute completion.

Faith idea: God

The Bible never deals with "proof" of God, though countless believers have sought to produce it over the centuries. It simply takes him for granted, assuring us of not just his existence but his fundamental goodness and kindness towards everyone, and encouraging us, if in doubt, to "taste and see that the Lord is good" (Psalm 34:8).

Patriarchs

A Family Begins

The story of God's people begins with Abraham, an unpromising candidate for founding a family, let alone a nation, since he was seventy-five and had a barren wife. But God called him to leave his homeland and "go to the land I will show you" (Genesis 12:1). It was in that land, Canaan, that God revealed his promises and plans as Abraham and his descendants became Israel's founding fathers, the patriarchs.

Names

Names were very important in biblical times, reflecting a person's history, character, or destiny. God changed the name of Abram ("exalted father") to Abraham ("father of many") to remind him of his promise. His son was named Isaac ("he laughs") to recall Sarah's laughter of disbelief at hearing the news she would become pregnant and it being turned into laughter of joy at his birth. His grandson Jacob was renamed Israel ("he struggles with God") after his wrestling match with a heavenly visitor to remind him that, while he had struggled all his life to prevail over others, he couldn't do this with God (Genesis 32:22–32; 35:9–10).

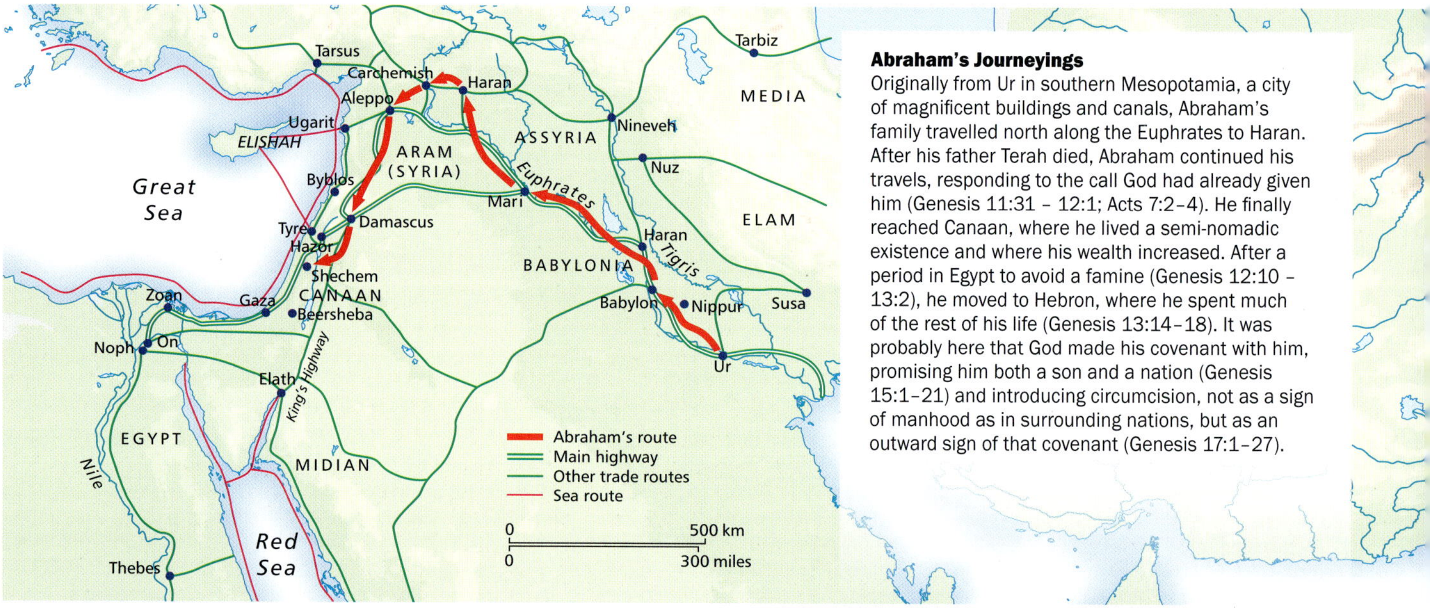

Abraham's Journeyings

Originally from Ur in southern Mesopotamia, a city of magnificent buildings and canals, Abraham's family travelled north along the Euphrates to Haran. After his father Terah died, Abraham continued his travels, responding to the call God had already given him (Genesis 11:31 - 12:1; Acts 7:2-4). He finally reached Canaan, where he lived a semi-nomadic existence and where his wealth increased. After a period in Egypt to avoid a famine (Genesis 12:10 - 13:2), he moved to Hebron, where he spent much of the rest of his life (Genesis 13:14-18). It was probably here that God made his covenant with him, promising him both a son and a nation (Genesis 15:1-21) and introducing circumcision, not as a sign of manhood as in surrounding nations, but as an outward sign of that covenant (Genesis 17:1-27).

Abraham

As a nomad, moving from place to place was nothing new for Abraham. What was new was doing so in faith in response to God. It was this faith that put him right with God (Genesis 15:6) and saw God's promises fulfilled, including the gift of a son to him and his wife Sarah (Genesis 21:1–7) – though that promise was strongly tested (Genesis 22:1–19).

But God's purposes for Abraham went far further than him. God also promised:

- His descendants would become a great nation (Genesis 12:1–3; 15:5).
- Every nation would be blessed through him (Genesis 12:3; 18:16–19).
- The land where he was living would one day belong to his descendants forever (Genesis 15:12–21).

Sodom and Gomorrah

Pressure on pasturelands from their growing herds and flocks led Abraham and his nephew, Lot, to separate. Lot chose to settle in the city of Sodom, south of the Dead Sea, which was fertile but also immoral and unstable (Genesis 13:1–13). Abraham rescued him from God's judgment on Sodom and nearby Gomorrah as burning sulphur, probably from erupting bitumen pits, rained down on them (Genesis 18:16 – 19:29).

Before Abraham met the living God, he would have worshipped Sin, the moon god, like his fellow-countrymen in Ur. Sin was often portrayed with the symbol of a crescent moon, just like that found in Islam today.

2200 | 2100 | 2000 | 1900 | 1800

2166–1991 BC Abraham
2091 BC Abraham moves to Canaan
2066–1886 BC Isaac
2006–1859 BC Jacob
1915–1850 BC Joseph

See also
Canaan pp. 68–69
Circumcision p. 88
Mesopotamia pp. 62–63

Isaac

After Abraham's death, his son Isaac became family head. While leadership normally passed to the eldest son, both Isaac and Jacob were second sons, showing God isn't bound by human traditions. Abraham's servant, sent to find a bride for Isaac, had brought back the beautiful Rebekah from Abraham's relatives in northern Mesopotamia (Genesis 24:1–67). Initially barren, she waited twenty years before bearing twin sons, Esau and Jacob. When Jacob was born, he was grasping his elder brother's heel, a prophetic foretaste of the future struggles between them.

During a famine, Isaac considered moving to Egypt but God appeared to him, confirming that his promise to Abraham was also a promise to him, leading him to stay, plant crops, and dig wells, eventually settling in Beersheba (Genesis 26:1–33).

Nomads

Besides the powerful kingdoms by the rivers of Mesopotamia and Egypt and the many tiny city-states in between, there were many nomadic peoples who lived in tents, like these Bedouin, constantly moving in search of pasture for their flocks and herds. This is how the biblical patriarchs lived.

Jacob

Jacob tricked Esau into selling him his birthright as firstborn son (Genesis 25:27–34) and then, encouraged by Rebekah, deceived Isaac, now blind, into giving him Esau's inheritance-blessing (Genesis 27:1–40). Jacob fled Esau's anger by going to his uncle Laban (Rebekah's brother) in Haran, encountering God on the way through a powerful dream (Genesis 28:10–22). In Haran he married two wives, Leah and Rachel, a situation thrust on him rather than chosen (Genesis 29:1–30), and fathered eleven of the twelve sons (Genesis 30:1–24) that would become the founders of Israel's twelve tribes. He returned to Canaan, and again God met him on the way (Genesis 32:22–32), wrestling with him until his strength was broken and changing his name to Israel ("he struggles with God"), which would become the name of the people descended from him. Rachel died on the way home while giving birth to Jacob's twelfth son, Benjamin (Genesis 35:16–20).

Joseph

As Jacob's favourite son, Joseph became the object of his brothers' jealousy, especially when Jacob gave him a beautiful robe and when Joseph developed an ability to interpret dreams, some of which seemed to belittle them. They decided to get rid of him, selling him to passing traders (Genesis 37:1–36), and he ended up in Egypt where he experienced many challenges to his faith (Genesis 39:1 – 41:57). Eventually becoming Pharaoh's right-hand man, he was able to bring his family to Egypt to escape the famine in Canaan, assuring his brothers that though "you intended to harm me… God intended it for good" (Genesis 50:20).

Faith idea: Faith

Faith is the conviction that God can always do what we cannot do, whatever the circumstances – though the patriarchs' stories show that trusting God can also involve sacrifice and risk, to demonstrate the seriousness of our faith. But what kept the patriarchs going was their conviction that God will always keep his promises.

Exodus

The Great Escape

As Joseph's descendants lived in Egypt for 430 years (Exodus 12:40), a new dynasty eventually arose that knew nothing of Egypt's obligations to him and them. Threatened by their growing numbers, the Egyptians forced them into slavery (Exodus 1:6–14). The Israelites called on God, who heard their cry (Exodus 2:24). But God's plan wasn't just to free them; it was to make them into a nation and take them back to the Promised Land.

Moses' early years

Exodus tells us that, though born a Hebrew, Moses was raised as an Egyptian, having been hidden by his mother to protect him from Pharaoh's slaughter of newborn Israelite sons and found by Pharaoh's daughter, who adopted him. He therefore grew up learning skills that would later prove so useful – leadership, writing, law, and warfare. At the age of forty he fled to Midian, after killing an Egyptian to defend a Hebrew slave. There he spent forty years, learning the skills of desert life that would also prove so useful later. The turning point was meeting God on Mount Sinai, who revealed himself as the God of his ancestors and as *Yahweh* ("I am"), sending him back to Egypt to free God's people (Exodus 3:1 – 4:31).

Above: Thutmose III, probably the pharaoh who enslaved the Israelites. His son, Amunhotep II, was probably the pharaoh at the time of the plagues.

Ten plagues

Now aged eighty, Moses delivered God's demands to Pharaoh, who rejected them outright, unwilling to lose his workforce. So God applied increasing pressure over the coming months through ten plagues (Exodus 7:14 – 12:51), each one not only a natural consequence of the previous one, but also a direct challenge to Egypt's gods; for everything struck was either seen as a god (like the Nile) or represented a god (like the fly). Finally death itself, which Egyptians prepared for so carefully, came without warning and took their firstborn. Only then did Pharaoh yield and free the Israelites. Their escape, known as "the exodus" (Greek for "departure"), was, according to the Bible's figures (Exodus 12:37), a massive people-movement of 600,000 men, plus women and children – perhaps two to three million people in all. But such large-scale migrations were not at all unusual in the Late Bronze Age.

Covenant and commandments

At Mount Sinai God made a covenant not with an individual (like with Abraham), but with a nation (Exodus 19:6), promising to bless and protect them, in return for which they would serve and obey him. God then gave them laws to live by, at the heart of which lay the Ten Commandments (Exodus 20:1–17). These were unpacked by further laws covering every aspect of life, recorded in Exodus and Leviticus, which helped weld them into a nation. The Ten Commandments were written on two stone tablets – two copies of the same ten laws, not five on each as often thought. Normally each covenant participant kept a copy; but since this covenant was entirely God's doing, both copies were kept by him in "the ark of the covenant" in the tabernacle.

Dates

Following the chronology of 1 Kings 6:1, the exodus occurred in 1446 BC, a date that also fits the 300 years mentioned in Judges 11:26. However, some believe that archaeological evidence of destroyed Canaanite cities in the thirteenth century BC points to a date for the exodus of c. 1290 BC instead. But since the identity of their destroyers cannot be ascertained, and since the Israelites were unlikely to destroy cities they wanted to live in, there seems little reason to modify the Bible's dating.

An Egyptian statuette of an Apis bull, with a sun disk (representing the god Ra) between its horns. This was what the golden calf, made by the Israelites as their god when they thought Moses wasn't returning from Mount Sinai (Exodus 32), probably looked like.

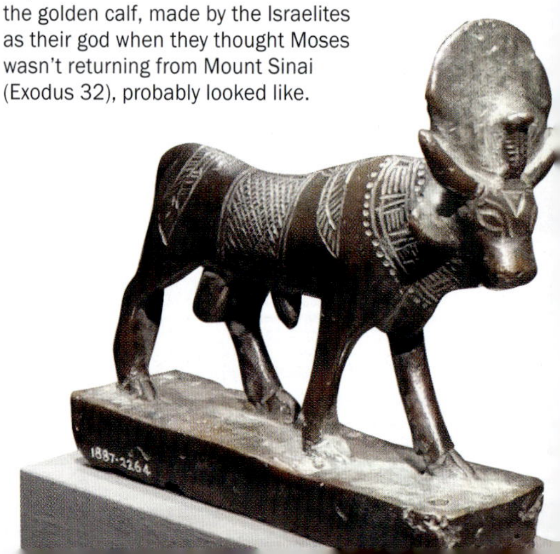

1900 | 1800 | 1700 | 1600 | 1500 | 1400

1876 BC Jacob & family settle in Egypt

1526–1406 BC Moses

1446 BC Crossing Reed Sea

1406 BC Joshua succeeds Moses; Israel enters the Promised Land

See also
The Law pp. 134–35
Passover pp. 138–39
Tabernacle p. 146

The journey home

While other options have been proposed, this map shows the traditional and most likely route taken by the Israelites.

1. The Israelites ate the Passover meal, while outside the Egyptian firstborn died (Exodus 12:14–30).

2. The Israelites were trapped between Pharaoh's army and the sea – not the Red Sea, as mistranslated in the Septuagint and perpetuated by tradition, but the "Reed Sea" (Hebrew, *Yam Suph*, "Sea of Reeds"), probably a marshy area in the Nile delta, where a strong wind (Exodus 14:21) could easily drive back the water for people on foot to cross, while heavy chariots got bogged down.

3. Initial euphoria turned to grumbling as the hardships of desert life hit them. But God miraculously provided "manna" and quail (Exodus 16:1–36).

4. When water supplies ran out, God told Moses to strike a rock, from which water miraculously erupted (Exodus 17:1–7).

5. At Mount Sinai God established Israel as "a holy nation" (Exodus 19:6), making his covenant with them (Exodus 24:1–8). Like any nation, they now needed laws to live by (Exodus 20–24) and ways of maintaining relationship with him (Exodus 25–40).

6. Spies sent into Canaan returned with mixed reports (Numbers 13:26–33), producing fear and unbelief (Numbers 14:1–10). As judgment, everyone over twenty years old would die in the wilderness, except faithful Joshua and Caleb (Numbers 14:11–45). The Israelites stayed here almost forty years.

7. The Israelites turned south then north, planning to enter Canaan from the east. But when Edom (descended from Esau) refused them passage, they bypassed it to the east (Numbers 20:14–21).

8. Moab also refused Israel passage, so Israel had to fight them, winning decisive victories at Jahaz, Heshbon, and Edrei (Numbers 21:21–33) and giving them a secure base for an attack on Canaan. Balaam, hired to curse Israel, could only bless them (Numbers 22–24). Moses commissioned Joshua as his successor (Numbers 27:12–23) and renewed God's covenant with Israel (Deuteronomy).

9. Within sight of the Promised Land, Moses died, aged 120, disqualified from entering because of his anger with God's people (Numbers 20:1–12).

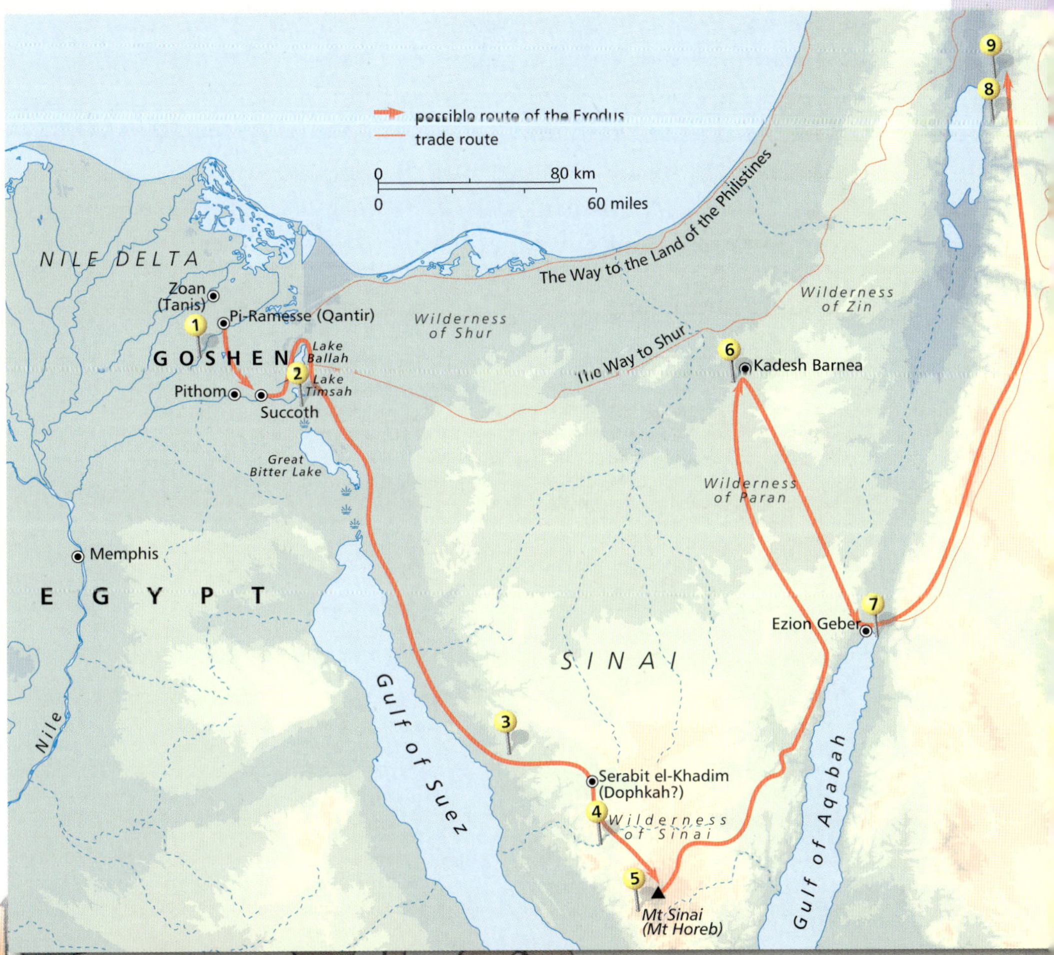

Faith idea: Covenant

Covenants – binding contracts – were common in the ancient world. But whereas they were always two-sided, involving obligations for both parties, in the Bible they are one-sided: it is God who makes covenant with people; all they can do is respond. A covenant is neither reward nor requirement, but rather a gracious expression of God's committed love to which he invites people to respond in trust and obedience.

Promised Land

Home at Last

With Moses dead, it was time for Joshua, his second-in-command, to become Israel's leader. God assured him of his presence and encouraged him to be strong (Joshua 1:2–9), for the time had come: the promises made to Abraham about the Promised Land hundreds of years earlier were about to be fulfilled. However, Canaan was already occupied by many independent city-states; but through a mixture of brilliant strategy and dependence on God, Joshua led Israel to claim their inheritance, though pockets of resistance would trouble them for generations to come.

Joshua's campaigns

1. Jordan
After the spies returned, Israel crossed the Jordan, whose waters, in flood from melting snow on Mount Hermon, were blocked upstream as the ark of the covenant was carried into the river (Joshua 3:1 - 4:24). Baal's power, symbolized in the flowing river, was nothing before the living God.

2. Gilgal
Circumcision, a practice neglected in the wilderness, was reinstituted to reaffirm commitment to God (Joshua 5:1–12) and Passover was celebrated for the first time in the Promised Land. The next day, the miraculous provision of manna ceased (Joshua 5:11).

3. Jericho
Joshua's first obstacle was the strongly fortified ancient city of Jericho, which controlled the pass through central Canaan. An angel revealed this battle was not his but God's (Joshua 5:13–15), underlined by the unusual strategy given for Jericho's defeat: a seven-day praise march after which the walls simply collapsed (Joshua 6:1–27).

4. Ai
Fifteen miles (24 km) west, Israel experienced defeat at Ai (Joshua 7:1–5) because of Achan's sin of having taken booty from Jericho. Once the sin was exposed (Joshua 7:6–27), Ai was taken by means of an ambush (Joshua 8:1–29).

5. Mount Ebal
Joshua built an altar and renewed the covenant (Joshua 8:30–35).

6. Gibeon
The Gibeonites tricked Israel into making peace, for which Israel demanded compulsory service from them (Joshua 9). Canaan was now cut into two.

7. Southern campaign
Every strategic city was subdued (Joshua 10), leaving Israel controlling southern Canaan.

8. Northern campaign
Joshua then headed north, defeating the king of Hazor's coalition. With Hazor destroyed and other towns overrun (Joshua 11), the bulk of the conquest was complete, thirty years after it had started. But pockets of resistance remained for many years to come.

9. Shechem
Joshua renewed the covenant and sent the people to their inheritance (Joshua 24). He died at the age of 110.

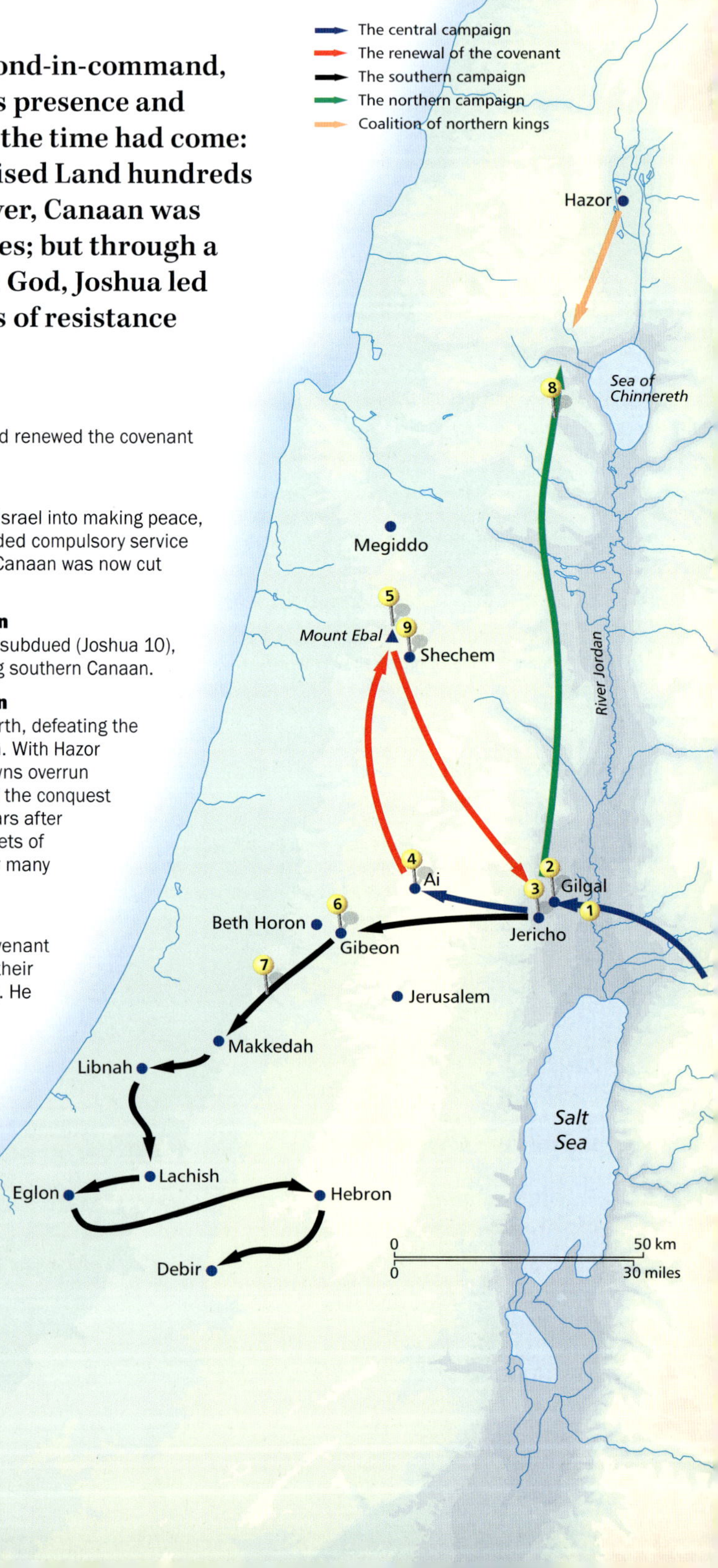

The granite stele of Merneptah, which confirms that a people known as Israel were definitely in Canaan by 1213 BC and that they had developed an agricultural lifestyle.

1400 | 1300 | 1200 | 1100

1406 BC Israel crosses the Jordan

1406–1375 BC Israel takes the Promised Land

1375–1050 BC The Judges

1200 BC Philistines begin to settle coastal plain

1105 BC Samuel born

See also
The Canaanites pp. 68–69
The Philistines pp. 70–71
The Holy Land pp. 52–53

Division of the land

With the land taken, Joshua then divided it between the twelve tribes. Reuben, Gad, and half the tribe of Manasseh returned to land east of the Jordan that they had previously requested (Numbers 32:1–42). Joshua cast lots to divide up Canaan among the remaining tribes. Joshua 13–19 is a map-in-words of the boundaries of each tribal area. The tabernacle was located at Shiloh in the middle of Canaan so everyone could reach it (Joshua 18:1). Six cities of refuge (three on each side of the Jordan) were established to ensure a fair trial for anyone accused of manslaughter, and towns were appointed for the Levites, who had no tribal area of their own.

Alternative settlement theories

Depending on how we date the exodus, the invasion of Canaan began in either 1406 BC or 1230 BC (and the scanty archaeological evidence could indicate either). However, since Israel intended to settle the land, it is hardly surprising that they didn't destroy everything before them and that therefore little evidence of destruction from that period has been found. The *Armana Letters*, written by Canaanite and Syrian rulers in the early fourteenth century BC, complain about the warlike activities of the Apiru, or Habiru (almost certainly a reference to the Hebrews, especially since one reference says they were former slaves), which points to the earlier date.

Some think the invasion was a much more piecemeal affair, or involved gradual and peaceful infiltration over a longer period until the Israelites became the dominant group, or that a social revolution occurred in Canaan. This view therefore sees the book of Joshua as the creation of later generations who wanted to glamorize Israel's origins. However, this is at odds with the Bible's own data.

Megiddo
Inhabited from around 7000 BC Megiddo, perched on a 700-foot (213 m) hill, guarded the international highway across the Jezreel Valley. It was one of the cities that was too well fortified for Israel to take at this time. This model dates from later Israelite times, showing lower levels beneath.

Judges

After Joshua's death, Israel quickly went into decline. Enticed by the sexuality of Canaanite religion, they forgot God and all he had done for them, becoming like the surrounding peoples. But God didn't give up on them. As an act of loving discipline, the Bible says, he allowed neighbours to attack them so they would cry out to him. The book of Judges records how God raised up twelve leaders ("judges"), empowered by his Spirit as occasion needed, to rescue them; but as soon as the danger passed, they slipped back into old ways, and so the respite was brief. This cycle of disobedience, distress, and deliverance continued for over 300 years. Perhaps the best-known judges are Gideon (6:1 – 8:32), Samson (13:1 – 16:31), Samuel (1 Samuel 1:1 – 25:1), and the only female judge, Deborah (Judges 4–5).

Most of the judges were "local heroes" and there was little sense of national cohesion at this time, summed up in the closing words of Judges: "In those days Israel had no king; everyone did as he saw fit" (Judges 21:25).

Ruth

The story of Ruth is set "in the days when the judges ruled" (Ruth 1:1). Ruth, a Moabite woman who married into an Israelite family fallen on hard times, is presented as a great example of selfless commitment to others and of God's ability to redeem people whatever their nation or circumstances.

Faith idea: Success

Moses' success lay, arguably, not so much in getting Israel to the Promised Land, but in producing someone who could take over and complete the task God had given him. Real success is about producing successors – successors who can hear the voice of God and obey it, just like Joshua did. If success ends with us, it isn't real success, as even Jesus recognized when he sent out the disciples he had trained to complete his mission.

Israel's First Kings

Right Request, Wrong Reason

The increasing Philistine threat from the west led Israel to think that the root of their weakness lay in not having a king, whereas the Bible says in reality it lay in their lack of trust in God. Despite Samuel's strong warning, they pressed him to give them one (1 Samuel 8:1–22), and God (already their King!) graciously agreed. Thus began Israel's transition from a loose federation of tribes to a monarchy.

Saul

Israel's first king, Saul, started out well. He was tall, strong, good-looking and, initially, humble – everything they wanted. But his initial success (1 Samuel 11:1–15) went to his head. He started thinking that, because he was king, he could do as he pleased, and twice he overruled the prophet Samuel's instructions, then blamed others when things went wrong (1 Samuel 13:1–15; 15:1–35). So God sent Samuel to tell him he had rejected him as king and had chosen another (1 Samuel 13:13–14).

Samuel thought that appointing a king had been a mistake; but in fact God had made provision for a king in the Law given 400 years earlier (Deuteronomy 17:14–20). So it seems the Israelites may have asked for the right thing, but for the wrong reason.

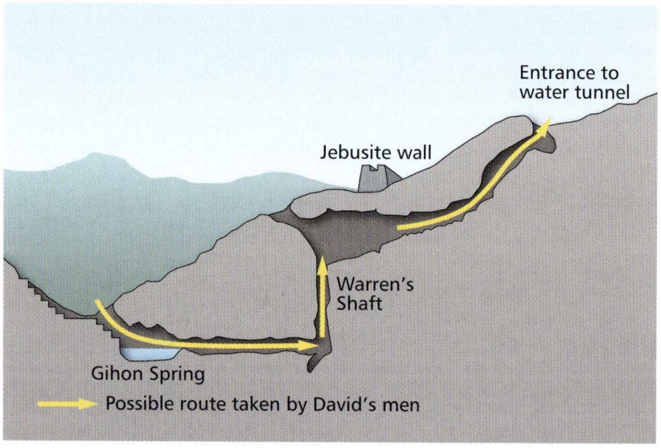

Jerusalem's capture

Located on the north–south tribal boundary, the Jebusite city of Zion was ideal for David's new capital. Over-confident in their fortifications, the Jebusites were overpowered by a surprise attack by David's men, who climbed the water shaft to the Gihon Spring to gain access to the city (2 Samuel 5:6–10).

David

David's father didn't even include him in the line-up when Samuel came looking for Israel's new king. Samuel was initially distracted by the appearance of David's brothers, but God reminded him that while "man looks at the outward appearance... the LORD looks at the heart" (1 Samuel 16:7). When David, who had been caring for the sheep, finally arrived, God told Samuel, "Rise and anoint him; he is the one" (16:12).

However, David's path to kingship wasn't easy. Desperate to retain power, and becoming increasingly mentally unstable, Saul became jealous and hounded David for the next ten years, despite David sparing Saul's life (1 Samuel 24:1–22; 26:1–25). Only after Saul's death was the way open for David to become king, initially over Judah, based at Hebron, and then seven years later, over a united kingdom, based at Jerusalem. Under his reign, the kingdom both expanded and became secure.

David was eager to build a temple for God, but instead God said he would build a "house" for David – a house made not of stones, but of descendants, promising him that one of those descendants would always be on the throne – a promise known as "the Davidic Covenant" (2 Samuel 7:1–29), which Christians believe is fulfilled in Jesus, a descendant of David.

These sling stones are like the one David used in his famous defeat of the Philistine champion, Goliath (1 Samuel 17). About the size of tennis balls, they could be lethal when released at high speed.

1100	1000	900	800

- 1050–1010 BC Reign of Saul
- 1010–1002 BC Reign of David in Judah
- 1002–970 BC Reign of David in Israel and Judah
- 970–930 BC Reign of Solomon
- 966–959 BC Construction of Temple

See also
Jerusalem pp. 154–55
The Philistines pp. 70–71
Temple pp. 146–47

Successes and failures

David was a good king and a man after God's heart (1 Samuel 13:14), though he knew as many failures as successes, as the chart below shows:

David's successes	David's failures
• United the nation under him as king (2 Samuel 5:3). • Established Jerusalem as the new capital (2 Samuel 5:6–10). • Recognized by Phoenicia, a significant trading nation (2 Samuel 5:11–12). • Subdued the Philistines and other enemies (2 Samuel 5:17–25; 8:1–14; 10:1–19). • Brought the ark to Jerusalem (2 Samuel 6:1–23). • Wrote psalms and encouraged worship.	• Failure in personal life » adultery with Bathsheba (2 Samuel 11). • Failure in family life » didn't deal with Amnon, his eldest son, who raped his half-sister Tamar (2 Samuel 13:1–22), nor Absalom, his third son, who avenged Tamar by killing Amnon (2 Samuel 13:23–39) » allowed Absalom to return from self-imposed exile and, under his nose, slowly gather support for a coup (2 Samuel 15) » paralysed by the ensuing civil war led by Absalom, ended only through Joab's killing of Absalom (2 Samuel 17:1 – 19:43). • Failure in leadership » took a census with disastrous consequences (2 Samuel 24:1–25) » failed to clarify the issue of succession and only narrowly averted another coup (1 Kings 1:28–53).

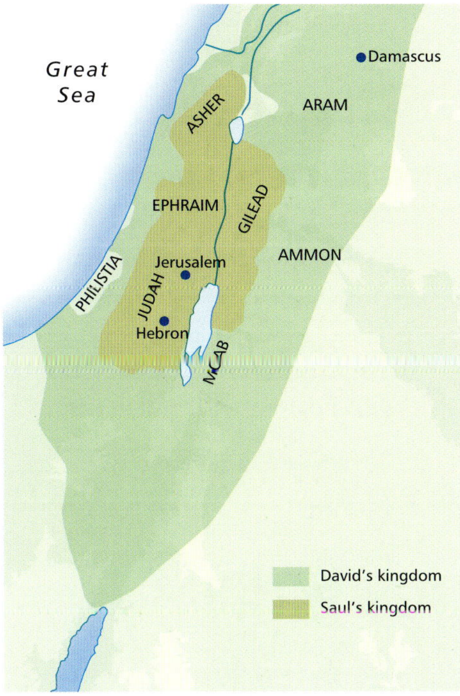

Israel's territory
Extent of Israel's territory under Saul and David. Under David, Israel at last controlled the land promised to Abraham. Under Solomon, it reached its furthest extent ever.

Solomon

In Solomon, David's son and successor, Israel got what it had asked for: "a king to lead us, such as all the other nations have" (1 Samuel 8:5); for although his forty-year reign gave Israel greater prosperity and influence than ever before, it also sowed the seeds of its destruction.

Solomon is best known for four things:

- **Wisdom**
  When God offered him any gift, Solomon chose wisdom (1 Kings 3:5–15). People from surrounding nations came to listen to his wisdom on wide-ranging topics (1 Kings 4:29–34).
- **Wealth**
  Solomon's renowned wealth attracted visitors, like the Queen of Sheba (1 Kings 10:1–13). While some wealth came from trade, some came from taxing his people and using them as forced labour for his building projects, producing resentment that later erupted and split the kingdom into two.
- **Wives**
  In biblical times, a man was considered wealthy if he had two wives; but Solomon showed his wealth through 700 wives and 300 women in his harem. This love of women was clearly a weakness, causing his heart to be stolen by other gods (1 Kings 11:1–6).
- **Worship**
  Solomon built the Temple his father David had planned. Taking seven years to complete, it followed a Canaanite pattern because of the Phoenician artisans he used. When completed, the ark of the covenant was installed and God's presence filled the Temple (1 Kings 8:1–10). Solomon's dedication prayer (1 Kings 8:22–61) shows a remarkable spirituality that, sadly, he lost later in life.

Wisdom Literature

Solomon's reign saw the production of much Wisdom Literature, dealing with life's big questions. These included Job (righteousness and suffering), Proverbs (guidance for life), Ecclesiastes (life's meaning), and Song of Songs (a celebration of love).

Faith idea: Kingship

God giving Israel a king wasn't simply a response to circumstances, but a picture of the kingly rule that would be brought through the Davidic king-messiah who would set up God's kingdom on earth, inviting all to come under his liberating rule. The New Testament shows how this was fulfilled in Jesus.

A Kingdom Divided

The Results of Folly

Solomon had built a great kingdom but had also sown the seeds of that kingdom's destruction, especially through the crippling burdens placed on his people to pay for his grand building projects and lavish lifestyle. It wasn't surprising therefore that, after his death, people sought some relief. But when his son, Rehoboam, refused to listen to their appeal, the consequences lasted down the centuries.

The divided kingdom

ISRAEL

1. Shechem was established by Jeroboam as Israel's capital (1 Kings 12:25).

2. Bethel and Dan became shrines, with golden calves (symbols of Canaanite religion) and their own priests (who were not Levites, as the Law required). Jeroboam wanted to deter people from going to the Jerusalem Temple, which he realized could remain a huge attraction (1 Kings 12:26–33). It is this sin that would be remembered for generations as "the sin of Jeroboam".

3. Samaria, fifty years later, was established by King Omri as a new capital to rival Jerusalem (1 Kings 16:23–24). Located on major trade routes, Israel would become more powerful and prosperous than Judah; but its strategic location was a mixed blessing, as international powers dominated and even invaded it at times. Within 200 years, it would be obliterated by Assyria, its people dispersed, never to return.

4. Aram, Ammon, and Moab all reasserted their independence over these years, taking advantage of their neighbours' weakness.

JUDAH

5. Jerusalem remained the capital of Judah. Although smaller (one-third the size) and less prosperous than the north, Judah would outlive Israel by almost 150 years, largely because of its isolated location in the Judean hills.

The cause of division

Eager to find relief from the crippling burdens imposed by Solomon, which had fallen mainly on the northern tribes, their representatives pleaded with Rehoboam. He foolishly rejected the advice of the elders in favour of the gung-ho approach of his young friends, who told him to make the lives of the northerners even harder in order to establish his authority. The northern tribes immediately rebelled, returning home and crowning Jeroboam, who wasn't a descendant of King David but simply one of Solomon's officials, as king instead (1 Kings 12:1–19), just as had been prophesied (1 Kings 11:9–13, 26–40). Rehoboam wanted to use force of arms to bring the north into submission, but the prophet Shemaiah restrained him through a word from God, thereby averting civil war (1 Kings 12:21–24). Rehoboam's folly had left him with just two of the twelve tribes. The kingdom was now divided – Israel in the north, Judah in the south – split along old tribal lines, never to reunite in the old way again.

Rising 300 feet (91.5 m) above the surrounding valleys, Samaria was ideally located for Omri's new northern capital. Rivalling Jerusalem in size, it frequently proved impregnable, and even Assyria would take three years to capture it (2 Kings 18:9–10). It was named after Shemer, from whom Omri bought the hill (1 Kings 16:21–24).

1000 | 900 | 800 | 700 | 600 | 500

930 BC Rehoboam comes to the throne; Israel's split from Judah; Jeroboam becomes king of Israel

930–721 BC Kingdom of Israel

930–586 BC Kingdom of Judah

See also
Assyria & Israel pp. 34–35
Babylon & Judah pp. 36–37
Prophets pp. 150–51

Pharaoh Shishak (945–924 BC), the first pharaoh called by name in the Old Testament, had given sanctuary to Jeroboam when he fled from Solomon (1 Kings 11:26–40). Once Jeroboam became king of Israel, Shishak took advantage of Judah's weakened position and attacked Jerusalem and other cities, as recorded by him in these inscriptions on the wall of the Temple of Amun in Thebes (modern Karnak). He took treasure from the Jerusalem Temple and royal palace, including Solomon's gold shields (1 Kings 14:25–26; 2 Chronicles 12:1–11).

Focus on the south

The book of Kings shows far more interest in Judah than Israel. This was because, at the time of writing, Israel had been completely destroyed, while Judah was in exile in Babylon, wondering whether it had a future. The writer was convinced that it did, because of God's promises made to King David. So he wrote the history of God's people, based on earlier sources, with an underlying motif that showed how obedience to God had always led to blessing, while disobedience had always led to curse. The lesson was obvious: Judah needed to obey God once again in the hope of being restored.

Kings of Israel and Judah

As this chart shows, Judah survived much longer than Israel, and was far more stable. Whereas Israel had twenty rulers over 210 years from several different dynasties (none of them descendants of David), Judah had twenty rulers over 345 years from just one dynasty (all of them David's descendants).

It can sometimes be hard to follow the story in Kings, as the writer constantly switches between Judah and Israel; but his approach is completely chronological and synchronistic, beginning with the king of Judah and then, after that king's death, looking at all Israel's kings who reigned during that period, before going back to Judah again.

His main interest is theological rather than political, judging each king by whether he did "right" or "evil" in the eyes of God.

Israel			Judah	
Jeroboam	930-909	930 BC	Rehoboam	930-913
			Abijah	913-910
Nadab	909-908		Asa	910-869
Baasha	908-886	900 BC		
Elah	886-885			
Zimri	885			
Tibni	885-880			
Omri	885-874			
Ahab	874-853			
			Jehoshaphat	872-848
Ahaziah	853-852			
Joram	852-841		Jehoram	848-841
Jehu	841-814		Ahaziah	841
			Athaliah	841-835
			Joash	835-796
Jehoahaz	814-798	800 BC		
Jehoash	798-782		Amaziah	796-767
Jeroboam II	793/782-753			
Zechariah	753		Azariah (Uzziah)	792/767-740
Shallum	752			
Menahem	752-742		Jotham	750/740-735
Pekahiah	742-740			
Pekah	752-732		Ahaz	735-715
Hoshea	732-722/721			
		700 BC	Hezekiah	715-686
			Manasseh	697-642
			Amon	642-640
			Josiah	640-609
			Jehoahaz	609
		600 BC	Jehoiakim	609-598
			Jehoiachin	598-597
			Zedekiah	597-586
		500 BC		

(Where dates overlap, this indicates a co-regency, common in the ancient world to ensure smooth succession.)

Faith idea: Servanthood

This period begins with Israel as a strong, united kingdom, but ends with it in division and disarray, and all because so many kings forgot the importance of servanthood. No matter what position we might hold, the Bible calls everyone to be servants of others, just like Jesus, who was always ready to serve, even though he was God's Son (e.g. Matthew 20:25–28; Philippians 2:5–7). Servanthood lies at the heart of God's kingdom.

Assyria and Israel's End

Judgment Day

After Solomon's kingdom split into two, Israel drifted not just from Judah but also from God, the Bible shows, and its kings were the chief culprits. Its strategic position between Egypt and Mesopotamia, secure during the strong reigns of David and Solomon, now became vulnerable, and ultimately it fell to the might of the new rising superpower in the east, Assyria.

Just as watchmen kept a lookout from their watchtowers, like this one, guarding their olive groves and vineyards, so the prophets saw themselves as keeping watch over the nation's life (see Hosea 9:18). Prophets like Amos and Hosea in the eighth century BC denounced sin of whatever kind (religious, political, social, or moral) and called people back to a godly way of living. Without this, judgment would surely come, they said.

Elijah and Elisha

The prophets Elijah and Elisha were at the forefront of the battle between followers of Yahweh and Baal, the Canaanite fertility god. While Elijah operated at a national level, Elisha was more involved with individual needs; but both experienced miracles at a level not seen since the exodus. Key events in their lives are outlined in the table below.

Major kings in Israel

Omri (885/880–874 BC)
Although the Bible only devotes six verses to Omri because of his sin (1 Kings 16:25), he was very successful, humanly speaking, establishing Samaria as Israel's new capital and defeating Moab, a fact confirmed by the Moabite Stone, which is now in the Louvre, Paris.

Ahab (874–853 BC)
Ahab was drawn into Baal worship by his Phoenician wife, Jezebel (1 Kings 16:29–33), which brought

Characteristics of Israel

Over its lifetime the northern nation of Israel was characterized by:

- **Political instability**
  Different dynasties continually replaced the previous one, often through bloodshed.
- **Religious syncretism**
  Worship of Yahweh was mixed with worship of Baal, involving idolatry, immorality, and even child sacrifice.
- **Ineffective leadership**
  Most kings were weak, and even the strong ones, Omri and Jeroboam II, were utterly godless.
- **International alliances**
  Israel's kings tried to prop up the ever-weakening nation through alliances with other nations.

Elijah ("My God is the Lord")	Elisha ("My God saves")
• Announced a three-year drought, during which he was miraculously fed by ravens (1 Kings 17:1–5), showing Yahweh alone controls nature. • Miraculously provided for a widow and raised her son from the dead (1 Kings 17:7–24). • Told Ahab the drought would soon end (1 Kings 18:1–2), leading to a contest with Baal's 450 prophets on Mount Carmel (1 Kings 18:16–46). • Fled to Horeb (Sinai) where he met God afresh (1 Kings 19:1–18). • Anointed Elisha as successor (1 Kings 19:19–21). • Pronounced judgment over Ahab and Jezebel after their annexation of Naboth's vineyard (1 Kings 21:1–28). • Miraculously taken into heaven (2 Kings 2:1–12).	• Became Elijah's successor (2 Kings 2:1–18). • Miraculously purified water (2 Kings 2:19–22). • Miraculously provided oil for a widow (2 Kings 4:1–7). • Raised a young man from the dead (2 Kings 4:8–37). • Purified poisoned food and miraculously fed 100 people (2 Kings 4:38–44). • Healed Naaman, a Syrian commander, of leprosy (2 Kings 5:1–27). • Miraculously restored an axe-head (2 Kings 6:1–7). • Prophesied the ending of Aram's siege of Samaria (2 Kings 6:8 - 7:20). • Told Hazael he would become king of Aram (2 Kings 8:7–15) and sent a prophet to anoint Jehu as king of Israel (2 Kings 9:1–13).

1000	900	800	700	600	500

930 BC Rehoboam comes to the throne
875–848 BC Ministry of Elijah
848–797 BC Ministry of Elisha
785–775 BC Ministry of Jonah
760–750 BC Ministry of Amos
750–715 BC Ministry of Hosea
722 BC Israel exiled
725–722 BC Siege of Samaria

See also
Assyria pp. 72–73
Canaanite religion pp. 68–69
Kings of Israel pp. 30–31

Sargon II's records

Sargon II's records note, "At the beginning of my reign I captured Samaria. I carried into captivity 27,290 people... People of other lands who never paid tribute I settled in Samaria."

many conflicts with Elijah (1 Kings 18:16 – 19:5; 21:1–28). In 857 BC, Ben-Hadad of Aram besieged Samaria, but Ahab defeated him, and again the following year at Aphek (1 Kings 20:1–34). Three years of peace and a coalition against Assyria ensued. But having allied with Judah, Ahab turned against Aram again and, despite elaborate deception, was killed in battle, his blood licked by dogs as Elijah had prophesied (1 Kings 21:19).

Jeroboam II (793/782–753 BC)
Bringing Israel to the height of its power and prosperity (2 Kings 14:23–29), Jeroboam II capitalized on a weakened Assyria to conquer Aram. Israel's shrines were crowded with pilgrims, but Amos saw through the veneer of religion to the underlying injustice and immorality.

Hoshea (732–722 BC)
Refusing to pay tribute to Assyria, Hoshea turned to Egypt for help. Assyria responded swiftly: it besieged Samaria, captured Hoshea, and deported the Israelites (2 Kings 17:3–6; 18:9–12).

Assyria's rise, Israel's fall

After a period of weakness, Assyria again became strong. Under Tiglath-Pileser III (745–727 BC), Assyria's expansionist ambitions grew and turned towards Israel. The history of this period is complicated, as Assyria subdued Israel, was shaken off, and subdued it again, until Assyria had finally had enough. After the death of Tiglath-Pileser III, Hoshea turned to Egypt for help, which provoked Shalmaneser V to besiege Samaria. The city resisted for three years, but finally fell in 722 BC to his successor Sargon II. Israel was conquered and its citizens deported across the Assyrian empire, never to return, while other people groups were settled in Israel (2 Kings 17:3–6, 24–33; 18:9–12). The history of the ten northern tribes was over. Assyria had done it; but the prophets saw that, from God's viewpoint, Assyria was but "the rod of my anger" (Isaiah 10:5), and Kings ends its account of Israel's history with a lengthy comment on why this happened (2 Kings 17:7–23).

While considerable mythology developed around these ten lost tribes, the truth is that we have no idea what happened to them. Some fled, most were dispersed and lost across Assyria, and some remained and intermarried with other peoples that Assyria brought there, becoming "Samaritans", despised by Jews in New Testament times because of their racial and religious impurity.

The conquered Israelites were deported to regions across the Assyrian empire.

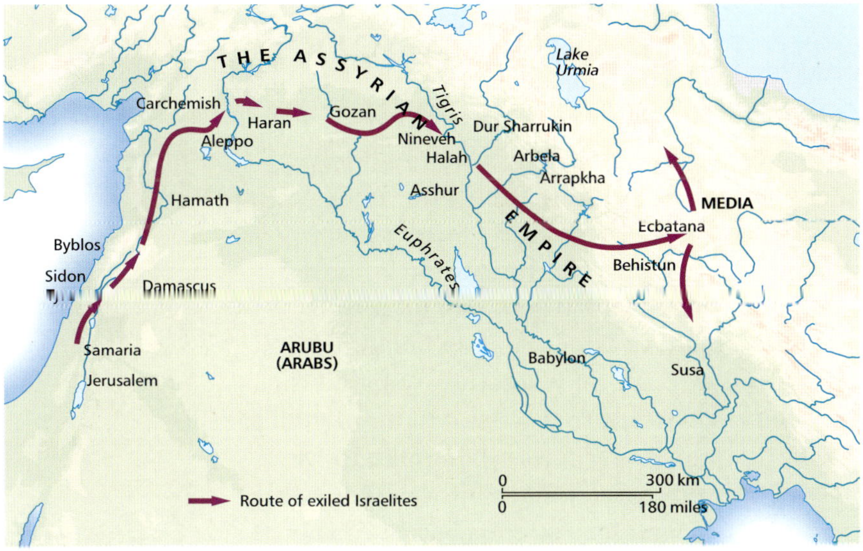

The Black Obelisk of Shalmaneser III. Each side has five rows of relief sculptures depicting tribute being brought by different conquered peoples. Above and below these reliefs are written descriptions of the main events of Shalmaneser's thirty-two military campaigns. One panel shows a leader, possibly King Jehu himself, bringing Israel's tribute.

Faith idea: Repentance

At the heart of the prophets' message was a call to repent – that is, for people to acknowledge that their previous way of living was wrong and that they would change direction and begin to live God's way. Only through repentance, the Bible says, can God's forgiveness, which he so much wants to give, be experienced.

Babylon and Judah's End

The Impossible Happens

Despite all Israel's turmoil in the years following the kingdom's division, Judah felt secure. After all, they not only had the Davidic dynasty, but also the Temple. Surely these would ensure God's blessing, they thought. However, they forgot Moses' warning that such blessing was dependent on obedience (Deuteronomy 28). So when they scorned the prophets' warnings that what had happened to Israel through Assyria would happen to them unless they changed, judgment was inevitable. Babylon besieged Jerusalem, destroyed the Temple, and took Judah into exile.

Siege of Lachish
A relief from Sennacherib's palace at Nineveh showing his siege of Lachish. Archers, spearmen, and sling-men march up ramps, and siege-engines and siege-towers stand against the walls. His choosing to portray this siege, rather than that against Jerusalem which failed, reflects typical Assyrian pride.

Rulers good and bad

Over the 350 years after the kingdom's division, Judah experienced both good kings and bad, as Kings and Chronicles demonstrate. Here are some examples:

Good rulers	Bad rulers
Jehoshaphat (872–848 BC) Taught God's Law; strengthened army and defences; defeated Moab and Ammon through a praise march.	***Jehoram*** (848–841 BC) Married Athaliah, Ahab and Jezebel's daughter; followed their wickedness; died a horrible death.
Joash (835–796 BC) Became king when seven years old; repaired the Temple.	***Athaliah*** (841–835 BC) Judah's only queen; tried to destroy the royal line but deposed by a coup.
Azariah (Uzziah) (792/767–740 BC) Long, stable reign; victorious over Philistines, Arabs, and Ammonites; encouraged agricultural development.	***Ahaz*** (735–715 BC) Encouraged worship of foreign gods; sacrificed his son; rejected Isaiah's appeal to trust God, trusting Assyria instead, to whom he became subordinate.
Hezekiah (715–686 BC) Removed paganism; re-organized Temple and worship; fortified cities; built tunnel for Jerusalem's water supply; trusted God when Assyria attacked Jerusalem.	***Manasseh*** (697–642 BC) Undid Hezekiah's work; took Judah back to Baal worship; practised sorcery and divination; placed pagan altars in the Temple; sacrificed his son.
Josiah (640–609 BC) Became king when eight years old; removed Baal worship; implemented "the Book of the Law", found during Temple repairs; renewed the covenant and celebrated Passover.	***Amon*** (642–640 BC) Behaved like his father, Manasseh; assassinated by his officials.

A foretaste of the future

Rehoboam (930–913 BC) had reigned just five years when he was faced with a major invasion by Egypt, with humiliating results (1 Kings 14:25–28). It was a foretaste of things to come, as was another event in 701 BC. Assyria had been sitting just a few miles north of Jerusalem since it had conquered Israel in 722 BC. Temporarily distracted by affairs elsewhere in its empire, giving Hezekiah time for his reforms, it finally turned its attention to Judah. Sennacherib invaded Phoenicia, defeated an Egyptian–Cushite army at Eltekeh, and then turned inland, destroying Lachish, just 25 miles (40 km) southwest of Jerusalem, and forty-six other cities. Hezekiah paid the heavy tribute demanded, even stripping gold from the Temple doors to do so (2 Kings 18:13–16). But, dissatisfied, Sennacherib sent his army to Jerusalem. Hezekiah spread out their threatening letter before God in the Temple, and Isaiah prophesied that God would save them (2 Kings 18:17 – 19:34; 2 Chronicles 32:1–23; Isaiah 36–37). That very night, the Bible says, 185,000 Assyrian soldiers suddenly died, leading Sennacherib to withdraw and return to Nineveh (2 Kings 19:35–36). For the moment, Jerusalem was spared.

1000	900	800	700	600	500

930 BC Division of the kingdom; Rehoboam becomes king of Judah

701 BC Assyria unsuccessfully besieges Jerusalem

612 BC Babylonians destroy Nineveh

597 BC Judah surrenders to Babylon

586 BC Babylonians destroy Jerusalem; nation exiled

See also
Babylon pp. 74–75
Kings of Judah p. 33
Prophets pp. 150–51

Key prophets

Key prophets over this period included:

- **Isaiah**, who prophesied both Judah's judgment and future salvation.
- **Micah**, who prophesied Samaria's downfall and the same for Judah unless people changed.
- **Nahum** and **Zephaniah**, who prophesied Nineveh's downfall.
- **Habakkuk**, who wrestled with God about his using godless nations like Babylon.
- **Jeremiah**, who prophesied the Temple itself would be destroyed if people didn't repent.

Jerusalem's fall

Initially a small state south of Assyria, Babylon had grown in power under Nabopolassar who, in 616 BC, invaded Assyria, capturing Nineveh in 612 BC. Babylon's defeat of the Assyrian–Egyptian army at Carchemish in 605 BC saw Assyria's final demise, and Babylon swallowed up its empire.

The victory at Carchemish persuaded Jehoiakim to submit to Babylon in 604 BC but, encouraged by Egypt, he rebelled three years later. In 598 BC Babylon retaliated; Jehoiakim was taken in shackles to Babylon and replaced by his son Jehoiachin. In 597 BC Jerusalem was besieged, Jehoiachin and many leading citizens were exiled to Babylon, joining those from an earlier deportation in 605 BC. Nebuchadnezzar then installed Zedekiah as king, but he too rebelled. So Babylon marched against Jerusalem, besieging it for two years. In 586 BC its walls were broken down, every important building including the Temple was destroyed, and its population was exiled to Babylon (2 Kings 25:1–21; 2 Chronicles 36:15–21; Jeremiah 52:1–30). Zedekiah's sons were killed in front of him, then his eyes were gouged out and he too was taken to Babylon. Judah's history seemed to be over.

The lost ark

After 586 BC the ark of the covenant (the gold-plated box containing the Ten Commandments that God gave Moses and that was seen as God's footstool on earth) disappeared from history, almost certainly broken up when Babylon looted the Temple. However, many (completely unfounded) legends grew up around it: Jeremiah hid it in a cave on Mount Nebo; Josiah hid it beneath Jerusalem; the Queen of Sheba had taken it to Ethiopia. Novels and films provide plenty more colourful suggestions!

Hezekiah's tunnel
Hezekiah built a 1,814-foot (553 m) tunnel, linking the Gihon Spring outside Jerusalem to the Siloam pool within it, to safeguard water supplies from the attacking Babylonians. The tunnel, which still exists, was dug from both ends and met in the middle.

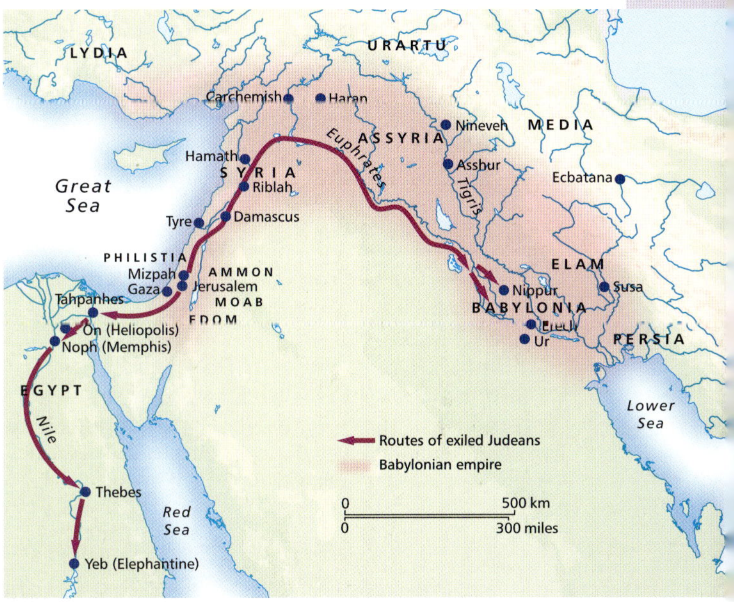

Sennacherib noted in this 15-inch (38 cm) high prism: "As for Hezekiah of Judah who had not submitted to my yoke, I surrounded and captured 46 of his strong towns, the forts, and uncountable smaller places in their neighbourhoods, by means of heaping up siege ramps, bringing up battering-rams, by foot soldiers fighting, by undermining, breaching and sapping... He himself I shut up in Jerusalem, his royal city, like a bird in a cage."

Faith idea: Judgment

The Bible says that, while God is gracious and patient, his judgment on sin inevitably comes, as the prophets repeatedly warned. They spoke of "the cup of God's wrath" – God's righteous anger stored up, ready to be poured out at any moment (e.g. Jeremiah 25:15–29). But whereas the Jews thought this was for God's enemies, Jeremiah warned it would also be for God's people unless they too repented.

Exile and Return

Making Sense of Disaster

The *Cyrus Cylinder*, a clay barrel recording Cyrus's own account of the conquest of Babylon through diverting the Euphrates for his army to march in along the dried-up river bed, where they were welcomed by its weary citizens. Like most such records of ancient kings, the cylinder is very boastful, with Cyrus claiming to be ruler of the four corners of the earth.

Jerusalem ransacked, the Temple destroyed, Judah exiled: all this led to questions. Where was God? What about his promises? Were Babylon's gods more powerful than Yahweh? The answers that God's people came to in Babylon would transform a *nation* into a *faith community* – *Judah* into *Judaism* – that would influence the world.

The development of Judaism

It was in Babylon that God's people gradually saw that their faith didn't depend on a particular place (the Temple) and started focusing on elements that could be practised anywhere. Over this time:

- A *special place* (Jerusalem) gave way in importance to a *special day* (sabbath).
- The *Temple* gave way to the *synagogue*, where they focused on prayer and reading the Law.
- *Priests* (now redundant) gave way to *scribes* and *rabbis* (copiers and teachers of the Law), who became central to Judaism's development.

Joshua, Judges, Samuel, and Kings (the history from entering Canaan to exile from it) received their final shape at this time, giving an underlying motif that obedience leads to blessing and disobedience leads to curse, a truth now self-evident from history.

The exile ends

With Babylon seemingly so invincible, it was hard to see how Jeremiah's prophecy of a seventy-year exile (Jeremiah 25:11–12) could ever come true; but a new power, Persia, was arising and Daniel warned Belshazzar that his days were numbered (Daniel 5:22–30). Jeremiah's prophecy was fulfilled when Cyrus conquered Babylon in October 539 BC, adding Babylon's empire to his own.

Cyrus adopted a more liberal approach to exiles, and in 538 BC he issued a decree permitting the Jews to return and rebuild the Temple, even restoring the Temple furnishings (though no mention is made of the ark of the covenant). However, many exiles had settled down and weren't keen to leave their new life behind, according to Josephus, the Jewish historian.

Life in Babylon

Unlike Assyria, Babylon let conquered peoples stay together and maintain their identity. So, as Jeremiah encouraged (Jeremiah 29:5–7), they built homes and settled down, adopting Aramaic, the Babylonian language. Many became wealthy and some, like Daniel, rose to high office; but many longed for home. "By the rivers of Babylon we sat and wept when we remembered Zion," went one song (Psalm 137:1). Babylon's mighty rivers, the Euphrates and Tigris, which to Babylon symbolized wealth and power, spoke to Judah only of defeat and despair.

700 600 500 400 300

- 605 BC First exile
- 597 BC Second exile
- 586 BC Final exile
- 539 BC Cyrus conquers Babylon
- 538 BC Jews return to Jerusalem
- 536 BC Work on the Temple begins
- 520 BC Haggai and Zechariah prophesy encouragement
- 458 BC Ezra arrives in Jerusalem
- 445 BC Nehemiah returns to Jerusalem and rebuilds the wall

See also
Babylon pp. 74–75
Persia pp. 76–77
Synagogue p. 147

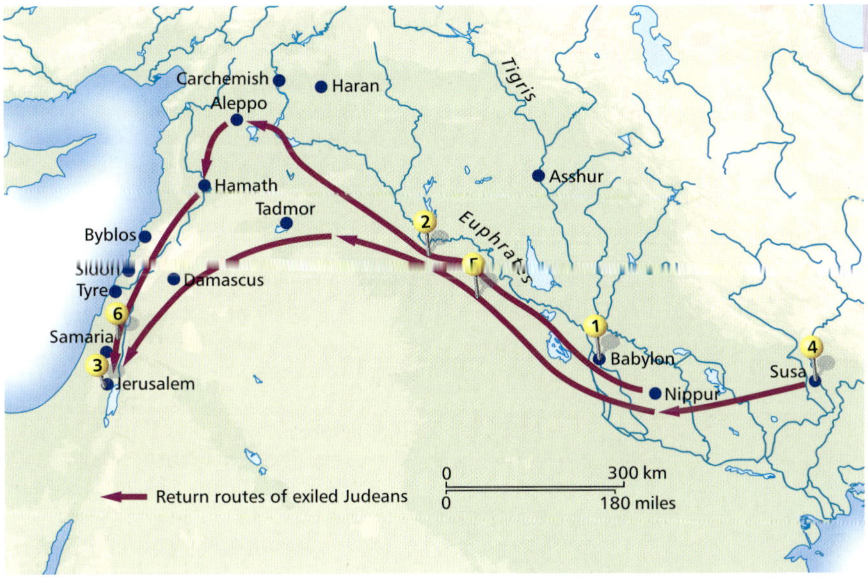

The exiles return

1. Daniel told Nebuchadnezzar his empire was about to crumble (539 BC).

2. Zerubbabel, Jehoiachin's grandson, led the first group of returning Jews (538–537 BC), who enthusiastically began to rebuild the Temple.

3. When work on the Temple stopped through weariness, Haggai and Zechariah encouraged people to complete it. Completed in 516 BC, it was nowhere near as grand as Solomon's. This "Second Temple" would be repaired and reconstructed until it was eventually replaced by Herod the Great.

4. Esther was one of those who didn't return, marrying King Xerxes (c. 460 BC) and saving the Jews still in exile.

5. Ezra returned with a second group and taught God's Law (458 BC).

6. Nehemiah returned with a third group and rebuilt Jerusalem's walls (445 BC).

Ezra, Nehemiah, Malachi

In 458 BC King Artaxerxes sent **Ezra** from Persia to Jerusalem to teach God's Law, backed by his authority and resources (Ezra 7:1–28). Appalled by the disobedience to the Law he discovered (like intermarriage with unbelievers), Ezra called God's people to a new way of living (Ezra 9:1 – 10:17). In 445 BC **Nehemiah**, a senior palace official, requested Artaxerxes' permission to go to Jerusalem to rebuild its walls and was appointed Judah's governor (Nehemiah 1:1 – 2:10). Challenging the Jews to end their disgrace, he stirred them into rebuilding the walls in just fifty-two days (Nehemiah 3:1–4, 23; 6:1–15) and spearheaded reforms to help the poor (Nehemiah 5:1–19). Ezra then gathered the people to teach them God's Law (Nehemiah 8:1–12). His work finished, Nehemiah went back to Persia in 433 BC, though returned for a second term in 432 BC (Nehemiah 13:6–31). **Malachi**, their contemporary, realized people were doubting the prophets' promises of a glorious future and rebuked their unbelief, encouraging them to believe "the Day of the LORD" was indeed coming, though with judgment if they didn't change their ways. The New Testament saw his promise of God's coming "messenger" (Malachi 3:1; 4:5) as fulfilled in John the Baptist.

Despite this return, by New Testament times a longing to be truly free from "spiritual exile" still dominated much Jewish thinking.

Daniel and Esther

Daniel and Esther found themselves at the heart of the Babylonian and Persian regimes, and it was there, rather than in Judah, that God used them to impact the surrounding culture. **Daniel**, deported to Babylon in 605 BC, attained high office at court (Daniel 1:1–21). Through many challenges to his faith (e.g. 6:1–28), he stayed faithful to God while serving Babylon's kings and challenging them that God alone is the supreme ruler and that only his kingdom will last forever (2:31–45; 7:1–28). Daniel never returned to Judah, giving some seventy years of public service to Babylon and dying there. **Esther**, who lived a century after Daniel, was a Jewish orphan chosen to marry King Xerxes I (486–465 BC). Through her position as queen, she foiled a plot to annihilate the Jews (Esther 3:1 – 9:17), an event still remembered in the Jewish festival of Purim.

Faith idea: Remnant

The prophets saw the existence of a "remnant" (a small surviving group of God's people) as evidence of God's ongoing faithfulness and love. No matter how bad things get, no matter how few God's people may be, God always keeps a remnant from which his purposes will spring once again, as this period of history shows.

Between the Two Testaments

The Silent Years

Turning from Malachi at the end of the Old Testament to Matthew at the beginning of the New, it's easy to miss that 400 years have passed by. But while God was no longer speaking through the prophets, he was certainly working. For through two huge changes on the world stage, he was preparing for the coming of Jesus, the promised Messiah.

The Greek empire

Greece, once weak and divided, was united by Philip II of Macedon and his son, Alexander the Great. In 334 BC, Alexander entered Asia Minor and defeated the Persian army at Granicus, sweeping through modern Turkey and, over the next twelve years until his death, taking everything before him – Asia, Syria, Palestine, Egypt, Persia, even reaching India. But Alexander's dream wasn't just to create an empire, but a way of life. He wanted to spread Greek culture, or Hellenism (from *Hellas*, "Greece"), leaving a legacy that couldn't be forgotten. Greek art, architecture, sport, customs, and ideas all flourished and Greek became the international language, which would help the spread of Christianity.

However, the man-centred Greek worldview clashed starkly with Judaism's God-centredness. Particularly offensive to Jews were stadiums, where athletes performed naked, and theatres, where plays were often erotic – an abuse of God-given sexuality and morality for Jews. Add to this the Greeks' polytheism and idolatry, and a clash was inevitable.

The Maccabean revolt

A key event occurred in 175 BC with the accession of **Antiochus IV Epiphanes.** Returning from successful victories over Ptolemy VI in 169 BC, he stripped the Jerusalem Temple of its wealth. The following year, because of resistance to Hellenization, he sacked Jerusalem and sought to eradicate Judaism – suspending sacrifices, forbidding circumcision and sabbath observance, forcing Jews to eat pork, destroying Jewish Scriptures, and erecting pagan altars across Judea. The final straw was placing a statue of Zeus in the Temple and sacrificing a pig (unclean to Jews) on the altar (Daniel's prophesied "abomination that causes desolation", Daniel 11:31). A priest called **Mattathias** killed a Seleucid officer when ordered to sacrifice on a Greek altar, sparking off a guerrilla war. When Mattathias died, his son, **Judas Maccabeus,** after whom the revolt became named, took over, marching on Jerusalem and reclaiming and purifying the Temple in 164 BC, an event commemorated in the festival of Hanukkah

Gold coin with the image of Antiochus IV Epiphanes, the Seleucid king who provoked the Maccabean revolt. The title Epiphanes means "god revealed", though his enemies changed this to Epimanes, meaning "mad".

The collapse of Alexander's empire

After Alexander's death – from poisoning, according to many ancient sources, though modern theories suggest malaria or typhoid – his vast empire was divided between his generals: two small empires (Macedonia and Thrace), and two huge ones (Egypt/North Africa, ruled by the Ptolemies, and Western Asia/Mesopotamia, ruled by the Seleucids). Once again this left Judah sandwiched between superpowers who would fight over it. Under the Ptolemies, the Jews experienced tolerance; but when the Seleucids took control in 198 BC, everything changed with their policy of compulsory Hellenization.

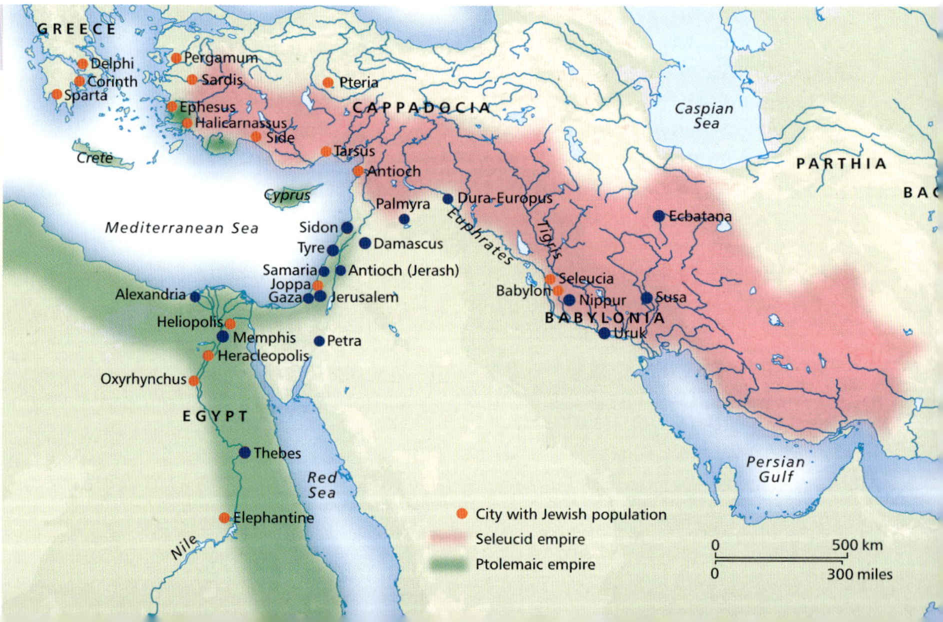

400 300 200 100 0

334 BC Alexander the Great invades Asia Minor
323 BC Alexander's empire breaks up
198 BC Seleucids take control of Judea
168 BC Maccabean revolt begins
128 BC Judea gains independence
63 BC Rome conquers Palestine

See also
The Deuterocanonical Books pp. 16–17
Hanukkah p. 139
The Greeks and Romans pp. 78–81

Jewish writings

Over this "inter-testamental" period a number of Jewish writings, known by Christians as "the Deuterocanonical Books" or "the Apocrypha", were written. Written in Greek, they never formed part of the Jewish Hebrew Scriptures and so are not accepted by all Christian traditions as Scripture. At the very least, they are highly informative about life and beliefs during this period.

Detail of a fourth-century BC floor mosaic in Pella, Philip II's capital and Alexander the Great's birthplace. This head of the god Dionysus shows how Greeks used black, grey, white, and reddish-brown pebbles to make their mosaics.

("Dedication"). The war dragged on for years, with the Seleucids granting increasing measures of autonomy and the **Hasmoneans** (after Hasmon, the father of Mattathias) increasingly establishing themselves as the ruling dynasty. Under their leadership Judea enjoyed a time of relative independence until Rome took Jerusalem in 63 BC.

The rise of Rome

If history teaches anything, it is that no empire lasts forever. That was as true of Greece as it had been of Assyria, Babylon, and Persia. For to its west, another new empire was growing. By 278 BC Rome had taken control of all Italy and had steadily expanded, defeating Carthage and Corinth in 146 BC and Athens in 86 BC. In the first century BC Julius Caesar conquered Gaul and Britain in the west, while Pompey conquered Syria and Palestine in the east. By New Testament times, Rome's empire was vast, covering Europe, Greece, Asia Minor, and North Africa. Its iron rule brought peace and stability; just laws and good administration prevailed; aqueducts carried fresh water; 50,000 miles (80,500 km) of roads linked every city; and the denarius became the universal currency. All this produced the Pax Romana ("Roman Peace"), which, together with Greece's gift of a world language, meant that the world could not have been better prepared for the spread of the Christian message.

The Diaspora

While some Jews had returned from the Babylonian exile, many stayed in Babylon or spread to other nations, reaching Morocco by 200 BC and India by 175 BC. This Diaspora ("Scattering") meant that Jewish communities could now be found across the Mediterranean, and there were more Jews outside Judea than inside it, with most of them reading their Scriptures in Greek (the version known as the Septuagint, which had added the Deuterocanonical Books). These scattered Jewish synagogues would become the favourite starting point for Christian missionary activity.

Faith idea: Sovereignty

This period of Israel's history shows that even great nations and world events are not beyond God's control. This sovereignty of God – his complete over-ruling of all circumstances, even those that would seem to be against us, in order to bring them, and us, into line with his good purposes – is a constant theme of the Bible and was one of Paul's underlying convictions of life (e.g. Romans 8:28–39).

Pompey and Judea
Left: Bust of Pompey, the Roman general who in 63 BC conquered Israel after its brief spell of independence, renaming it Judea. Four legions were based there to maintain peace and extract taxes, creating a highly charged atmosphere. While some appreciated Roman rule, the majority resented it, and following Herod the Great's death in 4 BC, there were many uprisings for the next seventy years as would-be messiahs tried to re-establish a Jewish kingdom.

The Life of Jesus

The Promised Messiah

As we come to the New Testament, the focus changes from a nation to a person. But it is still the same story, not a different one; for Jesus is, Christians believe, both the *continuation* and the *climax* of the Old Testament. The promises made to Abraham 2,000 years earlier were at last about to be fulfilled; the nation was about to get its long-promised messiah. But he would come in such a different way from what was expected that many simply missed him.

Messianic expectations

Mark begins his Gospel by recalling how the prophets foresaw that God's final intervention would begin with a messenger, a desert, and the coming of the Lord himself (Mark 1:1–3), which is just how Jesus' story began. In referring to the desert, Mark was striking a chord. Israel had come out of a desert twice in her history (Egypt and the exile); but there remained a huge feeling of still being in exile, for Isaiah's prophesied glorious return had never really happened. Surely something better must be coming, many people thought. And Mark says: it is! Through Jesus, the end of that exile was beginning. However, many missed him because they were looking for a particular type of messiah – a military and political deliverer who would remove the godless Gentiles and establish God's kingdom on earth, with Jerusalem as its capital. But Jesus' messiahship came, not with a sword, but with a cross.

The Desert

It was from the desert that John the Baptist came as the messiah's forerunner, calling people to repent and be baptized. It was also in the desert that Jesus was tempted by Satan, as he challenged the sort of messiah he had come to be.

Who was Jesus?

Mark begins by telling us that the gospel is about "Jesus Christ, the Son of God" (Mark 1:1).

1. Jesus Christ
"Christ" is not his name, but his role. "Christ" is the Greek for the Hebrew word *mashiah* ("messiah" or "anointed one"). In Old Testament times, prophets, priests, and kings were anointed with oil to symbolize God's Spirit being poured out on them for their work. "Messiah" came to be used of that ultimate prophet, priest and king, the descendant of King David, who would redeem God's people and introduce God's kingdom (e.g. Isaiah 9:6–7; 11:1–16; 42:1–7; Jeremiah 23:5–6; 33:14–16; Daniel 7:13–14; Micah 5:2–4). The New Testament claims that Jesus was this promised anointed one.

2. Son of God
But the New Testament claims Jesus was more than an anointed man; it says he was also the Son of God – not in some honorary way, but truly divine. He was God-become-man through the virgin birth and incarnation. But because this title could so easily be misunderstood, Jesus coined a completely different one for himself, one without associations: the Son of Man, a reference to Daniel's vision (Daniel 7:13) in which the kingdom was given to a man, yet one who was far more than a man.

10 BC | 0 | 10 AD | 20 | 30

31–14 BC Reign of Augustus
c.5 BC Jesus born
AD 14–37 Reign of Tiberius
AD 26–36 Pilate governor in Judea
AD 27–30 Jesus' ministry
AD 30 Jesus' crucifixion and resurrection

See also
Evidence for Jesus p. 21
The Gospels pp. 162–63
The Story of Jesus pp. 162–95

The Sea of Galilee, around which Jesus did so much of his ministry.

His birth

The Christmas story is one of the best-known stories in the world: the angel that told Mary she would become pregnant; the census that forced Joseph and Mary to travel to Bethlehem; Jesus' birth in a stable; the visits of shepherds and wise men (Magi); Herod's slaughtering of all baby boys under two. But behind these scenes lay a deeper mystery, Christians believe. As John puts it, "In the beginning was the Word, and the Word was with God, and the Word was God… the Word became flesh and made his dwelling among us" (John 1:1, 14). The New Testament's claim is that in Jesus, the Word, it was no one less than God himself who came to us.

His ministry

Around the age of thirty (Luke 3:23) Jesus began his public ministry, which lasted just three years. From shaky beginnings in Nazareth (Luke 4:16–20), his popularity spread far and wide as he demonstrated God's love through healing the sick, freeing the demonized, and teaching everyone about God's kingdom. His miracles were *demonstrations* of that kingdom, showing what life is like when God rules; his parables were *explanations* of it, showing how that kingdom works. He gathered an expression of God's new community around himself, with a core of twelve disciples, showing what life together under God's rule could look like. And yet, while his message and miracles attracted many, they also antagonized many, especially the vested religious and political powers who felt threatened by him.

His death

While his death seemed politically inevitable, the Bible claims it was actually part of God's plan and the very reason he came (e.g. Matthew 16:21; 20:25–28; John 12:23–33). After a whole number of trials with trumped-up charges, the Jewish leaders persuaded Pilate to have him crucified, a brutal execution reserved for the worst of criminals and traitors, and for Jews, a symbol of being under God's curse (Deuteronomy 21:23). Yet this death, which fulfilled ancient prophecies, often down to the smallest details (e.g. Psalm 22:16–18), was the means of mankind's sin being forgiven, Christians believe, just as Isaiah had foreseen (Isaiah 52:13 – 53:12) and as Jesus would later explain (Luke 24:25–27). His death was not a disaster, but rather the eternal plan of God for putting people into a right relationship with himself.

His resurrection

Crucified on Friday, by Sunday his disciples were claiming they had seen Jesus again, not as a spirit or "presence", but physically – though at first, none of them believed it. The resurrection confirmed for them that Jesus was indeed the messiah who had brought God's long-expected kingdom – and that this kingdom was no longer something to be awaited in the distant future, but that it was here right now, accessible to all who trusted him. The next stage of the story was under way.

Faith idea: The cross

Jesus said that the reason he came was not to live, but to die. This doesn't diminish his teaching, ethics, or miracles; rather, these all point to what he was dying for – the restoration of mankind's relationship with God to how it was at the beginning. The cross, the Bible says, was God's own way of dealing with human sin, which always leads to death. If there had been no cross, there could be no forgiveness, no relationship, no hope.

The Birth of the Church

Fired Up for Mission

After the resurrection, Jesus spent the next forty days teaching about God's kingdom. While it is clear that the disciples were still thinking in nationalistic terms (Acts 1:6), Jesus had something far bigger in mind that would involve them going to *all* nations, not just Israel (Matthew 28:18–20). But it was only when the Holy Spirit came that they started to understand, and a minor Jewish sect in Jerusalem was transformed into a worldwide movement, embracing both Jews and Gentiles. The promise made to Abraham 2,000 years earlier was starting to happen.

Pentecost

It was 9 a.m. and the disciples were getting ready to celebrate Pentecost, one of the three days when all Jewish men were required to attend the Temple in Jerusalem – which is why the Christian Pentecost event almost certainly took place in the Temple and not the Upper Room, as traditionally thought. Suddenly, what they could only describe as wind and fire rushed into the courtyard, and they were filled with the Holy Spirit and spoke in tongues (Acts 2:1–4). It was such an overwhelming experience that many of those watching at first thought they were drunk; but Peter explained that all this was simply the fulfilment of Joel's prophecy (Acts 2:15–21), offering others this experience of God's Spirit too if they would believe in Jesus (Acts 2:22–39). The church and its mission had been birthed, and on a most suitable occasion, for the Jewish festival of Pentecost celebrated two things: the giving of the Law and the harvest. Through the Holy Spirit, here was God's promised new law and new harvest: a law written not on stone but on hearts, and a harvest not of grain but of people.

Acts of the Apostles

The book of Acts was addressed to Theophilus (Acts 1:1), an unknown Roman official who was possibly Luke's patron, just like Luke's Gospel was (Luke 1:3). Since the style of writing of both books is identical, it seems clear therefore that Luke also wrote Acts. It is the second part of his two-volume work completing the story of "all that Jesus *began* to do and teach" (Acts 1:1), Luke's implication being that Jesus still had more to do through his followers.

Acts covers the life of the early church from Jesus' ascension (c. AD 30) to Paul's first imprisonment in Rome (c. AD 59–62). It is an utterly honest account, showing both the church's successes and its failures over this period.

The Nicanor Gate

The "Beautiful Gate", where Peter healed a crippled beggar (Acts 3:1–10) was almost certainly the Nicanor Gate in the Temple. Made of the highest quality bronze, which shone in the sun, it stood in the Court of the Women at the top of fifteen steps beyond which neither women nor the unclean (such as lepers) could pass. Begging for alms at such places was very common.

Healing was a common aspect of Christian ministry, as it had been with Jesus himself, and seems to have been an ongoing feature of early church life (Acts 3:1–10; 5:12–16; 8:6–8,13; 9:17–19, 32–42; 14:8–10; 15:12; 16:16–18; 19:11–12; 20:7–12; 28:3–5, 7–9).

The first twenty years of church life in Acts

Joys and successes:

- 3,000 baptized at Pentecost (2:41)
- Vibrant shared life (2:42-47; 4:32-37)
- Healings at the Temple (3:1–26; 5:12–16)
- Conversions of Samaritans (8:4–25) and an Ethiopian eunuch (8:26–40)
- First Gentile convert (10:1–48)
- Peter's miraculous escape from prison (12:1–19)
- Paul's first missionary journey (13:1 - 14:28)

Sadnesses and failures:

- Ananias and Sapphira try to cheat the church and are struck dead (5:1–11)
- Disagreements between Jewish and Gentile Christians (6:1–7)
- Martyrdom of Stephen (7:1–60)
- Doubts that Paul was truly converted (9:26–30)
- Unhappiness at Peter baptizing Gentiles without requiring them to become Jews (11:1–18)

See also
His ascension pp. 186–87
His followers pp. 192–93
Pentecost pp. 188–89

James and the Jerusalem church

James, the brother of Jesus and author of the New Testament letter that bears his name, quickly became the leader of the Jerusalem church. When Peter was miraculously released from jail, he told the servant to "tell James and the brothers about this" (Acts 12:17), and later Paul visited "James and all the elders" (Acts 21:18), indicating that James was obviously seen as the leader. He chaired the crucial Council of Jerusalem, concluding the discussions with a clear authority that was accepted by others (Acts 15:19). It isn't surprising, therefore, that Paul described him as a pillar of the church (Galatians 2:9). He was martyred in AD 62.

The Jerusalem church went through hard times, experiencing both persecution and poverty, and eventually needing support from the Gentile churches (e.g. Romans 15:25–26). Sadly, it eventually lost its pre-eminence through its inability to look beyond its Jewish roots, and Antioch would soon become far more significant in terms of the church's wider mission.

Ever-widening circles

In the thirty years following the resurrection, the church expanded rapidly, taking it way beyond its Jewish roots. Acts records the most significant breakthroughs of those years:

- Conversions among Samaritans, traditionally seen as unfaithful "half-Jews" (Acts 8:4–25).
- The conversion of an Ethiopian eunuch, whose condition excluded him from ever becoming a Jew (Acts 8:26–38).
- The conversion of the first Gentiles, a Roman centurion and his family and friends (Acts 10:1–48), as God gave them his Spirit before Peter had time to circumcise them, which he probably would have done.
- Conversions in Antioch, with its Gentile population from around the world (Acts 11:19–21).
- Conversions across Asia Minor (Turkey), Greece, and Rome as Paul began his travels (Acts 13:1 – 28:31).

But while Acts focuses on the church's growth across the Roman world, it was also spreading in other directions. Church tradition says that Thomas went to India and Matthew to Ethiopia and Arabia. The church was truly becoming an inter-racial and international community of God's people.

Faith idea: Filled with the Spirit

Whereas only special people, like leaders and prophets, had experienced God's Spirit in Old Testament times, Joel looked forward to a day when all God's people would receive him (Joel 2:28–32). Receiving the Spirit is seen in Acts as the norm of Christian experience (Acts 19:2), though this is described in various ways – being baptized with the Spirit, receiving the Spirit, being filled with the Spirit – suggesting that what is important is not the terminology but the reality.

On the right, the 3,500-seater amphitheatre in Caesarea Maritima where, according to Josephus, Herod Agrippa, who had James killed and Peter imprisoned, was struck down by an angel for claiming to be God (Acts 12:19–23).

The Growth of the Church

To the Ends of the Earth

Jesus had promised that his disciples would be his witnesses "to the ends of the earth" (Acts 1:8). Once they had grasped that the gospel really was for Gentiles as well as Jews, Christians began to push across the Roman world, reaching Syria by AD 40, Asia Minor by AD 48, Greece by AD 52, and Rome by AD 60. Their mission was under way.

Antioch

Antioch, the capital of the Roman province of Syria, lay on the Orontes River on a major trade route where people from many nations met. The church here was planted by Christians fleeing Jerusalem after Stephen's martyrdom. While some preached only to Jews, others crossed the barrier to Gentiles, many of whom responded (Acts 11:19–21). The nature of the city shaped the nature of the church: cosmopolitan and outward-looking. So while Jerusalem stayed entrenched in its Jewish roots, Antioch became the most significant base of the Christian mission.

Saul's conversion

A zealous Pharisee, Saul hunted down Christians; but he was stopped in his tracks by a powerful encounter with the risen Jesus (Acts 9:1–19). This changed the direction of his life, as Jesus commissioned him to take the gospel to the Gentiles, and he began to use his Roman name, Paul, rather than his Jewish one, Saul. He immediately started preaching in synagogues (Acts 9:20–22), but then withdrew to Arabia to reflect (Galatians 1:17). On returning to Damascus, he avoided an assassination attempt by being lowered over the city walls in a basket (Acts 9:23–25), a foretaste of trials he would face over the coming years (2 Corinthians 11:23–29).

Persecution – and victory

While Christianity seemed to be just another Jewish sect and therefore a *religio licta* (state-authorized religion), Rome let it be. But once emperors started claiming divinity and Christians refused to worship them, Rome's anger was unleashed. Persecution erupted under Nero (AD 54–68), who blamed Christians for the great fire of Rome (AD 64), throwing them to lions in the arena or using them as human candles. Peter and Paul were martyred at this time, Peter crucified upside-down, according to tradition, and Paul, as a Roman citizen, beheaded. Years later John was exiled to Patmos where he wrote Revelation. But despite this persecution, both Peter and Paul said that Christians should be good citizens (1 Peter 2:13–17; Romans 13:1–7). And John's Revelation shows that, despite all the devil's efforts, God will triumph at the end and the promise to Abraham will be fulfilled – a family of "every tribe and language and people and nation" (Revelation 5:9) gathered around Jesus in God's

Paul's journeys

The second half of Acts is a travelogue, recording Paul's journeys with his companions (Barnabas, Mark, Silas, Timothy, Luke, Priscilla and Aquila, and others) as they planted churches and returned to strengthen them. This map shows the journeys recorded in Acts.

40 50 60 70 80 90

- AD 35 Paul converted
- AD 46–47 Paul's first journey
- AD 50–52 Paul's second journey
- AD 53–57 Paul's third journey
- AD 59–62 Paul imprisoned in Rome
- AD 67/68 Paul's death
- AD 70 Romans destroy Jerusalem
- AD 90–95 John exiled on Patmos

See also
The Christian Faith pp. 158–59
Jesus' Message pp. 190–91
Travel pp. 112–13

New Testament letters

The New Testament contains twenty-one letters, the first thirteen (Romans–Philemon) written by Paul.

- **Romans** (AD 57) God's promises to Abraham are being fulfilled and Gentiles are included, not through keeping the Law, but through faith.
- **1 Corinthians** (AD 55) Love and the Holy Spirit's gifts are the key to every problem in the church.
- **2 Corinthians** (AD 55) A spiritual father's joy as he hears that things are going better.
- **Galatians** (AD 49/50) Gentiles do not have to become Jews before they can become Christians, nor keep the Jewish Law.
- **Ephesians** (AD 60) The blessings of being "in Christ" and being part of his church.
- **Philippians** (c. AD 60) Paul's joy at the church's friendship and God's goodness, despite his being imprisoned.
- **Colossians** (c. AD 60) Countering heresies about Jesus that were creeping into the church and claims to secret spiritual insights.
- **1 Thessalonians** (c. AD 50/51) Appreciation of the new church and encouragement to keep going in the light of Jesus' return.
- **2 Thessalonians** (AD 50/51) Correction of misunderstandings about Jesus' return.
- **1 Timothy** (c. AD 62) Practical encouragements to a young pastor on caring for the church.
- **2 Timothy** (c. AD 66/67) Final thoughts shared with a spiritual son in anticipation of Paul's impending execution.
- **Titus** (c. AD 63–65) Practical instructions for wise leadership of the church.
- **Philemon** (c. AD 60) Encouragement to receive a runaway slave who had become a Christian and needed a new start, just as Jesus had given Philemon a new start.
- **Hebrews** (pre-AD 70) Encouragement to Jewish Christians under pressure to return to Judaism to persevere in their Christian faith, for Jesus was better than everything they had left.
- **James** (c. AD 49/50) Written to Jewish Christians, encouraging them to stand firm and let their faith be expressed in practical ways.
- **1 Peter** (early AD 60s) A message of comfort and hope in the face of persecution and an encouragement to stand firm, remembering Jesus who suffered for them.
- **2 Peter** (early AD 60s) Addressing false teaching and a call to stand firm in the light of Jesus' return, which will bring God's justice.
- **1, 2, 3 John** (c. AD 85–95) Encouragement to share fellowship with God and one another and to avoid loving "the world" and being deceived by false teaching; 2 and 3 John are short personal notes.
- **Jude** (c. AD 65–85) A reminder from history of the danger of living godless lives and a call to persevere, trusting God who is able to keep us from falling.

The first Jewish revolt
Jews too suffered Rome's wrath when they stopped all foreign sacrifices, including those to Caesar. A war dragged on between AD 66 and 73, the height of which was the sacking of Jerusalem in AD 70 and the destruction of the Temple, never to be rebuilt. Some Zealots fled to Masada, a fortress-palace in the Judean desert, where they held out until AD 73. When the Romans finally breached the walls, having built a huge ramp, they found the Jews had taken their own lives.

Faith idea: Christian

"The disciples were called Christians first at Antioch" (Acts 11:26). Originally "Christian" ("Christ-follower") was a nickname given by others. The name emphasizes that being a Christian is not about belonging to a particular nation, family, or church, but rather choosing personally to follow Christ.

The Ancient Near East

The Setting of the Bible's Story

While the major part of the Bible's story is set in the tiny land of Canaan, that story cannot be understood apart from the stories of the nations surrounding it. These are examined more closely later (pp. 62–83); here we simply see the "big picture", noting how the nation of Israel, that was supposed to influence all the other nations, ended up again and again being influenced by them instead. Yet through it all, God's bigger purpose was at work.

Insights from archaeology

Our knowledge of all these ancient civilizations comes through two main sources: first, contemporary records (such as the mid-second millennium BC *Nuzi Tablets* recording in Akkadian some legal and social proceedings, which help illustrate earlier patriarchal customs, or the *Cyrus Cylinder* recording Persia's conquest of Babylon); second, the discoveries of archaeology, whose artefacts show not only what life was like but also provide evidence of events like invasions.

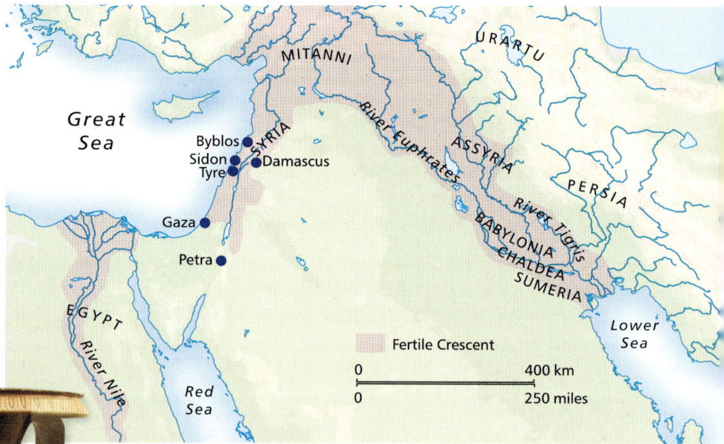

The Fertile Crescent
The Fertile Crescent was the belt of well-watered land stretching from Egypt with its River Nile, up along the Mediterranean coast of Canaan, and then down into Mesopotamia (modern Iraq), irrigated by its two main rivers, the Euphrates and the Tigris. Its fertility was understandably attractive, especially in a region with so many deserts and mountains, which explains why these lands were so often fought over.

Pottery

The constant changes of style in pottery (whose fragments are the most common archaeological discovery) are one of the greatest helps to archaeologists in dating sites. These pictures show the significant change of style between the simpler Iron Age style (above) and the beautiful craftsmanship of the late fourth century Hellenistic period reflected in this vase found in the tomb of Philip II of Macedon.

Tells
A "tell", or mound, although it may look just like a hill, is in fact the remains of a town. In ancient times, whole towns would often be destroyed by invaders; but rather than move away, the inhabitants simply rebuilt the city later. After all, bricks and wood were already there in abundance, as well as a good water supply, which was why the town was built there in the first place. But that meant that each time the town was destroyed and rebuilt (often several times over a millennium), it was on top of the previous ruins, so each city would be a little higher than the previous one. Archaeologists cut layers (strata) into these tells to reveal their history and can work out the date of each stratum from things like changing styles of pottery. This is the tell at Beit She'an (Bethshan) where King Saul's body was nailed to the city walls. The Graeco-Roman city of Scythopolis lies below.

See also
Nations pp. 62–83
The Bible and History pp. 20–21
The Promised Land pp. 30–31

The lands of the Bible

This map shows the world of Bible times and the nations whose history impacted God's people in various ways and at various times.

1. The Roman empire
By New Testament times the Roman empire covered most of Europe, the Middle East, and North Africa. While its Judean governor ordered Jesus' crucifixion, it unwittingly helped Christianity's expansion through its stability and excellent road network. The Jews experienced Rome's iron hand when Rome destroyed Jerusalem and its Temple in AD 70.

2. The Greek empire
Under Alexander the Great, the Greek empire spread as far as the borders of India. Its imposition of Greek culture and lifestyle brought it into conflict with Jews in the second century BC; but its provision of a world language significantly helped the preaching of the gospel.

3. Asia Minor
The Hittites built a powerful empire here between 1600 and 1200 BC, reaching south to Syria. In New Testament times, much of Paul's work took place in Asia Minor and many churches were planted here.

4. Mesopotamia
The Tigris–Euphrates Valley was home to several civilizations in the Old Testament period. In Abraham's time, the major civilizations were the Sumerians and Chaldeans; but later, Assyria, Babylonia, and Persia all developed here, and all had a great impact on Israel.

5. Assyria
Settling in the region c. 2300 BC, Assyria became a leading state between 1500 and 1100 BC, and expansion in the ninth and eighth centuries BC saw their empire reach Egypt. Assyria was responsible for the destruction of Israel and the dispersion of its ten northern tribes in 722 BC.

6. Babylon
Originating around 3000 BC, Babylon came to the height of its power in the seventh century BC when it conquered Assyria, swallowing up its empire. It conquered Judah, destroyed Jerusalem and the Temple in 586 BC, and exiled God's people to Babylon.

7. Persia
Appearing in the seventh century BC, Persia quickly became a powerful nation, stretching from Greece and Egypt in the west to Uzbekistan and the borders of India in the east. It was Persia that, in 538 BC, allowed the Jews to return to the Promised Land and rebuild the Temple.

8. Palestine
Known by different names at different periods (Canaan, Palestine, Israel, Judea) and seen by Jews as the land God promised to Abraham and his descendants, this was where most of the Bible's story took place.

9. Egypt
Developing in the Nile Valley around 3000 BC and becoming one of the ancient world's greatest civilizations, Egypt impinged on Bible history in various ways, at times as an enemy, but at times as a place of refuge.

Faith idea: Purpose

Israel's fourth prime minister, Golda Meir, once asked God why he chose Canaan as the Promised Land when it was the only Middle Eastern region that turned out to have no oil. But the Bible says God always has a purpose in everything, even what we don't understand. His purpose in choosing Canaan, it would become clear, was to put his people at the crossroads of civilization, so they could influence everything, especially through their messiah, Jesus. The preparation for his coming, Christians believe, shows that while God's plans may often seem slow in coming, they are never late.

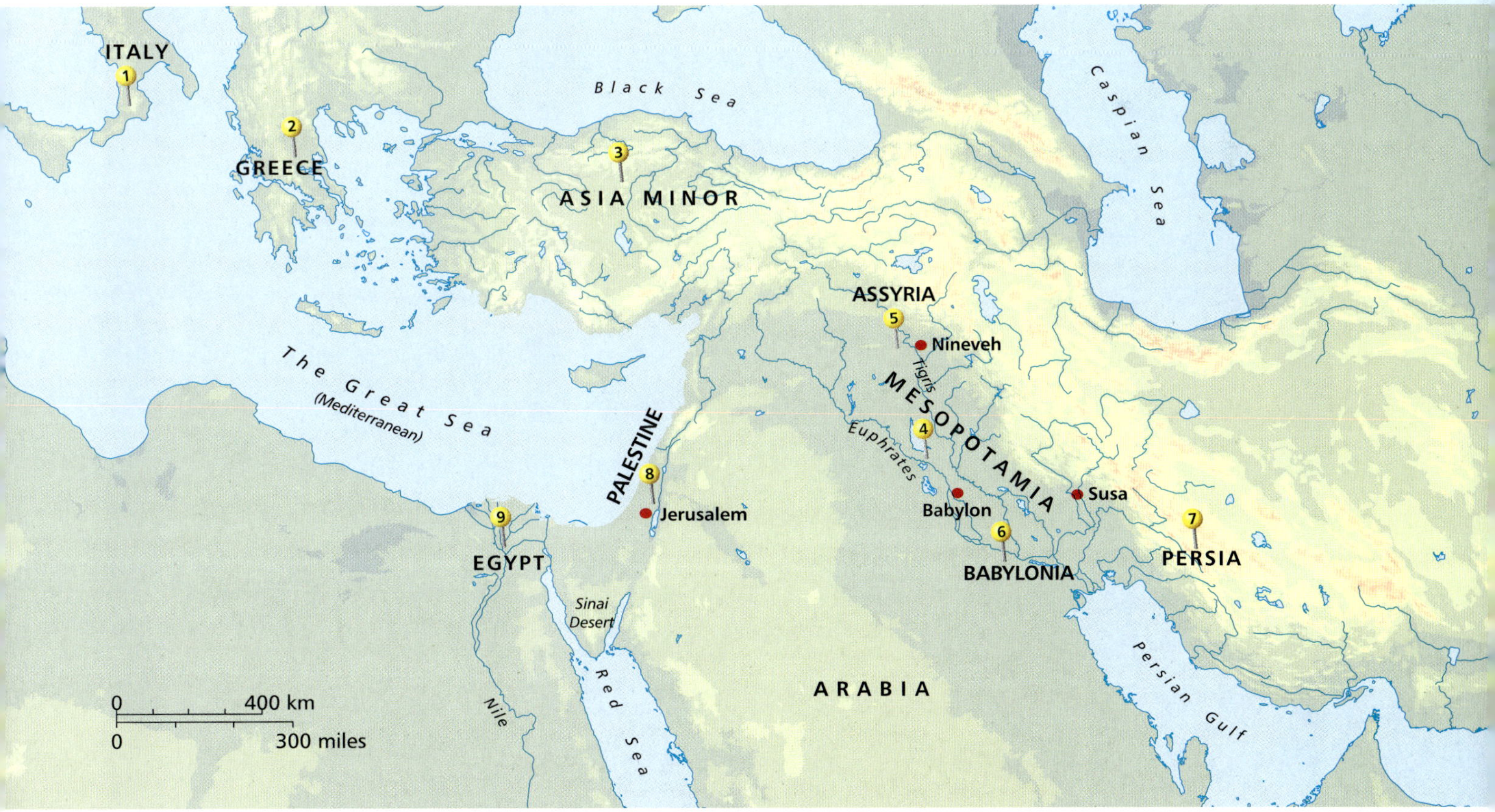

The Land of Canaan

A Land Flowing with Milk and Honey

God had called Moses to lead his people to "a land flowing with milk and honey" (Exodus 3:8) – symbols of the provision of both the basics and the good things of life. Although Moses never entered that land himself, he never lost sight of its promised goodness. Even in his final days, he was still describing Canaan as "a land with wheat and barley, vines and fig-trees, pomegranates, olive oil and honey; a land where bread will not be scarce and you will lack nothing" (Deuteronomy 8:8–9).

Canaan's geography

Canaan fell into distinct geographical regions:

1. The coastal plain
Comprised sand dunes, forest, and swamps at its southern end – not very useful land, which is why the Philistines were constantly seeking new territory. However, its northern end, the Plain of Sharon, was very fertile, and beyond Carmel were natural harbours from where the Phoenicians traded.

2. The Shephelah
Very fertile foothills, some 12–15 miles (19–24 km) wide, and therefore often fought over by Israel and the Philistines. Four valleys ran through it as corridors, with fortified cities like Gezer, Beth Shemesh, and Lachish guarding the roads.

3. The Central Highlands
Rising to 3,660 feet (1,115 m) near Bethel, these were the heart of Israelite territory and home to cities like Jerusalem and Hebron. International highways avoided this area, leaving it isolated and therefore protected.

4. The Plain of Megiddo
Formed an east-west plain between the Central Highlands and the Galilean hills. The main north-south road from Egypt to Mesopotamia crossed it, so it was strategic for both trade and war. Many battles occurred here and John, in Revelation, saw the end time battle (Armageddon) as happening here.

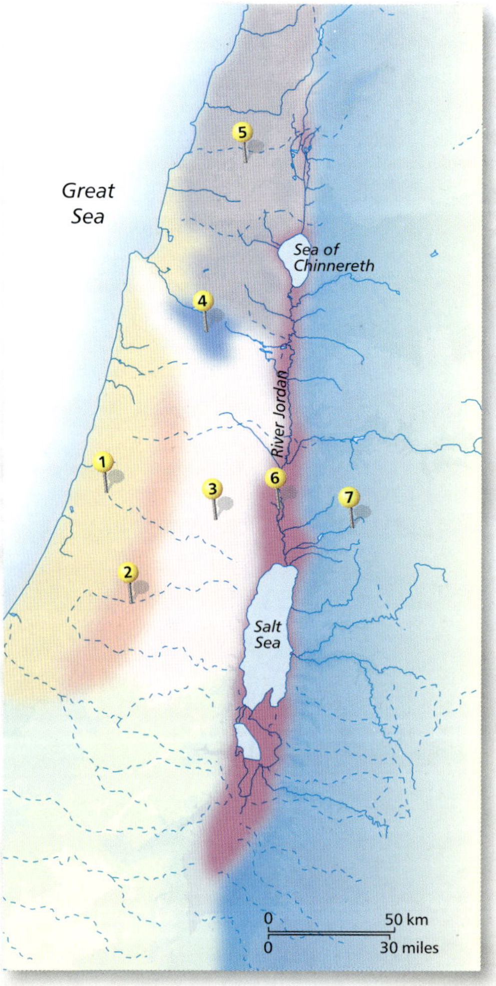

5. Galilee
Saw the continuation of the highlands, with hills rising to 3,950 feet (1,200 m) and then on to the mountains of Lebanon, climaxing in Mount Hermon at 9,232 feet (2,814 m). The lower Galilean hills were very fertile and the area became prosperous, aided by passing international trade. The Sea of Chinnereth, meaning "Harp" because of its shape (called the Sea of Galilee or Sea of Tiberius in New Testament times), was rich in fish. Galilee was where Jesus spent most of his life.

6. The Jordan Valley
Running from the Sea of Galilee in the north to the Dead (or Salt) Sea in the south, it is part of the Great Rift Valley. The Dead Sea is the lowest point on earth, more than 1,300 feet (400 m) below sea level, with its floor a further 1,400 feet down, and is 25 per cent salt. The river drops 2,380 feet (725 m) along its course, giving rise to its name (Jordan means "descender"). It is so winding that it covers nearly 200 miles (325 km), twice its direct distance. To the south of the Dead Sea is the Arabah Valley.

7. The Transjordan
To the east of the Jordan Valley, this was a mountainous area rising from 1,900 feet (580 m) east of Galilee to 6,560 feet (2000 m) southeast of the Dead Sea. It therefore attracted rainfall and provided good pasture for animals. Beyond it lay the Eastern desert.

See also
The Canaanites pp. 68–69
Farming pp. 104–05
Promised Land pp. 30–31

The River Jordan, in Lower Galilee, looking south.

Water

Moses described Canaan as "a land with streams and pools of water, with springs flowing in the valleys and hills" (Deuteronomy 8:7). Streams formed from the runoff rain on the hills, while pools and springs came from underground water sources. There were few streams west of the Jordan, so most places were dependent on springs and cisterns. Rain fell mainly in the winter (the "former rains" from mid-October and the "latter rains" in April/May) and increased with the height of the land, so the Galilean hills had more rain than the Judean hills. Dew, especially along the coastal region, also played an important part in watering the land, as moisture was blown in from the Mediterranean and fell to the ground as it cooled at night.

With no great rivers like those in Egypt and Mesopotamia that could be used for irrigation, the land was utterly dependent on rain. That is why Israel would be constantly faced with the question: who sends the rain, Baal or Yahweh? – a challenge the prophet Elijah was tireless in voicing (1 Kings 17:1; 18:1–2, 16–46). Droughts and ensuing famines weren't uncommon, especially when God's people were disobedient (Deuteronomy 28:23–24; Jeremiah 14:1–10).

Temperature

Canaan's varied geographical make-up produced significantly varying temperatures. It could be as hot as 50°C by the Dead Sea, yet cool and wet in Upper Galilee. Cooling breezes from the Mediterranean made the summer heat more tolerable, while "the east wind"– the *khamsin*, a hot dry wind from Arabia – could make life unbearable (e.g. Jonah 4:8).

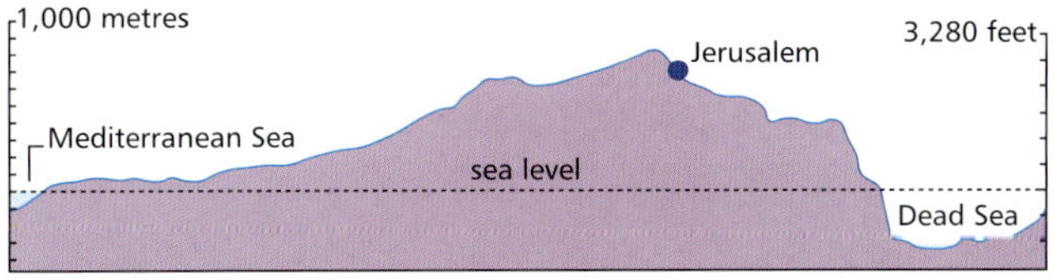

A cross-section of Canaan, showing how the land slopes up gently from the coast but then drops steeply towards the Jordan Valley and the Dead Sea.

Natural resources

Iron was plentiful, though not always of high quality, while copper was found mainly in Transjordan. While iron could be surface-mined, shafts had to be dug to reach copper. Primitive mining techniques are described in Job 28:1–11. The limestone of the Central Highlands and Galilee provided good stone for building, while limitless supplies of salt were available from the shores of the Dead Sea.

Earthquakes weren't unknown, and it may well have been timely earthquakes that caused the Jordan to stop flowing (see Joshua 3:15–16) and Jericho's walls to collapse (Joshua 6). Both Amos (1:1) and Zechariah mention a major earthquake happening during the reign of King Uzziah (Zechariah 14:5).

The Egyptian *Story of Sinuhe* (c.1950 BC), describing Sinuhe's flight from Egypt and stay in Canaan, confirms the Bible's description of the land. It says that "figs were in it and grapes. It had more wine than water. Abundant was its honey, plentiful were its olives. All kinds of fruit were on its trees. Barley and wheat were there, and limitless cattle of all kinds." This fragment is a copy dating from c. 1250 BC, probably from Thebes.

Faith idea: Dependence

Moses had warned Israel that enjoyment of the Promised Land wasn't automatic; it required dependence on God. One of the major ways this was tested was through their need to trust God to send rain, for Canaan had no great rivers for irrigation. The Bible says that real dependence is when we have nothing to fall back on other than God's promise alone.

The Holy Land

A Home for God's People

While Israel is often called "the holy land", the term actually occurs only once in the text of the Hebrew Bible – in Zechariah 2:12. Prophesying at the time of Judah's return from exile, Zechariah describes Israel as "the holy land" because the holy God had reclaimed it for his holy purposes – not just as a home for Abraham's descendants, but as a base from which salvation would extend to people of every land. The Old Testament more commonly refers to Israel as "the Promised Land", or simply "the land".

Division of the land

After conquering Canaan, Joshua divided it between the twelve tribes. Reuben, Gad, and half of Manasseh returned to land already assigned to them east of the River Jordan (Numbers 32:1–42), and Joshua divided Canaan among the remaining tribes, as shown in the map to the right. Dan ended up with two areas because their original allocation, between Ephraim and Judah, proved too difficult for them to take from the Amorites (Judges 1:34), so many migrated north to Galilee (Joshua 19:47; Judges 18:1–31).

The tabernacle was located at Shiloh, so everyone could reach it easily (Joshua 18:1).

God's tenants

"The land must not be sold permanently, because the land is mine and you are but aliens and my tenants" (Leviticus 25:23). Because God claimed the land as his, Israel was to see itself as merely a tenant, the Bible says, caring for it on God's behalf. This was expressed in many of their laws. For example, a tithe (one-tenth) of crops that the land produced and of the herds and flocks that fed from it was to be given to God (Leviticus 27:30–33); and land couldn't be sold freehold, only leasehold, with it returning to its original owners every fiftieth year (the Jubilee Year) to ensure no one ever ended up in perpetual poverty (Leviticus 25:8–31).

The Judean Desert

Key cities

Over the 2,000 years of Israel's history in the Bible, certain places would play a leading role in God's unfolding story. Among these were:

1. Capernaum, the base of Jesus' ministry (Matthew 4:12–16), where he taught and healed (e.g. Mark 1:21–34), yet which he lamented over for its unbelief (Matthew 11:23–24).

2. Nazareth, where Jesus grew up (Matthew 2:22–23) and where he was initially welcomed at the outset of his ministry, but then rejected when he said God's plan included Gentiles (Luke 4:16–30).

3. Megiddo, conquered by Joshua (Joshua 12:21) and fortified by Solomon (1 Kings 9:15). The plain below it was a frequent battleground, and Revelation (16:16) sees the last great battle, Armageddon ("mountain of Megiddo"), happening here.

4. Jezreel, location of Ahab's palace and where he stole Naboth's vineyard (1 Kings 21:1–28).

5. Caesarea, port where Peter first preached to Gentiles (Acts 10:1–48) and which Paul passed through several times (Acts 9:30; 18:22; 21:8). He was imprisoned here for two years before being sent to Rome (Acts 23:23 - 26:32).

6. Samaria, Omri's new northern capital (1 Kings 16:23–24) where Ahab later built an ornate palace (1 Kings 23:39) and a temple to Baal (1 Kings 16:32). After resisting two Syrian sieges, it finally fell to Assyria after a three-year siege, ending Israel's existence (2 Kings 17:3–6).

7. Shechem, where God promised the land to Abraham (Genesis 12:6–7), Joshua renewed the covenant (Joshua 24:1–27), and Jeroboam established his capital after the division of the kingdom (1 Kings 12:25).

8. Shiloh, location of the tabernacle (Joshua 18:1) and the ark of the covenant until the latter was captured by the Philistines (1 Samuel 4:1–11). Samuel grew up here (1 Samuel 1:24–28), but it was destroyed by the Philistines c. 1050 BC. Shiloh became a byword for an abandoned sanctuary (Jeremiah 7:12–15).

9. Bethel, renamed by Jacob after his dream (Genesis 28:10–22). The site of Abraham's first altar (Genesis 12:8–9), it became the centre of northern worship and the site of one of Jeroboam's golden calves (1 Kings 12:26–29).

See also
The Land of Canaan pp. 50–51
The Promised Land pp. 30–31
Temple pp. 146–47

10. Jericho, the first city taken by the Israelites (Joshua 5:13 - 6:27). This oasis, a home to a school of prophets (2 Kings 2:5), was where Jesus performed some miracles (e.g. Matthew 20:29–34) and met Zacchaeus (Luke 19:1–10).

11. Jerusalem, former Jebusite city captured by David and established as his capital 2 Samuel 5:6–10). It was here that Solomon built the Temple (2 Chronicles 2:1 - 7:22) that would be destroyed by Babylon in 586 bc (2 Kings 25:1–21). Often referred to as Zion (originally, the hill on which the city stood), the prophets and psalmists said Jerusalem was special to God (e.g. Psalm 48) and believed it would be the focus of God's end-time revelation (e.g. Isaiah 2:1–5). However, Jesus wept over its destiny because of its rejection of him (Matthew 23:37–39).

12. Bethlehem, Rachel's burial place (Genesis 35:19) and David's hometown, where he was anointed king (1 Samuel 16:1–13). Micah prophesied that the messiah would be born here (Micah 5:2; Matthew 2:6).

13. Lachish, captured by Joshua (Joshua 10:1–35) and later fortified by Rehoboam (2 Chronicles 11:5–12). Captured by Assyria, Sennacherib negotiated with Hezekiah from here until his army was struck by plague and he withdrew (2 Kings 18:13 - 19:36).

14. Hebron, Abraham's base (Genesis 13:18) where he received the promise of Isaac's birth (18:1–15) and where both Isaac and Jacob lived (35:27). Caleb took this city when Israel entered the land (Joshua 14:6–15), and David was crowned king here (2 Samuel 5:1–5).

15. Beersheba, where Abraham (Genesis 21:33), Isaac (26:23–25), and Jacob (46:1–4) all encountered God and which became a place of pilgrimage (Amos 5:5).

The extent of Israel
This map shows the approximate extent of the tribal territories, though Saul could do little more than secure Canaan's highlands during his reign (1050–1010 BC). However David (1010–970 BC) significantly extended and secured Israel's borders, and under him Israel at last gained complete control over the whole area God had promised to Abraham.

Faith idea: Holiness

The Bible describes God as "holy" – different from everything else – and calls those who follow him to reflect that holiness. For Israel, holiness was to be expressed in holy outward actions, through things like sacrifices, social obligations, and moral requirements that marked them out as "different", belonging to God. The New Testament, however, has little place for holy things, focusing instead on a holy person – Jesus – who alone, it claims, can make people holy as they follow him.

Plants, Flowers, and Spices

Not even Solomon ...

"Consider how the lilies grow. They do not labour or spin. Yet I tell you, not even Solomon in all his splendour was dressed like one of these. If that is how God clothes the grass of the field, which is here today, and tomorrow is thrown into the fire, how much more will he clothe you, O you of little faith!" (Luke 12:27–28; see also Matthew 6:28–30). Jesus often used things from the natural world to underline both the beauty of creation and mankind's uniqueness in it.

1. Aloe

A large plant whose resin and oil were used as perfume. Nicodemus anointed Jesus' body for burial with a mixture of aloes and myrrh (John 19:39–40).

1

2. Beans and lentils

Cooked as vegetables or dried and ground into flour (Ezekiel 4:9). Lentils were also made into soup (Genesis 25:34). Both were a good source of protein.

3. Bitter herbs

Leaves of wild plants with a bitter taste (like dandelion, endive, chicory). They were eaten in the Passover meal to remind Jews of the bitterness of slavery (Exodus 12:8).

4. Cassia

Fragrant bark from this tree was mixed with myrrh, cinnamon, and fragrant cane to produce the oil used for anointing priests (Exodus 30:23–24).

7a

5. Cereals

Part of the staple diet of Israel, used to make flour. Wheat produced the best flour for bread, while barley was used by the poor. Millet made the worst bread of all and was seen as food for times of famine. Barley was fed to horses and brewed for beer.

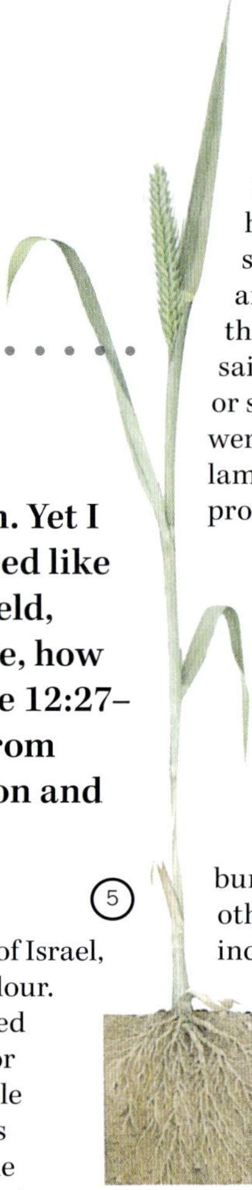

5

6. Cinnamon

Oil from the bark of cinnamon trees was used to flavour food and wine.

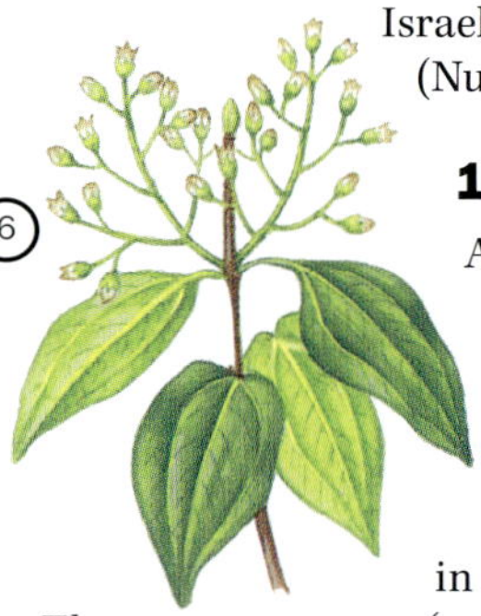

6

7. Cumin (a) and dill (b)

Used for spicing meat and flavouring bread and cakes. The Pharisees tithed even these tiny spice seeds, but Jesus rebuked them for doing this while neglecting more important issues (Matthew 23:23–24).

7b

8. Flax

Growing to about 18 inches (45 cm) high, its fibres were separated by steeping and combing and were then woven to make linen cloth for sails, fine clothing (Genesis 41:42), or shrouds (Mark 15:46). Its fibres were also used to make nets and lamp wicks, and its seeds crushed to produce linseed oil.

8

9. Frankincense

A gum collected by cutting the bark of its tree, which grew in southern Arabia and northeast Africa. It was transported in spice caravans (e.g. 1 Kings 10:2) and was very expensive. It gives off a sweet fragrance when burned and was used mixed with other spices to produce a special incense for use in the tabernacle (Exodus 30:34–37). It was one of the gifts brought by the Magi to Jesus at his birth (Matthew 2:11).

10. Garlic

Used for adding flavour to food, it was common in Egypt and was one of the foods (along with cucumbers, melons, leeks, and onions) that the Israelites missed when in the desert (Numbers 11:5).

11. Hyssop

A bushy fragrant plant growing out of rocks or walls (1 Kings 4:33). Its sprigs were used for sprinkling blood in rituals or sacrifices (e.g. Exodus 12:21–23; Leviticus 14:1–7), which is what David was thinking of when he asked God to "cleanse me with hyssop" (Psalm 51:7). A hyssop branch was used to affix the sponge soaked in wine vinegar that was offered to Jesus on the cross (John 19:29).

11

See also
Food and Drink pp. 98–99
The Land of Canaan pp. 50–51
Trees and Shrubs pp. 56–57

12

12. Lily

Refers to different flowers in the Bible – the scarlet tulip in Song of Songs 5:13, where lips are mentioned; or the lotus in 1 Kings 7:19, 26, where large flowers are envisaged on the Temple pillars and water reservoir. Elsewhere it may have been the wild blue hyacinth or the Madonna lily, which not only looked beautiful but whose bulb was also considered to be a delicacy.

13. Mandrake

A short-stemmed, large-leaved plant bearing orange-red berries resembling tomatoes, this plant was considered to promote fertility (Genesis 30:14–18).

14. Mint

A garden herb used for seasoning food.

15

15. Mustard

A plant growing to 4 feet (120 cm) high, but with very tiny black seeds used for flavouring and turned into oil. Jesus used this to illustrate the growth of God's kingdom (Matthew 13:31–32), and said that with faith as small as a mustard seed, his followers could do anything (Matthew 17:20).

16. Myrrh

A yellow-brownish gum from thorny bushes in southern Arabia and northeast Africa. It was the basis of the anointing oil used exclusively to consecrate the tabernacle, its furnishings, and priests (Exodus 30:22–33). It was one of the Magi's gifts to Jesus (Matthew 2:11) and was used by Nicodemus for anointing his body for burial. It was also used as a painkiller, mixed with wine, and was offered to Jesus on the cross, which he refused (Mark 15:22–23).

17

17. Papyrus

Grew in marshy areas (Job 8:11), especially in the Nile Delta, reaching 10 feet (3 m) tall. Its stems were cut into thin strips that were interwoven at right angles on a hard surface and pressed or beaten. When dry, they formed sheets of "paper" that could be pasted together to form a scroll. Papyrus was also used to make baskets (Exodus 2:3), boats (Job 9:26), rope, and sandals.

18. Rose

Almost certainly not the rose plant we know today, but more probably the narcissus, crocus, or mountain tulip (Isaiah 35:1; Song of Songs 2:1).

18

19. Spikenard (nard)

Used to make sweet-smelling ointment, imported from India and kept in alabaster jars to preserve its fragrance. This was the ointment used to anoint Jesus in Bethany (Mark 14:2–9; John 12:1–8).

19

20. Thistles

Over 120 kinds of thistle grew in Palestine, some as tall as 6 feet (2 m) high. The weeds in Jesus' parable of the wheat and the weeds (Matthew 13: 24–30) were darnel, indistinguishable from wheat in its early stages of growth. "Thorns" were plaited into a mock crown for Jesus by Roman soldiers before his crucifixion as "King of the Jews" (Mark 15:16–18).

20

21. Wormwood

The bitter-tasting absinthe, used in the Bible as a symbol of bitterness or sorrow (Revelation 8:10–11).

Faith idea: Frailty

"All men are like grass, and all their glory is like the flowers of the field. The grass withers and the flowers fall, because the breath of the Lord blows on them. Surely the people are grass. The grass withers and the flowers fall, but the word of our God stands for ever" (Isaiah 40:6–8; quoted in 1 Peter 1:24–25). As beautiful as flowers are, their temporary nature reminds us of the frailty of everything in this life, not least human existence. Only God and his word last forever, the Bible reminds us.

Trees and Shrubs

Pleasing to the Eye, Good for Food

"The Lord God made all kinds of trees grow out of the ground – trees that were pleasing to the eye and good for food" (Genesis 2:9). Genesis underlines how even things we take for granted, like trees, are part of God's good provision in creation. Besides their practical uses, such as food, fuel, and building material, they also play an important role in preventing soil erosion and controlling the climate. Here are some of the more important trees and shrubs in the Bible.

1. Acacia

Flat-topped and prickly trees that grew along dried-up riverbeds in the Sinai Desert and Arabah Valley. The ark of the covenant and its carrying poles were made from acacia wood (Exodus 25:10–16).

2. Almond

The first tree to blossom each year in Israel, its nuts were a favourite food and were also used to produce oil. God confirmed Aaron's authority by causing his almond rod to miraculously bud, flower, and fruit overnight (Numbers 17:1–11).

3. Balsam

Tall poplar trees that usually grow by water and whose leaves shake and rustle in the wind. God used this phenomenon to tell David when to attack the Philistines (2 Samuel 5:22–25).

4. Broom

A desert shrub that grows in dry sandy places. Its roots were used for making charcoal for fires (Job 30:4) or attached to arrows and set alight (Psalm 120:4).

5. Carob

Growing wild or cultivated, its pods were used as animal fodder, like those the prodigal son longed to eat (Luke 15:16).

6. Cedar

A huge flat-topped tree and the modern symbol of Lebanon, where it was plentiful in Bible times. Its wood is a warm red colour, very long-lasting, and can be carved well. It was used in constructing Solomon's Temple (1 Kings 6:14–18) and royal carriage (Song of Songs 3:7–10).

7. Cypress

A tall dark-green tree whose wood was used by Noah to make the ark (Genesis 6:14).

8. Date palm

A tall tree topped with 6-foot (2 m) leaves among which dates grow. The dates were enjoyed as food, while the leaves were used as symbols of victory, like those waved when Jesus rode into Jerusalem on Palm Sunday (John 12:13) and those waved by the saints in heaven (Revelation 9:9).

9. Fig

A medium-sized, slow-growing tree that produces sweet fruit for about ten months of the year. Its large leaves were made into garments by Adam and Eve (Genesis 3:7), but they were more commonly used as wrappings. The figs were eaten fresh (Isaiah 28:4) or dried into cakes (1 Samuel 25:18). Jesus cursed a fruitless fig tree as a symbol of God's judgment on fruitless Israel (Mark 11:1–14).

10. Fir and pine

Evergreens that grew on mountains and hills whose timber was used for building boats (Ezekiel 27:3–5), construction (1 Kings 5:8–9), and making musical instruments.

11. Laurel

Slow-growing evergreens with slender trunks and hard wood. Its leathery leaves were plaited into crowns and given to winning athletes (2 Timothy 4:7–8).

12. Myrtle

A wild shrub that grows on hillsides, with shiny evergreen leaves and a pleasant smell. Branches of myrtle were used for making shelters at the Jewish festival of Shelters (or Booths) (Nehemiah 8: 14–15).

See also
Farming pp. 104–05
Plants, flowers and spices pp. 54–55
The Land of Canaan pp. 50–51

15

13. Oak

Tall, long-living, strong trees found in several varieties, some of which are evergreen. The hard, long-lasting wood was used for making oars (Ezekiel 27:6) and carving idols (Isaiah 44:13–14). Oak trees were favoured locations for burying the dead (Genesis 35:8) and were often associated with idolatrous shrines (Isaiah 57:5; Ezekiel 6:13).

14. Olive

A small tree with grey-green leaves that produces berries containing a hard stone. The trees are slow growing, taking thirty years to mature, and are able to live for hundreds of years. Olives were eaten pickled, or crushed to produce oil for cooking, fuel for lamps, and skin lotion. The oil was also used in ancient Israel to anoint kings and priests for their work. Olive wood was carved and polished to make fine items, like the cherubim and doors in the Temple (1 Kings 6:23–35).

15. Pomegranate

A large shrub producing dark-green leaves and scarlet, bell-shaped flowers with large round fruit packed with juicy seeds. Its frequent mention in the Bible shows it was popular, as does its use in decorative art such as the embroidery on the high priest's robe (Exodus 28:31–35) and ornamentation in Solomon's Temple (1 Kings 7:16–20).

16. Sycamore

A kind of fig tree that likes warmer areas and cannot stand cold weather (Psalm 78:47). Amos tended sycamore figs (Amos 7:14). The tree's low-growing branches made it easy for Zacchaeus to climb one when he couldn't see Jesus because of the crowds (Luke 19:1–10).

17. Tamarisk

A bushy tree, with white or pink flowers and scaly leaves that excrete salt, that thrives in arid conditions and whose leafy branches provide welcome shade in the heat, as Saul appreciated (1 Samuel 22:6). Abraham planted a tamarisk tree in Beersheba (Genesis 21:33), symbolizing a peaceful and prosperous future, and Saul was buried beneath one (1 Samuel 31:13). Its bark was used for tanning and its wood for building and producing charcoal.

18. Vine

A vigorous climbing shrub with a short trunk and long branches producing clusters of green or black grapes. Vines were planted in rows on sunny slopes. Some grapes were pressed in winepresses to produce wine, while others were dried to make raisins. The vine became a national emblem of Israel, recalling the time when Moses sent spies into the Promised Land and the branch of grapes they brought back was so heavy that it took two men to carry it (Numbers 13:17–24). Jesus spoke of himself as the true Vine; that is, the new Israel (John 15:1).

Faith idea: God's provision

"God said, 'Let the land produce vegetation: seed-bearing plants and trees on the land that bear fruit with seed in it, according to their various kinds.' And it was so... And God saw that it was good" (Genesis 1:11–12). One aspect of God's goodness is his creation of a world with self-replicating abundant provision for us. The Bible says that he expects us to receive that provision gratefully, use it wisely, and share it generously with others.

6 10 10

Domestic and Working Animals

Gifts of God

As an agricultural people, the Israelites considered animals to be indispensable gifts of God. They used them for carrying loads, working on the farm, providing food, milk, and clothing, and occasionally even as pets. Here are some of the more common ones.

Working animals

Bullocks
Bullocks were used for pulling ploughs, heavy carts, and threshing sledges. They were also one of the prescribed animals for sacrifices (e.g. Leviticus 4:1–21).

Camels
Camels were invaluable to desert nomads, able to carry huge burdens of around 440 pounds (200 kg) and to go for days without water by drawing on the fat in their hump. The camel is particularly suited to desert life, with nostrils that close to thin slits to keep out the sand, eyes with long eyelashes to protect them, and lips and a tongue that can cope with eating thorns. Besides its carrying capacity, its dung could be dried and used as fuel, its milk drunk, and its hair used for clothing (like the garments worn by John the Baptist, Mark 1:6), though the Law forbade the Jews from eating its meat (Leviticus 11:4). Some peoples also used them in battle. While mentioned more often in the Old Testament than the New, the fact that Jesus used a camel in two humorous illustrations (Matthew 19:24; 23:24) shows they were still in use in New Testament times.

Donkeys and mules
The most common pack animals in Bible times, used by rich and poor alike for carrying loads or riding, the donkey was descended from the Nubian wild ass, and the mule was a crossbreed between horse and donkey. The most famous example of the use of a donkey in the Bible is when Jesus rode into Jerusalem on one on Palm Sunday, in fulfilment of Zechariah's messianic prophecy (Matthew 21:1–11).

Horses
Introduced into Israel in the tenth century BC, the horse was used only by the rich, or by kings and warriors in times of war. God told the Israelites not to trust in horses and chariots, since they were a symbol of human might (Isaiah 31:1), a principle King Solomon clearly did not understand, as he had thousands of them (1 Kings 4:26). Horses need better water and food supplies than donkeys and mules.

See also
Farming pp. 104–05
Fishing pp. 106–07
Food and Drink pp. 98–99

Food animals

Sheep

The fact that sheep were common in ancient Israel is reflected in there being many different words in Hebrew for "sheep", referring to their age, sex, and variety. Their wool was spun and woven to make clothing, and some were killed for their meat. They were among the most important Old Testament sacrifices, and John the Baptist described Jesus as "the Lamb of God" (John 1:29–36).

Goats

Goats were often hard to distinguish from sheep in appearance (which helps explain Jesus' parable of the sheep and goats in Matthew 25:31–46), but their eating habits were very different, with goats browsing for leaves and twigs rather than eating grass. Goats were kept for milk, cheese, meat, and hair for weaving into coarse cloth, and their skins were used for water bottles. They too were widely used as sacrifices, and in many cases a sheep or a goat could be offered (e.g. Leviticus 1:10).

Cattle

Cattle were kept to provide milk and meat, and leather from their skins. Bashan, northeast of the Sea of Galilee, was renowned for its cattle because of its rich pasturelands.

Fowl

First introduced to Israel from India through trading caravans, the Red Jungle fowl (the ancestor of modern chickens) was very common in ancient Israel. The fowl that were served at Solomon's table (1 Kings 4:23) were probably geese imported from Egypt. Jesus taught lessons based on hens and chickens (Luke 13:34).

Animals as pets

In contrast to life today, keeping pets was relatively rare in Israel. In fact, the only animal ever mentioned as a pet in the Old Testament is a lamb (2 Samuel 12:1–3). Wealthy Romans did keep pets, however, the most favoured of which were dogs, but also cats, fish, ferrets, blackbirds, parrots, monkeys, snakes, and even lions and tigers. In Greece, birds, dogs, goats, tortoises, and mice were all popular, and Greek vases portray hunters with their dogs. In Egypt, some dogs and cats were considered sacred and were even mummified.

The first clear archaeological evidence of domesticated dogs goes back to 9600 BC in Canaan. However, most references to dogs in the Bible are negative (e.g. 1 Samuel 17:42–43; 1 Kings 14:11; Proverbs 26:11), and there isn't even a word in Hebrew for "cat".

Animal welfare

While the Bible says that God gave mankind permission to use (Genesis 1:28) and eat (Genesis 9:3) the animals he had created, it also underlines that "a righteous man cares for the needs of his animal" (Proverbs 12:10). This was reflected in the Jewish Law that God gave to Moses, in which many laws provided for animal welfare. For example:

- The sabbath was to be a day of rest for animals as well as people (Exodus 20:8–10).
- Fields, vineyards, and olive groves were to be left fallow every six years so both the poor and wild animals could eat from them (Exodus 23:10–11).
- A donkey struggling under a load must be helped up, even if it belonged to an enemy (Exodus 23:5).
- Livestock were to be allowed to eat while they worked (Deuteronomy 25:4).

Such small but kind commands show that the Bible sets a high standard for animal welfare. However, the strict prohibition of animal idols and animal worship (Exodus 20:4–5) signals that, at the end of the day, animals remain part of the created order, given for people's use and enjoyment, but nothing more.

Faith idea: Dominion

The Bible says that man is not just another animal; he is the crown of God's creation, created on the same day as animals (so linked to them) but distinct from them by alone being made in God's image (Genesis 1:26–27). Animals are therefore not in any sense our "brothers", but our servants over whom we have been given "dominion" (authority and rule) (Genesis 1:28; 2:19; Psalm 8:6–9). But that dominion, the Bible teaches, should be caring not callous.

Wildlife

“God Made the Wild Animals” *(Genesis 1:25)*

The Bible’s simple account of creation, complex process though it no doubt was, highlights that all animal life was created by God (Genesis 1:20–24). Some large animals in the Bible (like the lion, bear, and ostrich) are no longer found in Israel; but here are some of the more common ones from Bible times.

Animals

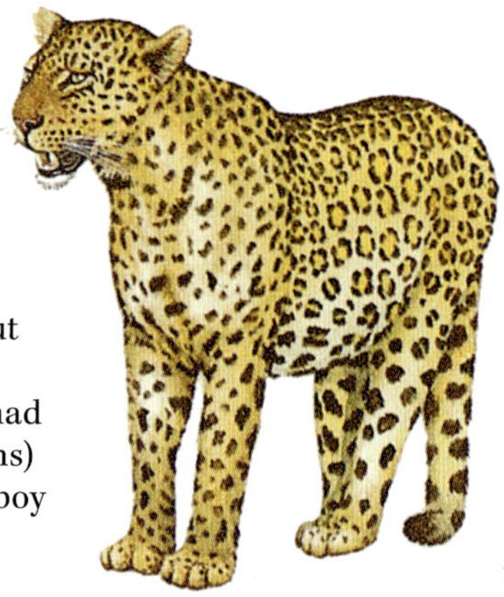

Bears
The Syrian brown bear, common in hills and woods, normally fed on berries, roots, honey, and eggs, but when hungry took lambs from flocks. King David had to fight off bears (and lions) when he was a shepherd boy (1 Samuel 17:34–37).

Deer
A variety of deer, gazelle, and ibex lived in Israel and were a major source of meat. As forests were cleared, life became harder for them and they gradually disappeared. They were used as images of gracefulness, swiftness, or gentleness (1 Chronicles 12:8; Song of Songs 2:8–9).

Foxes and jackals
Smaller cousins of the wolf, foxes hunt alone and often damage vines (Song of Songs 2:15), while jackals hunt in packs, scavenging at night, often in wild and desolate places, providing rich poetic and prophetic imagery.

Leopards
The leopard’s spotted coat acted as camouflage in forests and rocky areas so it could creep up on its prey unseen. The proverb about a leopard not being able to change its spots was quoted by Jeremiah (13:23).

Lions
Though common in Old Testament times, by New Testament times lions were rare in Israel, living in the thickets of the Jordan Valley. Assyrian and Babylonian kings enjoyed lion hunts and kept lions in cages or pits, as Daniel discovered (Daniel 6). The lion’s strength made it a symbol of power, and Jesus was called “the Lion of the tribe of Judah” (Revelation 5:5).

Wolves
Wolves were fierce hunters that usually fed on smaller animals, though sometimes might attack sheep or even cattle if hungry. The Bible describes deceptive leaders as wolves disguised as sheep (Matthew 7:15).

Birds

Doves and pigeons
Doves and pigeons were kept as domestic birds and used for food. Those too poor to sacrifice sheep or goats could offer two pigeons instead (Leviticus 5:7). A dove brought Noah an olive leaf, showing the floodwaters had receded (Genesis 8:8–12), and a dove rested on Jesus at his baptism as a symbol of God’s Spirit (Luke 3:21–22). Doves were proverbial symbols of innocence and gentleness (e.g. Matthew 10:16).

Eagles
These large birds of prey inspired awe (Proverbs 30:18–19) and admiration for their strength and powerful wings (Isaiah 40:30–31). God described himself as an eagle carrying Israel on his wings (Exodus 19:4); but the eagle could also be seen as an image of judgment (e.g. Ezekiel 17).

Ostriches
This large flightless bird was found throughout Arabia and Palestine in ancient times. Its unusual behaviour is well described in Job 39:13–18.

See also
Farming pp. 104–05
Fishing pp. 106–07
Domestic & Working animals pp. 58–59

Owls
Night-time hunters that swoop on small creatures and that inhabited ruined and deserted places (Isaiah 34:8–15), owls were seen as unclean by Jews.

Ravens
Large birds that will eat pretty much anything, ravens were used by God to miraculously feed Elijah during a time of famine (1 Kings 17:1–6).

Sparrows
"Sparrow" was used of any small bird suitable for eating, including larks and finches. Jesus used sparrows as an illustration of the extent of God's love (Matthew 10:29–31).

Quails
These small plump birds are migratory, covering long distances. When the Israelites were in the wilderness, God provided quail for them to eat by driving them inland with a strong wind (Numbers 11:31–32).

Vultures
Scavenging birds that lived off the carcasses of dead or wounded animals, they were proverbial of people waiting to pounce (Habakkuk 1:6–11). Jesus said his coming again would be as obvious as vultures gathering around a carcass (Matthew 24:28).

Reptiles

Lizards
A wide range of lizards was found in Israel, all of them unclean and forbidden as food (Leviticus 11:29–38). The lizard "found in kings' palaces" (Proverbs 30:28) was probably the gecko, whose toe pads allow it to climb walls and cross ceilings.

Snakes
The Bible doesn't distinguish between the variety of snakes living in Palestine and neighbouring lands. The snake appearing as a sign to Moses (Exodus 4:1–5) was probably a cobra, as these had special significance in Egypt, Pharaoh wearing one on his headdress as a symbol of authority. Some, like vipers, were poisonous (Numbers 21:6; Mark 16:18; Acts 28:1–5). The serpents in the wilderness (Numbers 21:4–9) were probably carpet vipers, whose venom can take two or three days to kill its victim, giving Moses time to make the bronze serpent God commanded him to set up. Jesus compared the scribes and Pharisees to a brood of vipers (Matthew 23:33), suddenly appearing like baby vipers, whose mother keeps her eggs within her until they are ready to hatch all at once.

Insects

Ants
Social insects living in colonies numbering up to millions, ants have a division of labour and are excellent at communicating and solving problems. The Bible sees them as examples of hard work and forethought (Proverbs 6:6–8).

Bees
While bees aren't mentioned often, they must have been prolific in a country described as "a land flowing with milk and *honey*". Honey was invaluable as a sweetener and as a tasty food. Most bees were wild and made their home in rocks and trees, and, in at least one case, a lion's carcass discovered by Samson (Judges 14:8).

Locusts
Locusts fly in huge swarms numbering up to hundreds of millions. They strip fields rapidly and devastate harvests (one of their names in Hebrew means "destroyer"). The Jewish Law allowed locusts to be eaten (Leviticus 11:20–23) and they were a good source of protein, which is why John the Baptist made them part of his diet (Matthew 3:4).

Moths
Moth larvae eat fabric such as clothes and blankets (see Isaiah 51:8), and so became proverbial of anything that eats something up (Matthew 6:19–20).

Faith idea: Creator

The Bible sees life in all its diversity not as an accident but as the handiwork of the Creator God, with even the routines of animal life as something he designed and is involved in (Job 38:39 – 41:34). That is why God is always seen as Father God, never as Mother Earth, as though creation were something independent of him. Rather, creation and everything in it is a reflection of his creativity, splendour, and care – a constant theme of the Bible.

Mesopotamia

Land of the Rivers

Mesopotamia isn't the name of a nation but rather a region. In fact, this name was never used by the people who lived there but was given to it much later by Greek historians, descriptive of its location (Mesopotamia means "between the rivers" in Greek). The area was home to several civilizations – Sumerians, Arameans, Chaldeans, Assyrians, Babylonians, and Persians. It would prove to be highly significant in terms of Israel's history, impacting the Bible's story at key points.

The Sumerians

Considered by many as the birthplace of civilization, some of the oldest settlements known to humankind have been found in Mesopotamia, going back as far as the seventh millennium BC. City-states (cities exercising influence over their surrounding region) began to develop in the mid-fourth millennium BC, growing up alongside the Tigris and Euphrates because of the possibilities for irrigation they afforded, as well as the trade they allowed to be developed. Two of the bigger city-states were Ur and Uruk, both mentioned in the Bible (where the latter is called Erech). Archaeological excavations at **Ur** suggest that its population may have been around 10,000 by 3200 BC, which was huge for those days, and its varied housing and buildings suggest a society that had developed different social strata. **Uruk** became the capital of a more extensive Sumerian dynasty, which, between 2900 and 2350 BC, drew together a coalition of city-states ruled by kings who are named in *The Sumerian King List*.

The origin of the Sumerians is uncertain, but they were responsible for many features of later civilization, including writing, art, architecture, and technology, such as the wheel and plough. After c. 2000 BC, however, intermarriage with other races, like immigrant Amorites, led to the gradual disappearance of the Sumerian identity.

Sumerian religion

Sumerians were polytheists, believing in many gods and goddesses; but each city had its own patron god to whom the main temple was dedicated and where the god was seen as living: Inanna, the goddess of love, fertility, and war, in Uruk; Nanna, also known as Sin, the moon god, in Ur; Sud, the grain goddess, in Shuruppak. There were also national gods like An, god of the sky. The Sumerians believed that the gods took human form and behaved like people, often interfering in human affairs.

Sumerian writing

Scholars believe that writing was invented in Sumeria, and early examples, dating from around 3300 BC, have been found on clay tablets in Uruk. Their writing system used around 700 pictorial signs and was used initially to record business transactions. By 2500 BC the Sumerian cuneiform ("wedge-shaped") writing system was being used. For examples of ancient literature from Mesopotamia, see "Ancient Mesopotamian Stories" (p. 23).

The region of Mesopotamia

This map shows the main city-states that developed along the banks of the Tigris (1,143 miles/1,840 km long) and the Euphrates (1,771 miles/2,850 km long), which both flow from the mountains of Turkey to the Persian Gulf. Mesopotamia covered lands in modern Iran and Iraq, as well as parts of Turkey and Syria, and would influence events in the Ancient Near East for four millennia.

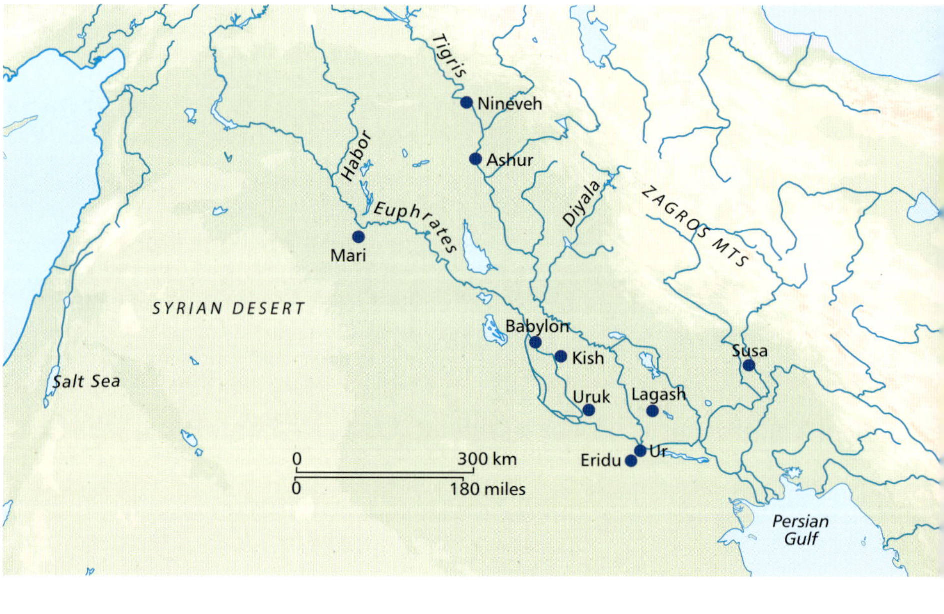

See also
The Assyrians pp. 72–73
The Babylonians pp. 74–75
Writing pp. 120–21

Connections with the Bible

- Abraham's father came from "Ur of the Chaldeans" (Genesis 11:28–31).
- Chaldean raiding parties stole Job's camels (Job 1:17).
- Daniel trained in "the language and literature of the Chaldeans" (Daniel 1:4, translated "Babylonians" in NIV).

For other connections with this region, see Assyrians, Babylonians, Persians.

Sumerian art

Sumerian art and architecture had a major influence on the culture of the Ancient Near East. Sculptures in clay, wood, and metal were highly advanced. Pottery was beginning to be produced in bulk on the potter's wheel or in moulds, rather than being hand-made. Beautiful jewellery was being made, showing there were highly skilled craftsmen; and the fact that their materials weren't local is evidence of travel and trade.

Akkadians

Unlike the Sumerians, who were native to Mesopotamia, the Akkadians were Semitic in origin but gradually spread through the region. Under King Sargon an Akkadian empire began to emerge after he conquered Sumerian cities in 2340 BC and established his rule from the Persian Gulf to Lebanon. His capital was Akkad, later known as Babylon, which would dominate the region for the next two millennia. He introduced a centralized taxation system, standardized weights and measures, and introduced Akkadian as the unifying language of business. While Sargon's empire lasted only until 2125 BC, it had long-lasting impact, awakening the thought that rulers could acquire territory well beyond their own cities, an idea that would inspire the future Assyrian and Babylonian empires.

By the end of the third millennium, Mesopotamia had two main centres of power: Akkad in the north and Ur in the south. After the collapse of the Akkadian empire, it was Ur that became the powerhouse of Mesopotamian life, though it too would disappear from the scene in 2004 BC, almost overnight, as Amorites came in from the west and Elamites from the east.

This beautiful goat statue, delicately crafted in gold, silver, and lapis lazuli, was found in the royal graves at Ur, and dates from c. 2600 BC.

Beer-drinking

A seal discovered in Tepe Gawra, a city occupied between 5000 and 1500 BC, has provided the earliest evidence of beer-drinking ever discovered anywhere in the world.

Faith idea: Monotheism

In contrast to Mesopotamia's polytheism (belief in many gods), the Bible emphasizes there is but one God (monotheism), underlined from its opening sentence: "In the beginning God created the heavens and the earth" – God, not the gods. Abraham, coming from Ur, would have believed in many gods and known the polytheistic creation stories; but when he encountered the living God (Genesis 12:1–9), he abandoned his polytheism, becoming the founding father of a worldwide family of believers in the one true God.

Ruins of the ziggurat (temple-tower) in the Sumerian city of Ur, constructed by King Ur-Nammu, founder of the Third Dynasty of Ur, in 2113 BC. The tower's base measures approximately 200 x 150 feet (60 x 45 m) and is one of the earliest examples of a design that became standard throughout Mesopotamia. The Tower of Babel (Genesis 11:1–9) would have looked like this.

The Egyptians

The Power of a River

Egypt was one of the most powerful nations in the ancient world, rivalling those of Mesopotamia. When Abraham visited it to avoid a famine (Genesis 12:10–20), it was already 1,000 years old. But by the first millennium BC its great days were over and it was little more than "a splintered reed" (Isaiah 36:4), incapable of supporting anyone, and would eventually be swallowed up by other empires. Through all of this, it often played a key role, for good or for bad, in the Bible's story.

The Nile

Without the Nile, Egypt would never have become the power that it did. Pouring out of Lake Victoria in Uganda, it flows north for 4,145 miles (6,670 km), finally breaking into a delta of swampy marshland before pouring into the Mediterranean. Swollen by Africa's melting snows and monsoon rains, it flooded annually between June and September in a season called *akhet* ("inundation"), seen by Egyptians as the coming of the god Hapi to bring fertility to the land. Crops were then planted, and by the time the river subsided in March/April, they were ready for harvesting. This reliable food supply was a significant contributor to Egypt's wealth.

Connections with the Bible

- Visited by Abraham to avoid a famine (Genesis 12:10–20).
- Home to Joseph, who rose to high position (Genesis 37:12 – 50:26).
- Setting for the exodus (Exodus 1–14).
- Subjugated Judah after Solomon's death (1 Kings 14:25–28).
- Seen as unreliable by the prophets (Isaiah 30–31; Jeremiah 46), confirmed by events as Egypt failed to protect Israel from Assyria (2 Kings 17:1–6).
- Place of refuge from Herod for the infant Jesus (Matthew 2:13–18).

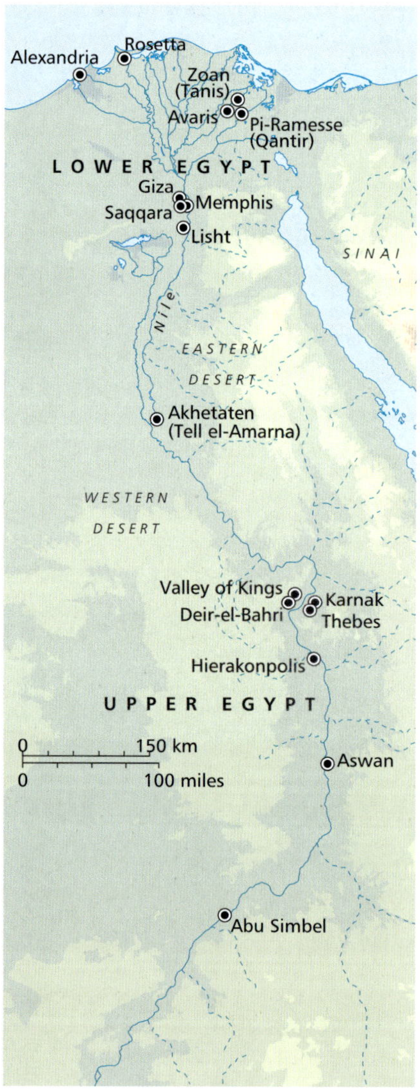

Map of ancient Egypt showing the main cities.

The history of Egypt

Historians divide Egypt's history into different periods:

- **The Archaic Period** (3100–c. 2691 BC), when Menes united Upper Egypt (the Nile Valley) and Lower Egypt (the Nile delta).
- **The Old Kingdom** (c. 2691–2136 BC), when the great pyramids were built as tombs for the pharaohs, the one at Giza being the best preserved of the seven wonders of the ancient world.
- **The First Intermediate Period** (2136–2023 BC), a time of social upheaval, possibly triggered by poor Nile floods and infiltration by Asiatics.
- **The Middle Kingdom** (2023–1795 BC), with its capital in Memphis, a time of considerable prosperity due to the annexation of gold-rich Nubia and better use of the Nile, increasing agricultural productivity. Fortresses along the northeastern border protected Egypt from incursions.
- **The Second Intermediate Period** (1795–1540 BC), when Egypt was ruled by the Hyksos, with a delta capital at Avaris.
- **The New Kingdom** (1540–1070 BC), beginning with the expulsion of the Hyksos by Ahmose, who established the Eighteenth Dynasty at Thebes (Luxor). Tuthmosis III (1479–1425 BC) undertook eighteen campaigns in Palestine and Syria to protect Egypt's borders through territorial expansion. Rameses II (1279–1213 BC) of the Nineteenth Dynasty established his capital at Pi-Rameses in the delta, giving it magnificent buildings, including the stunning Abu Simbel temple in the south, with its four enormous stone statues. Some scholars think the Israelite oppression detailed in Exodus fits better into his reign than the earlier period the Bible suggests.
- **The Third Intermediate Period** (1070–525 BC), when Egypt was ruled by Libyans, Cushites, and Assyrians, and, from 525 BC, by Persia.
- **The Greco-Roman Period**, which saw Egypt conquered in 332 BC by Alexander the Great, who founded the city of Alexandria. After his death, his empire was divided up and Egypt was ruled by the Greek-speaking Ptolemies until it was conquered by Rome in 30 BC.

See also
Death pp. 160–61
Hieroglyphics p. 120
Joseph pp. 164–65

Upper and Lower Egypt

Above: The unification of Egypt was symbolized by "the double crown" of Pharaoh (centre). It comprised the Red Crown of Lower Egypt (figure on left) and the conical White Crown of Upper Egypt (figure on right).

Above: Amenophis IV (Akhenaten; 1353–1337 BC) abandoned Egypt's traditional polytheism to worship one god, represented by the sun disk (Aten), seen in this picture. After his death, however, traditional polytheism was restored.

Egypt's gods

Ancient Egypt had many gods, like Ra (the sun god), Thoth and Khonsu (the moon gods), Hapi (god of the Nile), and Amun (god of air and sky). Pharaoh was the gods' go-between, representing the people by making offerings to the gods in return for blessings, and representing the gods by building and maintaining temples. Ordinary people couldn't enter the temples, only seeing the gods in processions on festival days, so would worship household gods or at local shrines. People wore amulets (charms) for protection, the most popular of which was the scarab beetle.

The afterlife

For Egyptians, the body was a home for the soul that departed at death, so personal possessions were buried with the body for the journey to the afterlife. The rich were mummified, as heat couldn't reach into their tombs to dry out their bodies; the poor were simply buried in dry sand. Mummification involved removing the brain and large organs, packing the body in salt to dry it out, and filling the cavities with fragrant resin. The body was covered with resin, wrapped in bandages, and placed in an elaborately decorated wooden coffin. Both Jacob and Joseph were mummified (Genesis 50:1–3, 26). New Kingdom pharaohs were buried in the Valley of the Kings, on the Nile's west bank opposite Thebes, as the west, the place of the sun's setting, was seen as symbolizing the ending of the old and the beginning of the new.

Spells and provisions were made to help the deceased pass through their journey into the underworld. Kings were believed to spend the afterlife with Ra (the sun god), riding his boat across the sky by day and passing through the realm of Osiris, the god of the underworld, by night to provide for their dead subjects.

Faith idea: Dreams

Egyptians saw dreams as divine predictions of the future, seeking to interpret them through dream manuals or dream specialists, which explains Pharaoh's eagerness to meet Joseph (Genesis 41). The Bible too says that God can speak through dreams, and many Bible characters encountered God or discovered his will through them. Joel anticipated the day when such dreams would be normal for all God's people (Joel 2:28).

The Egyptians used Nilometers to measure the height of the annual flood, and with it the level of taxation. This one took the form of rising steps to measure the increasing height of the river that flowed through a narrow tunnel into the courts of the Temple of Edfu.

The Hittites

People of the North

Often listed with other "-ites" in the Bible (e.g. Genesis 15:18–20; Exodus 3:17), it would be easy to think that the Hittites lived in Canaan. But in fact they came from Asia Minor, the bridgehead between Europe and Asia, bounded by the Black Sea and the Mediterranean. Between 1400 and 1200 BC they established one of the great empires of the Ancient Near East which, at its height, included central Turkey, northwestern Syria, and Upper Mesopotamia.

Origins

The Hittites were Indo-Europeans who settled in Anatolia (Turkey), deriving their name from the Hatti, the region's earlier inhabitants. But some groups then seem to have migrated south and settled in Syria and Canaan, and were certainly there by Abraham's time (Genesis 23:1–20), though some scholars think these Hittites were a separate people group, part of the indigenous Canaanite population, and that their common name was simply coincidental.

History of the Hittites

In their early years, the Hittites were a fairly disparate people; but as strong rulers started to unite them, they began to turn into more of an empire. Their history is then divided into three main periods:

- **The Old Kingdom** (c. 1600–1400 BC) Its greatest kings, Hattusili I and Mursili I, significantly expanded the Hittite kingdom towards Syria and Mesopotamia, defeating the Hurrians and Babylonians around 1531 BC. But after Mursili's assassination, the Hittite kingdom was weakened through in-fighting and a lack of any protocol for ensuring the royal succession.
- **The Middle Kingdom** (c. 1400–1340 BC) Under Tudhaliya II the nation was again pulled together, but remained weak in the face of northern enemies.

Hittite military

Above: The Hittites were famous for their use of chariots in battle, which they used to crash into the enemy to break up its infantry, its riders (sometimes three per chariot) armed with long spears and short daggers. Soldiers were called up as needed, though mercenaries were also employed, and they were noted for wearing different costumes for different campaigns. Pharaoh Rameses II described them as "women soldiers" because of their long hair. They developed clear military procedures, giving detailed rules to commanders on things like changing the guard, opening gates, patrolling routes, and organizing duty rosters. They were also pioneers in developing fortifications that could resist burning and tunnelling.

See also
The Ancient Near East pp. 48–49
Egypt pp. 64–65
Language pp. 120–21

- **The New Kingdom** (c. 1340–1200 BC) With the accession of Suppiluliumus I, the Hittites extended south, defeating Mitanni and Syria, with its key port of Ugarit, and becoming the major power north of Canaan. With its empire now bordering on Egypt, both powers contested control of the wealthy coastal cities, climaxing in 1275 BC when King Muwatalli fought a great battle at Kadesh against Pharaoh Rameses II. The outcome was indecisive, though Egypt claimed it as a great victory. Thereafter Hittite power began to decline due to civil war, rival claims to the throne, and external threats, leading to the abrupt (and still not fully explained) disappearance of the Hittite kingdom around 1200 BC.

Archaeological discoveries show that by the late fourteenth century BC, the Hittite capital Hattusa had a population of 40–50,000. It had an inner city with a royal residence, large administrative buildings, and a temple to the storm god, beyond which lay an outer city with elaborate and decorated gateways, stone-built temples and other buildings, and homes of timber and mud bricks. Outside the city walls were cemeteries, most of which contained cremation burials.

Religion

The Hittites worshipped hundreds of gods, happily incorporating elements of other religions as they encountered them. At the centre of their pantheon was the storm god Teshuba with his wife, the sun goddess Hebut. Many gods were expressed in human form with human emotions, but others had the form of animals or even objects, such as stones. The Hittites performed daily cultic rituals to bring food and drink to the gods.

Hittite texts reveal many details of their religious practices; for example, instructions for building a new temple, which has parallels with the description in Exodus of how the tabernacle was to be constructed. The behaviour of priests and temple officials is recorded, which also has parallel details in the Jewish Law. For example, temple kitchen assistants had to trim their hair and fingernails and wear clean garments, just like the Levites (Numbers 8:5–7); temple servants were allowed a daily portion of food from the temple, just like the Levites (Numbers 18:8–20); priests were to conduct festivals at appointed times according to appointed rules, just like the Mosaic priests (Leviticus 23:1–40). Such contemporary parallels are important in showing that the biblical priestly code was not something drawn up much later in Israel's history, as some scholars have suggested, but was in fact very common in this region at the time of Moses.

Hittite God

A Hittite storm god, identifiable by his axe, from a relief on the processional way in Carchemish. The gods of Hittite mythology were comparatively weak. For example, Telepinu, one of the storm gods, is portrayed in one myth as going off in anger, leaving creation to wilt. The crops stopped growing and animals stopped breeding. None of the gods could find him, and it was a bee that finally found him asleep under a tree and that stung him (literally!) into action. Only through magic could priests assuage his anger. Such stories contrast strongly with the Bible's picture of the living God who controls everything in creation, never abandoning it or falling asleep on the job.

Connections with the Bible

- Descended from Canaan, Noah's grandson (Genesis 10:15).
- Sold land to Abraham as burial plot for Sarah (Genesis 23:1–20).
- Esau married a Hittite woman who caused trouble in the family (Genesis 26:34–35; 27:46).
- Their territory promised to Abraham (Genesis 15:18–20).
- Hittites served in David's army (1 Samuel 26:6; 2 Samuel 11:1–27).

Faith idea: God's watchfulness

In contrast to the Hittite god Telepinu, who abandoned creation in anger and then fell asleep, the Bible says of the living God that "he who watches over you will not slumber; indeed, he who watches over Israel will neither slumber nor sleep" (Psalm 121:3–4). God is shown to be ever watchful over both his creation and his people, and nothing ever slips by him or catches him unawares.

The Canaanites

A Snare to Israel

The name Canaanites (meaning "traders") originally denoted people who lived along the coast, but was extended as a collective name for everyone living between the Mediterranean and the River Jordan in the Late Bronze Age (sixteenth to twelfth centuries BC). God had promised this land to Abraham (Genesis 12:6–7; 17:8) and had warned his descendants not to mix with its inhabitants (Deuteronomy 7:1–6); but they disobeyed, attracted by the strong sexuality of Canaanite religion. And so the Canaanites became a snare to Israel for many generations.

A land of city-states

Canaan's northern border extended to Tyre and Sidon, its eastern border to the Jordan, and its southern border from the Dead Sea through Kadesh Barnea to the Mediterranean, placing it between Egypt to the south and Syria, Anatolia, and Mesopotamia to the north. Since all these nations had territorial ambitions, it wasn't surprising that Canaan became a natural battleground.

The invading Israelites found a mixture of peoples living side by side – Hittites, Amorites, Perizites, Hivites, Jebusites – generically known as Canaanites, all descended from Canaan, Noah's grandson (Genesis 10:15–19). They lived in city-states, each with its own king and only loosely united, readily coming together in times of crisis (e.g. Joshua 11:1–5), but equally squabbling with each other at other times, as seen in Judges and the Armana Letters from fourteenth-century Egypt. Their cities were surrounded by defensive stone and earth walls, behind which their citizens would retreat at night or when attacked.

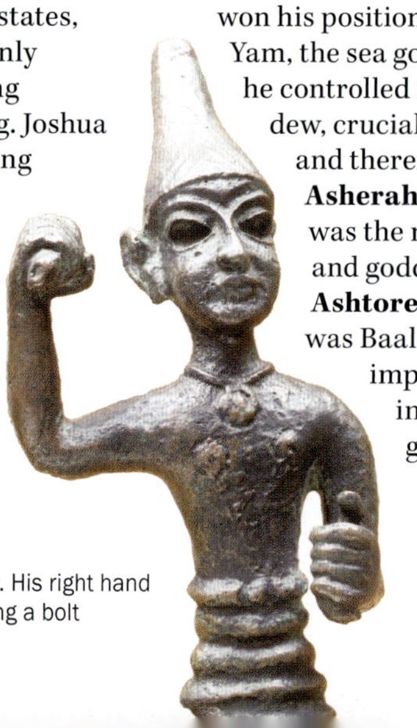

Baal, the god of fertility and weather. His right hand would have held a spear, representing a bolt of lightning.

Religion

It wasn't Canaanite culture that proved to be a threat to Israel, the Bible shows, but rather Canaanite religion. Much of our knowledge about this comes from cuneiform clay tablets from neighbouring Ugarit dating from c. 1400 BC. The Canaanites were followers of "fertility religions", in which nature's powers were personified and worshipped as essential to fruitfulness in both mankind and nature. **Baal** ("lord"), the son of **El** (the chief god), was the god of fertility and weather, often portrayed standing on a bull (a symbol of strength) and holding a spear of lightning. In Canaanite mythology, he won his position after defeating Yam, the sea god, in a battle, and he controlled rain, mists, and dew, crucial to good harvests and therefore survival. **Asherah**, El's consort, was the mother goddess and goddess of the sea; **Ashtoreth** (or **Astarte**) was Baal's consort. Other important gods included **Dagon** (the grain god), **Shamash** (the sun god), and **Reshef** (lord of war and the underworld). Both Baal and Asherah feature prominently in the Old Testament story, in which the influence of Canaanite religion is a recurring theme.

Below: The Canaanite goddess Asherah in classic posture highlighting her fertility.

A key aspect of Canaanite worship was ritual prostitution at cultic centres (e.g. Numbers 25:1–3), which was believed to bring fertility to the land. This explains why it was so attractive to Israel, offering as it did unlimited sex under the guise of religion, and equally why the prophets condemned it so unreservedly (e.g. Hosea 4:10–19). Such ungodliness, along with the child sacrifice practised by some (like the worshippers of Molech), helps explain why the Bible says God commanded Israel to completely remove the Canaanites from the land.

After Solomon's death (930 BC), the northern territory of Israel, founded from the beginning on idolatry (1 Kings 12:25–33), became strongly enticed by Canaanite religion and was challenged by prophets like Elijah and Elisha in the ninth century BC and Hosea in the eighth century BC, who said it was impossible to identify the worship of Baal with the worship of Yahweh, or even to try to blend the two (a practice known as syncretism). The author of Kings makes clear that this underlying idolatry was a key factor in Israel's downfall (2 Kings 17:7–23).

By New Testament times Jews had turned the name Baal-Zebul ("Prince Baal") into "Beelzebub" ("Lord of the flies") and used it of Satan, something Jesus himself picked up (Matthew 10:25; 12:24–28), underlining that anything that dehumanizes people through idolatry and sexual immorality is nothing less than satanic.

See also
Alternative Settlement Theories p. 29
The Land of Canaan pp. 50–51
The Promised Land pp. 30–31

The high place
The Canaanite high place at Megiddo, dating from the third millennium BC, which has a diameter of approximately 33 feet (10 m) and was probably covered with beaten earth to provide a flat surface. Sacrifices (normally animals or foodstuffs, though sometimes humans) were offered here, and sexual acts with temple prostitutes would also have taken place.

Connections with the Bible

- Canaanites inhabited the land when Abraham arrived (Genesis 12:6; 13:7).
- Abraham was promised their land, but only when Canaanite sin made their continuing to live there intolerable (Genesis 15:13–16).
- Canaanites joined together to fight Joshua (Joshua 9:1–2).
- A Canaanite/Phoenician craftsman (Hiram of Tyre) made furnishings for Solomon's Temple (1 Kings 5).
- King Ahab encouraged Baal worship (1 Kings 16:29–33).
- Baal's prophets were challenged by Elijah at Mount Carmel (1 Kings 18:16–46).

The alphabet

One of the greatest legacies the Canaanites left was the alphabet. Invented here between 2000 and 1600 BC, they used simple signs for each consonant, instead of the more complex cuneiform or hieroglyphics. There were no signs for vowels, however, just as in Hebrew, which was based on the Canaanite language.

Faith idea: Idolatry

Idolatry is unhesitatingly condemned in the Bible, pre-eminently in the Ten Commandments (Exodus 20:4–6). It is seen as foolish, for it involves worshipping something made by human hands (Isaiah 44:9–20), and illogical, for how can anyone know what God looks like and so make an image of him? Putting anything before God in our lives is condemned in the Bible as idolatry and dishonouring to him.

Mount Carmel
View from the top of Mount Carmel, the location of Elijah's contest with the prophets of Baal (1 Kings 18:16–46) during the reign of Ahab, who took Israel back into Baal worship (1 Kings 17:29–33). When their gods didn't answer, Baal's prophets slashed themselves (1 Kings 18:26–29), a common mark of grief and associated in Baal worship with mourning the death of a god, though possibly here as an expression of devotion. The Old Testament saw slashing or any form of bodily disfigurement or tattooing as pagan and unworthy of God's holy people (Leviticus 19:27–28; Deuteronomy 14:1). The outcome of the contest made clear that Yahweh, the living God, was more powerful than Baal and that it was he alone who sends the rain, as we see in the story's conclusion (1 Kings 18:41–46).

The Philistines

The Sea People

While the term "Philistine" is synonymous today with someone uncultured and boorish, nothing could be further from the truth. The Philistines were, in fact, a very cultured people; but they were also warlike. So as their coastal settlements in Canaan proved restrictive, they sought new territory inland, leading to clashes with the Israelites, who believed they had been promised this land by God. While the Philistines never controlled much of the interior, their legacy was to leave a name for the whole region – Palestine.

Origins

Egyptian records show the pharaohs of the thirteenth and twelfth centuries BC fighting off invasions from "the peoples of the sea". One of these groups was the Philistines, who had migrated from Crete and Greece. Their warriors sailed around the Mediterranean coast, while their families travelled alongside by land. They made their way through Syria and Canaan, leaving behind a swathe of destruction, and finally reached Egypt, where they were defeated by Rameses III in 1175 BC. So they retreated to land previously conquered, settling along Canaan's coastal strip in five city-states (Gaza, Ashkelon, Ashdod, Gath, and Ekron), which they violently destroyed and rebuilt on a bigger, more fortified scale, giving them control of the Via Maris, the international coastal highway between north and south.

Relationship with Israel

With both Israel and the Philistines wanting the same territory, conflict was inevitable. During the Judges period, the Philistines were a constant threat (e.g. Judges 13:1), leading to many Danites migrating north because they couldn't possess their allotted territory. It was the Philistine threat that led Israel to ask Samuel, last of the judges, for a king (1 Samuel 8). Israel was certainly terrified of the Philistines (1 Samuel 13:5–7) and Saul never managed to defeat them. It was their presence that led to his appointment as king, but also to his demise (1 Samuel 13:7–22), being utterly routed by them at the Battle of Mount Gilboa, where he and his son Jonathan lost their lives (1 Samuel 31). It was left to his successor, King David, to finally bring the Philistines to heel (e.g. 1 Samuel 5:17–25). The Philistines continued to live in Canaan until the eighth century BC, when they were defeated by Assyria, before being finally swallowed up by Babylon in the sixth century BC.

Military superiority

Perhaps more than any other factor, it was the possession of iron weaponry that was decisive in Philistine military supremacy. They gained their technology of iron-smelting from the Hittites whom they had defeated, and jealously guarded this secret, especially from Israel (1 Samuel 13:19–22). Part of Goliath's fearsomeness was not just his size (9 ft/3 m tall), but also his weaponry, having a spear with an iron tip weighing 600 shekels (15 lb/7 kg). It wasn't until King David's expansion of Israel's borders that the Israelites gained access to rich iron deposits in Edom (2 Samuel 8:14).

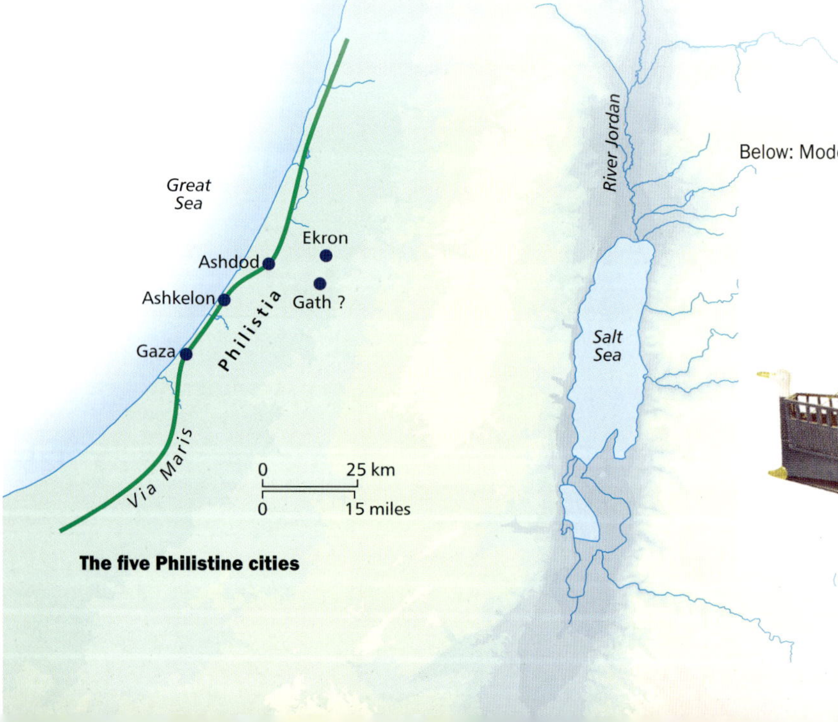

The five Philistine cities

Below: Model of a Philistine warship.

See also
Baal-Zebul p. 16
The Land of Canaan pp. 50–51
Warfare pp. 128–29

Faience tile from the mortuary temple of Rameses III depicting a Philistine wearing the traditional feathered-style headdress.

Samson is perhaps best remembered for his destruction of Dagon's temple (Judges 16:23–30). While no temple has yet been found at Gaza, excavations at Tell Qasile (near Tel Aviv) have revealed three temples built over one another from that period. The latest one, dating from the eleventh century BC, had two cedar-wood pillars resting on stone bases that supported the roof, just like those in Samson's story (Judges 16:26). Since only the weight of the roof held the pillars in place, it would have been quite feasible for them to be dislodged, bringing the whole temple down, just as in the Judges account.

Religion

The main Philistine gods were **Dagon** (the grain god), **Ashtoreth** (Baal's consort) and **Baal-Zebul** ("Prince Baal"). Dagon was widely worshipped throughout the Ancient Near East, with temples in Mesopotamia, Ugarit, and Canaan. In Canaan there were temples to him in Gaza, Ashdod, and Beth Shan, where Saul's mutilated body was put on display as a sign of Dagon's victory (1 Samuel 31:10; 1 Chronicles 10:10). That Dagon must have influenced Israelite life is reflected in the naming of an Israelite town, Beth Dagon, after him (Joshua 15:41). However, Dagon's powerlessness before Yahweh, the living God, is summed up in the Bible's story of his statue repeatedly falling on its face when the captured ark of the covenant was placed before it (1 Samuel 5:1–5).

Samson and the Philistines

Samson's inability to rule his sexual appetite led to his betrayal by a Philistine prostitute, Delilah, to whom he revealed the secret of his strength. Once weakened, he was captured and put to work grinding corn in prison (Judges 16:1–22). Excavations at Gaza have revealed such grinding-places.

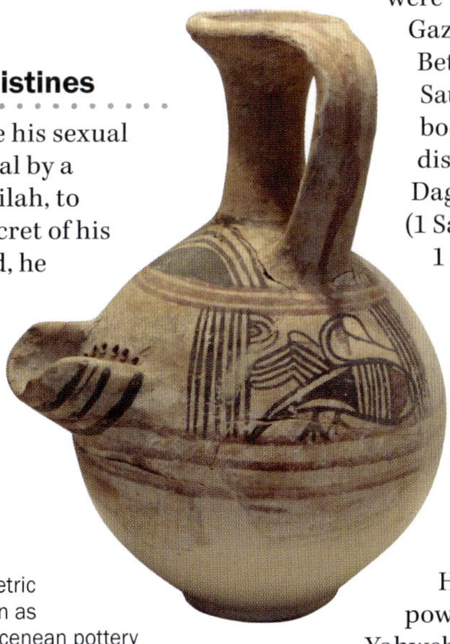

A Philistine beer jug with geometric designs in red and black, known as Bichrome ware. This type of Mycenean pottery was well known in Greece, Crete (Caphtor in the Bible), and Cyprus, further evidence that the Philistines migrated from those areas. Other aspects of Aegean culture that they brought with them included architecture and metallurgy.

Archaeological confirmation

The Bible's statement that Ekron's king was called Achish (1 Samuel 21:10) was authenticated by the discovery in 1996 of an inscription in a Philistine temple at Ekron, a pointer to the Bible's historical reliability.

Connections with the Bible

- Abraham "stayed in the land of the Philistines" (Genesis 21:34), earlier settlers who were more peaceful.
- Philistines captured the ark of the covenant, a devastating moment for Israel (1 Samuel 4:1–11), and destroyed Shiloh, Israel's first holy city (Psalm 78:58–64; Jeremiah 7:12–14).
- Samson was betrayed by a Philistine woman (Judges 16:1–31).
- David defeated the Philistine champion, Goliath (1 Samuel 17), and paid his bride-price in Philistine foreskins (1 Samuel 18:17–30).
- David pretended to serve Achish, King of Gath, while on the run from Saul (1 Samuel 21:10–15; 27:1–12), and it may have been here that he learned military tactics.

Faith idea: Magic

The Philistines were practitioners of divination (Isaiah 2:6) – reading omens to get guidance from the gods. All such attempts to read or manipulate the future, or to make contact with the dead or spirit-world, or any kind of "magic" – divination, sorcery, omen-interpretation, witchcraft, spell-casting, consulting mediums and spiritists – are unequivocally abhorred and warned against in the Bible as dangerous (e.g. Deuteronomy 17:9–13; Acts 8:9–24).

The Assyrians

The Rod of God's Anger

To most people, Assyrians symbolize cruel imperialism; but from their point of view they simply felt threatened by their neighbours in the deserts and mountains, for whom their well-watered lands were hugely attractive. So they felt they had little alternative but to embrace war to win peace. Israel, sandwiched between Assyria and Egypt, therefore found itself the object of their attention and, ultimately, their destruction – though Isaiah claimed this judgment wasn't Assyria's, but God's, who was using Assyria as "the rod of my anger" (Isaiah 10:5) to discipline his people.

History

Origins

The Assyrians, originally a Semitic people, settled in a small area of northern Mesopotamia around 2300 BC, naming both their country and capital after their chief god Ashur. The cities of Ashur and Nineveh, Assyria's second city, both lay on the River Tigris, which ensured ample water supplies and abundant harvests. They existed originally as independent city-states, but Ashuruballit I (c. 1364–1329 BC) consolidated them into a nation that became a leading power, pushing west to the Euphrates and Carchemish. Their power was broken, however, when Arameans (Syrians) invaded from the desert.

Growth

Over the next 300 years a series of strong kings regained lost lands and conquered new ones. Ashurnasirpal II (883–859 BC) and his son Shalmaneser III (858–824 BC) were both fearsome warriors, capturing many cities and making kings their vassals, though they often rebelled when Assyria withdrew. Tiglath-Pileser III (745–727 BC), however, not only pursued an expansionist policy but also imposed regional governors to keep a grip on conquered territories. After his death, Israel sought Egypt's help to throw off Assyrian domination, which provoked Shalmaneser V to besiege Israel's capital, Samaria. It fell after a three-year siege to his successor Sargon II in 722 BC (2 Kings 17:5–6). Israel was conquered and its citizens deported across the Assyrian empire (a common Assyrian policy), bringing an abrupt end to the history of the northern tribes (2 Kings 17:3–6; 18:9–12).

Decline

Under Esarhaddon (681–669 BC) and Ashurbanipal (669–627 BC), the Assyrian empire simply grew too big and was unable to tackle all its rebels at once. In 625 BC Babylon eventually won its independence, and with help from the Medes, it destroyed Nineveh in 612 BC, fulfilling Nahum's prophecy and bringing Assyria's empire to an end.

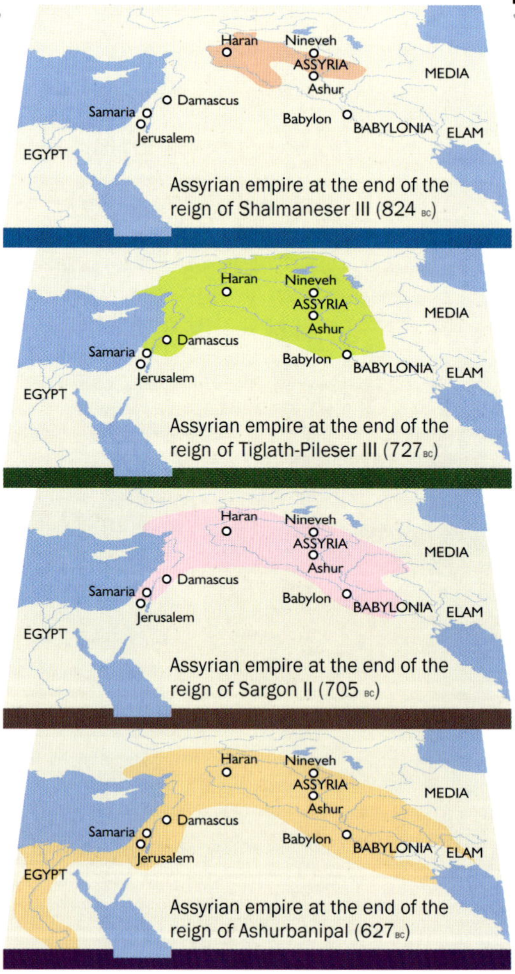

The growth of the Assyrian empire.

Religion

The Assyrians were polytheists, adopting the gods of ancient Mesopotamia, but also happily embracing new ones (1 Kings 17:27–33). Ashur was the national and supreme god, but there were many others covering every aspect of life. Each city had its own patron god, whose statue was paraded on festival days and who had a temple dedicated to him where, since the gods were unpredictable, offerings were made to win his favour. Stone reliefs in royal palaces portraying the king's victories were designed not just to honour the king or intimidate visitors but also to glorify the gods by showing their domination over the gods of conquered enemies.

Archaeological evidence shows that "prayer letters" were a common means of kings petitioning the gods for help. King Hezekiah of Judah used this well-established genre of spiritual communication when he wrote a prayer letter to God when he became critically ill (Isaiah 38).

See also
Assyria and Israel's End pp. 34–35
Mesopotamia pp. 62–63
Warfare pp. 128–29

Culture

Assyria's empire generated huge wealth, enabling its kings to seek to outdo one another in their construction of great palaces and temples whose walls were lined with magnificent low-reliefs of the king at leisure, worship, and war, originally painted in bright colours. Huge sculptures were made and palace furnishings were decorated with ivory and gold. Golden goblets were fashioned in the shape of animal heads, and fine jewellery was produced.

Assyrian culture was influenced by the Babylonians, especially reading and writing. They adopted Babylonian cuneiform script and thousands of clay tablets still survive, including the huge library of King Ashurbanipal, which claimed to have copies of every piece of literature and knowledge from the past. They also made advances in science, mathematics, and medicine, in part the result of their obsession with war. And the oldest known lock, some 4,000 years old, was discovered in Nineveh.

The Assyrian war machine
The Assyrian army was brutal, inflicting maximum suffering as a means of intimidation. This stone relief from Nimrud shows Assyrian soldiers destroying a city's walls with a battering ram. Conquered peoples were either forced to pay hefty tributes or were deported across the empire. It is estimated that the Assyrians deported some 4 million people.

A relief from Tiglath-Pileser III's palace showing him in his chariot.

The Assyrian king lists

Several copies of Assyrian king lists have been found, going right back to tribal times, which are hugely important in reconstructing the history of the Old Testament world.

Connections with the Bible

- Assyria is first mentioned as a region where Nimrod built great cities (Genesis 10:8–12).
- Tiglath-Pileser III (called by his Babylonian name Pul in the Bible) exacted tribute from Israel's King Menahem (2 Kings 15:19–20).
- Isaiah's prophecy of Immanuel (Isaiah 7) came in the context of Ahab's unwise appeal to Assyria for help against Israel and Syria (735 BC).
- Samaria was captured by Assyria in 722 BC after a three-year siege, leading to deportation of the Israelites (2 Kings 17).
- Hezekiah resisted Sennacherib's assault on Jerusalem by trusting God (2 Kings 18–19; Isaiah 36–37).
- Several prophets spoke about Assyria (Isaiah, Hosea, Joel, Amos, Micah, Nahum, Zephaniah).

Faith idea: Grace

In the first half of the ninth century BC, Jonah ran from God's call to preach to Nineveh, believing that they didn't deserve his love or forgiveness. When he eventually did go and they repented, he was very angry. But his story underlines a recurring theme of the Bible: God's grace – his undeserved kindness towards everyone, whoever they are, that cannot be earned and is not deserved, as Jonah thought, but that is available to anyone who repents.

The Babylonians

The Pride Before the Fall

"Is not this the great Babylon I have built?" boasted Nebuchadnezzar (Daniel 4:30). And indeed it was great, a city of immense splendour at the heart of a powerful empire stretching across the Middle East. Yet pride comes before a fall, as both Nebuchadnezzar and Belshazzar discovered (Daniel 4:31 – 5:31). Through a series of visions, God showed Daniel the fall not just of proud Babylon, but of other coming empires too (Daniel 2, 7, 8).

History

Already important by 2100 BC, the city of Babylon became the centre of the Old Babylonian empire under King Hammurabi (1792–1750 BC). However, after his death it soon declined, and it wasn't until Nabopolassar's Neo-Babylonian empire that it became significant again. In 616 BC Nabopolassar invaded Assyria, capturing Nineveh in 612 BC and freeing Babylonia from Assyrian control. The defeat of the Assyrian-Egyptian army by his son Nebuchadnezzar II at Carchemish in 605 BC finished off Assyria for good, and Babylon swallowed up its empire and its wealth. Nebuchadnezzar (mentioned in the Bible more than any other foreign ruler) not only expanded and enriched the empire but also set about grand building projects. But his vision didn't outlive him, and after his death Babylon had a series of weak rulers. When Nabonidus (556–539 BC) abandoned the worship of Marduk, withdrawing to the desert to worship Sin (the moon god), a series of subsequent plagues and famines were blamed on him. By the time he returned to Babylon ten years later, his position was greatly weakened, and when a little-known king from Persia called Cyrus knocked at Babylon's gates in 539 BC, the priests of Marduk overthrew Nabonidus and gladly welcomed Cyrus as their new ruler.

Law

While the empire that Hammurabi built collapsed at his death, he is remembered for his revision of Babylon's laws, engraved on this stele known as "The Law Code of Hammurabi". At the top Shamash, the sun god (seated), gives Hammurabi his symbols of power. These laws demonstrate that law codes existed in the early second millennium BC, and that Moses therefore could indeed have written his laws when the Bible claims.

A big difference between them is that Hammurabi's laws distinguished between social classes, whereas the Jewish Law treated everyone alike.

Religion

Gods

The Babylonians were polytheists. Among their many gods were **Anu** (king of heaven), **Ishtar** (goddess of war and love), and **Marduk** (creator of everything). Marduk became the patron god of Babylon and was very popular in the second millennium BC, eventually becoming king of all gods.

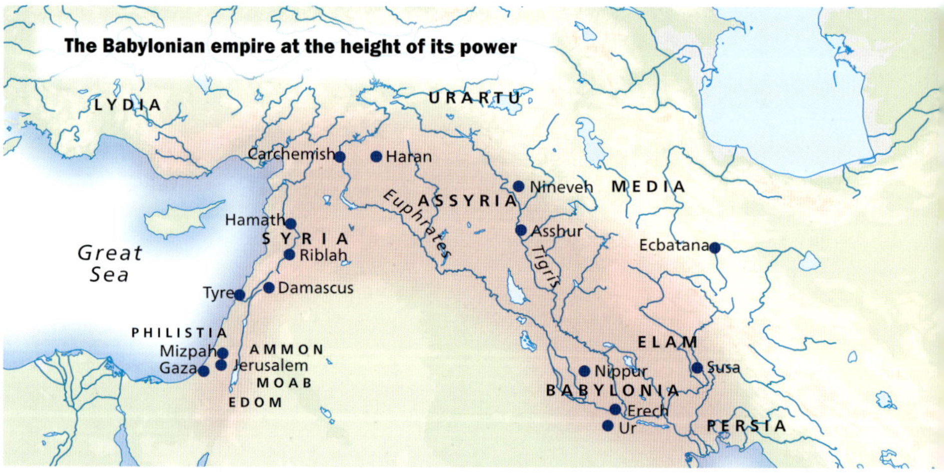

The Babylonian empire at the height of its power

See also
Ancient Mesopotamian Stories p. 23
Jerusalem's Fall p. 155
Mesopotamia pp. 62–63

Myths
Many myths about life's beginnings and early days originated in Babylon (see Ancient Mesopotamian Stories, p. 23). Their creation story, *Enuma Elish*, was recounted at the New Year Festival, celebrating Marduk's elevation after having conquered chaos and created the world.

Demons
The Babylonians believed the world was full of demons, waiting to pounce at any moment. Much superstition developed to protect oneself from them, such as the wearing of charms and amulets and the reciting of spells over the sick.

Divination
The Babylonians looked for "omens" as messages from the gods – things like inspecting animal livers to see whether they were unusual, noting the flight pattern of birds, or consulting astrologers on the movement of the stars (which were seen as gods).

Afterlife
Unlike the Egyptians, the Babylonians had little expectation of an afterlife. They believed that all the dead inhabited a dusty underworld where they lived on food offered by their descendants. If no offerings were made, they believed the dead returned to haunt the living.

The city of Babylon

Nebuchadnezzar was determined to make Babylon the greatest city in the world, using the vast riches from his conquests. Divided by the Euphrates with a bridge linking each side, Babylon was protected by a wide moat around double walls, the outer one 10 miles (16 km) long and 12 feet (3.7 m) thick, and the inner one 5½ miles (9 km) long and 21 feet (6.5 m) thick, wide enough for a four-horse chariot to turn on top. Every 55 feet (17 m) towers were placed in the walls, and the city had eight double gateways. Further protection came from a double eastern wall spanning 4½ miles (7.3 km) that protected buildings beyond the inner city, like the Summer Palace with its famous Hanging Gardens, reported by the Greek historian Herodotus as one of the seven wonders of the ancient world. The city covered 2,100 acres, and the palace within it 50 acres.

Connections with the Bible

- Babylon is first mentioned as a centre of Nimrod's kingdom (Genesis 10:10) and the location of the Tower of Babel (Genesis 11:4).
- Nebuchadnezzar invaded Judah (605 BC), taking treasure from the Temple. A first deportation saw some of Judah's nobles, including Daniel (Daniel 1:1–7), exiled to Babylon.
- Daniel served Babylon's kings, but used every opportunity to bring God's word to them, including prophesying Babylon's downfall (Daniel 2, 7).
- In 597 BC Nebuchadnezzar besieged Jerusalem in response to Judah's rebellion. Jehoiachin and 3,000 leading citizens were deported to Babylon (the second deportation) and treasure was again taken (2 Kings 24:10–16; Ezekiel 1:1–3).
- Zedekiah rebelled, leading to Jerusalem being besieged for two years and eventually falling in 586 BC. Its walls and Temple were destroyed, and a third deportation to Babylon followed (2 Kings 25:1–21; Jeremiah 52:1–30). A fourth occurred in 582 BC (Jeremiah 52:30).
- Babylon is used in Revelation as a symbol of powers that stand against God.

Faith idea: The day of the LORD

"The day of the LORD" was a common theme at this period, found in nine of the canonical prophets. God's people believed that this was the day when God would come in power, judge sin, and destroy his enemies. But the prophets said that the day of the LORD would also include God's own people if they didn't repent, for God's judgment is without discrimination, which is why the Bible says that everyone must be ready for it.

A reconstruction of the Ishtar Gate, one of Babylon's eight inner gates that was built c. 575 BC. Made of glazed brick, it was covered with figures of dragons (the symbol of Marduk) and bulls (the symbol of Adad, the weather god). From it the Processional Way, lined with blue glazed bricks with reliefs of lions (the symbol of Ishtar) in yellow, red, and white, led to the city centre with its great temples.

The Persians

Agents of God

Persia was one of the largest empires of the Ancient Near East; but although their language was Indo-European, it's not really clear where they came from. What is clear from the Bible's viewpoint, however, is that the timing of their rise to power fitted exactly with God's purposes for his people, so much so that Isaiah could prophesy about Cyrus, its king: "I am the LORD... who says of Cyrus, 'He is my shepherd and will accomplish all that I please'" (Isaiah 44:28).

History

The Persians were Indo-Europeans who entered Mesopotamia c. 1000 BC, but it was not until c. 650 BC that **Cyrus I** turned them into a nation. It was his grandson **Cyrus the Great** (ruled 559–530 BC) who turned that nation into an empire. Until then Persia had simply been a small territory known as Pars in southern Mesopotamia, but in 550 BC he conquered Ecbatana, the capital of the Medes, followed by their empire in Turkey and northwest India. He then turned his attention to Babylon, capturing the city without a battle on 12 October 539 BC (dated in *The Nabonidus Chronicle*) and swallowing up its empire. He now controlled land from the Aegean to the Indus River in India.

Cyrus died in battle and was succeeded by his son **Cambyses** (ruled 530–522 BC), who conquered Egypt. He in turn was succeeded by **Darius the Great** (ruled 522–486 BC) under whom the Persian empire reached its pinnacle, swallowing up Macedonia. He tried to expand further into Greece, but was defeated at the Battle of Marathon in 490 BC and died four years later. His son **Xerxes I**, or Ahasuerus (ruled 486–465 BC), assembled the largest army in ancient history to again try to take Greece, but the campaign was disastrous. His fleet was defeated at Salamis (480 BC) and his army decisively beaten at Platea (479 BC). His son **Artaxerxes I** (ruled 465–424 BC) was faced with the Egyptians and Greeks joining forces against him, and the war dragged on for ten years until a peace treaty was finally signed. Persia clung on to its empire for another 100 years until it was finally conquered in 333 BC by Alexander the Great.

Cyrus the Great

Unlike rulers before him, Cyrus the Great adopted a benevolent approach to conquered peoples, reversing the previous policy of deportations, allowing people some autonomy, encouraging local customs and religion, and even allowing people to return home. It was this policy that led to his decree in 538 BC allowing the Jews to go home and rebuild the Temple with state aid. While this may have been rooted in compassion, it was also a shrewd political move. He knew that a contented people were less likely to rebel, while his rebuilding of their temples curried favour with them. As a good polytheist, he also wanted the favour of local deities (Ezra 6:9–10; 7:23).

The *Cyrus Cylinder* (see p. 38) documents this policy of religious tolerance and Cyrus's freeing of conquered peoples, authenticating the Bible's own account (Ezra 1:2–4; 2 Chronicles 36:23).

Below right: This glazed brick relief of a Persian archer comes from the palace of Darius in Susa, where the story of Esther is set.

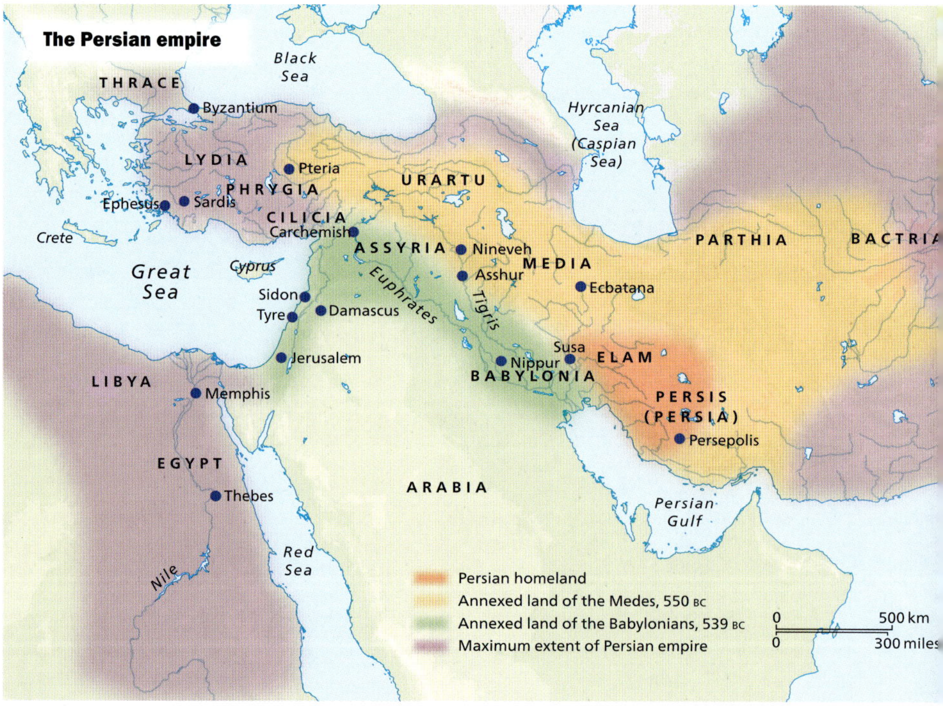

See also
Exile and Return pp. 38–39
Mesopotamia pp. 62–63

Government

Persia's ability to control distant lands was due to a mixture of wise policies and wise administration. Persia's empire was divided into twenty administrative districts, or *satrapies*, each with its own Persian governor or satrap (e.g. Ezra 8:36; Daniel 3:1–3), but which was also allowed a degree of local autonomy. Judea was part of the "Beyond the River" or Trans-Euphrates satrapy (Ezra 4:10; Nehemiah 2:7). Darius made further improvements to this system and introduced a new legal system, coinage, and postal service. Aramaic was used as the single administrative language of the empire, which explains why some parts of Ezra – those referring to the king's decrees (4:8 – 6:18; 7:12–16) – were written in Aramaic.

Arts and crafts

Persia's great wealth meant all kinds of arts and crafts flourished, and articles were brought from across the empire to adorn the king's palaces. This embossed gold ornament (above right) in the form of a lion-griffin comes from the Oxus treasure, a collection of 170 pieces of gold and silver jewellery and ornaments from the time of Cyrus the Great found by the River Oxus.

Religion

Ancient Persian gods were a mixture of nature gods and ideas, probably rooted in their early nomadic lifestyle. As part of their worship, Persians sacrificed animals and drank "haoma", an intoxicating drink that was believed to bring healing, strength, and sexual arousal. Hugely influential was Zoroaster (or Zarathushtra) who, at the age of thirty, had visions inspiring him to preach a new message focusing on Ahura-Mazda (the Wise Lord) as the supreme deity whose symbol was fire. He taught that the world and people were good but spoiled by attacks of evil. He therefore placed much emphasis on the importance of personal religion, calling men and women alike to choose between good and evil and to thereby determine their eternal destiny. His ideas found great favour at court, where they were promoted by the Magi, a priestly tribe of Medes who acted as royal chaplains. It was such Magi who visited Jesus at his birth (Matthew 2:1–12). Zoroastrians came under fierce persecution in the seventh century AD when Islam swept through Persia; many fled to India in the tenth century AD, becoming the forerunners of today's Parsi community.

Connections with the Bible

- King Cyrus's decree permitted the exiled Jews to return to the Promised Land (Ezra 1:2–4; 2 Chronicles 36:23).
- Esther's foiling of an attempt to exterminate the Jews (Esther 3:1 - 9:17) comes from the time of King Xerxes.
- Ezra and Nehemiah were sent back to Judah by King Artaxerxes (Ezra 7:1–28; Nehemiah 1:1 - 2:10).
- Haggai, Zechariah, and Malachi all prophesied against the background of the return from Persia.
- Magi from Persia visited Jesus at his birth (Matthew 2:1–12).

Faith idea: Goodness

Like Zoroastrianism, the Bible teaches that God is good and his creation is good, and in the light of this calls people to both be good and do good. But the Bible also says that human sin has marred this goodness (though not destroyed it, for the world is still God's and people are still in his image). Only through Jesus' death, the New Testament says, can that sin be dealt with and the hindrances to goodness be removed once and for all.

The Greeks

A Challenge and a Gift

While Greece isn't an obvious player in the Bible's story, its influence was greater than that of any preceding empire. For Jews, it was Greek culture that threatened to obliterate their way of life in the inter-testamental period and that led to a major revolt; while for Christians, Greek culture not only challenged their worldview but, positively, provided a world language that enabled the gospel to be shared anywhere.

History

Greece's origins go back to at least the late third millennium BC, when invaders from the north overran the area, establishing many independent city-states. Its first great civilization developed on Crete (Old Testament Caphtor), home to the **Minoans,** who reached their height around 1500 BC but who had completely collapsed by the turn of the millennium. Around 1400 BC the **Myceneans** rose to prominence on the mainland, and their language shows they were the first identifiable "Greeks". But by 1150 their civilization too had collapsed and internal conflicts characterized Greece for the next several hundred years.

Everything changed when **Philip II of Macedon** swept south, crushing the Greek army in 338 BC and uniting the nation. His victory was extended by his twenty-year-old son, **Alexander the Great**, who in 334 BC invaded the Persian empire, sweeping through it and replacing it with his own. Greece was now at the height of its power, one of the greatest empires the world had known, and one that would have been even greater had Alexander not died prematurely.

Having been tutored by Aristotle, Alexander wanted not just to conquer, however, but also to leave a legacy that couldn't be forgotten; so he began a programme of "Hellenization" – the introduction of Greek ideas and culture. Greek cities were established, like Sepphoris in Galilee; stadiums, gymnasia, and theatres sprang up everywhere; and Greek became the language of education and trade. Even after Greece's defeat by Rome, its influence long remained.

Alexander the Great's empire
Alexander's empire at its greatest. After his death, it disintegrated, divided among his generals into Macedon, Thrace, Mesopotamia, and Egypt.

Religion

The Greeks believed in many gods, chief of whom was Zeus, who lived on Mount Olympus and ruled the other gods – gods like Apollo (god of wisdom), Ares (god of war), Hades (god of the dead), Athena (goddess of art and war), Aphrodite (goddess of love), Demeter (goddess of harvest), and Dionysus (god of wine). To ensure they didn't offend any god they might not have known, the Athenians built an altar "To an Unknown God" (Acts 17:23), which Paul used to point them to Jesus. Greeks also had many "mystery religions" – secret societies where hidden spiritual truths were revealed only to their initiates. Paul sometimes used the language of mystery religions to engage with his hearers, saying God too had a mystery, a secret – but one that he has now shared with everybody through Jesus Christ.

Philosophy

As belief in the traditional gods waned, many Greeks turned to philosophy for answers to life's questions. Athens became home to many leading thinkers like Pericles, Socrates, and Plato, and playwrights like Sophocles and Euripides. Philosophical schools developed – Epicurean, Cynic, and Stoic – each with its own, and often very different, approach. Paul debated with Epicurean and Stoic philosophers in Athens (Acts 17:16–34).

Some philosophies taught "dualism" – that the body and spirit are utterly separate and that only the spirit matters. This produced one of two outcomes: either do what you like with your body because it is unimportant, or treat it harshly to keep it subdued. Both attitudes affected the early church and both were corrected by Paul in his letters, calling Christians to a more holistic view of humanity.

"Greeks"

The term "Greeks" is often used in the New Testament as a synonym for Gentiles.

See also
Break-up of Alexander's Empire p. 40
Language pp. 120–21
Maccabean Revolt p. 40

Sport

The Greeks loved sport, believing it had religious significance, and so dedicated it to the gods. Nowhere was this seen more clearly than in the Olympic Games, held every four years, when every city met at Olympia in southern Greece to compete against one another, causing even wars to stop over this period. Athletes trained at home for ten months, followed by one month's training in Olympia's gymnasium. Winners received no financial reward but were honoured with a laurel wreath, an image used by New Testament writers (e.g. 1 Corinthians 9:25; James 1:12; 1 Peter 5:4; Revelation 2:10). Cheats had their names and families engraved on stones near the stadium's entrance, as in this example, as a warning to others.

The pot which, according to some accounts, the fourth-century BC Cynic philosopher Diogenes inhabited in Corinth, just as he had in Athens. This action was just one of many designed to challenge the values of what for him was a corrupt society.

Connections with the Bible

- The rise of Greece was prophesied by Daniel (Daniel 2:1–43; 7:1–7).
- The Deuterocanonical book of 1 Maccabees recounts the Jewish revolt against the Hellenizing work of Antiochus Epiphanes IV.
- Jesus ministered to some Greeks (Mark 7:24–30; John 12:20–36).
- Paul's mission was largely in Greek cities in Asia Minor and Greece itself.
- The entire New Testament is written in Greek.

Democracy

Just prior to 500 BC Athens became the world's first democracy, having expelled a number of tyrants and established a popular assembly, believing that every male citizen should play a part in the affairs of "the city" (Greek *polis*, from which the word "politics" comes). While often seen as the highest form of politics today, democracy in fact finds no support in the Bible.

Faith idea: Apologetics

Apologetics (from the Greek apologia, *meaning "defence") is about presenting the rational basis for one's beliefs. The apostle Paul often did this in both his speaking and writing, especially in Greek settings – what he described as "defending and confirming the gospel" (Philippians 1:7). Christian apologetics seeks to show that faith is not a blind leap in the dark but has an utterly rational foundation to it.*

As protection against attack, most Greek city-states developed around a high, easily defendable stronghold called an acropolis. This is the one at Corinth, towering some 1,800 feet (c. 550 m) above the ruins of the Temple of Apollo in the newer city in the foreground. Paul almost certainly had this in mind when he encouraged the Corinthians to pull down the "strongholds" of their thinking (2 Corinthians 10:4–5).

The Romans

From City to Empire

Although modern Italy was peripheral to the biblical stage, it would nevertheless play an important, though conflicting, role in the Bible's story. For Jews, their faith was accepted by Rome as an authorized religion (*religio licta*), and yet it was Rome that destroyed their Temple. For Christians, Rome provided the peace that allowed them to travel and preach the gospel, and yet it was Rome that crucified Jesus and persecuted the church.

History

It was Romulus who, according to Roman mythology, founded Rome on the Palatine Hill on 21 April 753 BC, the date from which Romans reckoned their history. For centuries it remained a small and struggling city-state ruled by kings, some of them neighbouring Etruscans, but in 509 BC the Romans threw off Etruscan rule and established a republic. Over the coming years its power grew, aided by its location on the River Tiber just a few miles inland and on the main route along western Italy. It gradually conquered its neighbours until, by 278 BC, it controlled all of southern Italy.

Rome then cast its eyes further afield, defeating Carthage in North Africa after years of battle in 146 BC, giving it control of North Africa and the western Mediterranean. The same year it conquered Corinth, opening up Rome to Greek culture, and surrounding nations followed over the next 100 years. Julius Caesar went on to conquer Gaul and Britain in the west, and Pompey conquered Syria and Palestine in the east. By the first century AD Rome's empire was vast.

But this vast empire had its downsides. Corruption proved hard to control from distant Rome, and there were many struggles for power between rival generals. Julius Caesar defeated Pompey in 48 BC, becoming "dictator", but was assassinated four years later in the Roman Senate. His death started a civil war between Mark Antony and Octavian, and it was the latter who ultimately prevailed. In 27 BC he was given the title Augustus ("worthy of honour") and became Rome's first emperor, having established a peace that the New Testament would see as preparation for the coming of Jesus and the spread of the gospel.

Religion

Early Roman religion centred around belief in the divine power in nature, which they sought to harness to daily needs; so there were gods for almost every aspect of life, though only the main official gods of state like Jupiter were ever pictured as "persons". But after the conquest of Greece, Greek ideas and religion began to permeate Roman thinking. Gradually the old Roman gods were merged with the Greek gods, who were given Roman names, as seen in the chart opposite of "The Twelve Olympians", the gods who were thought to live on Mount Olympus as Zeus's extended family. Romans were very superstitious, giving much credence to omens and dreams, which is why Pilate's wife was so troubled by the dream she had about Jesus (Matthew 27:19). For most Romans religion had little impact on daily life, and the state was happy to let people believe whatever they liked as long as they were good citizens. Educated Romans came to see religion as a means to political ends and looked to Greek philosophy if they wanted answers to life's questions. For a more personal faith people looked to the "mystery religions" or foreign cults.

The Roman Empire

See also
Between the Two Testaments pp. 40–41
Greek Religion p. 78
Persecution p. 126

The Twelve Olympians

Greek name	Roman name	Sphere of influence
Zeus	Jupiter	Chief god
Hera	Juno	Marriage and motherhood
Athena	Minerva	War, wisdom, arts
Apollo	Apollo	Sun, prophecy, poetry, music, medicine
Artemis	Diana	Chastity, hunting, moon
Poseidon	Neptune	Sea, earthquakes, horses
Aphrodite	Venus	Love, beauty
Hermes	Mercury	Travel, commerce, invention, cunning
Ares	Mars	War
Demeter	Ceres	Agriculture, fertility, marriage
Dionysus	Bacchus	Wine, ecstasy
Hephaestus	Vulcan	Fire, metalworking

Connections with the Bible

- A Roman census led to Joseph and Mary returning to Bethlehem where Jesus was born (Luke 2:1–7), fulfilling Old Testament prophecy (Matthew 2:4–6; Micah 5:2).
- Jesus healed a Roman centurion's servant, impressed by his understanding of authority (Matthew 8:5–13).
- It was the Roman governor Pilate who tried Jesus and ordered his death (Matthew 27:11–26).
- Paul spent two years in Rome under house arrest (Acts 28:16, 30) but was released and imprisoned again later under Nero (AD 66–67), during which time he wrote 2 Timothy.
- Romans destroyed Jerusalem and its Temple in AD 70.

The city of Rome
Rome was a bustling cosmopolitan city with over a million inhabitants. While the wealthy lived in magnificent homes, the poor lived in tenement buildings, four to five storeys high, in crowded streets, so the city was constantly in tension, and emperors frequently bought peace by distributing free corn or organizing free shows. Some of the greatest shows took place in the Colosseum (or Flavian Amphitheatre, as it was originally called), which seated 50,000 people (top right). It used to be thought that many Christians were martyred there, thrown to wild animals or forced to fight gladiators, but there is no archaeological or literary evidence of this. Most were martyred at the nearby Circus Maximus.

Emperor worship

Because the Romans had so many gods, the step of seeing the emperor himself as a god wasn't a hard one. This had its origins in people's gratitude to Rome for the peace (*Pax Romana*) it brought. In 29 BC Pergamum in Asia Minor asked Octavian (Augustus) for permission to worship him as a gto be thoughtd the emperor duly granted it. This led John many years later to describe Pergamum as the city "where Satan has his throne" (Revelation 2:13), describing Rome as a great beast blaspheming against God because of this claim (Revelation 13:1–10). Honouring the emperor as a god spread rapidly, with cities vying to build temples to him. The emperor became known as "god", "son of a god", "saviour of the world" – titles Christians reserved for Jesus alone and so wouldn't use of the emperor, just as they wouldn't declare the oath of allegiance, "Caesar is Lord", which cost many Christians their lives.

Faith idea: Authorities

Both Paul (Romans 13:1–7) and Peter (1 Peter 2:13–17) urged Christians to submit to ruling authorities and pray for them. If they could write this about godless and cruel Roman emperors, how much more are Christians challenged to do the same today, even with governments not of their own political persuasion. Paul and Peter weren't approving of abuses of power, but were simply recognizing that even bad government is better than anarchy.

Other People Groups

"The Nations"

Many surrounding nations feature in the Bible's story, whether significantly or incidentally. The Bible foresees that one day all the nations will know the living God.

1. Turkey – besides the Hittites (pp. 66–67), several other people groups lived in modern Turkey. The Carians lived in the southwest and served as mercenaries. The Lydians had their capital at Sardis, a city enriched by gold deposits. The Phrygians, traders in copper and slaves, became part of Lydia in the seventh century BC. The Urartians, skilled in bronze-work, tried to dominate northern Syria in the eighth to seventh centuries BC to check Assyria's expansion, but Urartu was destroyed in the seventh century BC by Scythians.

2. The Hurrians appeared in Babylonia c. 2500 BC and scattered across the Ancient Near East. They were well established by the eighteenth century BC and established Mittani in Upper Mesopotamia by the sixteenth century BC. Groups also settled throughout Canaan. They became part of the Hittite empire by 1250 BC.

3. The Phoenicians lived in coastal city-states north of Canaan. One of their key ports was Byblos, where writing was probably invented, but it was surpassed by Tyre and Sidon after 1000 BC. Phoenicians were leading sea-traders, establishing colonies across the Mediterranean. Solomon used Phoenician products and expertise for his Temple (1 Kings 5).

4. The Cushites probably lived in Lower and Upper Nubia, sometimes translated "Ethiopia". Cush was very wealthy and exported precious minerals and spices down the Nile. Moses had a Cushite wife (Numbers 12:1); David had a Cushite messenger (2 Samuel 18:21); Philip baptized a Cushite convert (Acts 8:26–40) who served "the Candace", the Cushite queen.

5. The Arameans (Syrians) were a semi-nomadic tribe scattered across Mesopotamia and Syria. The Old Testament's patriarchs were Arameans (Deuteronomy 26:5). When the Hittite empire collapsed, Arameans in Syria became powerful city-states that flourished in the eleventh to eighth centuries BC. Naaman's pride in his city almost led to him not being healed (2 Kings 5:1–19). Israel had mixed relationships with Aram, especially Damascus, at times fighting them, at times trading with them. Aramaic became the international language of the whole region from 750 BC until Greek replaced it, though Aramaic remained the common language of the Jews.

6. The Amorites were a nomadic people from Mesopotamia who spread to Syria and Canaan. They were gradually absorbed by Reuben, Gad, and Manasseh (Joshua 12:1–6). "Amorites" was often used as a general term for Canaan's inhabitants (Genesis 15:16; Joshua 24:15).

7. The Ammonites, descended from Lot's daughters (Genesis 19:36–38), lived in southern Transjordan, between the Jabbok and Arnon rivers, enabling them to control trade along the King's Highway. Israel was forbidden to conquer them because of family ties (Deuteronomy 2:19), but Ammon still attacked them, especially in the period of the Judges (Judges 2:12–13; 10:6–18) and early monarchy (1 Samuel 11:1–14; 2 Samuel 10:1–19), but David defeated them (2 Samuel 11:1; 12:26–31). In the ninth century BC they joined a Transjordan League, stopping Assyria's advance and attacking Jehoshaphat, who experienced God's miraculous deliverance (2 Chronicles 20). They submitted to Assyria in 732 BC and were conquered by Babylon in 581 BC.

8. The Moabites lived east of the Jordan, between the Arnon and Zered rivers, though often fought Israel over the fertile plains to their north. Balak tried to stop Israel passing through Moab on the way to Canaan (Numbers 22–24) and Eglon oppressed Israel in the Judges period (Judges 3:12–30). Moab sometimes came under Israel's control (e.g. 2 Samuel 8:2) but also rebelled (e.g. 2 Kings 3). It ceased to exist when conquered by Babylon in 585 BC.

9. The Edomites were descendants of Esau, Isaac's son, and the rivalry between Esau and Jacob continued through their ancestors, leading to frequent conflicts (e.g. Numbers 20:14–21; 1 Samuel 14:47; 1 Kings 11:14; Isaiah 34:5). They lived in the mountains south of the Dead Sea, which provided almost impregnable strongholds. Obadiah's prophecy is directed against Edom.

10. The Amalekites were descendants of Amalek, Esau's grandson, living as nomads in Sinai and the Negev. Because they attacked the Israelites at the exodus, they were put under a permanent vow of destruction (Exodus 17:8–16). Both Saul (1 Samuel 15) and David (1 Samuel 30) fought them.

11. The Midianites were descendants of Abraham through his second wife Keturah (Genesis 25:1–4). They lived along the Red Sea, raiding and trading, and it was to Midianite traders that Joseph was sold by his brothers (Genesis 37:28). Moses had married a Midianite (Exodus 2:11–25), yet

See also
The Ancient Near East pp. 48–49
Nations pp. 62–83

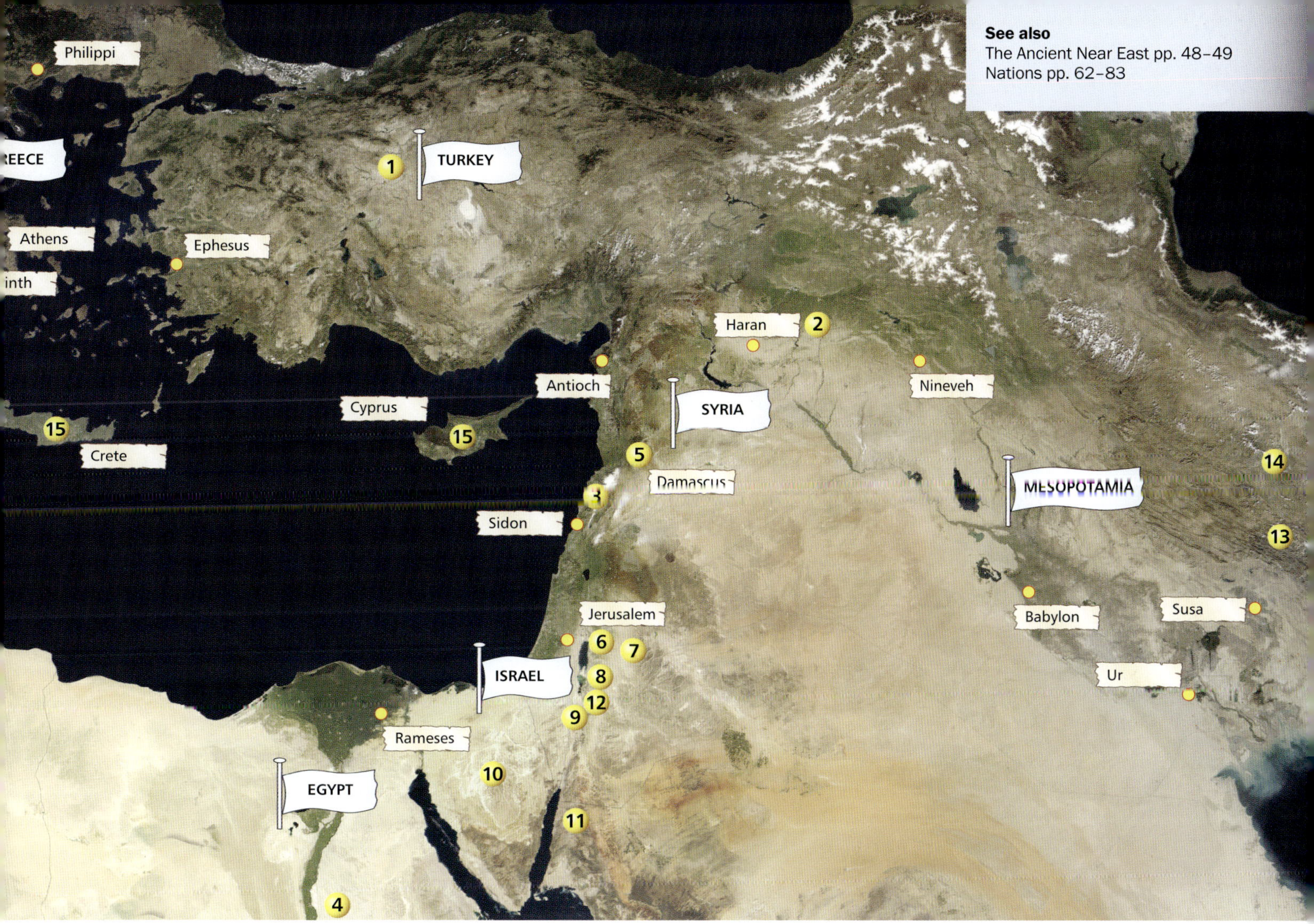

Midian resisted Israel when they tried to pass through on their way to Canaan, thereby becoming Israel's enemy (Numbers 25:16–18). They raided Israelite territory during the period of the Judges (Judges 6:1–6) but were defeated by Gideon (Judges 7).

12. The Nabateans were Arabs who settled in Edom and Moab. By the fourth century BC they were amassing great wealth from caravans that passed through their much-expanded territory with its capital at Petra. Their kingdom was at its height under Aretas IV (ruled 9 BC–40 AD). One of his daughters married Herod Antipas, son of Herod the Great, but he divorced her, bringing John the Baptist's condemnation (Mark 6:14–29). Aretas's governor in Damascus tried to arrest the apostle Paul (2 Corinthians 11:32–33).

13. The Elamites lived east of the Tigris, expanding and becoming prosperous, though often under the rule of neighbouring Assyria, who deported exiled Israelites here in 721 BC. Elam later became part of Persia, and a magnificent winter palace was established in Susa, which was the setting for Esther's story.

14. The Medes entered eastern Mesopotamia from the north around 1000 BC. In the seventh century BC they dominated Persia and, by allying with Scythia and Babylonia, brought about Assyria's fall in 612 BC. However, Persia ultimately became the dominant partner in their alliance with the rise of Cyrus the Great.

15. "The Islands" was Isaiah's term for Mediterranean coastal areas. Two key islands were Cyprus and Crete. Cypriots were among the first to hear and share the gospel (Acts 11:19–21) and Paul visited Cyprus, the home of Barnabas, on his first missionary journey (Acts 13:4–12). Crete, where the Minoan civilization had flourished, was visited by Paul on his eventful journey to Rome (Acts 27), and Titus was based here for a time.

Faith idea: The nations

While the Bible often speaks of "the nations" as those who oppose God – and there are plenty of examples of this in biblical history – it also looks forward to the end time when people of all nations will know God, just as he had always planned. When God called Abraham, it wasn't simply to found one nation, but rather to bless every nation (Genesis 12:3), as John saw in his vision (Revelation 5:9–10).

The Family

The Gift of the Relational God

The Bible never sees family as simply a social construct, but rather as God's gift to humanity. For Paul its origin lay in the very nature of Father God himself (Ephesians 3:14–15), describing him (through a play on words in Greek) as "the Father of all fatherhoods", the origin of all family life. Family is a key means of people expressing their humanity through relationships, just as God expresses himself in relationship within the "family" of the Trinity.

The primacy of family

The Bible's story begins with family as the central context of life and relationships, the setting for men and women to find fulfilment in one another and provide a safe place for bringing up children (Genesis 1:27–28; 2:19–25). While family is as flawed by sin as much as anything else – for in Genesis we see squabbling spouses, rival siblings, and deceitful children – it is through a family that God promises to establish his covenant purposes (Genesis 12:1–3; 15:1–19; 17:1–27). The primacy of family continues through the New Testament, with the church described as "the family of believers" (Galatians 6:10), Christians called brothers and sisters, and at the end of history the church being greeted by Jesus as his bride (Revelation 21:2).

Nation, tribe, clan, family

Life in ancient Israel was far less individualistic than Western life is today, with a sense of belonging to something bigger maintained through four levels of social structure:

- The **nation** was the entirety of Abraham's descendants, though in its early existence Israel was more like a tribal league than what we would call a nation today.
- The nation comprised twelve **tribes**, descended from the sons of Jacob, whose name was changed to Israel (Genesis 32:22–32): Reuben, Simeon, Levi, Judah, Issachar, and Zebulun (born to Jacob's first wife, Leah); Joseph and Benjamin (born to his second wife, Rachel); Dan and Naphtali (born to Rachel's servant, Bilhah); Gad and Asher (born to Leah's servant, Zilpah). There was no tribe named Joseph because Joseph's first two sons, Manasseh and Ephraim, were adopted by Jacob, and Joseph's inheritance was divided between them (Genesis 48) to replace Joseph and the descendants of Levi, who had no territorial inheritance because of their priestly ministry.
- Each tribe was made up of **clans** – groupings of families on a kinship and territorial basis – that had responsibility for protecting the families' land and was the first level of wider authority in matters of marriage, inheritance, administration, and warfare. However, with the rise of the monarchy and the centralization it imposed, the tribes and clans became less important.
- The clans comprised **families** or **households.** One of the Hebrew expressions for "household" is *bêt 'āb*, literally "the father's house", highlighting both the key role of the patriarch and that "family" meant more than simply parents and their children. The household included the patriarch and his wife, his sons and their wives (who joined their husband's household), his grandchildren, and wider family members dependent on him. When the patriarch died, his place was taken by his eldest son. The patriarch was responsible for the well-being of his entire household, as well as offering hospitality to visitors (Genesis 18). Clearly the inward-focused nuclear family of modern Western society is far removed from the biblical worldview.

See also
Children pp. 88–89
Homes pp. 92–93
Marriage pp. 86–87

Family life

The family was the key place for everything: religious and ethical teaching (Deuteronomy 6:9), as well as practical training – domestic skills for girls and the father's trade for boys, though everyone helped with the animals and at harvest. The father's authority was absolute, for he was responsible for the family's stability and well-being. In theory, his wife and daughters were his property, so life could be precarious for women. But they were by no means downtrodden, holding an influence in the family that was unknown in Assyrian households, and never being segregated but rather sharing in the whole of family life. The ideal wife of Proverbs 31:10–31 exercised considerable influence and responsibility.

Family order

Paul set out his understanding of God's ideal pattern for family life, just like in Roman "household codes" (Ephesians 5:21 – 6:4; Colossians 3:18–21). From a foundation of mutual submission for Christ's sake (Ephesians 5:21), he called for interdependent and complementary roles and responsibilities: a husband who sees himself as the family head, loving his wife as Christ loves the church, and training, though not exasperating, his children; a wife who submits to her husband's headship like the church submits to the headship of Jesus; children who honour and obey their parents. For Paul, this pattern wasn't simply cultural but part of what it meant to be full of God's Holy Spirit (Ephesians 5:18–21).

Inheritance

When a father died, his sons inherited his wealth, and his responsibilities. The eldest son was given a "double-portion" of the estate as he now became the patriarch and needed resources for supporting the wider family. When Elisha asked Elijah for "a double portion of your spirit" (2 Kings 2:9) he wasn't asking for a ministry twice as great, but was expressing his desire to continue Elijah's ministry as his spiritual son.

Genealogies

Because people didn't think of themselves as "individuals" but rather as members of their family, clan, and tribe, they maintained extensive genealogies (family records), of which the Bible records many. Sometimes these were short (e.g. Ruth 4:18–22), sometimes long (e.g. Matthew 1:1–16), but always establishing an irrefutable link with the past and an identity and legitimacy in the present. Genealogies were particularly important for hereditary offices like priest and king and for establishing land rights. The early Christians were at pains to show that Jesus was a true descendant of Abraham and David (Matthew 1; Luke 3) and therefore qualified to receive God's promises to them; but they also redefined genealogies by now including all those who follow Jesus as true descendants (e.g. Galatians 3:29).

A genealogy of Christ from *The Book of Kells*.

Faith idea: Adoption

While adoption as such was unknown in Israel, for provision for orphans came through other Jewish laws and customs, it was common among Greeks and Romans, who granted the adopted child all the privileges of a natural child, including inheritance rights. The New Testament says that, while only Jesus is God's Son by nature, through faith in him people can become God's adopted sons and know him as their Father (Romans 8:15–17; Ephesians 1:4–5), receiving all the privileges and inheritance that this entails.

Marriage

Two Becoming One

God's intention for intimate relationships, the Bible says, is for one man to live faithfully with one woman throughout their lives, the two becoming one (Genesis 2:24; Malachi 2:15; Matthew 19:4–6). However, not only did the Jews not always live up to this ideal, they often tried to find ways around it. But Jesus made the challenge of marriage even more demanding, such was his high esteem of it (Matthew 19:1–12).

Finding a wife

Israelite marriages were arranged by parents, normally within the same clan and ideally with a relative like a first cousin, though marriage between very close relatives was prohibited in the Law (Leviticus 18:1–18). Marriage to someone outside the faith was forbidden in both Old and New Testaments (Genesis 24:3–4; 2 Corinthians 6:14–18). Girls married young, twelve or thirteen being the minimum age, while men were usually in their late teens. Arranged marriages didn't mean they had no say in choosing a partner, however, as the story of Jacob shows (Genesis 29:9–18).

Betrothal

Marriage was a civil rather than religious matter. It began with betrothal, a legal commitment to proceed to marriage. This is why, when Joseph suspected Mary of unfaithfulness, it would have needed divorce to break the betrothal (Matthew 1:18–19). During this period the couple lived apart and no sexual relations occurred, a view maintained by the early church (Hebrews 13:4). Betrothal lasted up to a year while the man prepared the bride-price (*mohar*) – payment to compensate the bride's family for losing their daughter, either in money or in kind, like Jacob working to win Rachel (Genesis 29:16–20). Her father could use interest on the bride-price, but it was returned to her at her father's or husband's death. In exchange, the bride's father provided a dowry.

A Jewish Yemenite bride and groom wearing traditional garments and jewellery.

The wedding

The wedding took place when the bridegroom had completed his new home, so the timing could be uncertain (an image that lies behind Jesus' parable of the ten virgins, with its call to be ready for the bridegroom's unexpected arrival, Matthew 25:1–13). Accompanied by friends, he went to the bride's home in the evening where she was waiting, veiled, in her wedding dress, and wearing the jewellery given to her by the groom. In a simple ceremony, he declared that she was his wife and he was her husband, and the marriage was complete. The wedding banquet lasted up to a week (Genesis 29:27) and the whole village was invited, which explains why they ran out of wine at the wedding in Cana (John 2:1–11) and why Jesus produced such a large quantity of it. The marriage was consummated on the first night in the bridal chamber or *huppa* (the word used today of the canopy over the couple during the ceremony), and the bloodstained sheet was saved by the bride's parents as proof of her virginity at marriage against false claims for divorce (Deuteronomy 22:13–19).

See also
Children pp. 88–89
Family pp. 84–85
Homes pp. 92–93

How many wives?

In the early Old Testament period it was common for men to have more than one wife. At first, **polygamy** made economic sense (your children could work the fields and care for you when you were old); but as the expense of keeping several wives outweighed the potential gain from children the practice disappeared, except among the wealthy. Jesus reaffirmed that God's plan was for one man to be with one woman for life, however (Matthew 19:4–6).

Having a **concubine** – a slave taken as a secondary wife to produce an heir – was widespread, particularly among the wealthy. Sarah, frustrated by her barrenness, offered her slave to Abraham as a concubine (Genesis 16:1–4), though countless problems ensued (16:5–15; 21:8–21), and Leah and Rachel's servants became Jacob's concubines (Genesis 30:1–11). While concubinage died out in Israel, it was practised in Greece and Rome to provide sexual pleasure for men, though their children weren't legitimate. Against this background the early church refused to baptize men who had a concubine but wouldn't marry her.

Divorce

The Old Testament didn't ban divorce but certainly regulated it, and Moses required men who divorced their wives to give them a "certificate of divorce" (Deuteronomy 24:1–4). By New Testament times two approaches to divorce had developed in Judaism. Rabbi Shammai said Moses intended only marital unfaithfulness as a valid ground for divorce, but Rabbi Hillel took a more liberal interpretation, believing that "something that displeases him" (Deuteronomy 24:1) meant anything a man didn't like about his wife, even burning his dinner. Jesus not only took Shammai's approach but also went further, saying remarriage after divorce on any grounds except marital unfaithfulness was adultery. The starkness of his teaching is reflected in his disciples' incredulity (Matthew 19:1–12).

Ketubah

A decorated *ketubah* (Jewish marriage contract), outlining the husband's rights and responsibilities. The rabbis established the *ketubah* to deal with young men's inability to raise the bride-price (*mohar*) by combining the *mohar* with the sum agreed in the *ketubah,* which was then paid in the event of the marriage ending by death or divorce. It served to check freedom of divorce, for which no consent was required by the woman.

Singleness

Marriage was clearly the norm in ancient Israel, as there is no Hebrew word for "bachelor". Single women remained at home under their father's care until they married, so the modern issue of "singleness" (in the sense of an unmarried woman living alone) didn't occur; and widows were drawn into the extended family to be cared for. People who were genuinely single (like widows without families) were the object of special care (e.g. Deuteronomy 24:17–21; 1 Timothy 5:3–16). Some chose singleness for the sake of God's kingdom, like Jesus and Paul (who may have been a widower), and Paul saw celibacy as a gift of the Holy Spirit (1 Corinthians 7:7). Paul was not anti-marriage, but rather stressed that both marriage and singleness can have God's blessing, and that both must be lived out in true godliness.

Faith idea: Bride of Christ

The description of the church as Christ's bride (2 Corinthians 11:2; Ephesians 5:25–32; Revelation 19:7; 21:2, 9) is a powerful image of the union between Jesus and his church and his love for it. But it is also a provocation to the church to prepare itself for his coming again so that it is ready and beautiful, as any bride would be, for "the wedding of the Lamb" (Revelation 19:7–9).

Children

A Heritage from the Lord

"Sons are a heritage from the Lord, children a reward from him. Like arrows in the hands of a warrior are sons born in one's youth. Blessed is the man whose quiver is full of them" (Psalm 127:3–5). In a culture where the purpose of marriage was to have children, having many children was seen as a great blessing from God, especially sons who would provide protection and provision in your old age.

Birth

Birth wasn't always straightforward in Bible times. Some mothers died in childbirth, especially after difficult (Genesis 35:16–20) or premature (1 Samuel 4:19–22) deliveries. A safe delivery was therefore a joyous occasion and the child received as God's gift (Genesis 21:6; Isaiah 54:1; John 16:21). Midwives usually assisted the mother (Genesis 35:17), cutting the cord, washing the baby, rubbing its skin with salt to toughen it, and wrapping the baby in swaddling cloths (Luke 2:7) – long strips of linen tied tightly around the child in the belief this strengthened the bones. The cloths were loosened to rub the skin with olive oil and dust it with powdered myrtle leaves. While the Eastern Church believes Mary was alone when delivering Jesus, seeking to preserve the sanctity of the occasion, Middle Eastern custom makes this extremely unlikely.

Birth rituals

Naming

A baby was named at birth (Genesis 25:24–26), though sometimes, as with Jesus, at circumcision (Luke 2:21). The name had great significance for Jews, expressing beliefs or hopes, or the circumstances in which the child was born. For example, Elijah meant "Yahweh is God" at a time when Israel wasn't sure which god to follow, and Isaiah meant "God is salvation" when people weren't sure where to look for salvation.

Circumcision

Jewish boys were circumcised when eight days old (Leviticus 12:3), unlike in surrounding cultures where it was done to mark becoming an adult around the age of thirteen. For Jews circumcision was a sign that the child belonged to God's covenant people, a practice going back to Abraham, the founder of their nation (Genesis 17:9–14).

Purification

Childbirth made the mother ritually "unclean", which the Law saw as a barrier to worshipping God. So after forty days for a boy or eighty days for a girl, she sacrificed a pigeon and a lamb, or two pigeons if she was poor, to make her ritually clean again (Leviticus 12:1–8).

Redemption

The firstborn son was "redeemed", a practice originating at the exodus (Exodus 13:1), when God spared every firstborn Israelite from Egypt's tenth plague. The firstborn were therefore seen as God's, so had to be redeemed ("bought back") by paying five shekels to the priest as a reminder of his great redemption of Israel (Exodus 13:14–16).

Sons

Sons were important, for they continued the family name and led the extended family. So when a son was born, his mother became known as "Mother of…", like "Mary the mother of James" (Mark 16:1) or "Mary the mother of Jesus" (Acts 1:14). With little concept of an afterlife in Old Testament times, the sense of living on through your sons was crucial, so much so that if a man died childless, it was his brother's duty to father a child by his widow (Deuteronomy 25:5–10). It was his unwillingness to perform this duty that brought condemnation on Onan (Genesis 38:8–10). The custom appears to have been still operating in Jesus' time (Mark 12:19).

Traditional Jewish circumcision tools.

See also
Family pp. 84–85
Marriage pp. 86–87
Education pp. 90–91

Bar Mitzvah

A Jewish boy reading passages from the Torah to mark his reaching adulthood at the age of thirteen in his Bar Mitzvah ("Son of the Commandment") ceremony. From this point, he is old enough to understand and obey God's word. We are uncertain how this transition to adulthood was marked in Bible times, but something similar probably happened.

Child sacrifice

Many ancient peoples practised child sacrifice, to appeal to the gods in time of need (e.g. 2 Kings 3:26–27), to protect a city (e.g. 1 Kings 16:34), or to ensure fertility. Abraham's readiness to sacrifice Isaac shows he was familiar with human sacrifice, though he learned that this wasn't what the living God wanted (Genesis 22:1–19).

Below is the Valley of Ben Hinnom outside Jerusalem, where children, at dark points in Israel's history, were sacrificed to the Ammonite god Molech at Topheth (2 Kings 16:3; 17:17; Jeremiah 7:30–31). The bull-like idol was heated by a fierce fire within it and the child then placed on its red-hot, outstretched arms. Such practices were seen as an abomination (Leviticus 18:21; 20:2–5; Deuteronomy 12:31; Jeremiah 32:35), strongly condemned by the prophets (e.g. Isaiah 57:5; Ezekiel 23:36–39). King Josiah desecrated Topheth during his reforms (2 Kings 23:10; Jeremiah 32:35).

Childlessness

In ancient times, infertility was seen as great misfortune, if not God's judgment, and people handled this in different ways. Some, the Nuzi Tablets show, adopted servants as heirs, a practice Abraham considered (Genesis 15:2–3); infertile wives gave their maidservant to their husband to father a child through (e.g. Genesis 16:1–4); the Torah commanded a man to father a child through his deceased brother's wife for him (Deuteronomy 25:5–10); some resorted to infertility superstitions, like Leah and Rachel (Genesis 30:14–16). However, the Bible consistently commends those who trusted God in such circumstances, noting how people like Hannah, Samuel's mother (1 Samuel 1:1–28), and Zechariah and Elizabeth, John the Baptist's parents (Luke 1:5–25, 57–66), had their faith rewarded with children who were especially significant in God's purposes.

Jesus and children

Jesus loved children, even though he never had any of his own. He enjoyed spending time with them, refused to exclude them, and told his disciples they could learn from them (Matthew 19:13–15; 21:14–16; Mark 9:14–27).

Abortion

Abortion – the deliberate termination of pregnancy – was common in the ancient world, along with leaving children to die in the wild or on rubbish dumps or selling them into slavery. Jews and Christians consistently opposed this, evidenced in their writings outside the Bible, believing all life is sacred, God's gift from conception, full of potential and purpose (Psalm 139:13–16; Jeremiah 1:5).

Faith idea: Discipline

While the Bible rejects needless and provocative discipline (Ephesians 6:4), it sees proper loving discipline as essential to a child's well-being and good preparation for life (e.g. Proverbs 1:1–7; 6:23; 13:24; 19:18; 22:15; 29:17), and a lack of it as a recipe for disaster (e.g. Proverbs 5:22–23; 13:18; 15:10; 23:13–14). God too disciplines his children, the Bible says, not because he doesn't love them, but because he does (Proverbs 3:11; Hebrews 12:5–11).

Education

Knowledge and Wisdom

"The fear of the LORD is the beginning of knowledge" (Proverbs 1:7). This short proverb sums up the Bible's approach to education: that it is not simply about acquiring knowledge or satisfying curiosity or preparing us for work, but is intended to lead us to God, who alone gives meaning to everything.

Education in ancient Israel

Most education in ancient Israel happened at home (in fact, there was no word in Hebrew for "school"), and it was a parental duty to teach children about God at every opportunity (Deuteronomy 6:4–9). Instruction about prayer, ceremonies, and festivals was fundamental, as was the recounting of Israel's history (Exodus 13:14–16; Deuteronomy 6:20–25). Learning was by rote, aided by a variety of techniques and mnemonics to make things memorable. A common one, found in the Psalms (e.g. Psalms 9–10, 111–112, 119, 145), was having lines or stanzas beginning with successive letters of the alphabet.

Younger children were first taught by their mother; but the father then took responsibility for training his son in the family trade, while the mother trained daughters in household duties. Education was seen as a lifelong process, and there are many examples in the Bible of adults being taught God's word (e.g. Exodus 18:20; 2 Chronicles 17:7–9; Nehemiah 8:1–12). By contrast with this God-focused education, that of surrounding nations was generally more goal-orientated, preparing pupils for future service to the state. So when the Hellenizing Antiochus IV established a Greek-style "gymnasium" in Jerusalem in 167 BC, with its typical Greek curriculum of philosophy, rhetoric, poetry, drama, music, and athletics, its godless focus was resented by orthodox Jews and was a contributing factor to the Maccabean revolt.

A rabbi with young pupils.

Schools

Some boys in Old Testament times had opportunity for more formal training. For example, Samuel was trained by Eli (1 Samuel 1:24–28; 2:11, 18–26; 3:1–21), "schools of the prophets" were established (e.g. 2 Kings 2:3; 4:1; 6:1), and Isaiah had disciples (Isaiah 8:16). In later times more formal schools were organized in the synagogues. Around the age of five boys joined "the house of reading" (*beth sepher*) and at thirteen the more able proceeded to "the house of instruction" (*beth midrash*). Classes took place in the synagogue or even in the open air, and pupils sat on the floor around their teacher. Teaching methods focused on the spoken word and learning things by heart. Only if pupils showed exceptional ability did they undertake advanced study under a rabbi in Jerusalem, like the apostle Paul did (Acts 22:3), though such pupils were also expected to learn a trade, like Paul with his tent-making.

Scribes

After Israel's return from exile, scribes (originally royal recorders) took on new importance, not just copying the Law, but teaching and explaining it, like Ezra (Nehemiah 8:1–12) and Gamaliel (Acts 22:3) did. By New Testament times, they wielded considerable authority, comprising a large part of the Sanhedrin (Judaism's highest court) and holding other local offices. Since they weren't supposed to receive payment, many also had other professions. Their teachings

See also
Family pp. 84–85
Synagogue p. 147
Writing and Language pp. 120–21

A tablet from *The Instructions of Shurrupak*.

and interpretations came to be seen as authoritative as the Law itself, and by c. AD 200 they were compiled into the *Mishnah*. Jesus' teaching style contrasted strongly with theirs, for he simply made authoritative statements, unlike them with their practice of endlessly balancing one teacher's views against those of another.

Passing on wisdom

The transmission of wisdom from one generation to another was important in the Ancient Near East. In the Mesopotamian *Instructions of Shuruppak* dating from the mid-third millennium BC, Shuruppak begins his teachings with the words, "My son, I will instruct you." This same structure is found in Proverbs (e.g. 1:8; 2:1; 3:1, 11, 21; 4:1, 10, 20; 5:17; 6:1, 20; 7:1), a book that sees education as a father's transmission not just of knowledge but also of wisdom to the next generation.

The example of Daniel

Exiled as a young man to Babylon, Daniel stood out as "showing aptitude for every kind of learning" (Daniel 1:4) so was quickly chosen to serve in the Babylonian court. This meant being educated in "the language and literature of the Babylonians" (1:4), which would have included their ancient mythologies of origins, very different from what he had learned from the Jewish Scriptures and therefore an intellectual and spiritual challenge. Yet Daniel's education thus far allowed him to engage with this alien culture rather than to run from it, and God enabled him to become "ten times better than all the magicians and enchanters" of Babylon (1:20). His readiness to engage with an alien system contrasted strongly with the isolationist approach of the Qumran Community in New Testament times, and enabled him to influence Babylonian policy for almost seventy years.

Christians and education

The primary responsibility of parents for teaching their children continued in the early church, with Paul encouraging fathers to bring them up "in the training and instruction of the Lord" (Ephesians 6:4). But others in the Christian community also played a part, and Timothy was urged to teach "reliable men who will also be qualified to teach others" (2 Timothy 2:2), and Titus was told to encourage older women to "train the younger women to love their husbands and children" (Titus 2:4).

Christians have been hugely influential in the development of education over the centuries. Monks provided simple teaching; universities developed from religious orders; the Czech Jan Comenius (1592–1670) was an early champion of universal education; Robert Raikes (1736–1811) pioneered Sunday Schools in Britain, convinced that education was the best way of helping people out of poverty. Christians are still significant providers of education around the world.

Faith idea: Wisdom

While the Bible never despises knowledge (after all God, it claims, is all-knowing), it esteems wisdom more highly. Wisdom isn't just knowing the right things, but using that knowledge in the right way, at the right time. True wisdom is rooted in knowing God, and letting that shape every part of life: the intellectual (understanding the truth), the ethical (living the truth), and the practical (using the truth).

Dominus illuminatio mea

Latin for "The Lord is my light" – (left) a crest in the courtyard of Oxford's Bodleian Library, founded 1602. This is the motto of the University of Oxford, where education was founded on biblical worldviews that rejected any notion of a spiritual-secular divide. Because everything is part of a divinely ordered universe, united by its creator, its founders saw true education as not about becoming clever, but about becoming wise in how we see the parts of the whole fitting together.

Homes

The Heart of Jewish Life

Because the Bible's story covers at least two millennia, homes varied hugely over that time: from patriarchal tents, to settlers' stone houses, to kings' grand palaces – and all this within Canaan, let alone the nations around. But whatever the shape and style, the home was the heart of Jewish life.

Tents

Israel's patriarchs lived in tents, which suited their semi-nomadic lifestyle (though archaeology shows people were already living in cities, like Jericho and Hazor, by that time). The tent fabric, woven from goat's hair, was suspended by three rows of three poles, with the middle row slightly higher, hooked on by wooden rings and held firm by pegs and ropes. Once the roof was erected, it was enclosed by further panels and the tent was divided into two, the rear for women and children, the open front for visitors (e.g. Genesis 18:1–15). Sometimes the ground was covered with matting, but usually was left as bare earth, which explains why Achan's family shared his judgment for stealing treasure from Jericho, for it would have been impossible not to know of anything buried beneath their tent (Joshua 7:20–26). The tents were pitched in groups to provide protection and a sense of community, and continued to be used for some time after Israel entered Canaan, especially by herdsmen or soldiers.

In later times, Cilicium goat hair was used for tent-making, since it produced a stiffer material but one that was harder to work with. Tent-making therefore became a specialized occupation in Cilicia near Tarsus – one that the apostle Paul would learn (Acts 18:3).

Stone houses

As the Israelites settled in Canaan, they abandoned tents and began to live in houses, often built on three sides around a rectangular courtyard. In the hills, where limestone and basalt were widely available, and on the coast, where sandstone was found, the walls were made of stone, almost 3 feet (1 m) thick, with alcoves hollowed into them for storage. On the plains, mud-bricks were used, made of chopped straw, palm fibre, and bits of shell or charcoal, mixed with water and placed in wooden moulds. The bricks were then laid out in the sun to dry, or baked in kilns to make stronger foundation stones.

Roofs were made by covering beams with brushwood, earth, and clay, which is why the paralysed man's friends could dig through it to get him to Jesus (Mark 2:3–4). The Law required a parapet to be built around it so no one would fall off (Deuteronomy 22:8). A sheet or trellis with vines covered the roof, reached by a ladder or outside staircase, which was used for drying clothes and grain or as another room. It was probably such a suspended sheet that sparked Peter's rooftop vision (Acts 10:9–16). As skills improved, upper storeys became more common, like the guest room built for Elisha (2 Kings 4:10). By New Testament times, both tiled and pitched roofs were becoming common.

A Bedouin tent, similar to those used by the patriarchs.

See also
Villages, Towns, and Cities pp. 102–03
Daily Life pp. 96–97
Sanitation, Water, Lighting pp. 94–95

Floors were just hardened earth, though sometimes with stone chippings added. Greek influence led to mosaic floors being used in the homes of the wealthy, though Jews were careful to avoid pagan symbols in them.

Windows (just gaps in the walls) were few and small to keep the house cool in summer and warm in winter. Lattice shutters kept intruders out, and thick woollen curtains kept the cold out in winter. Doors were made of woven twigs, though later of wood or metal.

Most houses were divided into two areas: a lower area near the door for animals, and a rear area with raised platform where the family lived, the space beneath used for storage. There were no toilet or bathing facilities. In Roman cities, the poor lived in tenement blocks (*insulae*), where there was generally a shop on the ground floor and dwellings in the floors above, reached by an outside staircase.

Typical layout of an Israelite home.

Furniture

Most Israelite homes had little furniture. When the Shunammite woman made a room for Elisha, it simply had "a bed and a table, a chair and a lamp" (2 Kings 4:10). Beds were simple wool-filled mattresses, rolled out at night for the whole family to share (Luke 11:7) and packed away in the morning. Only the rich could afford beds, like King Og of Bashan, who had an enormous iron one (Deuteronomy 3:11), and stone tables, like those discovered in "the burnt house" in Jerusalem from AD 70, which belonged to a wealthy family.

Homes of the rich

The rich had very different homes from the poor. Solomon had a magnificent palace of dressed stones, lined with cedar (2 Kings 7:1–12) and with a huge ivory throne and golden household articles (1 Kings 10:18–22). Between the tenth and eighth centuries BC, a wealthy upper class emerged in Israel, reflected in lavish homes with gardens and courtyards. Some even had winter and summer homes (Amos 3:15) and were rebuked by the prophets for acquiring their wealth on the backs of the poor. By New Testament times, especially in Jerusalem, the rich had Roman-style houses with two colonnaded courtyards surrounded by rooms with mosaic floors and frescoed walls. Herod the Great had three palaces: a summer one in Jerusalem, a winter one in Jericho, and one in Masada as a retreat in times of trouble.

The ruins of what is probably Peter's house in Capernaum. One of a group of twelve homes made of black basalt and pebbles, it was built around a central courtyard containing ovens and grinding stones. Its plastered walls were covered with decorations, crosses, and inscriptions – some of them prayers to Christ, and some mentioning Peter, suggesting this home was venerated as a place of pilgrimage from early times. A modern church, St Peter's, opened in 1990, is now suspended over the site.

Faith idea: Jubilee

Every fiftieth year (the "Jubilee") the Bible said that all land must be returned to its original owners (Leviticus 25:8–17, 23–34) to ensure poverty didn't become endemic. Land could only be sold leasehold, its price reflecting the years remaining to Jubilee. God knew there would always be some who prospered and some who didn't, and knew of the human pull to selfishness of those who did; so this provision, sadly often ignored, was to ensure no one stayed in permanent poverty. This bias to the poor and a passion for freedom is a consistent feature of the Bible.

Sanitation, Water, and Lighting

Holy Living

"Be holy, because I am holy," God had told the Israelites in the desert (Leviticus 11:45). That holiness – cleanness, pureness, set-apartness – was to be reflected in every aspect of life, not just religion, and is seen in the Law's passion for Israel living a clean and wholesome life, even down to such basic things as latrines.

Early Israelite sanitation

It is highly probable that, without the Law's detailed guidance on public health, Israel wouldn't have survived during its wilderness journeys. The Jewish Law, especially Leviticus, dealt with matters like water supply, sewage disposal, public hygiene, and controlling disease. For example, it required latrines to be dug outside the Israelite camp, not just to ensure that disease didn't spread, but to reflect God's holiness among them (Deuteronomy 23:12–15), and food laws prohibited eating pork or animals that had died. All this helped prevent the spread of disease. Even burning captured cities to destruction had as much of a health as a holiness aspect, since sanitation and disease were often appalling during sieges.

Clean and unclean

The Law distinguished between things that were "clean" (and therefore permissible) and "unclean" (and therefore not permissible). While some distinctions were ritualistic, some were very practical. For example, "unclean" objects included animal carcasses and people with contagious diseases, and the Law gave detailed instructions as to what to do if contact was made with them, including careful washing and isolation (e.g. Leviticus 15:1–15). While relating to sanitation and protection from disease, such laws also served to underline how much God values the holiness that these acts represented.

The idea of "quarantine" comes from the Law's period of forty days' segregation for people with certain diseases or conditions (e.g. Leviticus 12:1–4). It was adopted by the Italians in the fourteenth century (*quarantena* being the Latin for a forty-day period), because they saw that Jews seemed to stay immune from certain plagues.

Water supplies

In ancient times, cities and villages needed to be located near water supplies (whether rivers or wells), which meant dwellings were often crowded together. Only with the invention of waterproof cisterns (large bell-shaped holes lined with lime plaster) around 1200 BC could settlements be built away from water sources and rainfall collected instead. Lachish was one of the first cities to be built away from a spring. Having one's own cistern was a dream (2 Kings 18:21), but normally everyone (usually women) had to repeatedly walk to the nearest well and draw water from it by dropping down a clay pot or wooden bucket tied to a rope. Cities, however, had many cisterns – fifty were discovered in Mizpah, and thirty-seven in the Temple area alone of Jerusalem.

By New Testament times more cisterns were in use, and the Romans brought water from reservoirs by aqueducts, though people were charged for it. In Rome itself, by the end of the first century AD, eleven aqueducts fed 591 public water basins, providing almost a million cubic metres of fresh water daily.

Hezekiah's tunnel

This tunnel was built by King Hezekiah around 710 BC to bring water from the Gihon Spring outside Jerusalem into the city at the Pool of Siloam (2 Kings 20:20), thus securing the city's water supply when under siege. An inscription on its walls records the excitement of the workers, who had started at opposite ends, when they broke through and met in the middle. The tunnel, barely large enough for an adult to squeeze through, is 1,750 feet (533 m) long and is S-shaped – possibly because the builders followed a natural crack in the limestone.

See also
Food and Drink pp. 98–99
Health and Healing pp. 124–25
Homes pp. 92–93

Public toilets in Ephesus, dating from the first century AD. The toilets were arranged around the mosaic-floored room with no partitions between them. Human waste dropped into a sewer with flowing water, and the small channel at foot level carried water for cleaning oneself. Sewage disposal through drains dates back to ancient Mesopotamian and Minoan civilizations.

Sanitation in later times

Sanitation varied greatly in New Testament times, though it was always better in the cities, especially near the Jerusalem Temple. Nothing that was a possible health risk, like a cemetery or tannery, was allowed within 50 cubits (about 75 feet, 25 m) of a city. The Romans introduced toilets with running water, which drained into cesspools and were cleared by carts at night, and also public baths. At Caesarea sewers drained into the sea. Rome itself had an extensive sewer network, though few homes were connected to it.

Romans bathed only once a week, though washed arms and legs daily. Jews probably bathed less often, though the various ritual washings, especially of the hands, that were required by the Law ensured they kept clean. Full-body ritual washings would be done in a *mikvah* (ritual bath), of which there were many at the Jerusalem Temple.

Lighting

The most basic lighting in Bible times was the oil lamp – in its simplest form, a saucer filled with olive oil with a wick of hemp or flax – placed on a lampstand (e.g. Luke 8:16) or suspended from the ceiling by a chain. In later Bible times, lamps became more ornate. The poor used candles, made from wax or tallow with the pith of a rush for a wick. For outside use, torches were used – either oil lamps suspended from poles, or bound twigs stuffed with vegetable matter or rags and soaked in resin, pitch, or oil.

Caldarium

Ruins of one of Herod's Roman-style bathhouses at Masada. The heavy floor of this *caldarium* ("hot room") was supported by 200 pillars, under which hot air was passed from a furnace outside. Water was thrown on the floor to create steam, and pipes were built into the walls to heat the room – an early form of central heating. Only the extremely rich could afford such luxuries in New Testament times.

Faith idea: Light

From beginning (Genesis 1:3–4) to end (Revelation 22:5), light in the Bible symbolizes God's nature and his conquest of all that is dark, so much so that John wrote, "God is light" (1 John 1:5). At the Feast of Tabernacles, when torches lit up Jerusalem, Jesus claimed to be "the light of the world" (John 8:12) and promised this light to his followers, who were also called to be "the light of the world", shining for everyone to see (Matthew 5:14–16; Ephesians 5:8–9).

Daily Life

Give Us Today Our Daily Bread

When Jesus encouraged his followers to pray, "Give us today our daily bread" (Matthew 6:11), it wasn't just some poetic imagery about provision. It was a recognition of the realities of life, for most people in Bible times had to be self-sufficient, living off the land, and therefore much of daily life focused around the land and its yearly cycle as people sought to gain their daily bread.

Living from the land

Throughout Bible times, most families made their living from the land. Every family had been given its own plot on entering Canaan, which was meant to stay within that family forever, or at least be returned to them in Jubilee Year (Leviticus 25:8–17, 23–34) as protection against generational poverty; but by New Testament times, much of the land was owned by foreigners with huge estates, with local farmers renting it from them (e.g. Matthew 21:33–34), often at exorbitant rates. In areas of poor cultivation, people kept sheep and goats rather than growing crops, though most families had a couple of animals that shared the house with them.

Daily routines

As in many parts of the world today, the whole family helped with the routine tasks of life so essential to survival. The men took responsibility for working the land or carrying out their trade, and for training their sons in the relevant skills. The women took responsibility for food and clothing. Their day started early – collecting water, baking bread, and getting milk from the goats to drink or turn into yoghurt and cheese. The rest of the day was taken up with cooking, cleaning, spinning, weaving, dyeing, sewing, and then helping in the fields or selling crafts in the town. Children were involved in the whole of family life from an early age (not the equivalent of "child labour" today, but rather essential to survival and important for training them in future life-skills). They carried the water, filled the oil lamps, and helped their mother with household tasks. Younger children would still find time to play with toys, however, while older boys would help their fathers, like King David did by watching over his father's sheep (1 Samuel 16:11; 17:34). Crafts were handed down the family from one generation

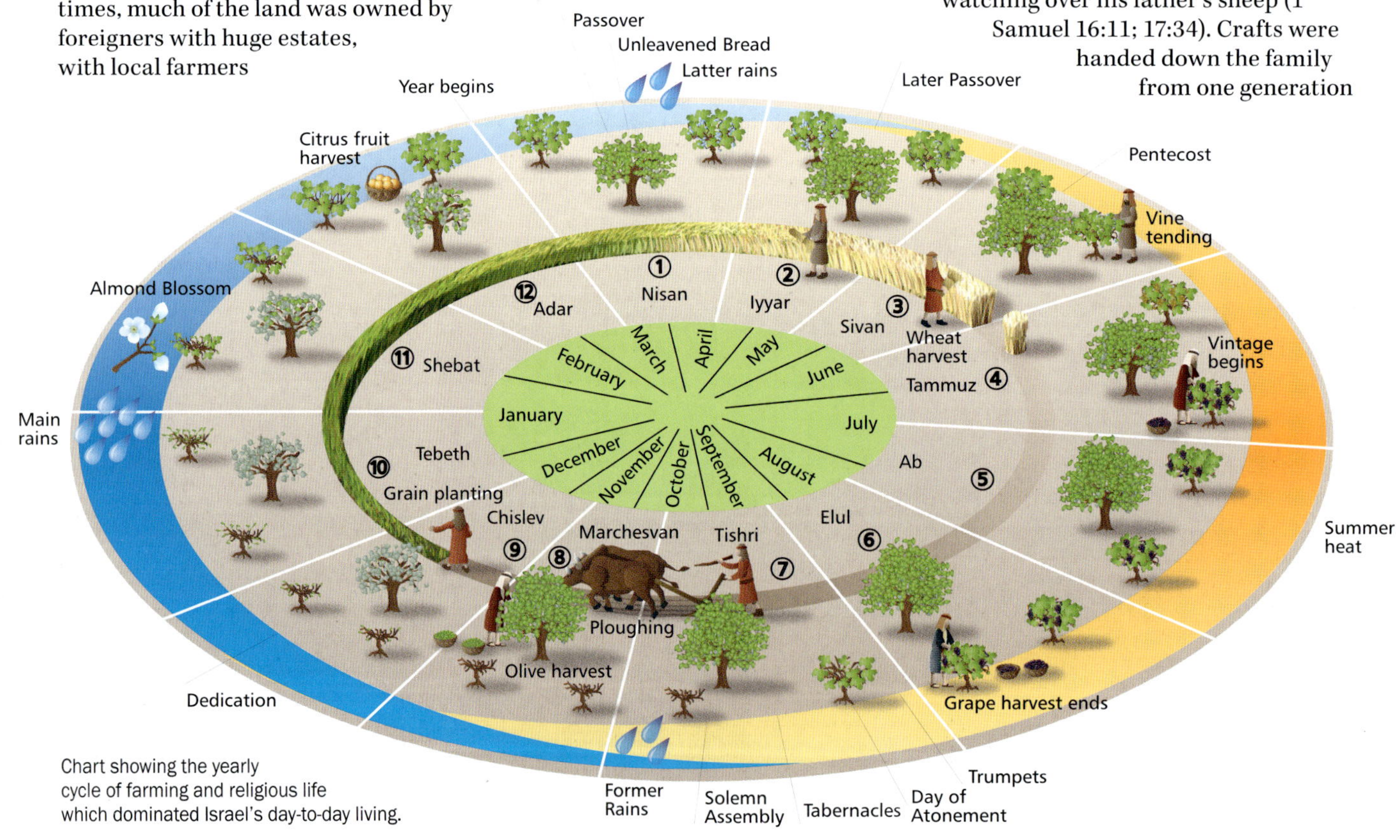

Chart showing the yearly cycle of farming and religious life which dominated Israel's day-to-day living.

See also
Farming pp. 104–05
Food and Drink pp. 98–99
Homes pp. 92–93

to another, and some villages specialized in certain crafts like pottery or ironmongery. The day ended when the family gathered together at sunset for the main meal of the day.

No matter how hard life is, young children have always found time to play. Many toys have been found from ancient times. This is a wooden pull-along toy dating from the tenth century BC.

Village life

Throughout most of the biblical period, the majority of Israelites lived in compact villages, especially in the eastern hill country, where there was a rapid growth in the number of villages between 1000 and 750 BC, perhaps the result of the developing bureaucracy of the monarchy that required more public buildings and so meant less space for ordinary homes in the towns. These villages retained close links with their nearby cities, however (e.g. Joshua 17:11), largely for protection but also for economic reasons. Some villages were built around a central square, but others developed in more random fashion.

The calendar

The earliest calendars focused around the seasons of the agricultural year and the religious ceremonies associated with them. Calendars in the great empires of Mesopotamia and Egypt were very accurate, but early Israel's calendar was less precise, apart from its focus on the festivals. Below is *The Gezer Calendar*, an inscription in Hebrew dating from the late tenth century BC that records the Israelite seasons of the farming year. It reads:

> *Two months of harvest, Two months of planting, Two months are late planting, One month of hoeing, One month of barley harvest, One month of harvest and festival, Two months of grape harvesting, One month of summer fruit.*

Not until the exile, but under Babylonian influence, did Israel work out a more accurate calendar (which still survives to this day) and replace Canaanite names of months with Babylonian ones. The New Testament writers generally dated events by reference either to the Jewish festivals (e.g. John 7:2, 14; 13:1) or to Gentile rulers (e.g. Luke 2:1; 3:1).

An enlarged replica of the Gezer Calendar.

Visitors

Receiving visitors was both a duty and a privilege in Israel (e.g. Genesis 18:1–5). Travellers didn't look for an inn (of which there were very few) but simply waited at the heart of the village or town until someone invited them home (e.g. Judges 19:14–21), where they would be given food, drink, and shelter. Such times were one of the few occasions when meat was eaten, and the visitor would be given the choicest cuts as a mark of honour (1 Samuel 9:22–24). With travel fraught with danger from both physical and social obstacles, such hospitality was essential and so followed certain conventions: invitation, screening, provision, and departure. It was the violation of such fundamental social customs that led to the destruction of Sodom, as much as its rampant immorality (Genesis 19:1–29).

For Greeks, hospitality was a mark of being civilized (Zeus, their chief god, was the god of hospitality); for Egyptians, it was something that ensured a favourable reception in the afterlife; and for Romans it was seen as a sacred duty. For Jews, however, it was rooted in the conviction that God himself was the host (e.g. Psalm 23:5; Song of Songs 2:4; Isaiah 25:6; Matthew 8:11) and that people should therefore reflect that to one another.

Faith idea: Hospitality

The Bible says that hospitality, not just for friends but also for strangers and those in need, is rooted in God himself, who "loves the alien, giving him food and clothing" (Deuteronomy 10:18) and who calls his people to do the same (10:19), remembering they too were once aliens as far as God was concerned (Exodus 23:9). Hospitality is seen as the proper response to God's love and provision (Deuteronomy 24:17–19), and its importance is underlined in the New Testament (e.g. Romans 12:13; Hebrews 13:2; 1 Peter 4:9).

Food and Drink

The Father's Provision

"Look at the birds of the air; they do not sow or reap or store away in barns, and yet your heavenly Father feeds them. Are you not much more valuable than they?" (Matthew 6:26). If God provides food for wildlife, Jesus said, how much more will he provide the basics of life for his people.

Bread

Bread was the staple of the Israelite diet. In fact, in Hebrew "to eat bread" meant "to have a meal". Wheat made the best flour, though the poor used barley. Grain was ground into flour and mixed with salt, water, and olive oil to form dough. Some fermented dough ("leaven") from the previous batch was kneaded into the fresh dough, which was then left to rise. Part of it was kept for leavening the next day's batch, and the rest was baked.

Baking bread

Egyptian model of a woman grinding grain, dating from the mid-third millennium BC. The grain was put on the lower fixed stone (the quern) and ground by pushing the upper stone (the handstone) backwards and forwards. This was replaced in late Old Testament times by more efficient millstones – two flat round stones, the bottom one fixed and the upper one turned by a handle – which needed two women to operate them (Matthew 24:41), one to pour the grain and the other to turn the wheel.

Fruit

Fruit was a key part of the Israelite diet and included grapes (eaten fresh or dried as raisins), figs (eaten fresh or dried), dates, pomegranates, melons (eaten fresh), olives (eaten fresh or pickled), and citrus fruits (by New Testament times).

Vegetables

Onions, leeks, and cucumbers were eaten fresh in season, while other vegetables were boiled. Beans, lentils, and peas were dried and stored in jars for making soups, like the one Esau sold his birthright for (Genesis 25:29–34). Lettuce, endive, chicory, and mustard all grew wild.

Above: Baking bread in a bread oven. If no oven was available, bread was baked on stones over hot coals (1 Kings 19:6). Sometimes the grain itself was roasted (1 Samuel 17:17).

Farm produce

Milk was used as a drink and to make cheese and yoghurt. It was sometimes curdled (Judges 5:25), artificially soured by being shaken in a skin bottle and left to ferment from the bacteria in the skin. By New Testament times many kept hens for their eggs, which were poached in olive oil. Eggs from quails, partridge, geese, and pigeons were also used.

See also
Farming pp. 104–05
Jewish Food Laws pp. 136–37
Water Supplies p. 94

Drinks

Since water was rarely good enough to drink, wine was the most common beverage, reflected in the fact that Hebrew has multiple words for "wine". Grapes were pressed and the juice strained before fermentation began. Mixed wines were created by adding spices, honey, or strong drink. Wine mixed with barley produced good vinegar, and when blended with myrrh formed an anaesthetic (Mark 15:23). Drinking wine wasn't forbidden in the Law, except for priests on duty (Leviticus 10:9) or those who had taken Nazirite vows (Numbers 6:1–4), but drunkenness was condemned in both the Old and New Testaments (e.g. Isaiah 28:1–8; Galatians 5:19–21; Ephesians 5:18) and was shown to have disastrous consequences (e.g. Genesis 9:20–24; 1 Kings 16:8–10; Proverbs 23: 20–21; Luke 12:44–46).

Amphora

Wine storage jars, dating from the third century BC. Commonly holding around 10 gallons (45 litres) of wine, the jars had pointed bottoms so they could be pushed into the ground to keep the wine cool. Flat-bottomed examples were used for wine, oil, and milk.

Meals

Breakfast was eaten on the way to the fields. Lunch was a light meal (Ruth 2:14), and the main meal (just one dish) was eaten by the whole family together at the end of the working day (Ruth 3:1–7). In patriarchal times, diners sat on the ground (Genesis 37:25), but later it became customary to sit at tables (1 Kings 13:20) or to recline (Esther 7:8). In New Testament times, diners reclined (Luke 7:36) on couches or mats around three sides of a low table. The feet were directed away from the table, which was why a woman could anoint Jesus' feet (Luke 7:36–38), and the left elbow rested on a cushion, leaving the right arm free to eat. People washed their hands before eating, as they ate from a communal dish (Matthew 26:23), using bread to pick up food and dip into the sauce. After the meal, a prayer of blessing was pronounced (Deuteronomy 8:10) and the diners washed their hands. Meals were a key setting for defining and establishing fellowship (Matthew 9:10–13), and the Lord's Supper (Holy Communion) occurred in the early church in the context of a meal (1 Corinthians 11:17–34).

Seasonings and sweeteners

Salt, found around the Red Sea, was used for both seasoning and preserving food. Favourite herbs included mint, dill, and cumin (Matthew 23:23). Honey from wild bees was used as a sweetener as well as a food (Judges 14:8–9; Matthew 3:4).

Fish

Fish was an important food by New Testament times, especially in Galilee, reflected in Jesus' miraculous feeding of crowds (Mark 6:32–43; 8:1–10). Small fish were dried in the sun, salted, and eaten with bread. Fresh fish was cooked over open fires (John 21:9–10).

Meat

Meat was only eaten on special occasions, like at the prodigal son's return (Luke 15:23) or at religious festivals. Mutton, goat, and birds were the most common meats, though the rich ate lamb, veal, and beef. The fat tail of the sheep was especially prized. Meat was normally boiled (1 Samuel 2:13), but the Passover lamb was roasted (Exodus 12:8).

Vegetarianism

While humankind may originally have been vegetarian (Genesis 1:29), after the flood God permitted people to eat meat and fish (Genesis 9:1–3). The New Testament says that vegetarianism can only be a matter of choice, therefore, and cannot be imposed on others (1 Corinthians 10:23–33; Romans 14:1–23).

Faith idea: Bread of life

"I am the bread of life. He who comes to me will never go hungry, and he who believes in me will never be thirsty" (John 6:35). As surely as bread was the staple of physical life, so Jesus promised to be the staple of life itself, physical and spiritual. Just as bread becomes part of us when we eat it, so Jesus envisaged a relationship with him in which he comes within us to feed us from within – a food that, unlike the manna in the wilderness, would satisfy forever (John 6:47–58).

Clothing and Cosmetics

The Gift of God

Clothing isn't just practical; it is God's gift, the Bible shows. When Adam and Eve tried to cover their nakedness with fig leaves (Genesis 3:7), God responded with as much kindness as judgment, making "garments of skin for Adam and his wife" (Genesis 3:21) before expelling them from Eden. This wasn't just covering their embarrassment; it was a token of his ongoing provision for the life now facing them. Giving clothes as a token of kindness would become a feature of life in the ancient world (e.g. Genesis 41:42).

Clothing styles

Clothing styles changed little in Palestine during the biblical period, the main difference being between rich and poor. While the poor only had the clothes they stood in, the rich had varied wardrobes for all seasons and occasions.

Men

As underwear, men wore a loincloth or skirt from waist to knee, and its absence was unusual and noteworthy (Mark 14:51–52). The Law required men to wear a cotton shirt with four tassels, called a tallith, as a reminder of their identity (Numbers 15:37–41). The undergarment, a calf-length tunic of wool, linen, or cotton (for the wealthy), was made from material folded in half and sewn or tied at the sides, with holes for the head and arms, and fastened at the waist with a girdle, made of leather or folded cloth. When working or running, the outer garment was tucked into the belt (Exodus 12:11; 1 Kings 18:46), known as "girding up your loins". By New Testament times, men wore a knee-length woollen cloak outdoors.

Women

Women wore a tunic like the man's, but ankle length, often dyed blue and with traditional embroidery, and some women wore shawls (Ruth 3:15). Their belts were more ornate than men's, and the rich had long silk girdles. When working, women lifted the tunic's hem to use as a bag, like Ruth did when gleaning (Ruth 2:17–18). By the eighth century BC, wealthy women wore elaborate outfits, which were denounced by Isaiah (Isaiah 3:18–23).

Asiatic clothing

Wall painting from the tomb of Khnum-hotep III, dating from the early nineteenth century BC, showing Asiatic travellers arriving in Egypt wearing brightly coloured garments, perhaps like those given to Joseph by his father (Genesis 37:3).

Making clothes

Most clothes were made from sheep's wool, goat's hair, or flax. Wool was combed, then spun into yarn and woven on a handloom. Linen, made from flax fibres, was spun and woven in the same way. The cloth was then dyed with dyes from plants, animals, and minerals. Black, blue, red, yellow, and green were all popular colours, but purple, expensive to produce, was only used by the wealthy. Analysis of cloth from the early second century AD shows that just three basic dyes (saffron yellow, indigo blue, and alazarin red) produced thirty-four different colours of thread.

See also
Crafts and Skills pp. 108–09
Priests' Garments p. 149
Swaddling Cloths p. 88

Headwear

Because the sun was so hot, the head, neck, and eyes needed protection by headwear – for men, a square of cloth, folded diagonally and fixed by a plaited wool band, allowing the folds to cover the neck. Sometimes they wore a cap with a fine wool shawl over it, especially during prayer. Women wore a veil to cover their head and shoulders, sometimes drawn across the face. By New Testament times, most women kept their head covered in public.

Cosmetics

Women wore dark eyeshadow, made by grinding minerals in oil or gum, both to protect the eyes against the sunlight and as a fashion. Lipstick was used, and red nail paint, from henna plants, was used on toenails and fingernails. Red oxide was used as rouge for the cheeks. Perfume, extracted from flowers, seeds, herbs, and fruit, was added to oil and rubbed into the skin to soothe it and hide body odours. Imported perfumes were very costly and kept in small alabaster jars (Matthew 26:6–9).

Hair and beards

In Old Testament times Jewish men had long hair. Some plaited it and some trimmed it, though the Law required that hair at the side of the head wasn't cut (Leviticus 19:27), a custom law still observed by Orthodox Jews. Most men wore beards, unlike Egyptians who were clean-shaven (Genesis 41:14). However, by New Testament times, hair was worn short and many men were clean-shaven.

Women plaited, braided, or curled their hair, keeping it in place by ivory combs. Paul's instruction to women to cover their heads (1 Corinthians 11:3–10) came against a background of women being expected to cover their hair in public, since hair was seen as sexually provocative, and such a desire to throw off cultural norms in pursuit of "freedom" was unacceptable for Christians, he said.

Footwear
Sandals (like in the mosaic above) were the normal footwear in Palestine, though the poor went barefoot. The simplest sandal was a cowhide sole with a leather strap (the thong) that passed between the big and second toes and was tied around the ankle. Soles were made from wood or dried grass, and in Egypt from papyrus. The rich wore leather slippers. Footwear was always removed before entering a house or holy place.

Miscellaneous facts

- The right sandal was put on and taken off before the left.
- Putting on shoes meant you were ready for a journey (Exodus 12:11).
- Enemy clothing was taken as booty after battle.
- Someone selling property gave his sandal to the purchaser (Ruth 4:7).
- Roman soldiers took the clothing of executed men (John 19:23).
- Fashionable clothes were a temptation then as now (Judges 7:21).

Jewellery

Necklaces, bracelets, anklets, and rings (for ears, noses, and fingers) were all worn by Jews for special occasions. Jewellery was made from gold, silver, and precious metals and set with precious or semi-precious stones. Ivory was carved to make hair combs and brooches. Wearing jewellery is never condemned in the Bible, and indeed at times it is seen as right and proper (e.g. Isaiah 61:10). But the ostentatious use of jewellery was condemned (Isaiah 3:16–23; 1 Timothy 2:9–10).

Bronze Age jewellery.

Faith idea: Handling anxiety

Recognizing how common anxiety was, Jesus said that his followers didn't need to be anxious – not even over such ordinary things as food and clothing (Matthew 6:28–33) – because they had a heavenly Father who cares about even the smallest details of people's lives. Paul encouraged Christians to bring whatever they were anxious about to God in prayer and there find peace (Philippians 4:5–7).

Villages, Towns, and Cities

Community Life

Unlike today, there was often little difference between villages, towns, and cities in Bible times. The chief difference wasn't size but defences, for towns and cities had defensive walls around them, whereas villages were "without walls and without gates and bars" (Ezekiel 38:11). But whatever their size, every settlement was an expression of mankind's longing for community.

Beersheba
Excavations at Beersheba have revealed structures from the time of the monarchy and shown the city's considerable size. This photo shows how towns and cities were built on top of mounds, or *tells*, for protection. Beersheba was Israel's southernmost city; hence the expression "from Dan to Beersheba", meaning "the whole kingdom".

Old Testament settlements

Villages in the Old Testament period were unwalled farming settlements, located near streams or springs. Excavations at Jericho show people settling in this way as early as 6000 BC. **Towns** developed around 4000 BC from a need to protect water supplies from nomads through strength of numbers. Many people still lived in surrounding villages, simply retreating to the town in time of threat. Towns were small, with only 150–200 dwellings and around 1,000 inhabitants, while villages comprised extended family units. The distinction between villages and towns wasn't great; hence, Bethlehem is described as both a town and a village (Luke 2:4; John 7:42). Post-New Testament Judaism defined a village as a place without a synagogue. **Cities** in Israel grew in number between 1000 and 750 BC as a result of the need for administrative centres for the developing monarchy; but they also diminished in size, for the growing need for public buildings meant less space for homes, leading many to migrate to villages.

Town life

Life in towns was very cramped, with houses tightly packed within its walls and no real streets or space between them. A common form of wall was the "casemate" – parallel stone walls filled with rubble to absorb shock, with partitions between them for storage or living, which was probably what Rahab's house in Jericho was like (Joshua 2:15). Key cities also had fortified towers along the walls from which weapons could be fired at attackers. There was no drainage, and rubbish was thrown out and left to pile up, meaning that the street level was sometimes higher than the doorsill, causing havoc in wet weather and leading many to prefer living in the countryside and villages. Originally, houses were similar in size, but during the eighth century BC a wealthy middle class developed that built grander homes in the better parts of town.

See also
Homes pp. 92–93
Jerusalem pp. 154–55
Sanitation, Water, Lighting pp. 94–95

Sepphoris

Below: The colonnaded street that ran through the heart of Sepphoris, a city of 30,000 people and capital of Galilee in New Testament times. While not mentioned in the Bible, it was just 4 miles (6.5 km) north of Nazareth. Since major building works, instigated by Herod Antipas, were underway throughout Jesus' lifetime, and since his father was in the building trade (Luke calls him a *tektōn*, meaning builder rather than carpenter), it is quite possible that they were both involved in building projects in this city that Josephus called "the ornament of all Galilee" (*Antiquities*, 18:7). Its streets were designed in a grid, paved with limestone and lined by large public buildings, as well as houses of varying sizes. It had a colonnaded main street, an amphitheatre seating around 4,000, and a public bathhouse fed from an underground reservoir served by a series of aqueducts. Its thoroughly Roman nature is seen in the way that it didn't join in the Jewish Revolt (AD 66–70), but sided with Rome. Jesus may well have been thinking of Sepphoris in its hilltop location when he told his disciples that "a city set on a hill cannot be hidden" (Matthew 5:14). One tradition says that Mary, Joseph's wife, came from here.

The fortified gateway

Above: Model of the gate at Megiddo during King Solomon's time. Fortified gateways were a key part of any town, and this one's L-shape and double gates made it easier to defend. As the largest open space, the gateway bustled with life, serving as market place, legal centre, and meeting place (e.g. Ruth 4:1; 2 Kings 7:1). The gates were closed and barred at night.

New Testament cities

Greek and Roman influence led to more careful town planning, with ordered streets, defined districts, taller buildings, and water and sewage services. Herod the Great rebuilt Samaria (renaming it **Sebaste**) and **Caesarea** in Roman style. The latter had a main street lined with shops, baths, and a theatre, crossed by smaller streets at right angles, and a 15,000-seater arena. It was developed into a major port with a magnificent harbour for 300 ships, with Herod's palace on a promontory overlooking it. Rome's main garrison was stationed here, and it was one of its centurions, Cornelius, who became one of the first Gentile converts to Christianity (Acts 10). An inscription naming Pontius Pilate, the Roman governor, has been found in the theatre's ruins.

Herod Antipas built **Sepphoris** as his capital, but then relocated to **Tiberias** on the western shore of Lake Galilee (also called the Sea of Tiberias). Built over seventeen underground hot mineral springs, Tiberias had a thoroughly Hellenistic design. It is quite likely that it was here that Jesus encountered the gluttons, drunkards, tax collectors, and sinners (Matthew 11:19) that the Pharisees accused him of mixing with.

Acts takes us to the great cities of the Greco-Roman world (like **Ephesus, Athens, Corinth,** and **Rome**) rather than the villages of Jesus' ministry. Paul recognized that, despite its challenges and immorality, the city was where most people lived and was therefore where the gospel needed to impact the most, and it was in such cities that he planted churches as a base for evangelism into the surrounding regions.

Faith idea: Community

Cain's building of the first city, the Bible shows, was an attempt to deal with isolation (Genesis 4:14–17). Thereafter cities often had negative associations, seen as places of opposition to God (e.g. Genesis 11:1–19) and destined to destruction (e.g. Revelation 18). But the city isn't abandoned, for in Revelation Babylon is replaced by "the new Jerusalem" (Revelation 21:2), a place of community and security. Meanwhile, the church is encouraged to express that community right now in anticipation of what is to come (e.g. 1 Corinthians 3:16; 12:12–31; Ephesians 2:11–22).

Farming

Living from the Land

When the Israelites settled in Canaan, they found a people who had been cultivating the land for centuries. It was natural, therefore, that these former nomadic herdsmen became farmers too. Almost everyone became involved in living from the land in some way or other, hence the many references to farming in the Bible.

A wooden fork and threshing sledge. Embedded with iron or stone pieces, the sledge was dragged across the grain by oxen to break it up.

The agricultural year

The farming year began each autumn when "the former rains" fell, softening the sun-baked ground for **sowing**. While the Babylonians used seed-planters, Palestinian farmers did this by "broadcasting" – carrying seed in a fold of their garments and scattering handfuls as they walked. Inevitably some got wasted or taken by birds, as Jesus portrayed in the parable of the sower (Matthew 13:1–23). Sowing was followed by **ploughing**, to push the seed into the ground to germinate (though sometimes the ground was also ploughed before sowing when it was very hard). The main rains came in January and February, helping the grain to grow, and giving an opportunity for planting peas, lentils, melons, and cucumbers. In March and April "the latter rains" fell, swelling the grain. **Harvesting** could then begin – flax and barley in April and May, and wheat in June. The stalks were cut with a sickle, tied into sheaves, and loaded onto carts to be taken to the "threshing floor" (a rocky outcrop or clay-covered patch of land) for **threshing**. Here the sheaves were beaten with sticks, or broken up by animals or a threshing sledge. The final stage was **winnowing**, as stalks were tossed into the air with a wooden fork, which allowed the lighter straw to be blown aside for collection as winter animal food, while the heavier grain fell to the ground for **sifting** and **storing** in jars, cisterns or barns.

Water

The great rivers of Mesopotamia and Egypt made irrigation possible. In Egypt, leather buckets tied to long counterbalanced poles allowed them to be dipped into the river, filled, and swung round to be emptied onto the fields, which were divided by mud walls that could be broken down or rebuilt to control water flow. Such irrigation made Egypt famous for its abundant grain, which is why people went there in times of famine (e.g. Genesis 42:1–5). In Babylon there was a network of irrigation and transport canals called "the waters of Babylon" (Psalm 137:1), which increased the area of land available for arable use in southern Mesopotamia. One such canal was the Kebar, alongside which Ezekiel had his vision (Ezekiel 1:1).

Irrigation wasn't possible in Canaan, however, as Moses had warned (Deuteronomy 11:10–12), for the Jordan was below sea level; so the Israelites were entirely dependent on God to send the rains. Sadly, they often turned to Canaanite fertility religions instead.

Vines

Vines were one of Palestine's three most important fruit crops, the others being olives and figs (see pp. 56–57). Vines were plentiful, as the spies sent into Canaan discovered (Numbers 13:23). Most were grown in carefully prepared vineyards (Isaiah 5:1–2; Mark 12:1), surrounded by walls or fences of prickly shrubs to keep out animals, with a watchtower as a lookout for thieves or foxes. They were pruned in spring to produce more fruit, an image used by Jesus (John 15:1–17). The grapes were harvested in August or September, which demanded rapid work so they didn't rot or get ruined by the coming rains. Jesus' parable of the vineyard workers (Matthew 20:1–16) shows how urgent farmers considered this work to be. The harvested grapes were gathered into baskets and taken away to be dried or turned into wine (see p. 99).

See also
A Year on the Land p. 96
Working Animals p. 58
Gezer Calendar p. 97

Farming and the Law

Many aspects of the Jewish Law regulated farming life. For example:

- Concern was to be shown to animals at work (Deuteronomy 22:10) or in need (Deuteronomy 22:1–4).
- Owners were responsible for their animals' actions (Exodus 21:28–36).
- A farmer burning weeds was responsible if the fire spread and destroyed neighbouring crops (Exodus 22:6).
- At harvest, crops had to be left at the field's edges for the poor to glean (Deuteronomy 24:19–22).
- Every seventh year (the Sabbatical Year) land had to be left fallow (Leviticus 25:1–7, 18–22), and any crops that grew were to be left for the poor and animals (Exodus 23:10–11).

Ploughs were simple and light for easy manoeuvring. Essentially a wooden stake with a point of bronze or iron, with a handle for guiding them, they were attached to a yoke and drawn by one or two oxen.

Sheep and goats

Sheep and goats were kept together and looked very similar, though a farmer could easily tell the difference, as Jesus noted in his parable of the sheep and goats (Matthew 25:31–46). Sheep were kept for wool, while goats were kept for milk, which was drunk or used to produce yoghurt and cheese. Some sheep were reared for food, and lambs were used as sacrifices. The shepherd's basic tools were his **rod** (a club for driving off wild animals), his longer **staff** with curved end (for guiding sheep or rescuing them), and a **sling** for hurling stones at wild animals that attacked (1 Samuel 17:34–37). Sheep were kept out on the hills, where life could be hard, as Jacob discovered (Genesis 31:40–41); but a good shepherd took his work seriously, seeking his sheep when lost (Luke 15:4–6) and even risking his life for them (John 10:11). At night, the sheep were gathered into a sheepfold built with dry-stone walls and thorn branches on top, with the shepherd acting as the door by lying across the opening (John 10:7–10).

Faith idea: The Good Shepherd

The Bible pictures God as a good shepherd, caring for his sheep (e.g. Genesis 48:15; Psalm 23; Isaiah 40:11; Ezekiel 34:7–31); so when Jesus used this imagery of himself (John 10:1–16), he must have been aware of the implications of his claim. But more than claiming it, he lived it out, the Gospels show, laying down his life as the Good Shepherd to rescue his sheep (John 10:11, 17–18), an image retained by the early church (e.g. Hebrews 13:20; 1 Peter 5:4).

Locusts

This is a swarm of locusts, like the one Joel described that devastated Judah (Joel 1:1 – 2:11). Locusts swarm in vast numbers, devouring fields within minutes and laying their eggs to cause future devastation, before rapidly moving on.

Fishing

Fishermen and Fishers of Men

The Israelites in Old Testament times knew little about fishing, reflected in the fact that Hebrew had only one word for "fish", from the tiniest tiddler to the great fish in the story of Jonah. But by New Testament times fishing had become a thriving industry, and it was from among fishermen that Jesus drew half of his disciples.

Fishing in Old Testament times

The Israelites were primarily a people of the land, for whom the sea was a fearsome place, full of fierce monsters like "Leviathan", whom they were challenged to see as under the control of the sovereign God (e.g. Job 41). By contrast, the Phoenicians were a great seafaring people who used boats on the Great Sea (the Mediterranean) for fishing and trading. Their main port was at Tyre from where fish were sent to Jerusalem for sale (Nehemiah 13:16). The Egyptians also loved fishing and had a great source of fish in the Nile, as the escaping Israelite slaves recalled (Numbers 11:5). The death of the fish in the first plague that came upon Egypt would have been a great disaster (Exodus 7:21). They also fished for sport, and social parties often went out on fishing trips.

Fishing in New Testament times

By New Testament times, a thriving fishing industry had developed in Palestine, based around the Sea of Galilee, where fourteen different kinds of fish were found, though mostly tilapia, carp, and sardines. Fish became an important part of the diet, and fish from Galilee were sent to Jerusalem's fish market and exported, along with the fish sauce produced from them, as far as Rome and Spain. The importance of fishing to the Galilean economy is reflected in place names from the time: Bethsaida, meaning "House of Fish", and Taricheae, meaning "Preserved Fish Town".

Fishing was impossible in the Dead Sea, however, because it was too salty, although Ezekiel saw its regeneration in the messianic kingdom (Ezekiel 47:7–12).

The fisherman's life

The life of fishermen was hard, and they were often out on the lake all night (Luke 5:5; John 21:3). When they returned the next morning, the fish had to be sorted and cleaned, and the net had to be cleaned, dried, and repaired. The good fish were put into baskets to be taken to the markets, and were normally salted to stop them going bad. Some were turned into fish sauce.

Fishing on Galilee was dangerous, as storms often blew up rapidly as the wind rushed through the steep surrounding valleys, like the Arbel Pass, causing violent storms to erupt "without warning" (Matthew 8:24). They were sometimes so fierce that even experienced fishermen could get frightened (Matthew 8:24–25).

Fishermen often clubbed together to buy a boat and then worked as partners, like Peter, James, and John (Luke 5:7, 10). When John records that Peter counted 153 fish in the miraculous catch after the resurrection (John 21:1–14), it wasn't because this number had some mystical significance, as suggested by some of the early church fathers. They wrongly believed that there were 153 kinds of fish in the ancient world and therefore saw this number as symbolizing the total number of

Using a cast net.

See also
Food and Drink (Fish) pp. 98–99
Trade and Commerce pp. 110–11
Travel pp. 112–13

nations among whom the disciples would go "fishing". In fact this was simply what fishermen did after a day's work – count the fish so they could share the catch, and the number that day was so huge that they could never forget it.

Tilapia (commonly called St Peter's fish) from the Sea of Galilee.

The fish became one of the most common early Christian symbols, often used as a "secret sign" for recognizing one another. The Greek word for fish was *ichthus*, and this was used as an acrostic, with each of its letters standing for a word: *Iēsous Christos Theou Uios Sōtēr* – Jesus Christ, Son of God, Saviour.

Fishing methods

Four ways of fishing are mentioned in the Bible:

- **Spearing** (Job 41:7) This was often done at night, a light being held over the edge of the boat to attract the fish, which were then speared with a harpoon.
- **Line and hook** (Matthew 17:27) A bone or iron hook was attached to a line and cast into the water by hand (not with a rod like today).
- **Cast net** (Matthew 4:18) This was a small circular net with weights on the edge to make it sink, which was thrown into the water by the fisherman, who stood on the shore or waded into the water. The fish were taken by surprise and caught in the net as it sank. The fisherman then dragged it back to the shore or boat.
- **Drag net** (Matthew 13:47–50) This was a larger net, up to 1,500 feet (450 m) long, with floats at the top and weights at the bottom, that was drawn out between two boats or between a boat on the lake and men on the shore. It trapped the fish and was then drawn into the boat or back to land (e.g. John 21:11).

Boats

The hull of a first-century AD boat recovered from the mud on the northwestern shore of the Sea of Galilee. Measuring 26½ feet (8 m) long, 7½ feet (2.3 m) wide, and 4½ feet (1.4 m) deep, it would have been able to carry 1 ton – either a crew of five to six with their catch, or the crew and ten passengers. It would have been propelled by oars or a single sail, and is typical of the boats that Jesus' fishermen-disciples would have used and in which he often found himself (e.g. Matthew 8:23; 9:1; 13:2; 14:13; 15:39).

Faith idea: Fishers of men

When Jesus chose his twelve disciples, at least half of them were hard-working fishermen (Matthew 4:18, 21; John 21:2). Perhaps it was their dogged determination to get a catch that made them suitable for the work he had in mind for them, of going into a hostile world and seeking to be "fishers of men" (Mark 1:17). This call still remains a challenge to his followers today, the New Testament shows.

Crafts and Skills

Gifts of the Creative God

From earliest times, humankind has been creative, reflected in Jubal, who created music, and Tubal-Cain, who forged bronze and iron (Genesis 4:21–22). This creativity, the Bible claims, comes from humankind being made in the image of a Creator God and creativity being a gift of his Spirit (Exodus 31:3–5). Originally everyone had to work with cloth, wood, stone, and metal themselves, but Israel's developing economy led to specialization. Craftsmen gathered in towns, organizing guilds called "families", whose members were "sons". By New Testament times such guilds were powerful and had political weight (e.g. Acts 19:23–41).

Pottery

Israelite pottery – mainly bowls, cups, jars, and lamps – was simple and relatively un-artistic. Nevertheless, by the time of the monarchy, pottery-making had become an industry, with potters joining together to make mass-produced items with their own trademark. There was even a royal guild of potters working for the king (1 Chronicles 4:23).

The pottery-making process began by extracting the local red clay and exposing it to the elements to break it up and remove impurities. Water was then added and it was trampled into mud, carefully removing the air, before being shaped, either by being pressed into a mould, or modelled freehand, or shaped on a wheel. Most potter's wheels in Bible times had two stones attached to an upright shaft, one of which was set into a hole and turned by the potter's foot, which then turned the upper stone on which the vessel was thrown. Once shaped, and decorated if needed, the object was fired in a kiln.

Leather-working

Leather was used for a variety of things: clothes, belts, footwear, bottles, and writing material. The animal was skinned and its fat and hair removed with scrapers. The skin was then tanned by drying it in the sun, smoking it, or treating it with plant juice. When ready, the hides were shaped and sewn. Jews despised tanners since their handling of dead animal skins made them "unclean" according to Jewish Law, so they often worked outside of town. Peter's stay at the home of Simon the tanner at Joppa (Acts 9:43; 10:6) shows how far he had come from his former Jewish scruples.

Gem-cutting

The Israelites used semi-precious stones, such as jasper, agate, and carnelian, which were cut and polished to make beads or engraved with designs to make seals. The high priest's breastplate was set with twelve semi-precious stones, each one representing one of the tribes of Israel (Exodus 28:15–21).

Glass-making

While glass-making wasn't common in Israel in Bible times, it had been produced in Egypt and Babylon for centuries. Initially the opaque glass was shaped around a core of sand; but by New Testament times the Romans had invented clear glass and the art of glass-blowing. These perfume bottles came from Alexandria.

Work tools

Leather-working tools discovered in an Israelite leather workshop in En Gedi: needles, scrapers, and piercing rods.

See also
Clothing and Cosmetics pp. 100–01
Musical instruments p. 140
The Temple p. 147

Building

Initially the Israelites showed little interest in building, apart from their simple homes, and it was only in the tenth century BC, under David and Solomon, that skilled building projects were undertaken, with help from Phoenician masons and joiners (2 Samuel 5:11–12; 1 Kings 5:1–18). Such large buildings were planned and directed by a "master-builder" (1 Corinthians 3:10) who oversaw all aspects of the construction, including measuring out (Revelation 11:1) and checking it was vertical, as it was built by using a plumb-line (Amos 7:7–8). Israel's greatest building project was King Herod's new temple. When completed in AD 62, long after his death, 18,000 people suddenly found themselves unemployed. Herod Antipas's extensive building programme meant skilled workers like stonemasons, carpenters, and metalworkers were much in demand in New Testament times.

Carpentry

The skills of an Israelite carpenter were wide-ranging, as he was called upon to produce anything in wood, ranging from items for construction (doors, windows, stairs, roofs), to furniture (couches, beds, chairs, tables), to utensils (carved bowls, spoons, boxes), to farming equipment (ploughs, yokes, threshing boards, carts). Phoenician carpenters built boats from local cypress, with cedar masts and oak oars, and Tyre provided specialist carpenters for David's palace and Solomon's Temple. Woodcarving was the work of specialists, for which hard wood (ebony, sandalwood, boxwood) was imported. Local woods (cedar, cypress, oak, ash, acacia) were used for common joinery work, and mulberry for agricultural implements.

Metalworking

Iron and copper were plentiful in Palestine, just as Moses had promised (Deuteronomy 8:9). **Copper** was extracted from the ore by smelting, either over a fire or in a small furnace that had leather bellows, and was then poured into a mould or hardened and shaped by cold-hammering. Around 2000 BC it was discovered that adding up to 4 per cent of tin made the copper harder and stronger, and this became known as **bronze** (though the Hebrew words for copper and bronze are the same). Many of the fine-worked articles in Solomon's Temple were bronze (1 Kings 7:38–47). The production of **iron** was learned from the Philistines, who initially safeguarded their monopoly (1 Samuel 13:19–22). Its use spread slowly, as it was difficult to produce. Ironsmiths were described by Isaiah as "he who strikes the anvil", while goldsmiths and bronze-workers were called "he who smoothes with the hammer" (Isaiah 41:7). Soldering, riveting, and casting-on were practised by these craftsmen, enabling them to produce intricate objects and jewellery, and not just items for daily use like plough-blades, hoes, axes, chisels, daggers, and swords.

Construction

Building blocks in the ruins at Ephesus. The circular protrusions fitted into holes on the stone that was laid above it for rigidity, like some children's building blocks today.

Ivory-carving

A ninth-century ivory carving of a sphinx discovered in the ruins of King Ahab's palace in Samaria, which the Bible says was "inlaid with ivory" (1 Kings 22:39).

Faith idea: Foundations

Building imagery is often found in the Bible, as in Jesus' parable of the wise and foolish builders (Matthew 7:24–27), in which he called people to ensure that their lives were built on firm foundations – the only sure one of which, he said, was hearing his words and obeying them. The church is likened to a building (1 Corinthians 3:9, 16) whose foundation and cornerstone is Christ (1 Peter 2:4–8), and Christians are therefore called to build upon it carefully (1 Corinthians 3:10–17).

Trade and Commerce

Buying and Selling

In Old Testament times, Israelite families generally produced only enough for their own needs, and there were few things they couldn't produce themselves. Any trade that did happen occurred locally, largely because of the difficulties of travel. But eventually markets began to develop around town gates, where produce from surrounding farms could be sold and where craftsmen could sell their wares. Gradually, trading became wider, both in diversity and extent. But while Palestine was well located at a junction of trade routes, it rarely took advantage of this.

The market in Beersheba, not greatly dissimilar to those of Bible times.

The market place

The market wasn't just a place of trade, but the centre of a town's activity. Here you could meet people (Matthew 23:7), find lodging (Judges 19:15–21), seek employment (Matthew 20:3; Acts 17:5), receive teaching (Nehemiah 8:1–3), or simply play (Matthew 11:16–17). By New Testament times, Jerusalem had several markets, one of which had been established in the Temple's outer courtyard and which was cleared by Jesus (e.g. Matthew 21:12–13). The rabbis appointed market inspectors to ensure deals were fair and scales were accurate, in accordance with Jewish Law (Leviticus 19:35–36). The prophets often saw what happened in the market as a barometer of spiritual life, for good or for bad (e.g. Nehemiah 10:31; 13:15–22; Amos 8:5–6).

Merchants

The great trading centres of Old Testament times were Tyre and Babylon, whose merchants controlled international trade and became very wealthy, producing great resentment (Isaiah 23; Ezekiel 27). Neither Judah nor Israel was an important trading nation because their capitals were inland and on mountains, so major highways bypassed them, and what little international trade there was seems to have been controlled by the king (1 Kings 20:34). By New Testament times, Rome was the commercial centre of the world, and most big merchants were Romans, though Jewish merchants appear to have become established in Rome and Alexandria. The same curse upon its insatiable trade-generated greed is pronounced on Rome (cryptically called "Babylon") in Revelation as on Tyre in the Old Testament (Revelation 18:11–24).

Israel's international trade

While there is evidence of international trade in the Near East as early as 5000 BC, it was only under King Solomon that international trade took off in Israel. A number of things lay behind this: the conquest of new territory that lay on trade routes; a need for imported raw materials for Israel's developing new industries; and the royal desire for luxury goods to reflect the king's status (1 Kings 10). By land came imports such as tin, lead, silver, timber, linen, and (from the east) gems, spices, and gold. By sea, through Ezion-Geber to the south, came gold, silver, precious stones, ivory, peacocks, and apes. But Israel began to export too, Ezekiel listing "wheat from Minnith and confections, honey, oil and balm" (Ezekiel 27:17) as part of its trading exports with Tyre.

Market place

The Roman *forum* and Greek *agora* were not only the market place but also the main place of public assembly. During the Hellenistic period, the Greeks surrounded their markets with *stoas* (colonnaded walkways). Preliminary trials were often held here (Acts 16:19) and philosophical or religious discussions often took place (Acts 17:17–18). Above (right) are the ruins of the Roman *agora* in Athens, along with a reconstructed colonnaded stoa.

See also
Money, Weights, and Measures pp. 116–17
Travel pp. 112–13

Luxury goods

Records show that under Roman rule no fewer than 118 different foreign luxury goods – including linen, silk, spices, perfumes, jewels, glass bowls, Greek wine, apples, and cheese – were imported to Palestine in New Testament times.

Roman taxes

The hatred of Roman domination was seen no clearer than in people's attitude to taxes and those who collected them. There were three main Roman taxes:

- **Land tax**, which was a percentage of the harvest's likely yield.
- **Poll tax**, which required a periodic census (e.g. Luke 2:1–5) and which cost a denarius, a day's wages.
- **Customs**, which involved tolls and duties imposed on goods, collected at ports and city gates. These were particularly burdensome, as goods were subject to multiple taxation on long journeys.

Despite the hatred with which Roman taxes were viewed, Jesus nevertheless told people to pay them (Matthew 22:15–22), and he even accepted former tax collectors like Matthew into his innermost circle (Matthew 9:8–13) as a demonstration of the transforming nature of God's kingdom.

Tax collectors

While the land tax and poll tax were collected by the Jewish authorities annually, indirect taxes were collected through "tax farming": that is, they were sold to the highest bidder who paid in advance to collect taxes from a particular district. This meant that Rome received its monies in advance, while the "tax farmer" was left to charge highly inflated rates so he could make a fat profit. While the rates were in theory regulated, the tax collector's power to determine the value of goods led to huge injustices, which to most people seemed little more than institutionalized robbery. It was these tax collectors who were so hated (e.g. Matthew 18:17; Luke 18:11), not simply because they collected taxes but because they were seen as collaborators with Rome; and chief tax collectors, like Zacchaeus, were hated even more, though that didn't stop Jesus including him either (Luke 19:1–10).

Caravans

Throughout Bible times, traders travelled together in "caravans" – convoys of camels and donkeys – for both protection and companionship. Caravans passed through Israel from all directions since its narrow corridor was a key link in the trade routes. It was to a caravan of passing Ishmaelite traders, whose camels were "loaded with spices, balm and myrrh" (Genesis 37:25), that Joseph was sold as they travelled down to Egypt. It was with "a very great caravan – with camels carrying spices, large quantities of gold, and precious stones" (1 Kings 10:2) that the Queen of Sheba visited Solomon from Arabia. Caravans were usually quite large (300 donkeys wasn't uncommon) and were often accompanied by guards for protection against robbers. Camels were the only pack animal that could survive the huge distances covered by some merchants.

Faith idea: Honesty

The Bible says that honesty – conveying truth through words and actions – is an essential aspect of God's character, and should therefore characterize his people in all they do. Dishonest dealings were forbidden in the Jewish Law (e.g. Deuteronomy 25:13–16) and are condemned throughout Scripture (e.g. Proverbs 11:1; Ezekiel 45:9–12), while honest, straightforward, and truthful speech is continually commanded and commended (e.g. Matthew 23:16–28; Ephesians 4:25–32).

Travel

Journeys in Life

Some of the Bible's greatest stories are about journeys. Abraham travelled from Mesopotamia to Canaan, in obedience to God; the Israelites crossed the Sinai desert, led to the Promised Land by God; Jesus walked through Palestine, preaching God's kingdom as he went; Paul crossed the Roman empire by land and sea, sharing the good news – all part of the greater journey of faith undertaken by God's people.

Walking

In Bible times most journeys (even long ones) were made on foot, with walkers able to cover little more than 3 miles (5 km) an hour. Some families, though not all, had an ass or a donkey to carry their loads. The Gospels show Jesus walking everywhere, and when he needed a donkey, he had to borrow one, reflecting his poverty. Most of Paul's journeys would have been on foot (Acts 20:13).

Carts and chariots

Wheeled transport was limited in Old Testament times, though evidence for wheeled vehicles goes back to the fourth millennium BC in Mesopotamia. Carts, pulled by oxen or donkeys, were used for carrying crops and goods (1 Samuel 6:11) and sometimes people (Genesis 46:5), while chariots were the preserve of the wealthy and military commanders (e.g. Exodus 14:6–7; 2 Samuel 15:1). By New Testament times Roman roads made the wider use of chariots possible, whether light chariots for racing, or carriages like the one used by the Ethiopian eunuch (Acts 8:26–31).

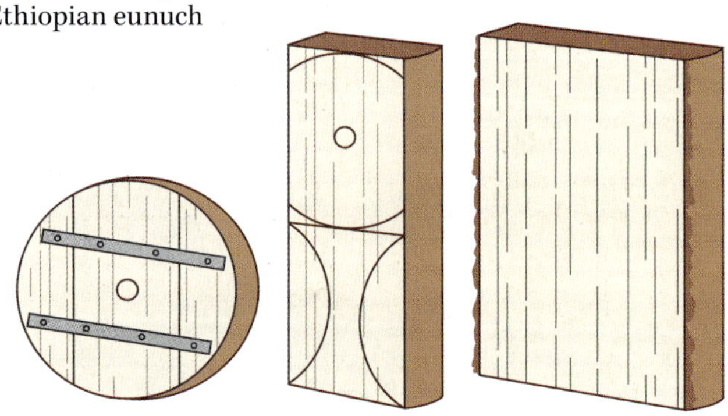

The earliest wheels were made by slicing timber into broad planks along the grain, cutting the plank in half and using one half as the centre of the wheel, while the other half was cut into two semi-circles. The three pieces were then joined together by strips of wood.

Roads

Until Roman times, most Palestinian roads were unpaved, beaten tracks. There were only two major roads: "The Way of the Sea" (Isaiah 9:1), skirting the coast from Memphis in Egypt to Tyre and Sidon, then turning east to Aleppo in Syria, where it joined a highway linking Mesopotamia and Asia Minor; and "The King's Highway" (Numbers 20:17), running south from Damascus, down the east side of the Jordan, and dividing south of the Dead Sea, one branch heading to Egypt and the other to the Red Sea. These two roads were linked by east–west roads through Jericho in the south and across the Plain of Jezreel in the north.

Rome's arrival integrated Palestine into a road network of over 50,000 miles (80,000 km) of highways and 200,000 miles

The road down which Paul walked to his final imprisonment in Rome. Roman roads were well constructed, with three separate layers: a foundation of stones mixed with cement; a rough core of gravel or rubble; and a top surface of stones fitted together. The road was cambered to let water drain into gutters, and major roads were between 20 and 26 feet (6 and 8 m) wide. They ran as straight as possible, using bridges and causeways wherever necessary.

A Roman milestone at Capernaum. Milestones were set every 1,000 paces, recording the distance from the road's beginning or the nearest city.

See also
Caravans p. 111
Visitors p. 97
Working Animals p. 58

(320,000 km) of secondary roads connecting every part of the empire. This not only facilitated the rapid movement of goods and imperial despatches but, more importantly, troops. This excellent road network considerably helped the spread of the Christian message.

Inns

While inns were sparse in Palestine in Old Testament times, the Romans built them at regular intervals of a day's journey. While primarily for imperial couriers, travellers also used them, and road maps showed their location and the services available. Many inns had a bad reputation, which was why Christians were urged to offer hospitality to one another (Romans 12:13; 1 Peter 4:9). Travellers staying in a place for longer periods would hire a room, like Paul did in Rome (Acts 28:30).

Ships and sailing

While Israel avoided the sea, seeing it as a fearsome thing, Phoenicia and Egypt were both great seafaring nations. Egyptians were building sea-going boats from c. 3000 BC, at first from reeds and then from wood. Phoenician boats were carefully constructed, with cedar masts, oak oars, cypress decks, and Egyptian linen sails (Ezekiel 27:5–9). Israel's only maritime success was under Solomon, who had a merchant fleet based at Ezion-Geber on the Gulf of Aqaba manned by Phoenician sailors (2 Chronicles 9:21).

By New Testament times, large ships were safely plying the Mediterranean, cleared of pirates by Rome. Shipbuilding had so improved that large corn ships, like the one Paul travelled on to Rome (Acts 27:6), which carried 276 passengers (Acts 27:37), could be 180 feet (55 m) long. Ships generally had one big sail on a single mast, though Roman warships also had rowers. Jews of the Diaspora (Dispersion) had to live within ninety days' journey of Jerusalem, and special boats were arranged to get them to Passover each year, often at hugely inflated prices.

Sailing was always at the mercy of the weather, and while it took only ten days to get from Rome to Alexandria in summer, winter winds increased that to two months.

Dangers

Travelling was both difficult and slow, and often dangerous. In fact, there were times in Israelite history when "it was not safe to travel about, for all the inhabitants of the lands were in great turmoil" (2 Chronicles 15:5). Even in Roman times, road travel could still be dangerous, as reflected in the parable of the good Samaritan (Luke 10:30). Travellers by sea also faced risks, both from piracy (considerably reduced by the Roman fleets) and the weather. The apostle Paul was shipwrecked four times, three mentioned in 2 Corinthians 11:25–26, and one experienced later in Acts 27:13–44.

The great rivers of Egypt and Mesopotamia offered natural highways. In Egypt, the Nile's current carried boats downstream, while the prevailing winds blew them upstream. Here is a temple carving of an Egyptian royal barge.

Faith idea: The walk of faith

The fact that walking was the primary mode of transport is reflected in its widespread metaphorical usage in the Bible. Believers are described as walking with God (e.g. Genesis 5:22; Micah 6:8; Revelation 3:4) – a picture of having a close relationship with him – and are called to walk in new ways (e.g. Colossians 3:5–8; 1 John 1:6–7) – a picture of the changed life that they are now called to.

Money

Blessing or Snare?

Contrary to popular thinking, the Bible has lots of practical advice about money. It recognizes that, handled properly, money can be a source of great blessing; but handled unwisely, it can be a snare. It is not money, it says, but "*the love of money* [that] is a root of all kinds of evil" (1 Timothy 6:10).

Money

In earliest times, things were bought not with money but with goods, perishable (barley, wheat, dates) and non-perishable (metals, timber, animals). By the third millennium BC precious metals (silver, copper, gold, electrum) were being used for purchases. In Palestine silver was the most common precious metal and was weighed out in "shekels" (Genesis 23:15–16; Jeremiah 32:9). Gold, being rarer, was used for international trading or tributes (1 Kings 9:11–14; 2 Kings 18:14). During the seventh century BC coins, representing the weight and worth of these metals, began to be used in Lydia, and Phoenician traders spread their use. This expanded further when coinage was standardized by Persia, which also allowed Jewish governors to issue small silver coins from c. 400 BC bearing the inscription "Yehud" (Judah). After the Maccabean revolt, Jews developed a native bronze coinage with various designs and the ruler's name in Hebrew and Greek.

By New Testament times three different currencies were circulating in Palestine: imperial money (Roman standard), provincial money (Greek standard), and local Jewish money.

Coins

Coins are helpful to archaeologists as they often carry the name and image of the ruler of an area at the time of production, helping them to date surrounding structures.

Old Testament

The basic Jewish currency in Old Testament times was the shekel, which remained a weight rather than a coin until post-exilic times. The following weights are approximations, as weights were not standardized for everywhere throughout the biblical period:

Gerah	= 0.6 g
Shekel	= 11.5 g (50 shekels = 1 mina)
Mina	= 600 g (60 minas = 1 talent)
Talent	= 30 kg

Money-changing

The circulation of so many currencies in Palestine in New Testament times meant moneychangers were inevitable, especially for Jews arriving from abroad for the great festivals who needed to pay their Temple tax. At such times the moneychangers moved their stalls into the Court of the Gentiles and charged exorbitant rates, causing Jesus to accuse them of robbery and throw them out (Matthew 21:12–13; Mark 11:15–17; Luke 19:45–46; John 2:13–16).

Money-lending

While money-lending was permitted, the Jewish Law forbade charging interest to fellow-Israelites (Exodus 22:25; Leviticus 25:35–37; Deuteronomy 23:19–20), and in the eighth century BC, when money-lending was happening on a large scale, the prophets challenged those who abused this. While interest on commercial loans was permitted in Babylon, there was no equivalent of this in Israel, where loans were considered an act of charity to help needy fellow-Israelites, not help for merchants expanding their business. Six-month agricultural loans were the most common type. The Law regulated collateral, requiring the return of outer garments at night (Exodus 22:26–27) and forbidding the taking

New Testament

Roman	Greek	Jewish
	Lepton (bronze) (plural, lepta)	
Quadrans (= 2 lepta)		
As (= 4 quadrans)		
Denarius (= 16 as)	Drachma (silver)	
	Di-drachma (= 2 drachmae)	(Used as a half-shekel)
	Stater (silver) (= 4 drachmae)	Shekel
Aureus (gold) (= 25 denarii)		
100 denarii =	Mina =	30 shekels
240 aurei =	Talent (= 60 minas)	

See also
Roman Taxes p. 111
Tax Collectors p. 111
Trade and Commerce pp. 110–11

Coins in the gospels

- The poor widow gave two lepta as an offering (Mark 12:42).
- One as could buy two sparrows (Matthew 10:29).
- A denarius was a labourer's daily wage (Matthew 20:9–10).
- A half-shekel (two drachmae) was the price of the Temple tax (Matthew 17:24).

Remains from a coin-maker's workshop. Bottom: bronze for making coins. Middle: small pouring funnels with coins attached. Top: coins after being struck. Left: pans from a small pair of scales. Coins were made individually and then pressed with seals to show their authenticity.

of millstones (Deuteronomy 24:6). Foreigners could be charged interest, however, though Jesus challenged the attitude of heart behind this (Luke 6:32–36). However, he did not forbid investment to earn income (Luke 19:23).

Banks

We don't know whether there were banks in Israel in Old Testament times, though they appeared in Babylon around 650 BC. Ordinary people hid their savings or valuables in the ground, like Achan (Joshua 7:21) and the servant in the parable of the talents (Matthew 25:25). By the second century BC the Temple treasury was being used as a bank, especially by the wealthy. Secular sources tell us that Pontius Pilate raided its funds to build an aqueduct.

Jesus and money

It surprises many to discover that, in the Gospels, Jesus taught more about money than prayer. In line with Jewish tradition, he had no problem with wealth as such. His concern was how that wealth was used, and what it could do to people. He tackled the former by encouraging generous giving to the poor (e.g. Matthew 6:2–4), and the latter by reminding people how wealth can hinder entering God's kingdom (Luke 18:18–30). His parable of the rich fool (Luke 12:13–21), told to someone wanting him to adjudicate on a family property dispute, underlined the foolishness of the insatiable desire for more.

Poverty and debt

While the Bible recognizes poverty can be the result of foolishness or laziness (e.g. Proverbs 6:9–11), it more often attributes it to others' greed and lust for power, and the prophets denounced leaders and a society that "crush", "deprive", "destroy", "grind", "trample on", and "oppress" the poor (e.g. Isaiah 3:13–15; Amos 4:1; 8:4). The Law sought to minimize debt, not only by commanding alms-giving and generous lending, but also by preventing the exploitation of those in debt (e.g. Leviticus 25:37–43; Deuteronomy 24:6) and cancelling all debts every seventh year (Deuteronomy 15:1–3), thereby preventing generational poverty. The early church continued this approach of caring for those in need (Acts 2:45; 4:32–35; Romans 15:25–26; 1 Corinthians 16:1–4; 2 Corinthians 8:1–15; James 2:1–19), and remembering the poor was a foundational apostolic principle (Galatians 2:9–10).

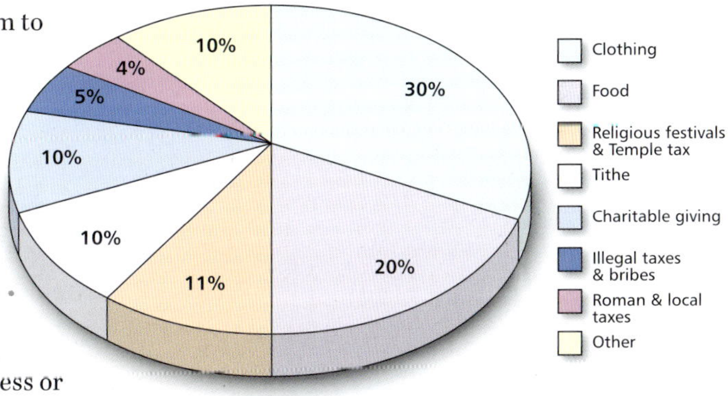

Typical outgoings of a Jewish working-class family in New Testament times.

Faith idea: Generosity

The Bible portrays God as unbelievably generous – like a king who freely forgave a debtor millions of pounds (Matthew 18:23–35). It therefore calls God's people to be generous too, especially to the needy (Matthew 25:31–46), reminding them that "whoever sows sparingly will also reap sparingly, and whoever sows generously will also reap generously" (2 Corinthians 9:6).

Weights and Measures

The Importance of Honesty

A variety of weights and measures were used in Bible times, and it was some time before standardization occurred. But throughout, the Bible is consistent in its demand that God's people should be honest in their use of them, maintaining accurate weights and measures, and denounces those who cheat others (Leviticus 19:35–36; Proverbs 11:1; 20:23; Amos 8:5).

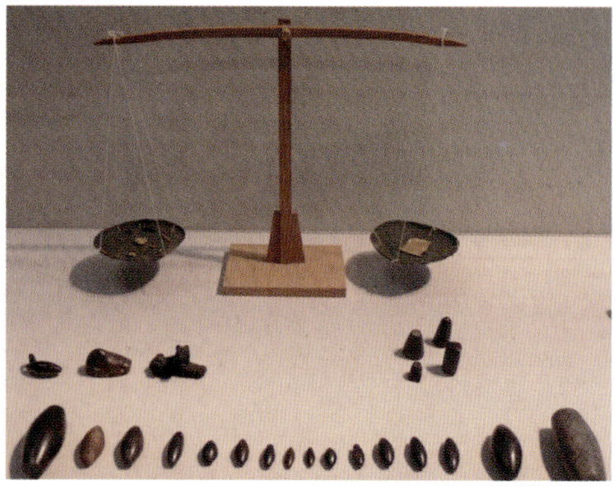

Weights

Ancient weights were made of stone or metal, often inscribed with their weight and standard. Because those standards varied over the biblical period, the following equivalents are approximations and, in some cases, averages.

Old Testament

1 gerah	=	0.6 g
10 gerahs	=	1 bekah (5.8 g)
2 bekahs	=	1 shekel (11.5 g)
1 pim	=	⅔ shekel (7.7 g)
50 shekels	=	1 mina (575 g)
60 minas	=	1 talent (34 kg)

New Testament

Litra/pound	=	327 g
Talent	=	20–40 kg

Dry measures

Homer (or Cor)	=	220 litres (6 bushels)
Lethek	=	110 litres (3 bushels)
Ephah	=	22 litres (⅗ bushel)
Seah	=	7.3 litres (13 pints)
Omer	=	2.2 litres (4 pints)
Cab	=	1.2 litres (2 pints)
Log	=	0.3 litre (½ pint)

Liquid measures

Bath	=	22 litres (5 gallons)
Hin	=	3.66–4 litres (7 pints)
Cab	=	1.2 litres (2 pints)
Log	=	0.3 litre (½ pint)

Persian period tin-bronze weight in the shape of a lion, a style going back to the late Assyrian period (eighth- to seventh-centuries BC). Most weights were carved into some sort of image, making them instantly recognizable.

MENE, MENE, TEKEL, PARSIN

During a banquet in which wine was flowing freely, King Belshazzar of Babylon brought out goblets taken from the Jerusalem Temple when it was destroyed in 586 BC. A hand suddenly appeared, writing on the wall: "MENE, MENE, TEKEL, PARSIN." Only Daniel could give its meaning (Daniel 5:26–28), which was based around weights and a play on words. MENE came from an Aramaic word meaning "to number", indicating the days of Belshazzar's empire were about to end, but it was also similar to the weight "mina". TEKEL came from an Aramaic word meaning "to weigh", meaning he had been weighed and found wanting, but was also a play on words on the weight "shekel". PARSIN came from an Aramaic word meaning "to divide", indicating his empire was about to be divided between Medes and Persians, but could also mean "half-shekel", as well as being a play on words on "Persians". So while the message initially seemed simply to be a list of weights – "a mina, a mina, a shekel, and half-shekel" – Daniel brought its true interpretation: Babylon had been weighed in God's scales and its time was up.

See also
A Year on the Land p. 96
Money pp. 114–15
Trade and Commerce pp. 110–11

Linear measures

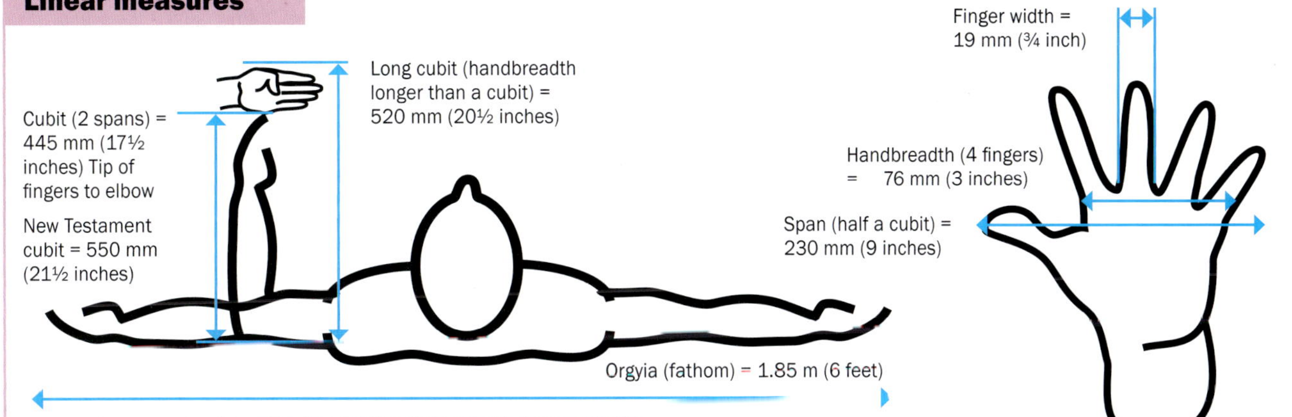

Reed (6 cubits) = 3 m (10 feet)
Mile (New Testament *milion*) = 1,000 paces – 1,478 m (1,618 yards)

Measuring time

Day

The most obvious measure of time is from sunrise to sunset – a day. But in Bible times, three different ways of measuring a day were used. While initially days were seen as beginning at sunrise, a later means of reckoning saw each day beginning at moonrise, so a day became "an evening and a morning", like in the Genesis creation account, and the evening was divided into three four-hour "watches". The Romans, however, divided morning and night into four three-hour watches in each.

Year

In Egypt, Israel had probably followed the Egyptian calendar of twelve months of thirty days each, with five days added at the end of each year. But a change occurred at Sinai when God decreed that the first month of the year (Nisan) was to be in spring to commemorate the exodus (Exodus 12:2). Thereafter their calendar, like the Western Semitic calendar, had a year of twelve lunar months (1 Kings 4:7), with each beginning when the thin crescent of the new moon was first visible at sunset. Since the month was considered to last twenty-nine/thirty days, a lunar year was eleven days shorter than a solar year, so a thirteenth month was added from time to time to ensure that the new year did not fall before spring.

Seasons

Israel often indicated the time of year by the season rather than by the name of the month. So they spoke of "the dry season" (April–September) and "the rainy season" (October–March), "seedtime" (November–December) and "harvest" (April–June). "The former rains" fell in September–October, and "the latter rains" in March–April.

Rulers

The New Testament sometimes reckons dates by reference to Gentile rulers, as in Luke 3:1 where John the Baptist's ministry is dated not only "in the fifteenth year of the reign of Tiberius Caesar" (AD 27–28), but also by reference to several other religious and secular rulers. For the most part, however, the New Testament notes time with reference to the Jewish religious calendar, especially John (John 2:13, 23; 5:1; 6:4; 7:2; 10:22) and Luke (Acts 2:1; 12:3; 18:21; 20:6, 16; 27:9).

Other measurements

Distance

- A bow-shot (Genesis 21:15–16).
- A sabbath day's journey (Acts 1:12) – the distance devout Jews could walk on the sabbath, limited to 2,000 cubits.
- A day's journey (1 Kings 19:3–4).
- A three-day journey (Genesis 30:36).

Area

Area was measured in a variety of ways. The expression "about half an acre" (1 Samuel 14:14) literally means "half a yoke". A yoke was the area ploughed by a yoke of oxen in one day, about an acre, called a *jugerum* by the Romans. Another way of measuring area was by the amount of seed required to sow the land (Leviticus 27:16). Elsewhere area is expressed simply by its constituent measurements (e.g. Ezekiel 40:47).

Diameter

Diameter was measured "from brim to brim" (2 Chronicles 4:2).

Faith idea: Consistency

"I the LORD do not change" (Malachi 3:6). Because God's nature is unchanging, he is utterly reliable and consistent in all he does, the Bible says, reflected even in things like the consistency of times and seasons promised to Noah (Genesis 8:22). The Jewish Law's call for accuracy and honesty in weights and measures was a daily reminder to God's people of the need to be consistent and reliable in all they do.

Government and Justice

Acting Justly, Loving Mercy

Since the Bible covers well over 2,000 years of history from Abraham to Jesus, Israel's system of government inevitably changed considerably over that period, especially when administered by conquering nations.

Government in early Israel

Patriarchal
Israel's earliest organization centred around the family, with the father being the chief authority – the patriarch – who was directly accountable to God. Abraham, Isaac, and Jacob all functioned in this way.

Theocratic
By the exodus, Abraham's family had grown into twelve families of clans, and God called Moses to be their leader and his mouthpiece (Exodus 3:11–22), confirming his authority (Numbers 12:1–15; 16:1–50). Moses led God's people on the basis of the Law received at Sinai, where Israel accepted God as their king (Exodus 19:3–8), thereby becoming a theocracy – a nation ruled by God.

Charismatic
In Canaan the Israelites initially operated as a confederacy of tribes, united only by ancestry and worship of Yahweh. During this period, God gave them Spirit-anointed "judges", raised up in response to particular needs (e.g. Judges 2:6–23). Their authority was limited and regional, however, until Samuel began to unite the nation.

Monarchy
The Philistine threat led Israel to demand a king, despite Samuel believing this betrayed theocracy (1 Samuel 8). Repeated disobedience led to God replacing Saul, Israel's first king (1 Samuel 13:13–14), but under David and Solomon the monarchy became stronger. Solomon's centralized control, through dividing Israel into twelve administrative districts that cut across tribal boundaries, weakened the power of tribal elders and increased his own; but it led to the kingdom dividing after his death (1 Kings 12:1–19). Monarchy continued in Israel and Judah with varying success until their conquest: Israel by Assyria in 722 BC and Judah by Babylon in 586 BC. Thereafter Israel never had a Davidic king again and was, apart from a brief period of independence, ruled by conquering nations.

Ruins of the city gates at Jerash, Jordan. It was at the city gates that Jewish elders sat to give their judgments (e.g. Ruth 4:1–12), thereby ensuring public visibility and openness in their rulings.

See also
Authorities p. 81
Israel's First Kings pp. 30–31
The Romans pp. 80–81

Elders

There was no "government control" in Israelite society like today. Decision-making and law enforcement were carried out locally by "elders" – heads of families, tribes, and clans. Elders, men of recognized experience and wisdom, existed from at least the time of the exodus (Exodus 3:16). In Canaan each city had its own elders, whose duties ranged from apprehending murderers (Deuteronomy 19:12) to settling marriage disputes (Deuteronomy 22:13–19). A national body of tribal elders dealt with the king on matters of national interest (e.g. 2 Samuel 5:1–3; 1 Kings 8:1; 2 Kings 23:1). By New Testament times elders, along with chief priests and scribes, were represented on the Sanhedrin, the Jewish High Court (e.g. Mark 15:1).

Elders remained the principal leaders in both Jewish and Gentile churches. In Acts 20 they are interchangeably called "elders" (v. 17), "overseers" (v. 28), and "shepherds/pastors" (v. 28). The use of "overseer" (Greek, *episkopos*) as a more senior level of leadership ("bishop") was a later church development.

Justice

When Moses became weary through having to judge every dispute, Jethro counselled him to appoint "capable men" as deputies to judge routine cases (Exodus 18:17–23). This system of judges was formalized in Deuteronomy, providing for judges in every town (Deuteronomy 16:18). Trials by jury were unknown, though sometimes elders were involved. Judgments by one judge opened the possibility of favouritism, which is why the Law called for impartiality (Leviticus 19:15) and why the prophets challenged any hint of legal corruption and constantly demanded justice (1 Kings 21:1–28; Amos 5:24). There were no lawyers, so most people represented themselves. Witnesses were required, and perjury was ruthlessly dealt with to ensure integrity in the legal process (Deuteronomy 19:15–21).

Crime and punishment

There was no distinction between criminal and civil offences in Israel. All crimes were committed against an individual or the covenant community, and the way to rectify this was through compensation for damage done (e.g. Exodus 21:18–36). Often this was just the value of the damage; but a thief had to compensate for stolen property with four or five times its value (Exodus 22:1), a strong deterrent against theft. Even in criminal offences, like rape or theft, the guilty person had to compensate the victim. The principle of "life for life, eye for eye, tooth for tooth…" (Exodus 21:24) was a restraining law, ensuring penalties were appropriate to the offence and no more. Assault was punished by fixed compensation, uniquely at that time even when a master assaulted his slave. Murder was seen as heinous everywhere and, with few exceptions, was punishable by death. However, the Jewish Law distinguished between murder and manslaughter (Exodus 21:12–14).

Roman government

By New Testament times the Jews were living under Roman rule. Rome governed its provinces in different ways: where peace was established, through proconsuls, appointed annually; where troops were needed to maintain order, through legates, prefects, and procurators, like Pilate, appointed for four or five years. Local kings, like Herod the Great, were permitted to rule in some areas as long as they obeyed Rome. Some cities, like Athens and Ephesus, were allowed to be self-governing ("free cities"), while others like Philippi were "colonies", enjoying the same rights as citizens in Rome itself. Certain "holy cities" retained some control over their affairs, like Jerusalem whose affairs were administered by the Sanhedrin.

Roman citizenship could be inherited, bought, or gifted, and one of Paul's ancestors had obtained this, which often proved useful to him, like when he appealed to Caesar to unblock legal proceedings against him (Acts 25:11).

Under Roman rule

Following Pompey's conquest, Judea became a Roman province. Rome appointed Herod the Great to rule it, first as governor (47 BC), then as king (40 BC). After his death in 4 BC, Rome divided his kingdom between his three sons, as shown below. But the ineffective Archelaus was replaced by a Roman governor, Pilate, who ruled (AD 26–36) in a heavy-handed and clumsy way and who was responsible for Jesus' crucifixion.

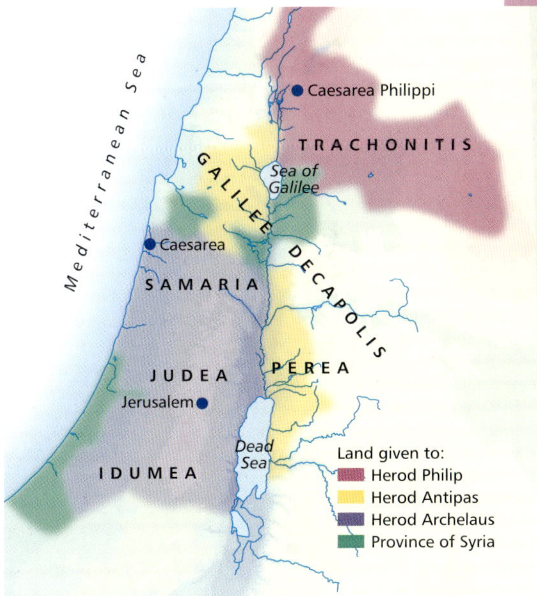

Faith idea: Justice

"What does the LORD require of you? To act justly and to love mercy and to walk humbly with your God" (Micah 6:8). The Bible teaches that justice and good government are important to God, who is the epitome of justice and good government. Those in authority are reminded they too have a master (Ephesians 6:9) and should exercise authority with justice, mercy, and kindness, just like God himself does.

Writing and Language

Tools of Communication

Writing and language can communicate both good and evil, so the Bible encourages people to use words carefully. It was arrogant words that led God to scatter people and confuse their language (Genesis 11:3–9), a judgment reversed at Pentecost (Acts 2:1–12).

Writing systems

The first writing systems comprised pictures, which communicate powerfully (think how we use simply a man's outline to indicate "men's toilet"). As the need for accuracy increased, these pictures became more abstract, becoming more symbol than picture. By 3100 BC **cuneiform** (wedge-shaped marks pressed into clay) had been invented in Sumeria, allowing signs to become more abstract and represent not only words but syllables, allowing writing to more accurately represent speech. The Akkadians adopted cuneiform, spreading it across their empire, and by the second millennium BC, Elamites, Hurrians, and Hittites were all using it.

Meanwhile in Egypt a different form of writing had developed: **hieroglyphics** ("sacred writing"), a system of picture word-signs (pictograms) used from c. 3000 BC. Hieroglyphs initially expressed the things they represented, but gradually came to express sounds. The original script was quickly adapted into *hieratic* script, a cursive form reduced to formal symbols; and by the seventh century BC it had developed into *demotic* ("popular") script, an even more abbreviated form. All three lasted until the fifth century AD.

A Sumerian contract written in pre-cuneiform script.

It was generally believed that the Phoenicians, around 1600 BC, invented the precursor of the modern **alphabet**, in which signs represented only individual vowels and consonants, thereby permitting a small number of signs to be used. However, archaeologists have recently found what may be an even earlier alphabetic script in Egypt dating c. 1900–1800 BC. The efficiency of the alphabet led to the decline of cuneiform, and in Syria-Palestine it was replaced by the alphabet-based Aramaic that became the common language of the Ancient Near East. Hebrew, the language of the Israelites, used the same alphabet as Aramaic, but was gradually replaced by it in the inter-testamental period, becoming the Jews' spoken language. Greeks adopted the Phoenician alphabet and standardized their writing from left to right, reversing the Semitic practice. The Romans then used this Greek alphabet, with a few adaptations, producing the script of Western Europe that still dominates the world today.

Writing materials

A wide range of writing materials was used in Bible times:

- **Stone**: used for monumental inscriptions, recording great deeds. Because chiselling was time-consuming, it was sometimes covered with plaster and inscribed with a stylus (Deuteronomy 27:1–8).
- **Metal**: used for decorative or commemorative objects. Silver amulets found in Jerusalem were inscribed with the words of Numbers 6:24–27. Stone and metal inscriptions were seen as particularly enduring (Job 19:23–24).
- **Wood**: coated with wax to produce a tablet that could be written on with a stylus (Isaiah 30:8) but easily rubbed out and re-used.

The Rosetta Stone

In 1799 the Rosetta Stone was discovered by Napoleon's soldiers during his Egyptian campaign. Inscribed to honour Ptolemy V in 196 BC, it was divided into three sections, each containing the same text in hieroglyphics, demotic, and Greek. It was French historian J. F. Champollion who grasped that the hieroglyphs represented not just letters but sounds and who, through comparison with the Greek, was able to decipher this script that had remained obscure since passing out of use in the fifth century AD.

See also
Codex p. 15
Education pp. 90–91
Scribes p. 14

- **Clay tablets** (Ezekiel 4:1): engraved with a stylus or reed. When baked, they became rock hard, so many examples have survived.
- **Ostraca**: fragments of broken pottery (potsherds) inscribed with a metal stylus or written on in ink. Used for notes or short letters.
- **Leather**: when treated, known as vellum or parchment. Written on with ink, and the preferred medium for writing the Scriptures (Jeremiah 36:17–18).
- **Papyrus**: made from the pith of reeds cut into strips, layered in alternate directions, and pressed into sheets that could be pasted together. The nearest thing to paper the ancient world could produce and popular because of its strong, smooth surface.
- **Ink**: made by mixing black carbon, water, and gum, with red oxide added if red ink was required.

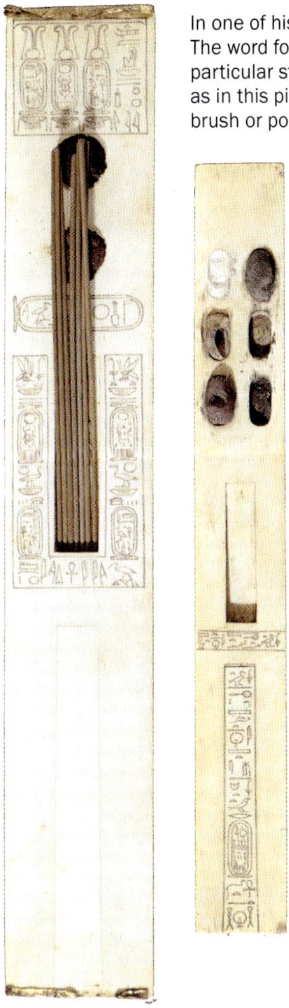

In one of his visions, Ezekiel saw a man with "a writing kit at his side" (Ezekiel 9:2). The word for "writing kit" here was based on an Egyptian word that identifies it as a particular style of palette, with slots for pens and two stores for black and red ink, as in this picture. Pens were rushes or reeds cut to a point that could serve as a brush or point depending on the character being drawn. The scribe had a knife to keep it sharp (Jeremiah 36:23).

The magnificent façade of the Library of Celsus in Ephesus, built AD 135. Libraries were common in the ancient world, preserving historical, literary, religious, and scientific texts. In Egypt, the first public lending library in the world was built in Alexandria c. 300 BC and had 600,000 scrolls.

Writing in the Bible

Writing appears from an early period in the Bible's history. Moses, trained in writing in Egypt, wrote history (Exodus 17:14), Law (Exodus 24:4), and a travel record (Numbers 33:2); Joshua wrote a copy of the Ten Commandments (Joshua 8:32) and the Law (Joshua 24:26); Samuel wrote a charter of kingship (1 Samuel 10:25); David wrote letters (2 Samuel 11:14) and kept administrative records (2 Chronicles 35:4); the prophets recorded their sayings (2 Chronicles 21:12; Isaiah 8:1; Jeremiah 30:2). Since writing skills were widely known in the ancient world, there is no reason why they should not have done this, as the Bible claims, and there is therefore no need to relegate their works to some later period.

Letter writing

Letter writing in the Graeco-Roman world followed a well-established formula, generally used in the New Testament letters:

- introduction identifying writer and recipients;
- greetings;
- thanksgiving for recipients;
- content of letter;
- concluding good wishes and farewell.

After writing, a scroll was sealed to protect its content (Isaiah 29:11; Daniel 12:4; Revelation 5:1–2).

Faith idea: Communication

The Bible says that God not only exists, but also communicates. It was his word that brought everything into existence (Genesis 1:3), and throughout the Old Testament he speaks to people in many different ways. His ultimate communication was through his Son Jesus, "the Word" (John 1:1, 14), who spoke his Father's words to people. Because Jesus claimed to be truth, his followers are called to be truthful in all their communication (Matthew 5:37; Ephesians 4:25–30; James 3:1–12; 1 Peter 3:9–12).

Leisure and Sport

Finding Refreshment

For ordinary people in ancient times, there was little "free" time, for they had to work long hours just to survive. However, they still managed to make time for recreational activities. For Jews this was particularly so on the sabbath and at the great religious festivals. The sabbath, the Jewish weekly day of rest, was not primarily for going to religious meetings, but for refreshment from labour and remembering God's "rest" after his work of creation, to enjoy what he had done (Exodus 20:8–11).

Children's games

There were no special recreational areas for children in Bible times. They simply played their games in the market place (Matthew 11:16) or open air (Zechariah 8:5). Games like hide-and-seek, hopscotch, and blind man's buff were popular, but also "pretend" games like "weddings and funerals" (Matthew 11:16). While girls in the Ancient Near East played with dolls, they didn't in Israel, for the Ten Commandments said images could not be made of anything in heaven or earth (Exodus 20:4). But whistles, rattles, tops, and hoops were all common toys.

Ball and target games

Ball games were very popular, though there were no bats or racquets. The leather balls were simply used for throwing or juggling. The game of marbles was also very popular. The marbles were rolled through a little wall with three archways and the aim was to knock down skittles on the other side. Target games were also popular – throwing stones into a hole at a distance, and shooting at targets with slings and bows and arrows. King David as a young shepherd boy would have done sling practice many times to become as skilful as he did (1 Samuel 17:34–37).

Wooden toy hippo on wheels.

Board and dice games

Draughts was played on boards made of clay, ebony, and ivory, and some boards stored the playing pieces in a compartment at the rear. Chess was played in Babylon before 2000 BC, as well as Ludo, Mancala, Solitaire, and a game called "The Royal Game". A popular Roman game was "Basileus" ("The Game of the King"), which is what the soldiers who gambled for Jesus' clothing probably played. The example above is carved into flagstones in the Convent of St Anne, the site of Jerusalem's Antonia Fortress.

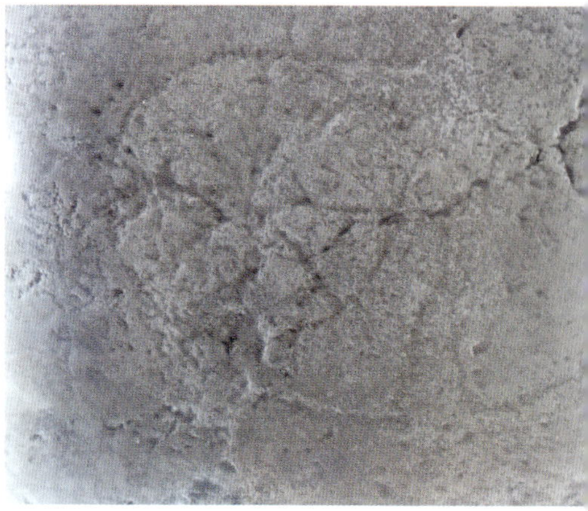

Although once thought to be the pavement where Pilate tried Jesus, it is now dated to the second century AD.

Other Jewish pastimes

Other Jewish recreational activities focused around the great religious festivals when singing, dancing, and story-telling were all common. There were even story-telling competitions and challenges to solve puzzles and riddles, something Samson enjoyed (Judges 14:12–14). Music and dancing also played an important role, both in entertainment and in Temple worship. In fact the Hebrew word *gil* means both to dance and to rejoice, showing the close link between the two in Jewish thinking. The Feast of Tabernacles was particularly associated with joyful dancing, and the Feast of Purim is described as "a day of joy and feasting, a day for giving presents to each other" (Esther 9:19).

Jesus and leisure

While Jesus gave himself fully to his ministry, he wasn't afraid to have leisure time, doing things like attending dinners (Luke 5:29–31), being a guest at a wedding (John 2:1–11), and enjoying time with children (Matthew 19:13–15). For him leisure also meant retreating from the busyness of life to get time for prayer and reflection (Mark 6:45–46), sometimes taking his disciples with him so they could "get some rest" (Mark 6:32). But he also taught people to beware

See also
Musical instruments p. 140
Olympic Games p. 79
Sabbath p. 138

Wrestling

Wrestling was popular in Bible times, including in Israel. The Old Testament story of Jacob wrestling a heavenly visitor uses the expression "hip and thigh" – a technical term for a particular wrestling throw. In Greece *pankration* (all-in wrestling) was a combination of wrestling and boxing, allowing any form of attack apart from biting or gouging the eyes. First introduced into the Olympic Games in 648 BC, it was considered the ultimate combat sport and was taken to India by Alexander the Great's armies, where it became one of the ancestors of martial arts. This wall painting depicting wrestlers comes from the tomb of Governor Baqet III, Beni Hassan, Middle Egypt.

of a self-indulgence that leads to complacency, like in his parable of the rich fool (Luke 12:13–21) whose attitude of "eat, drink, and be merry" (12:19) received God's response: "You fool! This very night your life will be demanded from you. Then who will get what you have prepared for yourself?" (12:20).

Athletics

The Greeks loved athletics – running, long jumping, boxing, wrestling, discus, and javelin throwing – as well as chariot racing, holding their Olympic Games every four years. Paul referred to the Greek games in a number of letters to Greek settings (1 Corinthians 9:24–27; Philippians 3:12–14; 2 Timothy 2:5). However, Jews found the games hugely offensive, as athletes not only performed naked, but the games also had religious links. That didn't stop Herod the Great introducing them in Judea, however, holding them every five years in honour of Caesar. He built a gymnasium, sports stadium, and hippodrome in Jerusalem, and a huge amphitheatre on its outskirts to which he invited gladiators from all over the world to come and fight.

Gladiatorial shows

Gladiators were generally slaves or criminals owned by the wealthy and trained to fight for public entertainment. The contests were bloody affairs, and at the end only one or two gladiators would be left standing to claim their prize – a bag of gold or freedom. There were different types of gladiators – some fighting with swords and shields, others with nets and tridents; sometimes they fought alone, sometimes in teams; and fights against wild animals were particularly popular. In the dreadful times of persecution under the emperors Nero (AD 54–68) and Domitian (AD 81–96) many Christians were forced to face gladiators and wild beasts, especially in Rome.

Faith idea: Enjoyment

Ecclesiastes observes that so many people spend so much of their life striving after things, especially wealth and success, that they don't have time to enjoy what they have worked for (Ecclesiastes 4:8). It therefore encourages people to enjoy life to the full (Ecclesiastes 2:24; 3:11–13, 22; 5:18–19; 8:15; 9:7–10; 11:9), receiving it as God's gift (3:13; 5:19; 9:7), for pleasure is not something to be avoided – something some early Christians, influenced by mystic cults, forgot. But nor is it something that should consume our lives, causing us to forget what is important.

Health and Healing

Searching for Wholeness

Because disease was so widespread, good health was seen as one of life's best blessings. The Old Testament therefore focused on maintaining health rather than curing sickness. Much of Jesus' ministry centred around healing – not for its own sake, but as a demonstration of the arrival of God's kingdom and foretaste of the end-time transformation.

Staying healthy

When Israel came upon bad water in the wilderness, God not only purified it but promised that, if they obeyed him, "I will not bring on you any of the diseases I brought on the Egyptians, for I am the LORD, who heals you" (Exodus 15:26). This wasn't an absolute promise they would never get ill, for even the godly got sick sometimes (e.g. 2 Kings 20:1; 2 Timothy 4:20), but rather an assurance that a healthy society would result from obedience to God's Law, with its wise rules for life (like what was safe to eat) and an excellent public health system (like isolating disease).

Disease

Heat, bad water, and poor diet meant diseases like **dysentery**, **cholera**, **typhoid**, and **beriberi** were common. Other common illnesses included:

- **Eye infections**, either from dust or flies that discharged infection into the eyes, which could develop into partial or total **blindness.** Both the blind and deaf were objects of special kindness in the Law (Leviticus 19:14), showing how common such conditions were.
- **Deafness** and **dumbness** – conditions Jesus often came across and healed (e.g. Mark 7:32–37). Such healings were particularly significant, for Isaiah had prophesied that they would be part of the messiah's work (Isaiah 29:18; 35:5–6).
- **Skin diseases**, including (but not only) leprosy. The priests examined patients (Leviticus 13) to confirm whether the condition was leprosy (requiring isolation) or some other skin disease.
- **Worms**, which caused bowel problems. Roundworms, which grow up to 16 inches (40 cm)long, can cause blockages if they interlock, and this may have been the cause of Herod Agrippa's death (Acts 12:23). Tapeworms were common from eating badly cooked meat, and other worms came from infections entering the body through bad water or cracks in feet.
- **Paralysis**, which had many causes, though some cases were probably the result of polio. Jesus healed many who were paralysed (e.g. Matthew 4:24; 9:1–8; 12:9–13).

Roman doctor's tools.

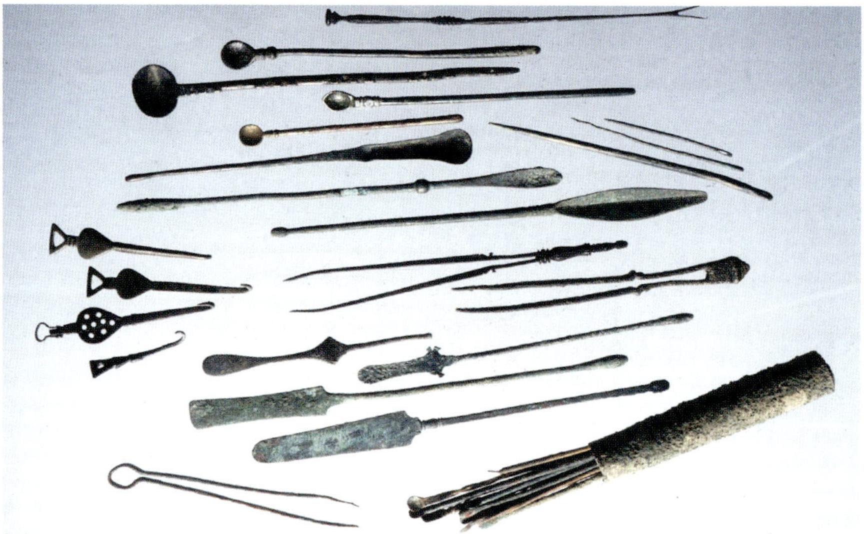

Doctors

Doctors were few in number and limited in skill, and many of their "cures" were often little more than superstitious remedies that proved ineffective (2 Chronicles 16:12) or made patients worse (Mark 5:26). The Greeks improved medical knowledge and care, and Hippocrates (c. 460–370 BC) laid down rules for doctors, many of which (like patient confidentiality) are still followed today. Rejecting beliefs that ascribed illness to supernatural forces, he looked for physical causes.

Doctors aren't often portrayed well in the Bible, probably because people thought they should trust God for healing. Job condemned his so-called comforters as "worthless physicians" (Job 13:4), and the woman with gynaecological problems was said to have spent all her money on doctors to no avail. However, it is clear from rabbinic writings that respect for medicine grew in the inter-testamental period. In the Book of Sirach, there is recognition that God gives doctors skills and "by them he heals and takes away pain", and Luke was known as "the beloved physician" (Colossians 4:14).

See also
Food and Drink pp. 98–99
Jesus: His Miracles pp. 174–75
Sanitation, Water, Lighting pp. 94–95

Calcified deposits from hot springs at Hierapolis (modern Pamukkale in Turkey), renowned as a healing spa. This is what lies behind Revelation's criticism of nearby Laodicea as neither hot nor cold (Revelation 3:15–16), for hot water piped from Hierapolis was lukewarm when it reached there, as well as full of sediment, while cold water from the mountains was tepid.

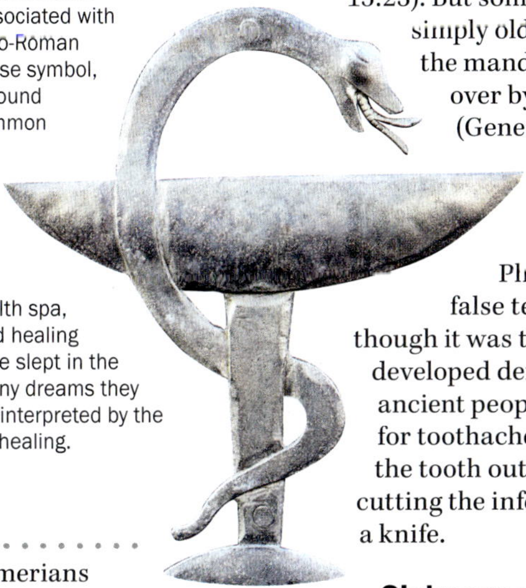

In New Testament times most physicians were associated with Asclepius, the Greco-Roman god of healing, whose symbol, a snake entwined round a staff, is still a common emblem of medical professions. There were many temples dedicated to him, which were a combination of health spa, medical school, and healing shrine. Some people slept in the temples believing any dreams they had there could be interpreted by the priests and lead to healing.

Remedies

The ancient Sumerians discovered the healing potential of many plants, including that of the willow tree's bark and leaves to act as a type of aspirin, and castor oil as a laxative. Egypt too developed animal and vegetable substances to treat disease. But this primitive medicine was mixed with magic spells to make them work, which is probably why people in the Bible avoided them. Many folk remedies were used in Israel, however, including oils and potions, like the famous balm of Gilead (Jeremiah 8:22), poultices of figs (Isaiah 38:21), and myrrh, used as a pain-killer (Mark 15:23). But some "cures" were simply old wives' tales, like the mandrake roots bartered over by Rachel and Leah (Genesis 30:14–16).

Dentistry

Both Egyptians and Phoenicians made false teeth of wood or ivory, though it was the Greeks who really developed dentistry. For most ancient peoples, the only solution for toothache was knocking the tooth out with a hammer or cutting the infected gum with a knife.

Sickness and sin

Because good health was seen as a mark of God's blessing, it was natural to assume that illness was a mark of his displeasure (e.g. 1 Samuel 5:9; Psalm 38:1–4). While the Bible says there were certainly situations where God sent illness as judgment or discipline (e.g. Exodus 12:29–30; Numbers 12:1–15; 1 Samuel 5:9; 2 Kings 19:35; Acts 12:23; 1 Corinthians 11:27–32), this didn't imply that *all* sickness is the result of sin. Indeed when this kind of link was put to Jesus, he specifically repudiated it (John 9:1–3). However, he also recognized that, because people aren't separate "bits" (body, soul, mind, spirit) but rather physical–psychological–spiritual entities, sin *can* sometimes affect health, like it did with the crippled man whose sin he dealt with before addressing his physical needs (Mark 2:1–12).

Faith idea: Wholeness

One of the Bible's promises is that people can know God's "shalom" (peace) – not just the absence of strife, but the presence of health, prosperity, security, friendship, and salvation at every level of existence, which only God can give. When Jesus told a woman to "go in peace and be freed from your suffering" (Mark 5:34), it was more than a parting blessing: it was his bestowal of shalom, the peace-bringing, life-releasing gift of God to his people.

Slavery

Serving Another

People fell into slavery for different reasons: some became slaves through conquest; some were captured by pirates and sold to the highest bidder; some were reduced to slavery by poverty; some were simply born into it. But while slavery existed in Israel, it was of a wholly different nature. And early church leaders shockingly wrote that one type of slavery was to be aspired to – slavery to God.

Slavery in Israel

There were two types of slavery in Israel. The first, and most common, was "economic slavery" in which the seriousness of debt was recognized by debtors having to sell themselves as slaves to pay off their debt (e.g. 2 Kings 4:1) – a sort of indentured labour. However, such slavery couldn't be forever, and the Law required that every seventh year such slaves should be freed, liberally provided for, and the debt counted as paid (Exodus 21:2–4; Deuteronomy 15:12–15, 18), though provision was made for any who wished to stay permanently (Exodus 21:5–6; Deuteronomy 15:16–17). Israelite slaves were to be well cared for, in contrast to many foreign practices (e.g. 1 Samuel 30:13), and women and children were especially protected (e.g. Exodus 21:6–11). If a master mistreated his slave, the slave was granted freedom (Exodus 21:26–27).

The second type of slavery was that of foreigners, which resolved the problem of prisoners of war in an age when death was the quickest solution. Foreigners could also be bought as slaves (Leviticus 25:44–46), such slavery being for life. However, runaway foreign slaves were granted sanctuary (Deuteronomy 23:15–16), which was quite exceptional, as most treaties provided for the extradition of runaway slaves and made hiding them a capital crime. But Israel was not to be part of this, perhaps to remind them that they too had once been runaway slaves.

Wall painting

Wall painting from an Eighteenth-Dynasty Egyptian tomb showing bricks being made from mud and straw. It was under this dynasty that the Israelites had been forced into slavery (Exodus 1:8–14). The Bible says that God heard their cry and rescued them (Exodus 3:7–10), and Israel was often told to remember this slavery and God's freeing them from it as a motivation for right living, a theme occurring right at the beginning of the Ten Commandments (Exodus 20:1; Deuteronomy 5:6).

See also
Exodus pp. 26–27
Jubilee Year p. 96
New Community pp. 178–79

Other ancient nations

Many ancient civilizations permitted slavery, and laws regulating it have been found in Sumer, Nuzi, Babylon, and Assyria. For example, the Code of Hammurabi restricted slavery for debt to three years, but permitted it for negligent landowners and spendthrift wives. Many slaves were trusted with huge responsibilities, as the story of Joseph in Egypt shows (Genesis 39:1–6).

A Sumerian branding iron used on runaway slaves from the mid-third millennium BC, with wording in cuneiform script.

Slavery in Rome

Slavery was common in the Roman world, with an estimated 85–90 per cent of the inhabitants of Rome and Italy being slaves or from slave origins by New Testament times. Slaves were the property of their master, completely at their disposal, and the head of a household could legally execute his slaves. But good slaves, especially skilled or educated ones, were often trusted with their master's property, and were allowed to worship with them, get married, and even live in separate houses. Slaves who ran away, however, were dealt with harshly, normally by death.

Slaves could be found in almost every profession, including agricultural, household, educational, and secretarial work. Mine and quarry slaves had the hardest and shortest lives. The apostle John was almost certainly one of those, exiled as he was to the quarries in the penal colony on Patmos (Revelation 1:9).

Freedom

Sometimes slaves could earn enough money on the side to buy their freedom. But since slavery was a life-long institution in the Gentile world, a way had to be developed to enable this, known as manumission. The slave went with his master to the temple, where he was sold by his master to the god or goddess to become his or her slave for life. In return, the money deposited into the temple by the slave was given to the master for him to buy another slave, less a percentage for the priests. The price paid was called a *lutron* (ransom) – the word used of the price Jesus paid to free people from sin (e.g. Mark 10:45; 1 Timothy 2:6).

Paul and slavery

In Paul's short letter to Philemon, he urged Philemon to take back his slave Onesimus, who had absconded, which under Roman law was punishable by death. During his time away, Onesimus had become a Christian and had been a real help to Paul. Now both Paul and Philemon had a dilemma. Jewish Law required Paul to give Onesimus refuge (Deuteronomy 23:15–16), whereas Roman law required him to return him. Philemon, as a master, had absolute rights over Onesimus; but as a Christian, he needed to resolve what forgiveness meant. So Paul appealed to Philemon to give Onesimus a new start, just as Jesus had given Philemon himself a new start – a request that went way beyond anything found in any other contemporary documents, a request not just for leniency, but for nothing less than freedom.

Paul knew he couldn't change an entrenched social structure like slavery overnight, though he encouraged slaves to get their freedom if possible (1 Corinthians 7:21) and said slave trading was incompatible with Christianity (1 Timothy 1:9–11). However, he certainly undermined its foundations. While he might not have been able to change slaves' legal status, he could certainly change how they were treated in the Christian community, applying the Christian faith to both slaves and masters in terms of their relationship with one another (Ephesians 6:5–9; Colossians 3:22–25) and reminding everyone that "there is neither Jew nor Greek, slave nor free, male nor female, for you are all one in Christ Jesus" (Galatians 3:28).

A Roman slave tag asking whoever finds the runaway slave to return him to his master.

Faith idea: Spiritual slavery

Jesus said that "everyone who sins is a slave to sin" (John 8:31), and Peter said that "a man is a slave to whatever has mastered him" (2 Peter 2:19). But through the price that Jesus paid on the cross, the Bible says it is possible to be freed from spiritual slavery to become not just God's slave, but God's child (e.g. Romans 6:15 – 8:17). The promise of Jesus was that "if the Son sets you free, you will be free indeed" (John 8:36).

Warfare

Swords and Ploughshares

While warfare was simply part of life in the ancient world, for Israel its purpose was much more limited: their establishment in the Promised Land. The fact that others also wanted that land, however, would bring them face to face with the most brutal armies of those days. Little wonder the prophets therefore looked forward to a day when swords would be beaten into ploughshares (Micah 4:2).

Israel at war

Unlike surrounding empires, Israel didn't have militaristic aims. Its sole purpose in taking up arms was to gain, and keep, the land God had promised to Abraham, which couldn't be given to him in his day, God had said, "for the sin of the Amorites has not yet reached its full measure" (Genesis 15:16) – that is, their sin hadn't reached the appalling levels it would reach (with things like child sacrifice) that would make it apparent to everyone that the only solution was to remove them. Joshua, therefore, led Israel into a "holy war", one that saw its battles not just as a fight for territory but also as a religious act. The amazing thing, from a military point of view, is that his men weren't trained soldiers, just nomads. They therefore had to learn that success would only come through obedience to God, as the contrasting stories of Jericho and Ai showed (Joshua 6–8).

Victories over enemies during the period of the Judges were spasmodic, causing Israel to ask for "a king to lead us, such as all the other nations have" (1 Samuel 8:5). Saul established Israel's first standing army; but his leadership was ineffective, and it was David who really developed a professional army, calling up men from the tribes on a rota basis, ensuring that a trained army was always ready. Solomon developed the army further, adding cavalry and 1,400 chariots, enabling Israel to reach the borders promised by God. Thereafter it was a story of decline as first Israel, then Judah, turned from trusting God, who therefore abandoned them to the onslaught of Assyria and Babylon. After they returned from exile, Israel never had an established army again.

Ancient warfare

The earliest weapons were simply wooden and stone clubs, and soldiers fought mainly on foot. It wasn't until the Late Bronze Age (c. 1550–1200 BC, in this part of the world) that chariots were extensively used, bringing speed and shock into warfare. The Iron Age (c. 1200–1000 BC), with its superior weapons, saw the rise of massive armies of heavy infantry, and battles lasted only as long as the line held (sometimes just hours). While heavy infantry had full armour and moved in large, close formations, light infantry had little or no armour, relying on speed and skill instead. The great armies, like those of Alexander the Great, used light and heavy infantry working together and always had a core of well-trained professionals.

Religious artefacts were often taken into battle, which is what lay behind Israel taking the ark of the covenant into battle against the Philistines. God wouldn't bow to their superstition, however, and let the ark be captured (1 Samuel 4:1–11).

The Standard of Ur

This mysterious object, measuring 19½ inches (50 cm) long and 8½ inches (22 cm) high and found at Ur, is believed to have been carried on a pole as a standard. It is one of the earliest depictions of the Sumerian army and dates from the mid-third millennium BC. The two main panels depict war and peace. This side ("War") shows chariots pulled by donkeys trampling enemies underfoot, cloaked infantry carrying spears, and enemies being killed with axes, while others are paraded naked and presented to the king who holds a spear. The other side ("Peace") depicts a peacetime banquet, perhaps the celebrations after victory.

See also
Assyrian War Machine p. 73
The Philistines pp. 70–71
Siege of Lachish p. 36

Siege warfare

Siege warfare was an important strategy in ancient times. The attacking army surrounded the city, blocking access and cutting off food and water supplies. Sometimes this show of force alone caused the city to surrender, as Sennacherib hoped would happen when he surrounded Jerusalem (2 Kings 18:17 – 19:36); sometimes the city was starved into submission or left to the ravages of plague; and sometimes it was besieged by using assault ladders, battering rams, digging tunnels under the walls, or building ramps up to the walls (e.g. Ezekiel 26:7–9). This photo shows the huge siege ramp (bottom left) built by the Romans to capture the fortress of Masada in AD 73.

After battle, it was usual to kill, mutilate, or enslave all male adults, while women and children were taken captive. City walls were broken down and major buildings destroyed (e.g. 2 Kings 25:8–10), and soldiers were allowed to take whatever plunder they could find.

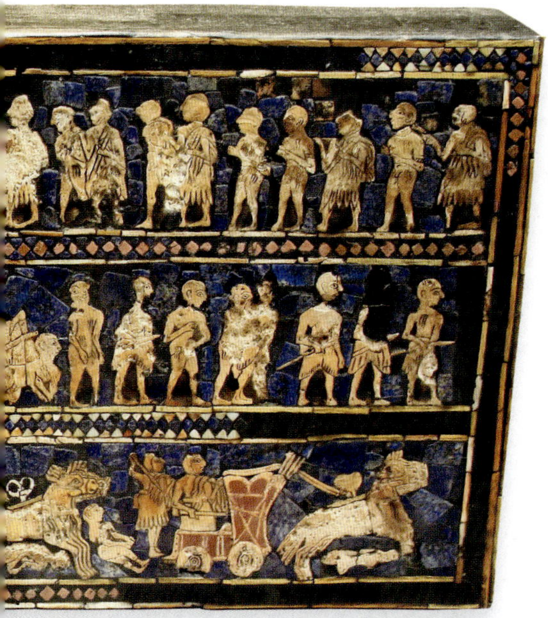

Battle by champion

The story of David and Goliath (1 Samuel 17) was an example of "battle by champion", in which armies decided the outcome of battle by having their best warriors fight one another to the death. Whoever won determined which nation won. But this was more than a battle between champions; it was seen as a battle between gods, as David understood (17:45–47).

The Roman war machine

It was Augustus (63 BC–AD 14) who developed the Imperial Legion, a structure that remained largely unchanged throughout the first century AD.
Legions were recruited only from Roman citizens and played a vital role in the expansion and stability of the empire. By New Testament times there were twenty-eight legions with 150,000–170,000 soldiers, and two of these legions were always stationed in Palestine. Their weapons included the catapult (for hurling javelins), ballista (for hurling heavy rocks), onager (for hurling lighter stones), and siege towers. Individual soldiers wore upper-body armour and helmets, and carried a dagger, sword, and javelin. They had two types of shield: a smaller round one for fighting at close quarters, and a full-length curved one that they could hide behind or lock together as a wall or ceiling. It was this equipment that Paul saw on the Roman soldier guarding him and that stirred him to write of the Christian's armour in the battle against evil (Ephesians 6:13–17).

Faith idea: Pacifism

Against the background of a violent world, Jesus renounced all expressions of violence, rejecting the popular expectations of a military messiah who would conquer Israel's enemies, and telling his followers rather to overcome their enemies through unexpected kindness and turning the other cheek (Matthew 5:38–41). The prophets' longed-for ploughshares would be won, he said, through a cross not through a sword (e.g. Matthew 16:21–28).

God

The One Lord

"The fool says in his heart, 'There is no God'" (Psalm 14:1). The Bible nowhere seeks to prove God's existence, since it was rooted in a worldview where that was obvious to anyone but a fool. Rather, it shows what God is like, how people can know him, and the difference this makes to life.

The one God

From its outset, the Bible is utterly monotheistic: "In the beginning *God*..." – not *a* god, or *the* gods, but *God*. Belief in one God lay at the heart of Israelite faith, underlined in Moses' words that became their confession of faith: "Hear, O Israel: The Lord our God, the Lord is one" (Deuteronomy 6:4). In the light of that Israel was urged to "love the Lord your God with all your heart and with all your soul and with all your strength" (Deuteronomy 6:5), for there was no other god for whom they needed to keep something in reserve.

Sometimes Israel wavered in this monotheism, however, blending worship of the Lord (Yahweh) with that of other gods (e.g. Judges 2:10–15). But the prophets constantly challenged this, declaring this was the cause of their problems, not the solution to them (1 Kings 18:16–18; 2 Kings 17:7–20).

God's nature

While it is impossible to summarize everything the Bible says about God, here are some key features:

- **Eternal**
  God has no beginning or end; he simply "is", not needing to adapt to time or circumstances. He is "the Eternal God" (Genesis 21:33; Deuteronomy 33:27).
- **Transcendent**
  God is outside of creation (1 Kings 8:27), so cannot be found in it unless he reveals himself (Matthew 11:25).
- **Creator**
  As the one who made everything from nothing (Hebrews 11:3), God is above creation and is not to be confused with it.
- **Spirit**
  God is invisible and incorporeal (1 Timothy 1:17; 6:15–16), so cannot be seen unless he breaks into our dimension (John 1:18).
- **Present everywhere (omnipresent)**
  God can be everywhere simultaneously, so there is nowhere to hide (Psalm 139:1–16; Jeremiah 23:23–24).
- **All-knowing (omniscient)**
  God has all knowledge: factual (Job 37:16), moral (Hebrews 4:13), personal (Psalm 139), and historical (Isaiah 46:10).
- **All-powerful (omnipotent)**
  He is "God Almighty" (Genesis 17:1), so nothing is impossible for him (Job 42:2; Jeremiah 32:27), "the Sovereign Lord" (used almost 300 times) who works everything together for good (Romans 8:28–39).
- **Unchanging**
  His being (Psalm 102:26–27), nature (Malachi 3:6), truth (Isaiah 40:6–8), and purposes (Numbers 23:19) don't change. He is dependable and faithful (2 Timothy 2:13; Hebrews 10:23).
- **Holy**
  God is distinct, set apart (the meaning of holy), yet not self-protectively so. His holiness both calls people to be holy (Leviticus 11:45) and makes them holy (Leviticus 20:8).

"Mountain of Moses"

Jebel Musa (Arabic for "Mountain of Moses"), the traditional site of Mount Sinai, where Moses received the Ten Commandments. Here God revealed himself as "the Lord, the Lord, the compassionate and gracious God, slow to anger, abounding in love and faithfulness, maintaining love to thousands, and forgiving wickedness, rebellion and sin" (Exodus 34:6–7). This revelation became a consistent theme of Scripture (e.g. Psalm 86:15; 103:7–18; Joel 2:13).

See also
Canaanite Religion pp. 68–69
Idolatry p. 69
Jesus' Teaching about God pp. 170–71

God's names and titles

Some key names of God in the early chapters of the Bible include:

Name or title	Significance
God (*Elohim*)	Transcendent Creator God (Genesis 1:1–2)
God Most High (*El Elyon*)	Supremacy above other so-called gods (Genesis 14:19–20)
God the Seer (*El Roeh*)	Watchfulness over his people (Genesis 16:13)
God Almighty (*El Shaddai*)	Invincible power (Genesis 17:1)
God the provider (*Yahweh Yireh*)	Ability to provide for people (Genesis 22:14)
God of Israel (*El Eloho Israel*)	Care of Israel (Genesis 33:20)
Lord (*Yahweh*, or Jehovah)	God of relationship (Exodus 3:14–15)
Lord (*Adonai*)	Master of everything (Joshua 3:11)
The living God	In contrast to idols and the Canaanite fertility gods who were believed to die and rise again each year (Deuteronomy 5:26)

Other later titles include *Yahweh Shalom*, "the Lord my peace" (Judges 6:24), *Yahweh Tsidkenu*, "the Lord my righteousness" (Jeremiah 23:6), and *Yahweh Shammah*, "the Lord who is there" (Ezekiel 48:35).

Yahweh

How God's name, YHWH, appears in Hebrew (below, reading from right to left). Having no vowels, we are uncertain of its pronunciation, but it was probably *Yahweh* – the only *personal* name of God in the Bible (all others are titles or descriptions), revealed to Moses at the burning bush (Exodus 3:1–15). Through a Hebrew play on words, God told Moses his name was "I AM" (3:14) but said, "You can call me HE IS" (3:15, the Lord, *Yahweh*). After the exile, this name was deemed so holy that it was forbidden to speak it. Instead, Jews substituted the word *shem* (Aramaic for "the name") or *adonai* (Hebrew for "my Lord"). This tradition was followed in the Septuagint (the Greek translation of the Hebrew Scriptures), which used *kurios* ("Lord"), and was continued in many English versions that translate "Yahweh" as Lord (written in lower case capitals).

יהוה

Describing God

Because God is so mysterious and "other", the Bible uses anthropomorphisms (the attributing of human characteristics) to describe him. This isn't simply inevitable; it underlines an important biblical teaching: that God isn't a "force" but is *personal*, and without this it would be impossible to have *relationship* with him. Many descriptions of God, therefore, are those of a close relationship – loving parent, devoted husband, caring mother or father. The most consistent description of him is "Father", Jesus' favourite title for him (used 168 times in the Gospels) – a strong indication that this expresses something fundamental about God, rather than being a mere picture.

Egyptian gods

Gold statuettes of the Egyptian gods Isis, Osiris, and Horus, c. 889–886 BC. While representations of gods were common in surrounding nations, the Ten Commandments forbade making them (Exodus 20:1–4; Deuteronomy 5:6–10), since it was impossible to represent God in any meaningful way, and idolatry was opposed. It was still commonplace in New Testament times, remaining a challenge to the first Christians (1 Corinthians 8; 2 Corinthians 6:14–17; Galatians 5:19–21; 1 John 5:21).

Faith idea: Revelation

Because God is so great and mysterious, we could never find him ourselves, the Bible insists. But it also says that, in his love, God comes looking for people instead, choosing to reveal himself. The Bible not only records people's encounters with that revelation, but is itself a revelation of who God is and what he is like, and an invitation to everyone to experience that revelation for themselves.

Covenant

God's Contract

"Covenant" is one of the Bible's key undergirding ideas. While an archaic word today, relegated to the realms of law and property, in Bible times covenants were common and everyone knew what they were: binding contracts between two parties. The Bible says that God used this concept to express the kind of relationship he wanted with people.

Covenant formulas

Covenants followed a standard pattern in the ancient world:

- *preamble*: outlining the main parties;
- *prologue*: the history bringing them to this point;
- *stipulations*: requirements of the covenant on both parties;
- *witnesses*: testifying to the covenant;
- *oath*: affirming the covenant;
- *blessings and curses*: consequences of keeping and breaking the covenant;
- *provision for preservation and renewal*: ensuring the covenant could be maintained;
- *ratification*: making and sealing the covenant.

Covenants in the ancient world

Covenants – the committing of two or more parties to the rights and responsibilities demanded by their relationship – were widespread in the Ancient Near East. Making and keeping them was a serious matter, and breaking them could mean death. This is reflected in how Abraham entered into covenant with God in Genesis 15, in which animals were cut in half and laid on opposite slopes. Normally the two participants then walked through the divided animals, as a way of saying, "May this happen to me if I break this covenant." (In fact, the Hebrew for "make a covenant" is "cut a covenant", referring to this practice.) But what stood out about this covenant with Abraham was that only God (symbolized by the smoking brazier and blazing torch) passed between the animals, while Abraham was left watching, underlining his inability to contribute anything to this covenant that God alone was making.

There were three main types of covenant in the ancient world:

- **Royal grant** – an unconditional grant of a gift or land in exchange for faithful service. It was normally perpetual, providing the grantee's descendants continued to be loyal (e.g. 1 Samuel 27:5–6; Esther 8:1).
- **Parity** – made between equals, binding them to mutual friendship and support (e.g. Genesis 31:44–54; 1 Kings 5:12).
- **Suzerain-vassal** – a claim of absolute sovereignty by a great king over a subject-king, offering protection in return for loyalty and exclusive dependence (e.g. Joshua 9:6–15; Ezekiel 17:11–18).

Yet, despite the commonness of covenants, the ones made with Israel were unique, for they were all the gracious gift and revelation of God.

Old Testament covenants follow the standard pattern of those times (see Covenant formulas, above) as we see in the covenant renewal at Shechem (Joshua 24) and in the whole book of Deuteronomy, which renews the covenant between God and Israel before entering Canaan. Beginning with recollection (chs 1–4), Moses recalls their thirty-eight year history since leaving Mount Sinai. The requirements of the covenant follow (chs 5–26), in which the Ten Commandments have a central place (5:1–33) and are then unpacked in wide-ranging religious, social, and legal laws for life in the Promised Land (chs 12–26). The book closes with ratification of the covenant as Moses outlines curses for disobedience and blessings for obedience before the covenant is renewed (chs 27–30).

Sealing covenants

Covenants were sealed in one of three ways: by sharing a meal (e.g. Genesis 26:28–31), offering a sacrifice (e.g. Exodus 24:4–8), or making an oath (e.g. 2 Kings 11:4). Jesus placed a meal at the heart of the covenant he made between God and people, seeing the bread as his body and the wine as his blood that would be given in sacrifice at the cross (Matthew 26:26–29). Christians still share bread and wine, both as a reminder of that sacrifice and as a renewal of their covenant with God. The initiatory external covenant sign for Christians is now baptism (e.g. Colossians 2:11–12).

See also
Ark of the Covenant p. 146
Circumcision p. 88
Ten Commandments pp. 134–35

Key covenants in ancient Israel

Covenant	Scripture	Type	Characteristics	Outward sign
Noah	Genesis 9:8–17	Royal grant	Unconditional promise the world would never be flooded again.	Rainbow
Abraham (part 1)	Genesis 15:1–21	Royal grant	In response to Abraham's faith, God unconditionally makes him "righteous" and promises Canaan to his descendants.	Circumcision
(part 2)	Genesis 17		Confirmation of the covenant already made; Canaan promised again, but they must keep the covenant (17:9–10).	
Moses	Exodus 19–24	Suzerain-vassal	God's adoption of Israel as "a kingdom of priests and a holy nation" (19:6), pledging to be their God and bring them into their destiny, but conditional on their keeping his Law and living as his people.	The Law
Phineas	Numbers 25:10–13	Royal grant	Promise to Aaron's grandson, Phineas, that his descendants would be Israel's priests forever.	Eternal priesthood
David	2 Samuel 7:5–16	Royal grant	Unconditional promise to establish David's descendants as Israel's rulers forever.	David's descendants (for Christians, fulfilled in Jesus)

The promised new covenant

Sadly, Israel's desire to keep the covenant deteriorated. The prophets repeatedly called people back to it, warning them of judgment if they didn't, but the downhill slide continued. Jeremiah prophesied that the covenant was now so utterly broken that it could no longer be restored; it could only be replaced. He prophesied that God would establish "a new covenant" (Jeremiah 31:31–34), written on hearts rather than on stone tablets. Ezekiel too prophesied this new covenant, seeing it as a work of God's Spirit (Ezekiel 36:25–27).

The theme of new covenant is picked up strongly in the New Testament where it is seen as new, yet also a continuation of the covenant made with Abraham (Acts 3:24–25; Galatians 3:15–20). Sealed with the blood of Jesus (Matthew 26:27–28), this covenant provides forgiveness (Hebrews 8:7–12; Romans 11:26–27) and brings people into relationship with God and one another (Ephesians 2:11–22; Hebrews 12:22–24).

Faith idea: New Testament

*When Christians expanded the Hebrew Scriptures, with its story of Israel, to include the story of Israel's messiah and the church, they called the first part of the story the Old Covenant and the second part the New Covenant. The term "new covenant" (*kainē diathēkē*) came from the New Testament itself (Luke 22:20; 2 Corinthians 3:6; Hebrews 9:15), using the Septuagint translation of Jeremiah 31:31, where covenant was seen as relationship with God. By extension, it came to describe the book telling the story of that relationship, and was translated into Latin as* Novum Testamentum *(New Testament).*

The Bible says God chose the rainbow as a sign of his covenant with Noah, promising the human race would never again be destroyed by a flood (Genesis 6–9). All key biblical covenants had some sort of external sign. This photo shows a rainbow over Jerusalem.

The Law

God's Gift to Israel

After their escape from Egypt, God led Israel to Mount Sinai where he established them as "a holy nation" (Exodus 19:6) and made a covenant with them (Exodus 24:1–8). Like any nation, they now needed laws to live by. But before God gave them a single commandment, he reminded them, "I am the LORD your God, who brought you out of Egypt, out of the land of slavery" (Exodus 20:2), showing that the Law wasn't a list of do's and don'ts to help people find God, but rather his gift to an already redeemed people.

The Ten Commandments

The Ten Commandments (Exodus 20:1–17; Deuteronomy 5:6–21) were the heart of God's Law for Israel, though the term "the Ten *Commandments*" isn't really accurate, for in Hebrew they are called "the Ten *Words*" (e.g. Exodus 34:28; Deuteronomy 4:13). Because these "words" aren't numbered, they are listed differently by different Christian traditions.

The Ten Commandments were first spoken by the voice of God in the hearing of the whole nation (Exodus 19:16 – 20:19), and only afterwards written on stone tablets, "inscribed by the finger of God" (Exodus 31:18; 32:16; 34:1). They follow the pattern of a covenant treaty (see p. 132), beginning by identifying the covenant suzerain ("I am the LORD your God..."), recounting their history ("...who brought you out of Egypt, out of the land of slavery..."), and then the obligations of the vassal ("You shall have no other gods before me..."). The two versions of the Ten Commandments have slight variations – for example, Deuteronomy 5:21 adds "land" to things not to be coveted – but this was normal "covenant renewal" practice, allowing successive generations to be drawn into it. Since the adults with whom God had made the covenant at Sinai had died in the wilderness (Numbers 14:26–35), the covenant needed renewing with the next generation; and with entry to the Promised Land imminent, it was appropriate to adjust it for the new situation.

Ten Commandments

Classic depictions of Moses show him holding the two tablets of the Ten Commandments with five commandments on each tablet, like in this painting. However, the tablets would have been copies of the same ten laws. Normally each party to the covenant kept a copy, but since this covenant was entirely God's doing, both copies were kept by Moses and placed inside the ark of the covenant in the tabernacle.

See also
Ark of the Covenant p. 146
Covenant pp. 132–33
Exodus pp. 26–27

The Ten Commandments and the Law

The Bible distinguishes between the Ten Commandments and the rest of the Law. For example, "Moses went and told the people all the LORD's *words* and *laws*" (Exodus 24:1), "words" referring to the Ten Commandments and "laws" to "the Book of the Covenant" (Exodus 24:7), which is summarized in Exodus 21:1 – 23:19 and is unpacked in the rest of Exodus, Leviticus, and Deuteronomy. The same distinction is found in Deuteronomy, where the Ten Commandments are recorded (5:6–21), with the comment: "these are the commandments the LORD proclaimed… *and he added nothing more*" (5:22). A further unpacking of these commandments then follows, beginning with the words, "These are the commands, decrees and laws the LORD your God directed me to teach you to observe *in the land that you are crossing the Jordan to possess*" (Deuteronomy 6:1), suggesting that while the Ten Commandments are God's "words" for everyone (underlined by their being written in stone), the further laws were specific to Israel and their life in the Promised Land. While some of these laws were *casuistic* ("If… then"), others were *apodictic* (absolute law); however, all were designed to reflect God's holiness, goodness, and justice.

The Law and Jesus

Jesus both taught obedience to the Law (e.g. Luke 10:25–28) and obeyed it himself (e.g. Matthew 17:24–27), saying he hadn't come to abolish it but to fulfil it and that "not the smallest letter, not the least stroke of a pen, will by any means disappear from the Law until everything is accomplished" (Matthew 5:18). Such language shows his high esteem for God's Law, even in its smallest detail; but it also indicates its incompleteness, for he said he came to "fulfil" it (literally, "to bring it to its completion"). He called for a righteousness that "surpasses that of the Pharisees and the teachers of the law" (Matthew 5:20); but since their punctilious Law-keeping was legendary, he clearly had a different sort of righteousness in mind, one that could be brought about only by his death. He had little time for their many oral interpretations (e.g. Matthew 5:21–48), constantly taking people back to the heart of God's Law (e.g. Mark 2:23–28).

The Ur-Nammu Law Code, the oldest known law code in existence, written in cuneiform on a clay cylinder, dating from c. 2100 to 2050 BC.

The Law and the church

As the gospel spread, the issue arose of whether people needed to become Jews in order to become Christians (e.g. Acts 15:1). Acts shows how such thinking was steadily broken down. First, half-Jews (Samaritans) were converted (8:4–17), then a man who could never become a Jew, the Ethiopian eunuch (8:26–40), then Gentiles (10:1–48), then Gentiles in the wider world (13:1–3ff) – a mission so successful that a council had to be convened at Jerusalem in AD 49/50 to determine how to handle Gentile converts (Acts 15:1–35). It was agreed that circumcision wasn't required of them, but that for the good of their relationship with God and with Jewish Christians, Gentile converts should comply with four requirements: abstaining from food offered to idols, sexual immorality, eating non-kosher meat, and drinking blood (15:20–21).

Though a devout Pharisee himself, Paul consistently resisted arguments that Gentiles should keep the Law, and even rebuked Peter when he wavered on this (Galatians 2:11–14). He was constantly dogged by "Judaizers" – Christians who insisted converted Gentiles should be circumcised and keep the Law – but he steadfastly opposed this, as the letter to the Galatians reflects.

Faith idea: Legalism

Jesus often challenged the Pharisees' legalism – the belief that God's favour depended on obedience to the Law in its smallest details – exposing their punctilious tithing of tiny herbs while neglecting basics like justice and mercy (Matthew 23:23), fulfilling the letter of the Law but missing the spirit of it. Legalism fatally misunderstands the Law's purpose, the New Testament says: that is, that it existed to bring people to Christ, who alone can save (e.g. Galatians 3:10–14, 23–25). Religious legalism still occurs whenever human traditions take priority over God's heart and people's needs.

Jewish Identity Markers

Externals and Internals

Jewish religious practices developed considerably over the biblical period from what were often simple and practical origins into crucial and complex fundamentals of the faith. It was such developments that Jesus so often challenged – not because they were necessarily bad, but because their time had come. He claimed they were no longer the hallmarks of God's people, as they were now being refocused not around rituals but around a person: himself.

Animals

Of all the Jewish "unclean" animals, the pig became the most notorious. So when Antiochus IV Epiphanes was enraged at resistance to his Hellenization programme in Judea in 168 BC, he made his point not only by forbidding circumcision and sacrifices, but also by forcing Jews to eat pork and by sacrificing a pig in the Temple. That the pig was still the height of uncleanness in Jesus' time is reflected in his parable of the prodigal son (Luke 15:11–31), where the son is reduced to feeding pigs, the ultimate indignity for the religious leaders to whom Jesus told the story.

Part of the reason for pigs being seen as so unclean was probably their cultural and religious connotations. In Egypt pigs were sacred to the god Seth and were used in sacrifice, while in Mesopotamia they were used as offerings to underworld deities, as they were later in Greece and Rome. The prohibition on eating pork may therefore have been an attempt to keep Israel from any association with sacrifices to demons or the dead.

Dietary laws

The permission given to Noah to eat "everything that lives and moves" (Genesis 9:3) was restricted in the Jewish Law, given centuries later to Moses, with its lists of "clean" (permitted) or "unclean" (forbidden) animals. These lists (Leviticus 11:1–47; Deuteronomy 14:3–21) permitted meat from "any animal that has a split hoof completely divided and that chews the cud" (Leviticus 11:3), so included sheep, cattle, and deer. Fish were permitted if they had "fins and scales" (Leviticus 11:9) and birds if they were not birds of prey or scavengers. While good health reasons lay behind such laws, their primary reason was "holiness" (Leviticus 11:44–45), marking Israel out as belonging to God, for no other nation had such comprehensive food regulations. Jews still follow these dietary laws.

One of the challenges the early church faced was whether such laws were binding on Christians. It took a powerful vision to convince Peter they no longer were (Acts 10:1 – 11:18), and Paul too stressed that they weren't part of the Christian faith (Romans 14:1 – 15:13).

Ritual cleansing

The Old Testament reflects the conviction that physical cleanliness is somehow related to what God is like, and this was reflected in the Law. The earliest reference to ritual washing is at Mount Sinai, when Israel was told to "wash their clothes" (Exodus 19:10) before meeting God, a reminder of the gulf between them. Ritual cleansing found various expressions in the Law. For example:

- washing hands and feet by priests (Exodus 30:17–21);
- washing some sacrifices (e.g. Leviticus 1:9, 13) and blood-splattered priestly garments (Leviticus 6:27);
- washing after contact with death (Leviticus 11:24–25; 17:15; Numbers 19:11–13);
- washing in cases of leprosy (Leviticus 14:1–9);
- washing after bodily discharges (Leviticus 15).

Although some of these laws had hygienic purposes, their deeper significance was ritual purity, symbolic of the need for cleansing. Sadly, Israel elevated these external actions beyond the symbolic, as though performing them in themselves had intrinsic value.

See also
Food pp. 98–99
Sabbath p. 138
The Law pp. 134–35

Jewish man ritually washing his hands before praying at the Western Wall ("the Kotel") in Jerusalem.

Circumcision

In circumcision God took something that already existed and used it as the sign of the covenant with Abraham and his descendants (Genesis 17:9–14). Boys were circumcised when eight days old (Genesis 17:12), a timing later confirmed in the Law (Leviticus 12:3), though the descendants of Ishmael (the Arabs) were circumcised at thirteen like he was (Genesis 17:24–25). Circumcision became *the* sign of national identity, and those wanting to become part of Israel had to submit to it (e.g. Genesis 34:8–17), a belief that spilled over into the early church until challenged (e.g. Acts 15:5–21). For a photo of circumcision tools, see p. 88.

But not only did these rituals acquire intrinsic value, they also spread. For example, while priests had to wash before performing their duties (Exodus 40:13), by Jesus' day such ritual washings had become commonplace among all the devout, washing their hands first thing in the morning and before each meal. While the Law didn't require this, "the tradition of the elders" (Mark 7:5) had developed many regulations about how such things should be done. It was Jesus' failure to keep these rules that brought him into conflict with religious leaders, and he accused them of letting go of "the commands of God and… holding on to the traditions of men" (Mark 7:8). He stressed that it is what comes out of people's hearts rather than what goes into people's stomachs that makes them unclean (Mark 7:1–23).

Jesus' attitude

What were seen as key identity markers of first-century Judaism were often the very things that Jesus challenged, stressing that God's true people aren't characterized by externals like ritual washings (Mark 7:1–8), sabbath observance (e.g. Mark 2:23–28), or fasting (Mark 2:18–22). What mattered to God was the heart (Mark 7:14–23). Nevertheless, the New Testament constantly asserts that Jesus fulfilled all the true demands of the ritual Law through his death on the cross, which is why Christians are no longer bound by them (e.g. Ephesians 2:15; Colossians 2:14; Hebrews 10:1–14).

Faith idea: The heart

The Bible constantly underlines the importance of the heart, the very core of our being that makes us who we are – personality, mind, will, emotions, and affections. Both Old Testament prophets (e.g. 1 Samuel 15:22) and Jesus himself (e.g. Mark 7:1–23) stressed the priority of the heart over external observance. As Samuel said, "Man looks at the outward appearance, but the LORD looks at the heart" (1 Samuel 16:7).

A Jewish mezuzah
These wooden or metal cases, affixed to the front doorpost of Jewish homes, contain parchment inscribed with Deuteronomy 6:4–9 and 11.13–21 and are touched and kissed on entering and leaving. The Jewish historian Josephus (c. AD 37–100) spoke of it as an old and well-established custom even in his day. In post-New Testament times it was sometimes attributed with the power of warding off evil spirits.

Jewish Festivals and Holy Days

Celebrating God's Goodness

Celebrating festivals was an important part of Jewish faith, seen as God's gift to his people to help them remember his interventions in the past and rejoice in his blessings in the present. Almost all were associated with happiness and feasting.

Sabbath

The origins of the sabbath lie not in the Ten Commandments (Exodus 20:8–11), but in the creation story where, on day seven, God "rested from all his work. And God blessed the seventh day and made it holy" (Genesis 2:2–3). The word "rested" comes from the Hebrew root for "sabbath", thus establishing the divine pattern for healthy living: six days of work, followed by one day of rest. Sabbath, beginning just before sunset on Friday night and lasting until just after sunset on Saturday night, was marked as different by stopping all routine work so people could rest and be refreshed. While all other nations had annual festivals, only Israel had a weekly sabbath.

By New Testament times, sabbath-keeping had become burdensome, however, with endless rules defining what was and wasn't work. Religious leaders even objected to Jesus healing people; but he reminded them that "the Sabbath was made for man not man for the Sabbath" (Mark 2:27).

A Jewish mother lights the "Shabbat" candle, marking the beginning of sabbath.

The Jewish religious year

Passover (14 Abib/Nisan)
Through a family meal, Passover recalled God's deliverance of Israel from slavery in Egypt. Today various foods highlight different aspects of the story: a sweet paste represents the mud used to make bricks; salt water, their ancestors' tears; a hard-boiled egg, their hardship; bitter herbs, their bitter slavery; a lamb shank bone, the sacrificial lambs; unleavened bread, their hasty escape; and parsley, a sign of fresh hope.

See Exodus 12:1–30; Leviticus 23:5; Numbers 9:1–14; Deuteronomy 16:1–8.

Unleavened Bread (15–21 Abib)
Unleavened bread (bread without yeast) was eaten at Passover and throughout the following week to recall the hurried preparations when Pharaoh finally allowed the Israelites to leave Egypt.

See Exodus 12:15–20; 13:3–10; 23:15; Leviticus 23:6–8; Numbers 28:17–25; Deuteronomy 16:9–12.

Firstfruits (16 Abib)
This festival acknowledged God's provision by bringing the first sheaf from the barley harvest to the priest, who waved it before God and offered burnt and grain offerings.

See Leviticus 23:9–14.

Weeks/Pentecost (6 Sivan)
In this festival celebrating the wheat harvest, two loaves made from its flour were waved before God, and sacrifices were offered. It occurred fifty days after Passover, so was later called Pentecost (Greek for "fiftieth"). By New Testament times it also celebrated God's gift of the Law to Moses.

See Exodus 23:16; Leviticus 23:15–22; Numbers 28:26–31; Deuteronomy 16:9–12.

Trumpets/Rosh Hashanah/New Year (1 Tishri)
While trumpet-blasts marked the beginning of every month (important when calendars were unavailable), at the Feast of Trumpets many trumpets were blown to mark the end of the agricultural year and the start of a new year, celebrated with a day of rest. It was not until later times it was called Rosh Hashanah.

See Leviticus 23:23–25; Numbers 29:1–6.

Day of Atonement/Yom Kippur (10 Tishri)
On this solemn day, the whole nation fasted and offered sacrifices to atone for their sin. Wearing only a simple white linen garment, the high priest sacrificed a bull for his own sin and that of the priests, taking its blood into "the Holy of Holies", the most sacred

See also
A Year on the Land p. 96
Exodus pp. 26–27
Farming pp. 104–05

part of the tabernacle or Temple (the only occasion he could do this), where he sprinkled it on the ark. He then took a goat and sacrificed it for the people's sin, sprinkling some blood in the Holy of Holies and smearing some on the altar's horns to cleanse the sanctuary. Then he took a second goat, known as the "scapegoat", laid his hands on its head, confessed Israel's sin over it, and sent it off into the desert as a sign their sin had been taken away.

See Leviticus 16:1–34; 23:26–32; Numbers 29:7–11.

Tabernacles/Booths (15–21 Tishri)
During this week-long festival celebrating the climax of harvest, the Israelites lived in "booths" (shelters) to remember their journey to the Promised Land and God's bountiful provision. The festivities ended in "a day of solemn assembly". By New Testament times, this was one of the most popular festivals.

See Exodus 23:16; Leviticus 23:33–43; Numbers 29:12–40; Deuteronomy 16:13–15.

Sacred Assembly (22 Tishri)
This was a day of assembly, rest, and sacrifices to mark the close of the agricultural cycle of feasts.

See Leviticus 23:36; Numbers 29:35–38.

Hanukkah (25 Chislev)
Also called Dedication or the Festival of Lights, this festival from later Judaism celebrated the rededication of the Temple by Judas Maccabeus in 165 BC (see p. 40).

Purim (14–15 Adar)
This festival recalled the thwarting of attempts to exterminate the Jews in Persia. The story of Esther is read, people dress up as key figures in the story, and presents are exchanged.

See Esther 9:18–32

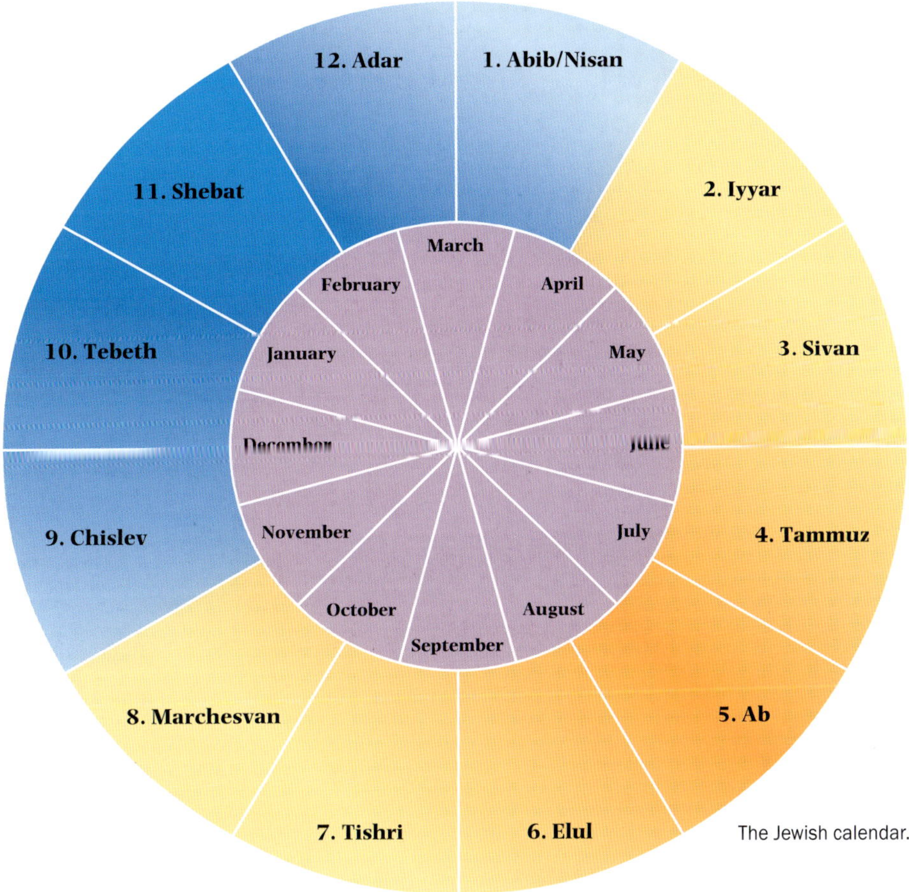

The Jewish calendar.

Christians and festivals

Some Jewish festivals were adopted by Christians. The **weekly day of rest** was continued, though changed from Saturday to Sunday ("the first day of the week", e.g. Acts 20:7) to celebrate Jesus' resurrection, which Christians believed gave them true "rest". **Passover** took on new meaning for them, recalling Christ's death on the cross, which brought a deliverance greater than that of Israel from Egypt. **Pentecost** came to mark the occasion of God's gift of his Holy Spirit, transforming dispirited disciples into an empowered church (Acts 2:1–47). The keeping of other Jewish festivals or special days was seen purely as a matter of personal preference (e.g. Colossians 2:16–23; Romans 14:5–23).

The three great festivals

Passover, Pentecost, and Tabernacles were three festivals for which all Jewish men had to appear before God in the Temple (Deuteronomy 16:16).

A *shofar*, ready for use at a wedding. Made from a ram's horn, this ceremonial instrument recalls God's promise to Abraham when he provided a ram to sacrifice instead of his son (Genesis 22:1–19).

Faith idea: Remembrance

Festivals and holy days built into life a pattern of remembrance to ensure God's people stayed mindful of the past, grateful for the present, and trusting for the future. For Christians their key remembrance event is Holy Communion (also called the Lord's Supper or Mass), when they remember through bread and wine Christ's sacrifice on the cross and his promise to come again.

Worship

Honouring God

While the expression of worship changed over the biblical period, the heart of it remained the same: honouring the God who made us and joyfully responding to his blessings. Yet there is no suggestion in the Bible that God "needs" people's worship, as though he were insecure or somehow the less if he didn't receive it. Worship adds nothing to God, but it adds much to the worshippers, reminding them of who they are and of their dependence on him.

Worship anywhere

In the early parts of the Bible, there were no set places for worship. Adam and Eve enjoyed God's presence in the Garden of Eden; the patriarchs worshipped God wherever they were in the open air; Moses worshipped God at a burning bush and on a mountaintop. Sometimes standing stones or altars were erected where memorable spiritual experiences had happened; but it was only later that particular places acquired special significance, like Shiloh where the tabernacle was erected, or Jerusalem where the Temple was built. Sadly such sanctuaries often became the objects of people's confidence, rather than the God they pointed to, as the prophets exposed (e.g. Jeremiah 7:1–15). Christians rediscovered that true worship isn't dependent on a special or particular place, just like Jesus said (John 4:21–24). As Paul put it, "The God who made the world and everything in it is the Lord of heaven and earth and does not live in temples built by human hands" (Acts 17:24).

Expressions of worship

There are many different expressions of worship in the Bible, including:

- praying (e.g. Acts 2:42; Revelation 8:3)
- singing (e.g. 2 Chronicles 5:13–14; Ephesians 5:19)
- music (e.g. 2 Samuel 6:5; 1 Chronicles 6:31–32)
- dancing (e.g. Exodus 15:20; Luke 15:25)
- silence (e.g. Psalm 4:3–4; Revelation 8:1)
- sacrifices (e.g. Genesis 46:1; 1 Kings 8:62–64)
- breaking bread (e.g. Acts 20:7; 1 Corinthians 10:16–17; 11:23–34)
- fasting (e.g. Nehemiah 1:4; Matthew 6:16–18).

A sistrum. This example comes from Egypt, 12th–10th centuries BC.

Instruments

The first biblical reference to musical instruments is in Genesis 4:21, where Jubal is described as "the father of all who play the harp and flute". While few relics of ancient instruments have been found, the Psalms attest to their varied use, and King David appointed 4,000 Levites as Temple musicians (1 Chronicles 23:5). Biblical instruments included:

- **Stringed instruments**, like the 8–10 stringed *kinnor* (lyre) and 10–20 stringed *navel* (harp).
- **Percussion instruments**, like the *timbrel* (made of skin stretched across a hoop), *cymbals* (pairs of cup-like metal plates that were clashed together), and the *sistrum* (discs on metal rods that jingled when shaken).
- **Wind instruments**, like the *halil* (a reed instrument of wood or bone), the *qeren* (a wooden or metal horn), the *hazozra* (a straight metal trumpet), and the *shofar* (a ram's horn).

Bedouin musician playing the *rababa*, a one-stringed instrument.

See also
Places of Worship pp. 146–47
Prayer pp. 142–43
Sacrifice pp. 148–49

Olive wood carving of the Last Supper.

Sharing bread and wine

The night before his execution Jesus shared the Passover meal with his disciples. But changing the traditional wording over the bread and wine, he gave the meal a whole new meaning, placing himself at the centre of Israel's story. Through him, he was saying, the new exodus that Israel had been longing for was about to begin, and the promised new covenant was about to be made, bringing forgiveness of sins (Matthew 26:28). The early church placed sharing bread and wine at the heart of their worship (Acts 2:42; 20:7; 1 Corinthians 11:23–34), as Christians still do when they "do this in remembrance of me" (Luke 22:19). It has different names (the Lord's Supper, Holy Communion, Breaking of Bread, the Mass) and is celebrated in different styles, from the very informal to the highly ritualistic.

The Psalms

Psalms is the Bible's hymnbook, its Hebrew title *Tehillim* ("Songs of Praise") highlighting that they were originally songs to be sung, not prayers to be prayed. The title "Psalms" comes from the Greek title *Psalmos* ("Music Played on Instruments").

King David is associated with seventy-three psalms, while the rest were written over a period of 1,000 years, between the time of Moses (Psalm 90) and the return from exile (Psalm 137). Some are corporate, expressing worship or remembering God's intervention in history; others are personal, expressing love for God, sorrow for sin, struggle in difficulties, even anger towards others. Some, like "the Songs of Ascent" (Psalms 120–134), were written for pilgrims as they travelled to Jerusalem, while the *Hallel* ("Praise") Psalms (113–118) were sung at festivals. The Temple would have been full of the sound of the Levitical choirs singing psalms each day, accompanying the morning and evening sacrifices, as well as at processions and assemblies.

Faith idea: Praise

The Bible says that praise is the appropriate human response to God, both in terms of expressing gratitude for his goodness and honouring him for who he is. It also records examples of how praise reversed impossible situations, like Joshua's victory at Jericho (Joshua 6:20), Jehoshaphat's defeat of Moab and Ammon (2 Chronicles 20:15–30), and the collapse of the walls of the jail holding Paul and Silas (Acts 16:25–34).

New Testament worship

The first Christians initially continued to worship at the Temple but supplemented this with meetings in homes (Acts 2:47) that had four main elements: the apostles' teaching, fellowship, breaking bread, and prayer (Acts 2:42). Many Jewish Christians elsewhere initially attended their local synagogue, whose service (comprising Scripture reading, prayer, and a sermon) formed the model for Christian services. Gentile converts had a more informal worship style with plural, spontaneous participation led by the Holy Spirit (1 Corinthians 14:26–40), though even here the Lord's Supper remained a central feature (1 Corinthians 11:17–34).

Christian creeds and hymns

The New Testament church believed certain fixed truths about their faith that were not just written in the New Testament documents but were also recited as creeds (statements of faith) or sung as hymns. Examples include:

- Jesus is Lord! (1 Corinthians 12:3; Philippians 2:11).
- One Lord, one faith, one baptism, one God and father of all, who is over all and through all and in all (Ephesians 4:5).
- There is one God and one mediator between God and men, the man Christ Jesus, who gave himself as a ransom for all men (1 Timothy 2:5).
- He appeared in a body, was vindicated by the Spirit, was seen by angels, was preached among the nations, was believed on in the world, was taken up in glory (1 Timothy 3:16).

The fullest creedal statement or hymn is in Philippians 2:5–11, which expresses Christ's incarnation, humiliation, and exaltation.

Prayer

Talking to God

Prayer in the Bible isn't seen as the recitation of religious formulas, but rather as conversation with God out of relationship with him. People genuinely believed, and experienced, that prayer made a difference; so we find hundreds of references to people praying and dozens of prayers recorded, some short, some long. But common to them all was a conviction that God hears and answers when we talk to him.

Prayer in the Old Testament

Prayer in the Old Testament ranges from the prayers of individuals in personal need, to the prayers of prophets and kings in times of national need. But not all prayer was need-orientated. Much expressed thanksgiving, worship, or recollection of God's past interventions. As well as spontaneous prayers, more formal prayers for set occasions are also recorded, and many of these are found in the Psalms. The content of some psalms seems shocking at first, like asking God to smash your enemy's teeth. But such prayers recorded what people felt, not what God himself felt. Their inclusion in the Bible is meant to show that people can be honest in prayer and that God is big enough to cope with even their darkest thoughts.

During the exile, daily prayer acquired new importance for the Jews since they could no longer worship in the Temple. By New Testament times there were three set times of prayer: the third hour (9 a.m.), the ninth hour when the evening sacrifice was offered (3 p.m.), and sunset.

Postures for prayer

The Bible records a variety of ways in which people prayed, suggesting there is no "right" way of doing it. Postures include:

- sitting (e.g. Nehemiah 1:4; Luke 10:13)
- standing (e.g. 1 Kings 8:22; Mark 11:25)
- kneeling (e.g. Ezra 9:5; Acts 9:40)
- bowing (e.g. Exodus 34:8–9; Matthew 2:11)
- prostrating (e.g. Joshua 5:13–14; Luke 17:15–16)
- lifting hands (e.g. Exodus 17:10–16; 1 Timothy 2:8).

A Jewish man praying, wearing the prayer-shawl (*tallith*) with its distinctive stripes and tassels – here in black, though often in blue or a combination of both colours. God had told the Jews to wear tassels to remember they were his people (Numbers 15:38–39), but by Jesus' time, the Pharisees wore extra-long tassels as an ostentatious mark of piety, which Jesus rebuked (Matthew 23:5). The man is also wearing phylacteries (*tefillin*), bound to his left arm and forehead. These black boxes, containing Scripture, are worn in literal fulfilment of God's command to remember his commands and to "tie them as symbols on your hands and bind them on your foreheads" (Deuteronomy 6:8).

See also
Sacrifice pp. 148–49
The Supernatural pp. 144–45
Worship pp. 140–41

Prayer and the early church

Prayer played a fundamental role in the early church's life from its very beginnings and was found at every key point of its life (e.g. Acts 1:14, 24–26; 2:42; 3:1; 4:23–31; 6:1–6). Paul was a man of prayer, no doubt rooted in his Pharisaic background; yet his relationship with Jesus brought new life to his praying, and some of his letters contain wonderful prayers (e.g. Ephesians 1:15–23; 3:14–21; Philippians 1.3–10, Colossians 1:9–14).

Jesus and prayer

Prayer played a key role in Jesus' life, and he took whatever steps were needed to spend time talking to his heavenly Father, whether getting up early in the morning (Mark 1:35), or staying awake at night (Mark 14:32–42), or getting away from everyone (Mark 6:45–46). For Jesus, prayer was simply conversation with his heavenly Father, so needed no special places, no special rituals, and no special language. He encouraged people to pray simply (Matthew 6:5–8), with faith (Matthew 7:7–11), and not to give up (Luke 18:1–8). He said God had little time for religious people who made a great show of their prayers, but had a big heart for people who humbly threw themselves on his mercy (Luke 18:9–14). His teaching on the simplicity and intimacy of prayer is best summed up in what has become known as the Lord's Prayer.

Prayer and fasting

Fasting is the practice of abstaining from food, partially or totally, for a period of time to devote oneself more fully to God and seek him in prayer. It is about "humbly submitting oneself to God" (the actual meaning of the Hebrew word "fast"), showing that nothing is more important than seeking him, not even eating.

Fasting is voluntary in Scripture, the only fast actually commanded being on the Day of Atonement (Leviticus 16:29–31). But after the exile other fasts were introduced: in the fourth month (to lament the destruction of Jerusalem's walls), the fifth month (to lament the Temple's destruction), the seventh month (to commemorate the assassination of Judah's governor), and the tenth month (to lament the siege of Jerusalem).

By Jesus' time, Judaism had made fasting a twice-weekly requirement for the devout (Luke 18:12) and it had become an outward demonstration of piety. Nevertheless Jesus still practised fasting (Matthew 4:1–2) and anticipated that his followers would, though with a different spirit (Matthew 6:16–18). The early church continued the practice (Acts 13:2–3; 14:23).

The Bible mentions several types of fast:

- **The normal fast** – abstaining from food, but not water (e.g. Luke 4:1–2), and generally lasting just one day, from sunrise to sunset (Judges 20:26), or a twenty-four-hour period (Leviticus 23:26–32).
- **The partial fast** – abstaining from particular foods for a period (e.g. Daniel 1:8–20).
- **The complete fast** – abstaining from both food and water in exceptional circumstances (e.g. Esther 4:15–16).
- **The special fast** – lasting forty days and found only at key times, like when Jesus faced Satan's temptations (Matthew 4:1–11), or when Moses received the Ten Commandments (Exodus 34:28).

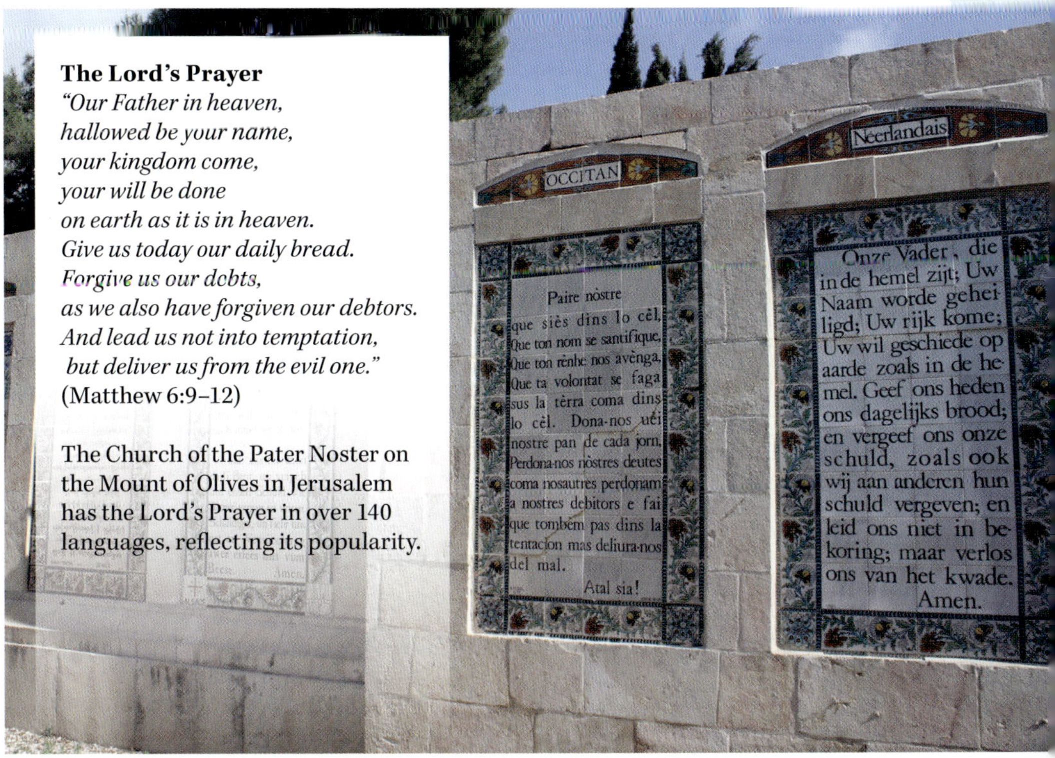

The Lord's Prayer

"Our Father in heaven,
hallowed be your name,
your kingdom come,
your will be done
on earth as it is in heaven.
Give us today our daily bread.
Forgive us our debts,
as we also have forgiven our debtors.
And lead us not into temptation,
but deliver us from the evil one."
(Matthew 6:9–12)

The Church of the Pater Noster on the Mount of Olives in Jerusalem has the Lord's Prayer in over 140 languages, reflecting its popularity.

Faith idea: God's fatherhood

At the heart of Jesus' praying was a conviction that God is a loving heavenly Father who knows people's needs before they even ask (Matthew 6:5–8) and who can be trusted (Matthew 7:9–11). God's fatherhood is not an anthropomorphism; he is not like *a father, the Bible says; he* is *a father – not in terms of procreation, but in terms of his love, provision, grace, and strong protection. It is confidence in knowing him as Father that increases confidence in prayer, Jesus said.*

The Supernatural

The World Beyond

While many Westerners are sceptical of claims of the miraculous or a "world beyond", dismissing such things as primitive superstition, the Bible takes it as a given that such a world not only exists, but that it affects this world too. Hence angels and demons, miracles, and signs aren't seen as unusual or unexpected, but wholly normal. Indeed non-supernatural faith is barely faith at all.

Miracles

In the Old Testament, miracles are relatively rare, generally confined to dark periods, like when Israel was enslaved in Egypt and the ten plagues challenged Pharaoh and his gods, or when Elijah and Elisha stood against the wickedness of Baal worship. By contrast, there is an outburst of miracles with the coming of Jesus – one-third of Mark concerns miracles, in fact. But these weren't designed to attract followers, or even primarily to express compassion. Jesus saw them as demonstrations of God's kingdom, showing how life is transformed when God rules.

Raising of the dead

The Bible's greatest supernatural events are people being raised from the dead, found in both the Old and New Testaments (e.g. 1 Kings 17:17–24; 2 Kings 4:8–37; Mark 5:21–42; John 11:1–44), underlining the Bible's conviction that death is not the end of life. The reality of the raising of Lazarus is reflected in how it provoked Jesus' opponents to get rid of him (John 11:45–57).

The central biblical event is Jesus' resurrection – seen not as mere resuscitation back to this life, but as transformation by God's power into a form suitable for life in his future kingdom. While challenging to modern thinking, the Bible is clear that "if Christ has not been raised, our preaching is useless and so is your faith" (1 Corinthians 15:14).

Dreams and visions

It was widely accepted in Bible times that God could speak through dreams. They are particularly common in the Old Testament (e.g. Genesis 28:12–22; 31:10–13; 37:5–11; 41:1–40; 1 Kings 3:5–15; Daniel 2:1–48), but are also found in the New Testament, especially around Jesus' birth where, through a dream, Mary's conceiving is explained to Joseph (Matthew 1:20), the Magi are warned not to return to Herod (2:12), and Joseph is given direction (2:13, 22). Visions are similar to dreams, except they occur while the recipient is awake (e.g. Genesis 15:1–21; 1 Samuel 3:1–18; Isaiah 1:1; Acts 9:10–16; 10:9–16). Peter reminded his Pentecost audience that renewed dreams and visions were a consequence of the outpouring of God's Spirit (Acts 2:17).

Angels

Though generally portrayed in art with wings, angels in the Bible are much more "human", at times even being mistaken for people, though they are spirit-beings; and they never have wings, something that only cherubim (Ezekiel 10:3–5) and seraphim (Isaiah 6:2), higher ranks of angels, have. The word "angel" means "messenger", for their role was to bring God's message (e.g. Luke 1:26–38), though also his blessing (Genesis 24:40), intervention (Genesis 22:9–12), help (Daniel 6:22), protection (Psalm 91:11), direction (Acts 8:26), and even judgment (Genesis 19:1–29). Jesus said that even children, not always esteemed in the ancient world, have guardian angels (Matthew 18:10).

Despite the importance of angels, they were not to be worshipped, and when angel worship crept into the church in Colosse – under the

See also
God pp. 130–31
Jesus: His Miracles pp. 174–75
Jesus: His Resurrection pp. 184–85

influence of Gnostic-like cults that believed God's transcendence meant he could only be worshipped through intermediaries – Paul quickly corrected it (Colossians 2:18).

Satan

Three Bible passages provide some insights into the origins of Satan. **Ezekiel**, prophesying against the king of Tyre (chapter 28), suddenly moves from describing the king and his pride (verses 1–10) to describing the one who stood behind his actions, who was there in the Garden of Eden (verses 11–15), who was a "guardian cherub" (verse 14) and "blameless" (verse 15), but whose pride led to his eviction "from the mount of God" (verses 16–17). Likewise **Isaiah**, prophesying about the king of Assyria, saw the "morning star" ("Lucifer" in the Latin Vulgate translation) at work behind him, and the pride that brought about his wanting equality with God which led to his expulsion (Isaiah 14:12–15). Finally, **John** saw "an enormous red dragon" being cast out of heaven, taking with him one-third of the angels (Revelation 12:1–6). From early times many Christians have seen these as descriptions of Satan's fall, the fall of one who was once one of the highest angels, but who became proud, wanting to rival God, and who was therefore cast out of heaven.

While Satan appears rarely in the Old Testament, and is even of little interest, the coming of Jesus seemed to provoke an outbreak of his activity. Jesus overcame him simply with the word of God (Matthew 4:1–11), and Paul urged Christians to resist him with the spiritual armour God provides (Ephesians 6:10–18).

A bronze statue of Pazuzu, an Assyrian and Babylonian demon, whose image was engraved on amulets to protect the wearer from other demons.

Demons

Demons are fallen angels, the Bible seems to suggest – though since John saw only a third of the "stars" (angels) being taken by Satan (Revelation 12:3–4), that means they are well outnumbered. Though powerful, they are seen as subject to God, with even Satan having to get permission to test Job (Job 1:6–12). This contrasted strongly with contemporary worldviews, like the Babylonian belief that demons were constantly waiting to pounce on people at any moment. While some demons work wickedly on earth, reflected in the deliverance miracles of Jesus, others are confined to spiritual dungeons (2 Peter 2:4; Jude 6), though the final defeat of all is assured (Revelation 12:7–12).

Forbidden practices

While utterly open to the supernatural world, the Bible says some expressions of contacting that world are dangerous and forbidden by God (e.g. Deuteronomy 18:9–13).

These occult practices included:

- **Magic or sorcery**: trying to manipulate the gods through spells, chants, curses, etc.
- **Divination**: trying to discover the gods' will through consulting animals' livers, or looking for unpredictable events, like unusual flights of birds.
- **Astrology**: seeking guidance from the movement of the stars, seen as linked to the gods. Babylonian astrologers first worked out the zodiac.
- **Spiritism**: trying to contact the dead or the spirit-world.

Faith idea: Lordship

For Christians, Jesus' supernatural miracles demonstrate his lordship – his absolute supremacy – over every aspect of life, both physical (reflected in his healings) and spiritual (reflected in his casting out demons). A central Christian belief is that we enjoy life at its best when we engage with the supernatural through acknowledging Jesus as Lord, letting him rule every part of life.

Places of Worship

The God Who Cannot be Contained

When King Solomon dedicated the Temple, he prayed, "But will God really dwell on earth? The heavens, even the highest heaven, cannot contain you. How much less this temple I have built!" (1 Kings 8:27). He recognized that God needed no "house" for people to worship him, not even one as splendid as this; for God could be found and worshipped anywhere.

The ark of the covenant
The ark of the covenant (Exodus 25:10–22), Israel's most holy artefact, was an acacia-wood box measuring 4x2x2 feet (1.2x0.6x0.6 m) covered with gold and containing the Ten Commandments (Exodus 40:20; Deuteronomy 10:5), a jar of manna, and Aaron's rod that had budded (Hebrews 9:4) – symbols of God's word, provision, and power. It had poles through rings at each corner for the Levites to carry it when Israel moved camp. Its cover, "the mercy seat", had two gold cherubim with outstretched wings, symbolizing God's protecting presence.

Places of encounter

Early Israelite religion had no special places of worship, for the patriarchs believed God could be worshipped anywhere. While certain places came to be seen as "holy" through their association with God's intervention or revelation – like the great trees at Mamre (Genesis 13:18; 18:1) or Jacob's stone at Bethel (Genesis 28:10–22) – such places served merely as reminders of what God had done, never as places that "contained" God.

The tabernacle

The tabernacle was the first real focus of Israelite corporate worship. Measuring 45x15x15 feet (13.7x4.5x4.5 m) and erected at the heart of their camp, it symbolized how God would "tabernacle" ("dwell") among them, providing a focus for worship and sacrifice on their journey from Mount Sinai to the Promised Land.

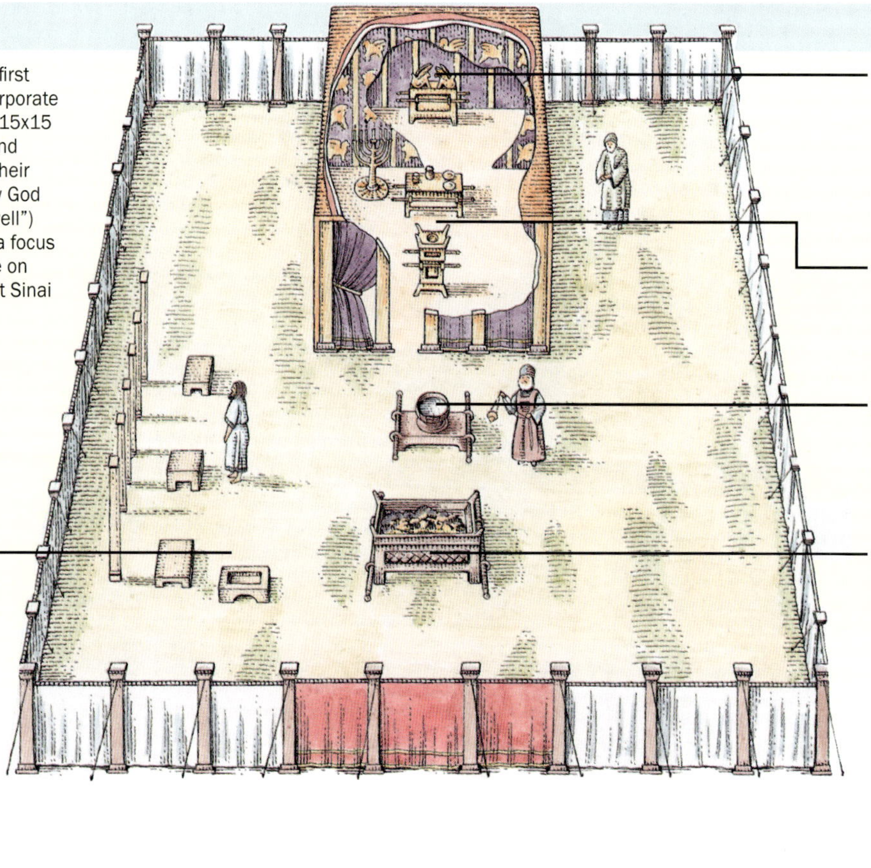

Holy of Holies, containing the ark of the covenant, separated from the Holy Place by a curtain. Only the high priest could enter on the annual Day of Atonement.

Holy Place, containing a golden lampstand (menorah), golden incense altar, and golden table for twelve loaves.

Bronze laver, used by priests for washing before offering sacrifices.

Outer court (150x75 feet or 45.7x22.8 m), formed by a high linen screen.

Bronze altar (7½ feet square x 4½ feet high, or 2.2 m square x 1.3 m high), used for daily morning and afternoon sacrifices.

See also
Priests pp. 148–49
Sacrifice pp. 148–49
Worship pp. 140–41

Solomon's Temple

Solomon's Temple was Israel's first permanent place of worship. Taking seven years to build, it followed the pattern of Canaanite temples because of the Phoenician artisans he used. Priests entered through a large porch, with freestanding pillars on either side, which led into the Holy Place, beyond which lay the Holy of Holies with the ark of the covenant. While the Holy Place was illuminated by candles and light from high windows, the Holy of Holies was completely dark.

This Temple stood from 960 to 586 BC, when the Babylonians besieged Jerusalem, destroying it and removing its treasures. While rumours abound about the ark of the covenant, it was probably taken to Babylon as a trophy or melted down. A second Temple was rebuilt after the exile, though on a much smaller scale, grieving those who remembered the magnificent original Temple (Ezra 3:8–13).

1. Temple, measuring 90x30 feet and 45 feet high (27.4x9.1x13.71 m high) and standing on a raised plinth. Only the priests entered the Temple; ordinary people gathered outside.

2. Entrance porch, measuring 15x30 feet (4.5x9.1 m), with two huge freestanding pillars.

3. Holy Place, lined with carved cedar panels, containing ten golden lampstands, a golden incense altar, and a golden table for the holy bread.

4. Holy of Holies, with walls covered with gold and containing the ark of the covenant.

5. Store rooms surrounding the Temple on three floors.

6. Bronze laver for washing, supported by twelve bronze bulls.

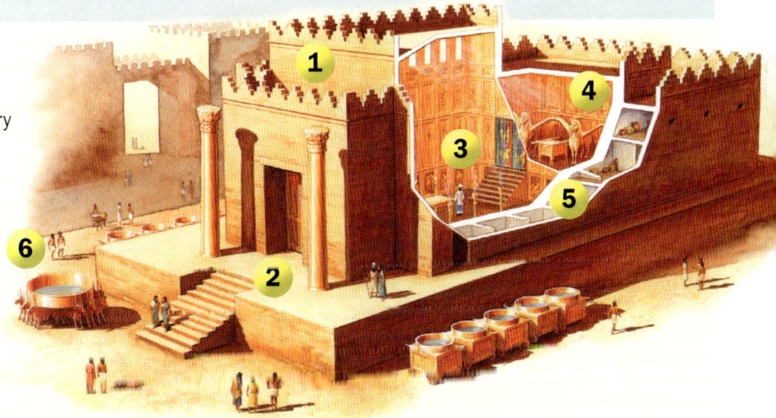

Herod's Temple

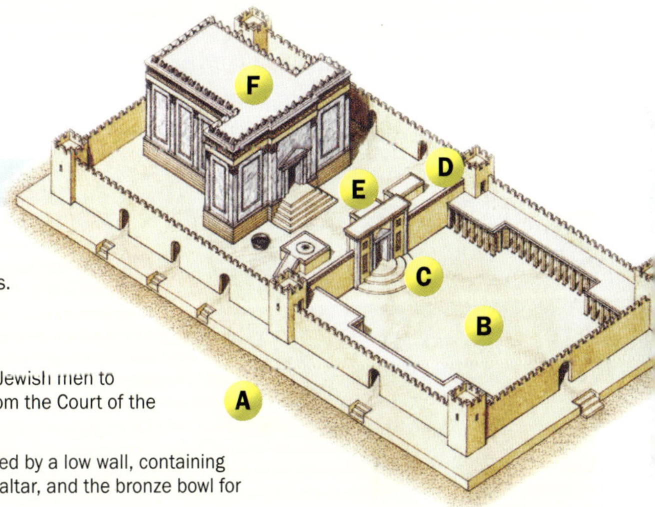

Of Herod's many building projects, his greatest was the rebuilding of the Temple. Begun in 20 BC and not finished until AD 64, long after his death, it was meant to win over his subjects and impress Rome, but did neither. His subjects hated him because he was an Idumean, and Rome destroyed the Temple in AD 70 at the end of the Jewish rebellion. All that remains today is the western retaining wall of the Temple platform, known by Jews as "the Kotel". The site now contains a mosque, a source of great contention between Jews and Muslims.

A. Court of the Gentiles, the furthest Gentiles could go. Jesus removed merchants and moneychangers trading here because they hindered the Gentiles from praying (Matthew 21:12–17; John 2:12–25).

B. Court of the Women, where thirteen trumpet-like moneyboxes collected donations.

C. Nicanor Gate, reached by fifteen steps.

D. Court of Israel, reserved for Jewish men to present sacrifices, separated from the Court of the Priests by a low barrier.

E. Court of the Priests, separated by a low wall, containing the places for slaughtering, the altar, and the bronze bowl for ritual washings.

F. Temple Sanctuary, containing the Holy Place and, behind a heavy curtain, the Holy of Holies.

The synagogue

Synagogues originated during the Babylonian exile when, with Jerusalem distant and the Temple destroyed, Jews needed a new focus for preserving their beliefs. The synagogue (Greek for "gathering") met that need, as Jews simply gathered together, often in the open air. Synagogue buildings had seating on all sides, with a single door that often faced Jerusalem.

The synagogue wasn't a place for sacrifice – something later Judaism believed could only be done in the Temple – but for Scripture-reading, sermons, and prayer. More than anything else the synagogue helped preserve Jewish identity during the exile.

Christian places of worship

Jewish Christians initially continued to meet in synagogues, while those in Jerusalem met in the Temple courtyards (Acts 2:46). But from the beginning, the relational nature of their faith meant the most common meeting places were homes (Acts 2:46), where worship happened in the context of a meal and genuine fellowship. Homes played a key role in the Gentile mission (e.g. Acts 16:15; 18:26; 21:16). It wasn't until Emperor Constantine's conversion in AD 312 and his legalization of Christianity the following year that Christians started to have buildings of their own in which to worship.

Faith idea: Church

While we often use the word "church" to mean a religious building, this wasn't how the New Testament used it. For early Christians, "church" (Greek, ekklesia*) always meant the people, never the place, just like in the Septuagint, the Greek Old Testament, where the word meant "assembly". The first Christians were returning to the heart of patriarchal faith, with its conviction that God could be worshipped anywhere, and that sanctuaries were therefore unnecessary.*

Sacrifices and Priests

Renewing Relationship

Virtually every ancient civilization practised sacrifice, hoping to appease the gods or win their favour. But Israel saw sacrifice differently. Sacrifice was not their gift to God, but God's gift to them (Leviticus 17:11). Whereas Adam and Eve had tried to hide their sin (Genesis 3:7–11), the sacrificial system enabled people to face up to it as the essential prerequisite for renewing fellowship with God.

The process of sacrifice

There were three key elements to Jewish sacrifice:

1. The sinner
You had to acknowledge your sin by laying your hand on the animal's head, thereby acknowledging that you were the sinner and deserved to die, but imploring God to accept this substitute instead. The priest didn't kill the animal, but you yourself did (e.g. Leviticus 1:3–5), though eventually this changed, probably after the exile.

2. The sacrifice
The sacrifice was always an animal, for the Law forbade human sacrifices (Leviticus 20:1–5) – though sadly some kings, influenced by foreign practices, ignored this (e.g. 2 Kings 21:1–6). The animal had to be male, since these were the most expensive, underlining that dealing with sin wasn't a cheap matter, and perfect, for only the best was good enough for God.

3. The priest
While you yourself slaughtered the animal, you couldn't offer your sacrifice. This task was reserved for the priest, demonstrating the necessity of an intermediary between sinful people and a holy God. As you slit the animal's throat, the priest caught its blood in a bowl and took it to the altar on your behalf (e.g. Leviticus 1:5).

Priests and Levites

Priests traced their origins to Aaron, Moses' brother, and his four sons, whose descendants alone could succeed them. To reflect the holiness of their duties, God gave detailed regulations concerning both their dress and their work, which included teaching God's Law, acting as judges and public health inspectors, and seeking God's will through the Urim and Thummim stones, as well as offering sacrifices.

Levites were appointed to assist the priests as a result of their zeal at the golden calf incident (Exodus 32:25–29). Their duties were distributed between Levi's three sons and their descendants (Numbers 3:14–20): *Gershonites* were responsible for the tabernacle's curtains, coverings, and cords; *Koathites* for its contents, like the ark and other artefacts; and *Merarites* for the outer structures of its enclosure (Numbers 3:21–37).

A tenth-century BC altar from Beersheba. The horns were where the blood was smeared to effect cleansing (Exodus 29:12), though in some sacrifices it was sprinkled on the altar's sides (Leviticus 5:5). The horns also provided sanctuary for anyone grasping them (1 Kings 1:50–53).

Altars were to be made of uncut stone (Exodus 20:25), perhaps to reflect their sanctity. While this was followed in the early Israelite period (Deuteronomy 27:5; Joshua 8:31), it wasn't always followed later (e.g. 1 Kings 6:7), as in the example below.

See also
Jesus' Death pp. 184–85
Places of Worship pp. 146–47
Sanitation pp. 94–95

Old Testament offerings

Name	References	Elements	Purpose
Burnt offering	Leviticus 1; 6:8–13; 8:18–21; 16:24	Bull, ram, dove, or pigeon.	To atone for unintentional sin. Offered morning and evening for all Israel (Exodus 29:38–42). Could be offered by individuals to express thanksgiving and dedication.
Grain offering	Leviticus 2; 6:14–23; Numbers 28:12–13	Fine flour, oil, and incense; could be baked into cakes.	The only bloodless offering, used along with burnt, fellowship, and sin offerings. To recognize God's goodness and provision.
Fellowship (or peace) offering	Leviticus 3; 7:11–34	Any animal from herd or flock.	To re-establish friendship with God and others. The only sacrifice where the worshipper could eat part of it.
Sin offering	Leviticus 4:1 – 5:13; 6:24–30; 8:14–17; 16:3–22; Numbers 15:22–29	Bull (for priests), male goat (for leaders), female goat or lamb (for Israelites), dove or pigeon (for the poor), fine flour (for the very poor).	To atone for unintentional sin (there was no provision for dealing with wilful sin, Numbers 15:30–31). Offered where restitution was impossible. While the previous three offerings were voluntary, this was compulsory.
Guilt offering	Leviticus 5:14 – 6:7; 7:1–6	Ram or lamb.	Offered where restitution was possible and therefore required, e.g. stolen property had to be returned with 20 per cent of its value added.

Where more than one offering was required, the order was always: first, the sin or guilt offering; second, the burnt offering; third, the fellowship and grain offering. This order underlined that sin had to be dealt with first and recommitment to God made before fellowship with him and others could be re-established.

The priests' garments

The high priest:
Robe, made of blue cloth with bells on the hem to announce his entry into the tabernacle.
Ephod, made from gold, blue, purple, and scarlet yarns. Two onyx stones, engraved with the twelve tribes' names, were fastened to its straps, allowing him to symbolically bring them before God.
Breastpiece, containing twelve precious stones, one for each tribe, attached by a braided gold chain, with a pouch containing the Urim and Thummim.
Turban, with a gold plate inscribed with the words "Holy to the LORD".

Priests:
Ordinary priests wore simple outfits of linen tunics, sashes, and headbands.

Faith idea: Atonement

Atonement comes from a Hebrew root meaning "to cover". The Bible says it is only as our sins are "covered" or "dealt with" that sinners can approach a holy God. The New Testament teaches that Jesus fulfilled every aspect of Old Testament sacrifice, providing the perfect substitutionary sacrifice that made it possible for him, God's Son, to "make atonement for the sins of the people" (Hebrews 2:17; see also Romans 3:23–25).

Christians and sacrifice

Considering the centrality of sacrifice in Judaism, it is staggering that Christians so quickly believed that Jesus had completely fulfilled and superseded it. They claimed he had fulfilled the three elements of a sacrifice: he had taken the place of the sinner, had offered himself as the sacrifice, and had acted as the priest. Hebrews in particular, written for Christians from a Jewish background, explores these themes in depth, concluding that Old Testament sacrifices were simply "shadows" (Hebrews 10:1), pointing to the reality of Christ's sacrificial death that alone cleanses, opens the way to God, and makes all other sacrifices redundant.

Carving of the *Agnus Dei* (Latin for "Lamb of God"). This representation of Jesus as the sacrificial lamb has been part of Christian iconography from earliest times. From the Middle Ages it included a banner with a red cross resting on the lamb's shoulder, representing the blood he shed to atone for human sin.

Prophecy and Prophets

Bringing God's Word

Throughout the Bible there is a conviction that, unlike pagan gods, Israel's God was a God who speaks. By contrast, idols are mocked as having "mouths, but cannot speak, eyes, but they cannot see; they have ears, but cannot hear" (Psalm 135:16–17). But Israel's God was a speaking God, and it was through the prophets that his message came.

What is prophecy?

Prophecy is speaking a message directly from God. This doesn't mean prophets were seen as some kind of divine loudspeaker, their personality and thinking bypassed as God "took them over" – something reflected in the prophets' very different language and style (contrast the rough style of a country boy like Elijah with the polished court language of Isaiah). Peter explained its operation like this: "Prophecy never had its origin in the will of man, but men spoke from God as they were carried along by the Holy Spirit" (2 Peter 1:21). The expression "carried along" was used of a ship's sail catching the wind. Peter was saying that the prophets "hoisted their sail of faith" to catch the wind of God's Spirit, which led their thinking in exactly the direction that God wanted it led, but without squashing their approach or personality. This explains why they were all so different and why, unlike pagan prophecy, true Israelite prophecy wasn't "ecstatic" but under the prophet's control, as Paul reminded Christians in New Testament times (1 Corinthians 14:29–33).

The prophets' message

In Old Testament times, prophecy had two main aspects – forthtelling (declaring God's truth) and foretelling (declaring God's plans). There were three focal points to their message:

- **God**, who alone was Creator, Redeemer, Lord of history, Covenant-Maker, Protector, and Provider. In the light of this, the prophets challenged apostasy, idolatry, ingratitude, and lack of faith.
- **Israel**, which was called to live differently in order to show God to the nations. In the light of this, the prophets challenged social and legal injustice.
- **The land**, held in trust by Israel on God's behalf. In the light of this, the prophets challenged land abuses, politics and economics run for the benefit of the wealthy, and arrogance that thought Israel had an automatic right to blessing.

In short, every aspect of life, personal and national, was covered by the prophets' ministry.

Between the Old and New Testaments, however, there was prophetic silence, the last recorded canonical prophecy coming from Malachi (c. 440 BC). God's people had stopped listening, so God stopped speaking. Not until the coming of John the Baptist and Jesus was there an outbreak of prophecy once again (Luke 1:67–79; 2:28–38; 3:1–20), preparing for the new Messianic Age.

New Testament prophecy

In New Testament times, prophecy underwent a significant change. With Israel no longer a theocratic nation, the national aspects of the prophets' work diminished. But Joel had prophesied that one day God's Spirit would be given, not just to special people, but to everyone, with the consequence that "your sons and daughters will prophesy, your old men will dream dreams, your young men will see visions" (Joel 2:28, quoted by Peter at Pentecost, Acts 2:17). With the gift now broadened – so much so that Paul could say, "You

Prophetic delivery

While most prophecies were delivered as addresses, some were brought in other ways, including: parables (e.g. 2 Samuel 12:1–14), song (e.g. Isaiah 5), letter (e.g. Jeremiah 29:1–23), drama (e.g. Ezekiel 4–5), and symbolic actions (e.g. Jeremiah's buying of a field, Jeremiah 32).

Mount Carmel, where Elijah won a prayer contest with the prophets of Baal, leading to their destruction and the release again of rain on the land (1 Kings 18:16–46).

See also
Elijah and Elisha p. 34
Malachi p. 39
The Supernatural pp. 144–45

can all prophesy" (1 Corinthians 14:31) – its purpose also broadened, focusing on "strengthening, encouragement, and comfort" (1 Corinthians 14:3).

The prophets' settings

Setting the prophets against their historical background is crucial to understanding their message. This chart shows their most commonly accepted dates and settings.

Israel		Judah	
Elijah	875–848		
Elisha	848–797		
Jonah	785–775		
Amos	760–750		
Hosea	750–715	**Micah**	**750–686**
		Isaiah (of Jerusalem)	740–682
		Nahum	663–612
		Zephaniah	640–609
		Jeremiah	626–585
		Habakkuk	c. 605
		Obadiah	605?

Exile

Jeremiah	585– (in Egypt)
Ezekiel	593–571
Daniel	605–530

Isaiah (of Babylon) mid sixth-century.

(Some scholars think a disciple of Isaiah – "Isaiah of Babylon" – wrote chapters 40 onwards because of their different tone, but this is largely based on their rejection of the possibility of long-range prophecy. The consistency of style suggests one single author.)

Restoration

Haggai	520
Zechariah	520–480
Malachi	440–430

Uncertain

Joel (anywhere between 835 and 515!)

Ezekiel had been looking forward to becoming a priest, but then he was suddenly exiled to Babylon where, through an amazing vision, he was called to be a prophet (Ezekiel 1:1 – 3:15). While much of his message prophesied judgment, he nevertheless extended hope for the future, seeing in his vision of the valley of dry bones that God would rebuild Judah out of the dry bones it had become (37:1–14).

False prophets

Because the prophet had such influence, there was great concern that people should not be led astray by false prophets, those who "fill you with false hopes. They speak visions from their own minds, not from the mouth of the LORD" (Jeremiah 23:16). Moses legislated for this, outlining in Deuteronomy 18:14–22 three types of prophecy and how to handle them:

- **True prophecy** (vv. 18–19), characterized by bringing God's word. Such prophecy is to be accepted.
- **False prophecy** (v. 20), characterized by presumptuous speech or words in the name of another god. Prophet to be stoned.
- **Wrong prophecy** (vv. 21–22), characterized by the prophet thinking he had God's word, but he didn't, and so it didn't come true. Such prophets were not to be stoned, simply ignored and not feared.

The New Testament too underlined the importance of testing prophecy (1 Corinthians 14:29), stressing it is the content of a prophetic word, not its delivery, that determines its truthfulness (1 Corinthians 12:1–3).

Faith idea: Hearing God

While only special people heard God speak in Old Testament times, Joel said that a characteristic of the Messianic Age would be that ordinary believers would hear him in a variety of ways (Joel 2:28). The repeated call in Revelation – "He who has an ear, let him hear what the Spirit says to the churches" – shows the New Testament's conviction that hearing God's Spirit remains a reality for those who will take the time to listen.

Groups and Sects

A Divided People

The late second century BC saw the rise of several religious and political parties in Palestine. It would be these groups, rather than the secular authorities, that would oppose Jesus and his message of God's radical kingdom, for they disliked what he said about the way that kingdom was coming. So they conspired to get rid of him.

Hasidim

The Hasidim ("pious ones") weren't an organized sect but rather pious, faithful, Law-keeping Jews who resisted the attempts of Alexander the Great and his successors to Hellenize the Jewish way of life and culture. In the second century BC some of them joined the Maccabees in their armed resistance, and it was from such groups that both the Pharisees and Essenes emerged.

Caves near Qumran in which were found the Dead Sea Scrolls, copied by the Essene community there. See p. 20.

Pharisees

The Pharisees were the largest religious group in New Testament times, though still only numbering around 6,000. The name (probably meaning "separatists") was originally given derogatively when they were expelled from the Sanhedrin under John Hyrcanus (135–104 BC), but later acquired a positive sense of those who separated themselves from ritual uncleanness. Being a Pharisee wasn't a job (most were middle-class merchants), but rather a way of life. They believed that scrupulous obedience to God's Law was the duty of every Jew, and they led by example, not only keeping the 613 commandments the rabbis had identified in that Law, but also a host of additional oral traditions based upon it that had been developed over generations that applied the ancient Law to current life. These were known as "the tradition of the elders" (Mark 7:3–5) or the *Halakah* (Hebrew for "walk").

While often parodied as hypocrites concerned only with externals, their stress on purity and obedience wasn't an end in itself but, in their eyes, something crucial to maintaining Israel's identity, believing this alone could pave the way for God coming to liberate his people. They therefore put great stress on identity markers like circumcision, tithing, sabbath, ritual washing, ritually clean foods, and keeping the festivals. All this led to a clash with Jesus, who said God wanted his people to transform an impure world, not be separated from it.

Essenes

The Essenes were a much smaller and more exclusive sect than the Pharisees, whom they saw as "givers of easy interpretations". Like the Hasidim they grew up as a protest movement against Hellenization, appalled at the laxity of fellow-Jews in keeping God's Law. While some lived among ordinary people, most established alternative monastic communities, like the one at Qumran, where they could live out their ideals in an ascetic lifestyle

See also
Dead Sea Scrolls p. 21
Scribes pp. 14–15
The Law pp. 134–35

of brotherly love and strict adherence to the Law. Here in the isolation of the desert they waited for God to act in what they believed would be the end of the age. Many of their ideas were similar to those of John the Baptist and Jesus; but while the Essenes were waiting for God's future intervention, both John and Jesus proclaimed that this intervention was beginning with Jesus.

Sadducees

The Sadducees, whose name probably derives from Zadok, Solomon's high priest, were a much smaller group than the Pharisees, yet far more significant, for they were the aristocratic families that controlled the high priesthood and the Temple. Josephus wrote that they "persuade only the well-to-do and have no popular following. But the Pharisees have the masses as allies." Unlike the Pharisees, they accepted only the Torah (the first five books of the Scriptures) as God's word, so excluded any doctrines not found in it, like the resurrection of the dead (Mark 12:18–27); and also unlike the Pharisees, they thought that strict purity was only incumbent on priests, not everyone.

They were supporters of Rome, for Rome supported the status quo, and so they were afraid of Jesus, who was upsetting the delicate political balance, because that would lead to their losing influence. But they also disagreed theologically with him, especially with his attitude to the Temple (Matthew 26:59–61). While they had little in common with the Pharisees, they nevertheless joined them in opposing Jesus, and it was their man Caiaphas, the high priest, who was ultimately responsible for ensuring Jesus' execution (John 18:14).

John's Gospel

John's Gospel often groups together the leaders of these different religious groups, simply describing them as "the Jews".

Zealots

Unlike the Essenes, the Zealots weren't prepared to wait for God to act; they wanted to help him out. Founded by Judas the Galilean in AD 6, they were guerrilla fighters who believed that Israel had no king but God alone, and so vehemently opposed Rome's rule. Preferring daggers to prayer, they fought to bring God's kingdom and were responsible for several revolts, one of which led to Jerusalem's destruction in AD 70. One of Jesus' disciples, Simon, had been a Zealot (Mark 3:17–18). When Jesus advocated non-violent resistance to enemies, he was directly opposing the Zealots' view of revolution. This photo shows the stronghold of Masada in the Judean Desert near the Dead Sea, where King Herod built a fortress and palace in 36 BC. After Jerusalem's destruction, a group of Zealots retreated here to make their last stand. Rome built a huge siege ramp to capture the fortress, but on finally breaking through they discovered that the Zealots – over 900 men, women and children – had taken their own lives to avoid being captured.

Herodians

These were supporters of King Herod, who hoped for his rule to be restored in Judea, currently ruled by the Roman governor Pilate, and so were troubled by anyone who might cause Rome to tighten its direct control. They often tried to catch Jesus out, such as over the issue of paying taxes to Caesar (Matthew 22:15–22). From early in Jesus' ministry the Herodians and Pharisees (strange bedfellows indeed) plotted together against him (Mark 3:6), though for very different reasons.

Faith idea: Acceptance

Against this background of clashing vested interests and expectations, Jesus portrayed a refreshing picture of God as hugely welcoming of all (e.g. Matthew 22:8–10) and modelled this in the community he gathered around him, which embraced both the collaborating tax payer (Matthew) and the Zealot (Simon). Fundamental to following Jesus is a willingness to "accept one another... just as Christ accepted you" (Romans 15:7).

Jerusalem

The Holy City

From the time it became David's royal city, Jerusalem always held a key place in Israel's history and was seen as being special to God (e.g. Psalms 99:1–2; 132:13–14) and the focal point of his reign on earth (e.g. Psalms 2:6–9; 110:1–2). Nevertheless, its blessing wasn't automatic, and when Israel refused to abandon their godless ways, God abandoned their beloved city.

Its history

Jerusalem, first mentioned in the Bible as Salem, the city of Melchizedek (Genesis 14:18), became significant from the time when David, against all expectations, captured this former Jebusite stronghold and made it the capital of his newly united kingdom around 1000 BC (2 Samuel 5:6–9). He built a palace here, fortified its walls, and made it the centre of worship by bringing the ark of the covenant into the city (2 Samuel 6:1–19). Its tiny site of 12 acres with a population of around 2,000 was extended northward by Solomon to cover 32 acres, and it was here that he built the Temple on land his father David had purchased for that purpose. Later kings, like Hezekiah and Manasseh, developed the city further westward, and it was frequently refortified during the seventh and sixth centuries BC, as threats from Mesopotamia increased. Uzziah built well-defended towers in strategic places along the walls (2 Chronicles 26:9, 15), and Hezekiah built a tunnel from the Gihon Spring to the Pool of Siloam to ensure a water supply during the anticipated siege by the Assyrians (2 Kings 20:22). By this time Jerusalem covered some 125 acres and had a population of around 25,000.

The city survived until the Babylonians attacked and destroyed it in 586 BC. After the exile the walls were rebuilt under Nehemiah, and further fortifications were added westward by the Maccabees. However, it was Herod the Great who was responsible for the city's vast redevelopment, turning it into a grand city in the Roman style, dominated by the Temple, covering about a fifth of the city's area, which by now had grown to 230 acres.

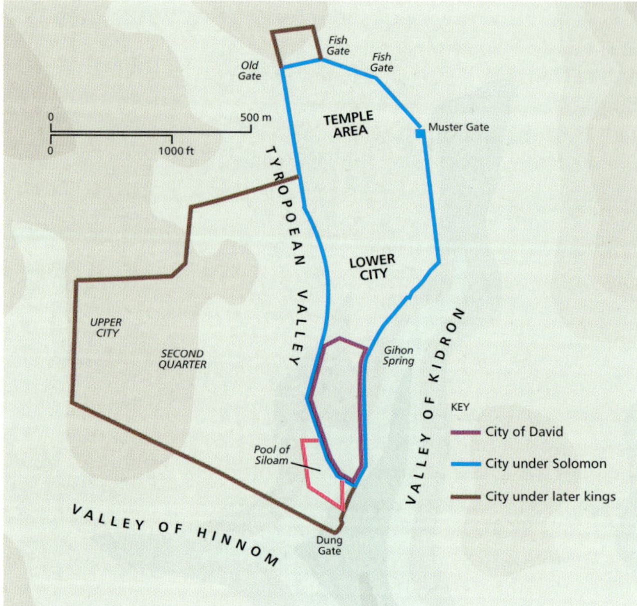

Jerusalem in Old Testament times

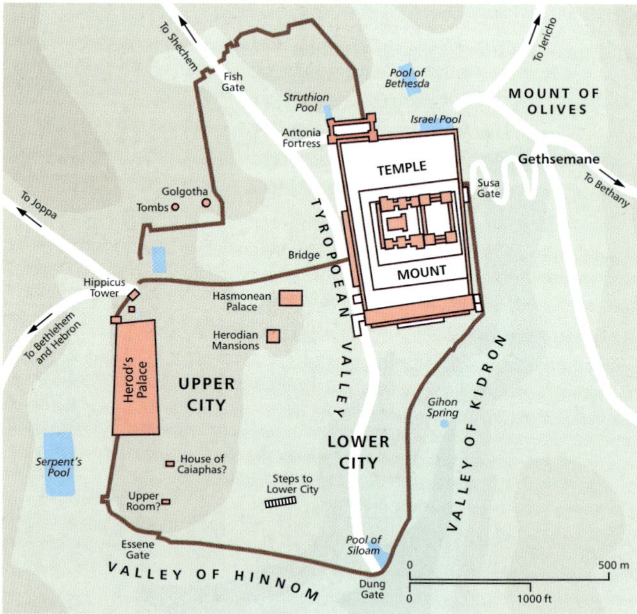

Jerusalem in New Testament times

The holy city

Jerusalem became known as "the holy city" (though the expression is used of historic Jerusalem in the Bible only seven times) because of its association with the holy Temple where God was seen to dwell. Other expressions for Jerusalem include "holy hill" (e.g. Psalm 2:6; Daniel 9:16; Joel 3:17) or "mountain of the Lord" (Isaiah 2:2–3; Micah 4:1–2), referring to the hill of Mount Zion, the heart of the ancient city, or simply (and much more commonly) "Zion" (e.g. Psalms 9:11–14; 48:9–14).

See also
Groups and Sects pp. 152–53
Jerusalem's Fall p. 37
Temple pp. 146–47

The Western Wall (the Kotel)

All that remains of the Temple are these huge limestone blocks in what is now known by Jews as "the Kotel" ("The Wall"), one of the retaining walls built by Herod the Great for the Temple platform. For devout Jews, this is the holiest spot for prayer, and many prayers are written on slips of paper and stuffed into the cracks. The stones, all with fine-chiselled borders, weigh between 2 and 8 tons each, while one 13-metre-long stone in the foundations weighs a staggering 570 tons – a remarkable feat of engineering, and one that caused Jesus' disciples to be amazed (Matthew 13:1).

The destruction of Jerusalem

Twice in the biblical period Jerusalem and its Temple were destroyed – the first time by the Babylonians in 586 BC and the second time by the Romans in AD 70. Neither is seen by the Bible as a mere event of history, however, but rather the judgment of God. The prophets consistently warned that unless Judah repented, the same fate that had befallen the northern territory of Israel would also befall it, and people's claims that Jerusalem would be safe because it had the Temple were quickly dismissed by Jeremiah (7:1–8). Even the rebuilding of the Temple in a more glorious manner than before wouldn't protect it, Jesus said, prophesying that every stone would be pulled down (Matthew 13:1–2), as indeed it was by the Romans, when they ransacked it, desecrated it by setting up their standards in it (fulfilling Daniel's prophesied "abomination that causes desolation", Daniel 11:31), and set it on fire. The Temple was now finished with, irrelevant to God's future purposes. It had been destroyed, not by the Romans, but by God himself.

Jerusalem and Christianity

While early Christians always showed compassion for their poorer brothers and sisters in Jerusalem (e.g. Romans 15:25–27; 1 Corinthians 16:1–3), they understood that its role as "the holy city" was now over, and that it was a city of old slavery rather than new freedom (Galatians 4:24–31). Certainly the idea of some Christians today that the Temple will be rebuilt in the end times finds no encouragement in the New Testament. Rather it stresses that the time of God's dealing with holy places is over, and the writer of Hebrews seems to sum up the early church's attitude to Jerusalem when he says, "Jesus also suffered outside the city gate to make the people holy through his own blood. Let us, then, go to him outside the camp, bearing the disgrace he bore. For here we do not have an enduring city, but we are looking for the city that is to come" (Hebrews 13:12–14).

Jerusalem

A model of first-century AD Jerusalem, viewed from the east. The city was dominated by the Temple, covering one-fifth of the city. Above the Temple towered the Fortress of Antonia, named in honour of Mark Antony, housing the Roman garrison of 600 soldiers. To its west were the homes of the wealthy and Herod's palace, while below it the homes of the poor huddled together in narrow streets. Jerusalem's population was around 30,000 in Jesus' time, though this swelled to five times that number at the great festivals.

Faith idea: New Jerusalem

One of the final things John saw in his vision of the end time was "the Holy City, the new Jerusalem, coming down out of heaven from God, prepared as a bride beautifully dressed for her husband" (Revelation 21:2). This is the Bible's closing reassurance of an eternal home with God for believers where "there will be no more death or mourning or crying or pain, for the old order of things has passed away" (21:4) – a home, not in heaven, but on a renewed earth. The Bible's story that began in a beautiful garden ends in a beautiful city.

Life's Big Questions

Finding God in Life's Challenges

Despite their belief in God's goodness, the Bible's authors weren't afraid to ask God hard questions or even argue with him when faced with life's puzzling circumstances. Although found throughout the Bible, it is particularly in the Wisdom literature (Job, Proverbs, Ecclesiastes, Song of Songs) that the big philosophical questions of life are found – questions that have abiding relevance.

Why do good people suffer?

This age-old question underlies **Job**, a story that asks: if there is a God, and if God is just, why do good people suffer? Job was a good and godly man who lost everything – family, health, possessions – and wanted to understand why. Three friends gave the conventional answer that great suffering must surely come from great sin. But Job knew this wasn't the case, and wasn't satisfied by this answer, as Jesus wouldn't be (Luke 13:1–5; John 9:1–3). Another friend then berated Job for justifying himself and questioning God's justice; but his view of God was utterly unfeeling and unhelpful.

This traditional Jewish "theodicy" (a vindication of God's existence and justice in the light of evil) failed to deal with Job's fundamental problem – his physical and emotional pain. His answer finally came, not through theological or philosophical argument, but through a fresh revelation of God's presence, power, and justice through which he at last found contentment – though not answers (Job 42:4–6).

Why does evil exist?

Two main lines of thinking about this developed in Judaism. One said that, since God created everything, he must also be responsible for evil. But how can a good God cause evil? For Job this remained a mystery; but others believed bad things were God's tool to discipline his people (e.g. 2 Samuel 7:14; Isaiah 10:1–19; Hebrews 12:4–13). Towards the end of the Old Testament period, however, a dualistic view emerged, seeing two competing (though not equal) forces at work – God and Satan. The New Testament picks this up, showing Jesus in battle against Satan (e.g. Matthew 4:1–11) and demons (e.g. Mark 1:23–28, 34), seeing Satan as ruling "the dominion of darkness" (Colossians 1:13), and urging Christ's followers to battle against him (e.g. Ephesians 6:10–18), assured that his overthrow one day is inevitable (e.g. Revelation 20:1–15).

Is there any point to goodness?

Proverbs answers with a resounding "yes", convinced that *doing* good will always lead to *experiencing* good. Through its collection of short sayings it outlines God's wise ways for life, but also shows what happens when people don't follow those ways. Every aspect of life is covered – family, marriage, home, work, poverty, justice, attitudes – the message underlined by powerful images and dramatic contrasts, showing that goodness always brings its own reward.

One key aspect of Job's story wasn't revealed to him, but only the reader: the fact that God and man have an enemy, "the satan", meaning "accuser" (Job 1:8 – 2:10; see also Genesis 3:1–24; Zechariah 3:1–2; Matthew 4:1–11; Revelation 12:1–17). But the story also shows that despite Satan's work – portrayed here in William Blake's *Satan Smiting Job with Sore Boils* – he is ultimately thwarted and God's people are vindicated.

See also
Death, Burial, and Beyond pp. 160–61
Satan p. 145
Wisdom pp. 90–91

Is life meaningless?

Life is unfair, work is pointless, and pleasure never really satisfies – so what's the point? This is the apparently pessimistic outlook of **Ecclesiastes**. But its truth is deeper. Writing as an old man looking back on life, "the Teacher" (1:1) concluded that life was a mystery, the greatest of which was people who rush around, work hard, and still don't find meaning in life; and they all end up dead anyway! So, is there any point? Yes. Life is but "a breath" (the literal meaning of the Hebrew word used thirty-five times and which is generally translated, rather unhelpfully, as "meaningless"), so we should make the most of it while we have it, recognizing our human limitations, and realizing that God alone brings true meaning to life.

Seasons

"There is a time for everything, and a season for every activity under heaven" (Ecclesiastes 3:1) – the opening of a poem about life's different phases and the need to accept the release and restraint that each different phase brings to get the best out of life.

What about injustice?

In Bible times, as today, huge injustices occurred, leaving many confused and crying out to God (e.g. Exodus 2:23; Job 19:7; Isaiah 40:27; Jeremiah 12:1; Habakkuk 1:2–4). But if injustice exists, it's not because God wants it, or is indifferent to it, but because of sinful people's greedy pursuit of possessions and power. The Bible is clear that God hates injustice, since it denies his very nature, and the Ten Commandments express his justice outworked in community. Of course, God could do away with injustice in a moment, the Bible says, but this would involve destroying everyone, for everyone expresses or condones injustice at times. For the moment God waits, challenging injustice through his prophets (e.g. 1 Kings 21:1–29; Jeremiah 22:13) and calling his people to model a different lifestyle (e.g. Matthew 5–7). But the Bible warns that a day of judgment is coming when every act of injustice will finally be called to account (e.g. Romans 2:5–11; 2 Peter 2:4–12; Revelation 20:11–15).

Why is there persecution?

In both the Old and New Testaments God's people experienced persecution from those whose rejection of God found expression in anger against his people (e.g. Esther 3:1–15; Acts 12:1–4). This inevitably caused God's people to ask "Why?" and Revelation, written during Roman persecution, answered this through its behind the scenes glimpse of history. Through a series of "sevens" – seven letters to churches (1:1 – 3:22), seven seals broken to unfold history (4:1 – 8:1), seven trumpets of warning (8:2 – 11:19), seven visions of battle (12:1 – 15:4), seven bowls of judgment (15:5 – 16:21), seven visions of Babylon's fall (17:1 – 19:10), and seven visions of victory and final judgment (19:1 – 21:4) – the church is reassured that, despite persecution, Jesus is coming again and ultimate victory is assured for all who remain faithful to him (21:5 – 22:21).

Faith idea: The fear of the LORD

The Bible encourages us to bring our questions to God, unafraid that he will be angry with us for doing so. But it also encourages us to develop a healthy "fear of the LORD". This is not about being afraid of God, but rather having a healthy respect for who he is and living accordingly, for only then can we discover what life is really all about.

The Christian Faith

Following Jesus

Christianity is not a religion but a relationship – a relationship with God through Jesus Christ. At its very heart, it is about following Jesus (Matthew 4:19), who leads people to the Father. The whole of Christianity focuses on him – his coming, life, teaching, death, resurrection, and coming again – with its claim that knowing him changes everything.

Distinctive Christian beliefs

Although rooted in the Old Testament, and so sharing many beliefs with it, Christianity was at the same time radically different; for while Jews were waiting for God's kingdom, Jesus said it was already here because he, the King of the kingdom, was here. Key Christian beliefs about him include:

Incarnation
"The incarnation" (from the Latin *in carne*, "in the flesh") is the teaching that Jesus wasn't simply a prophet or holy man, but none less than God himself who had come in human flesh. He is God's eternal Son, who was with his Father eternally (John 1:1–14; Philippians 2:5–11; Colossians 1:15–20; 1 John 1:1–3) and who was therefore everything that God himself was.

The cross
When Jesus was crucified, he was offering himself as a sacrifice (Romans 3:25; 5:6–7) and as a ransom (Romans 3:24; Ephesians 1:7–8) for others in order to win God's "not guilty" verdict for them (Romans 3:21–26; 5:1–2; 8:1–2) and to reconcile them to God and others (Romans 5:9–11; Ephesians 2:14–22).

Resurrection
Belief in Christ's resurrection is foundational to the assurance of forgiveness and hope for the future (e.g. 1 Corinthians 15:12–58). The resurrection was God's seal of approval on Jesus' sacrifice, without which there is no Christian message (1 Corinthians 15: 17).

Ascension
After his resurrection Jesus returned to his heavenly Father (Luke 24:50–52; Acts 1:1–11), though in a different form from how he came, for he took his humanity with him. This ascension convinced his followers he was now exalted in heaven, reigning over his enemies (Acts 2:32–33; 5:30–31; Ephesians 4:7–10; Colossians 1:2; Hebrews 4:14; 1 Peter 3:22).

The Holy Spirit
After his ascension, Jesus sent his Spirit to his followers (Acts 2:1–14), not as a one-off to "get the church going", but an ongoing experience for all who believed (Acts 4:31; 8:14–16; 9:17–19; 10:44–48). For Paul, life in the Spirit *was* Christianity, and anything else was sub-Christian.

Trinity
Christians believe in one God, but also believe that the Father, Son, and Holy Spirit are all that one God – "the Trinity". This belief arose as the first Christians discovered that in dealing with Jesus they were dealing with God, and then that in dealing with the Holy Spirit they were dealing with Jesus, who was himself God. Yet they remained convinced there were not three gods, but one; and this doctrine of the Trinity was their way of trying to explain this complexity of the one God's being and his fundamentally relational nature.

Christian symbols

The most common Christian symbols are the cross and crucifix. The cross (empty to recall Christ's resurrection) was used from earliest times, while the crucifix (Jesus nailed to the cross to recall his suffering and death) only appeared in the fifth century. The earliest symbol, however, was the fish – in Greek, *ichthus*, which was used as an acrostic for *Iēsous Christos Theou Uios Sōtēr* – Jesus Christ, Son of God, Saviour.

See also
God pp. 130–31
The Life of Jesus pp. 42–43
Sharing Bread and Wine p. 132

Distinctive Christian practices

Two practices in particular characterize Christianity, both called "sacraments" (from the Latin *sacramentum*, meaning "oath") – an outward sign of an inward spiritual gift:

Baptism
Just as circumcision was the outward sign of relationship with God in the Old Testament, so baptism became the outward sign in the New Testament. Jesus himself was baptized (Matthew 3:13–17; Mark 1:9–11; Luke 3:21–22; John 1:29–34) and commanded his disciples to baptize those who believed (Matthew 28:19). Current baptismal practice varies: some churches baptize only those who have made a conscious decision to follow Jesus, saying there are no examples of infant baptism (or "christening") in the Bible, while others, basing their practice on post-apostolic tradition, will baptize the infants of believers, seeing it as a parallel to circumcision in the Old Testament.

The Lord's Supper
The early church put sharing bread and wine at the heart of their worship, recalling Jesus' last supper with his disciples (Acts 2:42; 20:7; 1 Corinthians 11:23–34). Most Christians still do this, though call it by different names (the Lord's Supper, Holy Communion, Breaking of Bread, the Mass) and celebrate it in different styles, from very informal to highly ritualistic. While for many this remains the central feature of worship, others celebrate it less frequently, and some (like the Salvation Army) do not celebrate it at all.

Other sacraments
Some Christians, particularly from high church traditions (those with a strong emphasis on formality and ritual), also accept five other sacraments: confirmation, Holy Orders, confession, anointing the sick, and marriage. Most Protestant denominations, believing these rites do not actually convey God's grace, prefer to call them "ordinances".

A large ancient Roman bath used as a baptistery in St Stephen's Cathedral, Metz, France, showing that baptism by immersion must have been practised there.

Distinctive Christian living

Christianity isn't about following lists of rules, but about having a relationship with God through Jesus. There are no *conditions* for beginning that relationship, as it is entirely based on God's grace (Ephesians 2:8); but there are *consequences*, for Christians believe it is impossible to know Jesus and stay the same. That is why the New Testament calls Christians to show the difference Jesus has made through the way they live (e.g. 2 Corinthians 5:14–15; Ephesians 4:1 – 6:9).

Faith idea: Freedom

Christianity is about freedom – freedom from keeping rules in the hope this will put us right with God or win his favour. Trying to win God's favour through keeping rules or following rituals means abandoning the freedom Jesus won for us at the cross and returning to slavery, Paul stressed (Galatians 5:1).
True freedom is about being led by the Holy Spirit rather than being driven by duty or pressurized by others; it is doing what is right because we can, not because we must.

Church

In the New Testament the "church" wasn't a building or denomination, but God's people. The Greek word for church, *ekklesia* (literally "called out ones"), was originally a political term ("assembly"), but became used of those whom Jesus had "called out" of this world to become his new people.

Death, Burial, and Beyond

Life's End

From the very beginning, people have tried to avoid death (Genesis 4:14); yet it is the certain destiny of all (Psalm 89:48; Ecclesiastes 8:8) – not merely a biological inevitability but, the Bible says, a spiritual consequence: "the wages of sin" (Romans 6:23) which none can avoid (Romans 5:12–21). Yet the Bible also reveals hope for the future, rooted in the death and resurrection of Jesus Christ.

First-century burials

Entrance to a first-century AD tomb, showing the rolling stone in place. Chambers were cut from the rock, from which shafts were dug as burial places. Bodies were washed, anointed with spices, wrapped in linen, and placed in the first chamber. A rolling stone was placed across the entrance to protect the body from thieves or scavenging animals. Once the body had decomposed, which could take up to two years in Israel's dry climate, its bones were gathered and placed in a stone box called an ossuary. When Joseph of Arimathea offered his tomb for Jesus' burial (Mark 15:42–47), he was envisaging such a usage of it, with the bones to be gathered and reburied in due course.

Causes of death

Burial site investigations show that the main cause of death in ancient Israel was infectious disease, aggravated by its location at a trade crossroads where passing travellers helped spread disease. Life expectancy was short and, despite the psalmist's optimistic seventy– to eighty–year lifespan (Psalm 90:10), half the population died before the age of eighteen, and if ordinary people survived to forty they had done well. So when people lived to an old age, it was frequently noted.

Burial

Israelite practice was to bury bodies in the family tomb; for example, Sarah, Abraham, Isaac, Rebekah, Leah, and Jacob were all buried in the cave of Machpelah (Genesis 23:19; 25:9; 49:31; 50:13). The poor, however, were buried in shallow graves outside the city (e.g. 2 Kings 23:6; Jeremiah 26:23), their graves marked with a whitewashed stone to warn people not to touch them and so become defiled. Burial occurred within a day because of the heat – Lazarus's body would have been decomposing by the fourth day, hence Martha's protestations when Jesus suggested opening his tomb (John 11:39). Coffins weren't used; the body was simply wrapped in linen and carried to the burial place on a bier (e.g. 2 Samuel 3:31). Mourners who had touched the body were seen as ritually unclean for seven days (Numbers 19:11–22). Cremation wasn't practised, apart from in extreme situations (1 Samuel 31:12–13), and in later rabbinic literature it was condemned.

Old Testament views of death

Most peoples in the Ancient Near East believed that at death everyone went to the underworld. The Old Testament called this "*Sheol*", or *Hades* in Greek, "the land of gloom and deep shadow… the land of deepest night, of deep shadow and disorder" (Job 10:21–22), and going there was a one-way journey (2 Samuel 12:23). Initially it was seen as the destiny of good and bad alike, only gradually becoming seen as the destiny of the wicked (though with no thought of punishment attached to it). However, there was little clarity about what happened to the righteous after death, although there were occasional glimpses of hope: "God will redeem my life from the grave; he will surely take me to himself" (Psalm 49:15); "I know that my Redeemer lives, and that in the end he will stand upon the earth. And after my skin has been destroyed, yet in my flesh I will see God;
I myself will see him with my own eyes – I, and not another" (Job 19:25–27). Such glimpses were rare, however, which is why having sons was so important, for only through them could your name and family be perpetuated.

See also
Jesus: His Return pp. 194–95
Jesus: Death and Resurrection p. 184
Raising of the Dead p. 144

Mourning

Wailing women from a fourteenth-century BC Egyptian tomb painting. Such professional mourners (always women) were common throughout the ancient world. Mourning was expressed in different ways: tearing one's clothes, wearing sackcloth, putting dust or ash on the head, fasting, beating the chest, and wailing (Genesis 37:34; 2 Samuel 3:31; Nehemiah 9:1; Luke 23:48). Mourning normally lasted seven days (Genesis 50:10; 1 Samuel 31:13), though could last longer for important people (e.g. Exodus 34:8).

Hope for the future

Only in later Old Testament times did Israel start thinking about life after death, reflected in occasional glimpses of hope from the prophets (Isaiah 26:19; Ezekiel 37:11–13; Daniel 12:2). Jewish inter-testamental literature developed this thinking, though opinions were greatly divided, as we see in the conflict between Sadducees, who rejected the idea of resurrection, and the Pharisees, who didn't (Matthew 22:23–32; Acts 23:6–9). Some began to see *Sheol* as having two sections: one ("Abraham's side") for the righteous, and the other ("Hades") where the wicked awaited judgment – a concept alluded to in the parable of the rich man and Lazarus (Luke 16:19–31).

In contrast to such uncertainty, Jesus proclaimed clear hope for the future (e.g. Matthew 25; John 14:1–3). For his followers, his death, resurrection, and ascension broke the fear of death (Hebrews 2:14–15) and convinced them of the reality of a future life (e.g. 1 Corinthians 15:50–57; Philippians 3:7–14; 1 Thessalonians 4:13–18). Revelation, written to churches facing persecution and martyrdom, ends on a glorious note of hope for the future, with evil conquered, pain removed, death destroyed, and life lived in God's presence forever (Revelation 20:7 – 22:6).

What happens after death?

The New Testament says that death is simply a "departure" (Luke 9:31; Philippians 1:23; 2 Timothy 4:6–8; 2 Peter 1:13–15) in which believers leave their bodies and immediately enter God's presence. That is why Jesus promised the man crucified alongside him, "*Today* you will be with me in paradise" (Luke 23:43) – no delay, purgatory, soul-sleep, or reincarnation. The New Testament assures believers that at death they will be "with Christ, which is far better" (Philippians 1:23).

Jewish ossuaries from the Roman period.

Faith idea: Hope

Hope lies at the heart of Christianity, rooted in Jesus' resurrection. His disciples' absolute conviction that he was risen was the bedrock of their faith, enabling them to face hardship in the present and giving them hope for the future. Through the cross and resurrection Christians have a firm hope that, whatever happens in life, God is at work for their ultimate good and that nothing, not even death, can separate them from him (Romans 8:28–39).

The Gospels

Four Accounts, One Story

The Gospels are the part of the Bible that records the life of Jesus. But to see them as mere biographies is to miss the point. After all, so much is missing. What did he look like? How was he educated? What happened in the first thirty years? – everything we might reasonably expect in a modern biography. And not only are key facts missing, but there is disproportionate interest in the last week of his life (one-third of Mark, one-half of John). Clearly the authors' purpose was not mere story telling; rather, they saw it as a sharing of "good news".

Many early church leaders thought four Gospels was the ideal number, as four was seen as symbolizing totality or universality in those days. In AD 160 Tatian, a theologian and apologist, tried condensing the four into one (his *Diatesseron*) but found that each Gospel's unique perspective made his task impossible.

What is a Gospel?

Four books in the New Testament are called "Gospels". Gospel (*euangelion* in Greek) means "good news". Although it is now a religious word, it originally had a secular meaning. When the emperor had news, he sent messengers across his empire to town squares where they cried out, "*Euangelion! Euangelion!*", and everyone came running to find out more. And it was this word that the Gospel writers took to describe their works, seeing them as announcements of good news.

No book had ever been called a *euangelion* before; but there was simply no literary category for what they wanted to write about Jesus. Books had been described as *bioi* ("lives"), like Plutarch's *Life of Alexander*; *praxeis* ("deeds"), like Arian's *Anabasis*; *apomnemoneumata* ("memoirs"), like Xenophon's *Life of Socrates*; but none of these would do, for what they wanted to write was history, biography, memoirs, sayings – all this, and more; and so they created a brand new literary genre – "*euangelion*", reflecting that here was unashamed, impassioned "good news" about Jesus that was worth listening to. But because good news isn't good news unless it's true, they were also concerned to give an accurate picture of what had actually happened.

Why four?

Just as different media sources give different viewpoints in reporting events today, so it is with the Gospels; each has its own "angle". Matthew, Mark, and Luke have a similar content and order of material, so are called by scholars "Synoptic" ("same viewpoint") Gospels. John, however, uses a quite different approach, selecting just seven of Jesus' miracles and seven of his teachings (for in Jewish thinking seven was the perfect number), though he knew many more (John 20:30–31), in order to focus on their significance.

Illustration from the *Book of Kells* (c. AD 800), an illuminated Latin manuscript of the four Gospels. It reflects the Celtic monks' understanding of each Gospel's particular emphasis. Clockwise from top left it portrays Jesus as: a man (Matthew), reflecting Jesus' humanity; a lion (Mark), reflecting Jesus' royalty; an eagle (John), reflecting Jesus' anointing by the Holy Spirit; an ox (Luke), reflecting Jesus' sacrifice.

See also
Can We Trust The Bible? pp. 20–21
Creation of New Testament pp. 18–19
Gospel of Thomas p. 19

Key features of the Gospels

	Matthew	Mark	Luke	John
Author	One of the twelve disciples	Part of the wider group of disciples; Peter's assistant in Rome	Doctor and Paul's companion; the only Gentile writer in the New Testament	One of the twelve disciples
Date	Mid-AD 60s	Late AD 50s	c. AD 59–61	c. AD 85
Target audience	Jewish Christians	Gentiles (non-Jews)	Gentiles (non-Jews)	Jews and Gentiles
Style	Teaching gathered into long blocks	Fast-moving, action-packed, simple language, abrupt ending	Well-researched, accurate detail	Highly selective; lengthy teaching and discussions
Jesus seen as	• The messiah who fulfils Israel's hopes • Son of God • Great teacher • A 'greater Moses'	• Son of Man who suffers for us • Son of God who overcomes evil • Promised messiah • Teacher (rabbi)	• Messiah • Man of the Spirit • King David's promised descendant • The man for everyone	• Pre-existent "Word" • God-become-man • The Father's unique Son • Messiah
Birth stories	Yes	No	Yes	Cosmic beginnings
Key points	• A "better law" • Denunciation of Pharisees • Kingdom of heaven • Discipleship • Judgment upon Israel	• Presence of God's kingdom • Jesus' power • Call to discipleship • Jesus as a different sort of messiah • The necessity of Jesus' death	• Care for the despised and disadvantaged • The Holy Spirit • Healing • Prayer • God's new community	• Seven "signs" and "discourses" that reveal Jesus' identity • Seven "I am" sayings • Jesus' relationship with God • Contains some of the Bible's best-known verses
Particularly useful for	Understanding how Jesus fits in to the Old Testament	Starting to learn about Jesus	Seeing Jesus' compassion for the needy	Thinking more reflectively about Jesus

Can we trust the Gospels?

While the Gospels themselves acknowledge they have an "angle" (e.g. John 20:30–31), this doesn't take away from their reliability. Luke, for example, emphasized the historical research behind his Gospel, including careful investigation of eyewitnesses (Luke 1:1–4); and wherever we can check his facts, even down to minor geographical and political details, they prove to be accurate. Recent discoveries of first-century Jewish rabbinic writings, like the Dead Sea Scrolls, show that the picture we get of Jesus in the Gospels fits exactly with what we now know of life, thought, and beliefs in first-century Judaism. We can therefore be more confident than ever that the Gospels' account of Jesus, while impassioned, is also highly trustworthy and provides a solid basis for a modern-day search for the historical Jesus.

Where the Gospels sometimes appear contradictory, this probably reflects the fact that they are recording similar teaching given on different occasions, rather like a preacher or politician might use similar speeches or illustrations in different settings today.

Faith idea: Testimony

In Jesus' final words he promised that the Holy Spirit would enable his disciples to "be my witnesses" (Acts 1:8; see also John 15:26–27) – that is, to bring their testimony of what they had discovered about him, just as the Gospels seek to do. Such witness would lead to martyrdom for many (e.g. Acts 7; Revelation 6:9), and the Greek for "witness" (martys) *became the root of the word "martyr": someone who witnessed to the point of death. Christians are still called to bear witness to their own experience of Jesus.*

His Coming

The God Who Breaks In

With generations of preparation in place – the story of the Old Testament – the time at last arrived for the coming of the longed-for messiah, though he would prove to be even greater than ever expected. For "when the time had fully come, God sent his Son" (Galatians 4:4). Nothing less than God himself coming, the New Testament claims, would suffice for the next stage in the plan.

Messiah's arrival

As the Old Testament progressed, there was growing belief that God would one day send his "messiah" – in Hebrew, *mašiah* ("anointed one"), or in Greek, *Christos*. The title came from Israel's practice of anointing priests and kings for God's work. Israel had therefore had many "anointed ones"; but they increasingly expected an ultimate "anointed one": *the* messiah, anointed by God to free his people. Mark begins his Gospel by declaring that Jesus was that long-awaited messiah: "The beginning of the gospel about Jesus Christ [Messiah], the Son of God" (Mark 1:1). Here was a messiah of a completely different order from what people expected: a messiah who was no less than God himself.

Angelic visitors

People in the first century weren't naïve: they knew as well as we do how pregnancy happened. That's why, when God sent the angel Gabriel to tell Mary she would conceive and give birth to God's Son (what Christians call "the annunciation"), she replied, "How will this be since I am a virgin?" (Luke 1:34). It's also why Joseph, her fiancé, decided to cancel the marriage (Matthew 1:18–19). It took an angelic visit in a dream to convince him Mary was telling the truth, that her child had indeed been conceived miraculously, not through any man, and that this was the long-awaited Saviour (Matthew 1:20–21). Even Mary needed a "sign" that this was truly God at work – given when her barren relative Elizabeth became pregnant like the angel had said she would (Luke 1:36–45).

Mary's Magnificat

When Mary discovered Elizabeth was pregnant, she burst into singing (Luke 1:46–55), a song Christians call the "Magnificat", from its opening word in Latin, which is still used by many churches in worship. From the fourth century, Mary gradually acquired a more central place in many Christians' thinking, primarily through a desire to maintain Jesus' true humanity. She became known as "the Mother of God" to underline that it was God himself who was born to her. Although some theologians were unhappy with this title, the trend continued, leading to the increased importance of Mary.

Nazareth's Church of the Annunciation, traditional site of the annunciation. Although the Roman Catholic basilica dates only from the 1960s, Christians have worshipped on this spot from earliest times. An alternative site is marked by the Greek Orthodox Church built over the town's water source.

See also
Angels pp. 144–45
Dreams and Visions p. 144
His Birth pp. 166–67

The virgin birth

While many dismiss the virgin birth – Mary's conception of Jesus without human intervention – as impossible, seeing it as merely a literary device for conveying that Jesus was somehow "special", it remains central to the traditional Christian understanding of who Jesus is and why he came. Through the virgin birth, God was starting humanity all over again through Jesus: a brand new, perfect human being, created in Mary's womb by God's Spirit, thus avoiding inherited sin. It is this sinlessness that made it possible for Jesus to die for people, paying the price not of his own sin (since he had none), but ours. Remove *his* virgin birth and you remove *our* forgiveness.

While the belief in Mary's "perpetual virginity" (remaining a virgin throughout her life) arose in later church history, this isn't claimed in the New Testament itself, which simply notes that "Joseph had no union with her *until* she gave birth to a son" (Matthew 1:25).

Incarnation

At the heart of Christianity is the belief that Jesus wasn't merely a good man, but God himself come into this world with full and true humanity. Christians call this "the incarnation" (from the Latin *in carne*, meaning "in the flesh"), underlining that Jesus was the same eternal being that he had always been, but existing now in a different form, just like a butterfly is the same being as the caterpillar it came from. Look at Jesus, the New Testament claims, and you are looking at the eternal God.

Nowhere is this seen more starkly than in John's prologue, which begins, not with birth narratives like the Synoptics, but with the cosmic dimension of who Jesus was. "In the beginning was the Word, and the Word was with God, and the Word was God" (John 1:1) – no mistaking there who he thought Jesus was. But then he continues: "And the Word became flesh and made his dwelling among us" (1:14). It was this God, and no one less, John was saying, who became the man Jesus.

Mosaic at the Church of the Annunciation depicting Gabriel telling Mary she would bear God's Son. The early church saw the virgin birth as fulfilling Isaiah's prophecy: "The virgin will be with child and will give birth to a son, and they will call him Immanuel – which means, 'God with us'" (Isaiah 7:14; Matthew 1:23).

The Trinity

How can God be one (a fundamental Old Testament truth), yet also three? While this mystery of "the Trinity" is never set out formally in the New Testament, it was the conclusion that church leaders reached on the basis of the New Testament's teaching that Father, Son, and Spirit are all God. The first recorded use of "Trinity" (Latin, *Trinitas*) occured around AD 180, though a final agreed doctrine wasn't formulated until AD 325 at the Council of Nicea.

This illustration, originally with Latin text, called "the Shield of the Trinity", dates from the twelfth-century AD. Many other illustrations of the Trinity have been suggested, including that of the cube which, while having three equal dimensions, makes only one cube. Just as the one cube is impossible without its three dimensions, so the one God cannot exist without being Father, Son, and Holy Spirit all at the same time, such is his complex nature.

Faith idea: Humility

The Bible says that although Jesus was "in very nature God, [he] did not consider equality with God as something to be grasped, but made himself nothing, taking the very nature of a servant, being made in human likeness. And being found in appearance as a man, he humbled himself and became obedient to death – even death on a cross!" (Philippians 2:6–8). Such humility is seen as the model for Christians to follow (Philippians 2:5).

His Birth and Childhood

The Real Christmas Story

While the events of Christmas are one of the world's best-known stories, re-enacted annually in countless nativity plays, this story is also one of the least understood. For behind its simplicity lies a truth of unimaginable importance, Christians believe: this baby was none other than God himself.

Jesus' birth

Although tradition locates Jesus' birth in a stable "because there was no room for them in the inn" (Luke 2:7), the word "inn" really means "guest room" (as in Luke 22:11) – when Luke means "inn" he uses a different Greek word (as in Luke 10:34). Homes generally had a "guest room", but the return of the wider family for the census probably meant the family home was packed when Joseph and Mary arrived, the usual three-day journey perhaps extended by her condition. An adjacent cave, often used for storage and animals, would therefore have provided a warm, private place for the birth.

The manger

"She wrapped him in cloths and placed him in a manger" (Luke 2:7). A manger (feeding trough), generally made of stone, like this one, would have made an excellent crib once lined with straw. After his birth, Jesus would have been rubbed with salt to cleanse and toughen his skin, and had strips of cloth wrapped around him, as this was believed to help the bones grow straight and strong.

Why Bethlehem?

Although his parents lived in Nazareth, Jesus was born in Bethlehem, 6 miles (10 km) south of Jerusalem. The human reason for this was the census called by Quirinius, Rome's governor of Syria. Censuses were used for assessing taxes and involved everyone returning to their native home (Luke 2:1–4). But God was also at work, the Bible says; for Bethlehem, Micah had prophesied, was where the messiah would be born (Micah 5:2–4; John 7:41–42). While men usually represented their families in such matters, the province of Syria also taxed women, which may explain why Mary accompanied him. But equally, Joseph may have preferred taking her to leaving her in Nazareth where rumours about her pregnancy were probably still rife.

When was Jesus born?

While we aren't actually sure when Jesus was born, it wasn't on 25 December nor in AD 0. It was somewhere between 6 and 3 BC, most probably 5 BC, a date that fits both the first census of Quirinius and the appearance of a tailed comet, confirmed by ancient Chinese records and modern astronomy (though some think the "star of Bethlehem" was more probably a conjunction of planets). Our modern calendar was simply miscalculated by the monk Dionysius in AD 525.

But not only is the year wrong, so is the date. Jesus was probably born in April, during lambing season, when it was warm enough for shepherds to be "keeping watch over their flocks at night" (Luke 2:8). This also fits Chinese records that note a comet's appearance between 9 March and 6 April. The date 25 December wasn't adopted until the fourth century by the Western church to replace the pagan festival of Sol Invictus ("Invincible Sun"). The Eastern Orthodox Church, following the Gregorian calendar, celebrates Christmas on 7 January.

See also
Angels pp. 144–45
Birth, Birth Rituals p. 88
Circumcision p. 88

The fourteen-pointed silver star under the altar in Bethlehem's Church of the Nativity, the traditional spot of Jesus' birth.

The visit of shepherds

Through an angel, shepherds were the first to hear of the Saviour's birth (Luke 2:8–20). They needed a 'sign' – not because they were despised and 'unclean' (an urban myth!), but because they needed reassurance that ordinary, working people were included in the "good news" of the Saviour. This painting is from the Shepherds' Field Chapel in Bethlehem.

Visitors from the East

While tradition sees Jesus' final visitors as kings, they were in fact Arabian "Magi". Babylon and Persia were great centres of astronomy and astrology, where Magi served as priests, astronomers, and royal advisers. In Old Testament times Daniel had been appointed Chief of the Magi (Daniel 2:48), and it may have been from him that Magi learned of God's coming saviour. They brought gifts, symbolizing Jesus' future: gold, the most precious metal, symbolizing his kingship; frankincense, burned in worship, his priestly role; myrrh, used for embalming, his death for all.

We don't know how many Magi visited (the traditional number three is based solely on the number of gifts brought), nor when they came. It was probably several weeks after the birth, for the family was now in "the house" (Matthew 2:11), into which they had presumably moved after the other family members had departed; and Herod's massacre of boys up to two years old (Matthew 2:16–18) suggests that, even allowing for Herod wanting a margin of error, quite a period of time had elapsed.

From Bethlehem to Nazareth

Warned by an angel of Herod's infanticide, the holy family fled to Egypt (Matthew 2:13–15), where there had been Jewish settlements since the exile. Here they remained until Herod's death in 4 BC, which Matthew sees as a parallel with what happened to Israel when it too spent time in Egypt before returning to the Promised Land (Matthew 2:17–18). Herod was replaced in Judea and Samaria by Archelaus, a cruel ruler; so having been warned of this in a dream, Joseph took his family back to Galilee and settled in Nazareth again (Matthew 2:19–23).

Silent years

We know nothing of Jesus' early life, apart from a visit to Jerusalem when he was twelve (Luke 2:41–52) and the fact he was trained as a "carpenter" (Mark 6:3) – though the Greek word really means "builder", which may explain why Jesus used building illustrations. Since he isn't mentioned again, Joseph probably died while Jesus was a teenager, which would explain why, as eldest son, Jesus stayed at home until he was thirty, fulfilling his responsibility as the head of the household. Only when his siblings (Matthew 12:47; 13:55) were old enough did he leave to begin his ministry.

Faith idea: Saviour

The name "Jesus" means "the LORD saves". But while Jews believed it was others who needed saving, the angel said, "He will save his people from their sins" (Matthew 1:21). Jesus came as saviour (Luke 2:11) for the whole world, starting with Israel. And his salvation is something that must be experienced personally, not on the basis of nationality or religious tradition, but on the basis of faith in him alone.

His Launch

The Work Begins

Around the age of thirty (Luke 3:23) Jesus left Nazareth to begin his public ministry, which lasted just three years. After a time of preparation in the desert, he returned to Galilee, where some received his message but others rejected him – mixed reactions that were prophetic of what the next three years would hold.

Preparing the way

Before royal visits, messengers were sent ahead, calling people to prepare, and Isaiah had prophesied that such a messenger would precede Messiah's coming. That messenger was John the Baptist (Mark 1:1–4), whose pointing to Jesus began in his mother Elizabeth's womb (Luke 1:39–45). John preached "a baptism of repentance for the forgiveness of sins" (Mark 1:4) and called for changed living (Luke 3:7–18). While many Old Testament prophets had made such calls, what was shocking was John's insistence on marking this by baptism, something Jews only demanded of Gentile converts, thereby saying Jews too were outsiders. While many ordinary people responded to John's message, the religious leaders were offended by it (Matthew 3:7–10; Luke 3:7–9). He was eventually imprisoned and beheaded by Herod Antipas (Matthew 14:1–12).

The Judean desert where John preached. Deserts had played key roles in Israel's history, and the prophets had said Messiah would come from here (e.g. Isaiah 40:3–5). Little wonder huge crowds gathered when John started preaching there (Matthew 3:5), his ascetic lifestyle (Mark 1:6) reflecting that of Elijah, whose reappearance was expected before Messiah's coming (Malachi 4:5–6).

Jesus' baptism

Jesus' first step was to be baptized by John in the Jordan (Matthew 3:13–17; Mark 1:9–11; Luke 3:21–22; John 1:29–34). Although John was reluctant to baptize him, Jesus said it was the right thing to do. As he was baptized, the Holy Spirit came on him, and a voice from heaven declared, "You are my Son, whom I love; with you I am well pleased" (Luke 3:22). Accredited as Messiah and God's son, his work could now begin.

The photo shows a modern baptism in the river Jordan.

Wilderness temptations

After his baptism, Jesus was led by God's Spirit into the wilderness, where he spent forty days praying and fasting and where the devil tempted him (Matthew 4:1–11; Mark 1:12–13; Luke 4:1–13). Centuries earlier, God had led Israel through the Sinai wilderness, where they had faced many tests, failing them all; but here now was the man representing the new Israel and he also faced tests, but triumphed. In overcoming these temptations, Jesus resolved at the outset that:

- he would depend on God's word, quoting it (all from Deuteronomy, the book of Israel's wilderness years) to show his high view of its authority;
- he would not pursue a worldly form of messiahship, gathering followers by signs and establishing God's kingdom by force, but would walk the path of humble dependence.

See also
Baptism p. 159
Discipleship p. 171
Prayer and Fasting p. 143

His ministry begins

While it is impossible to be certain about the exact chronology of Jesus' ministry, the early months probably looked something like this:

1. Left his childhood home;

2. Baptized by John (Matthew 3:13–17; Mark 1:9–11; Luke 3:21–22; John 1:29–34);

3. Tempted by the devil (Matthew 4:1–11; Mark 1:12–13; Luke 4:1–13);

4. First miracle performed at a wedding (John 2:1–11);

5. Temple's outer courtyard cleansed of merchants whose activities prevented the Gentiles from praying (John 2:13–25);

6. Visited Samaria, avoided by pious Jews, breaking social taboos by speaking with a Samaritan woman, leading to many believing (John 4:1–42);

7. Rejected in Nazareth (Matthew 4:12–17; Luke 4:14–30);

8. Moved to new base in Capernaum (Luke 4:31).

Rejection in Nazareth

While Jesus experienced initial popularity (Luke 4:15), his message soon alienated many. One sabbath he was invited to read the Scriptures and preach in the local synagogue (Luke 4:16–30). He read from Isaiah's prophecy of Messiah bringing God's new age of freedom (Isaiah 61:1–2), something they could all agree with. But when he added, "Today this scripture is fulfilled in your hearing" (Luke 4:21) – in other words, claiming that this age was beginning right now – the atmosphere started to change. And when he then gave hope to Gentiles through the Old Testament stories he quoted, it was the final straw: they drove him out and tried to throw him off a cliff. But he miraculously escaped and left Nazareth, never to return.

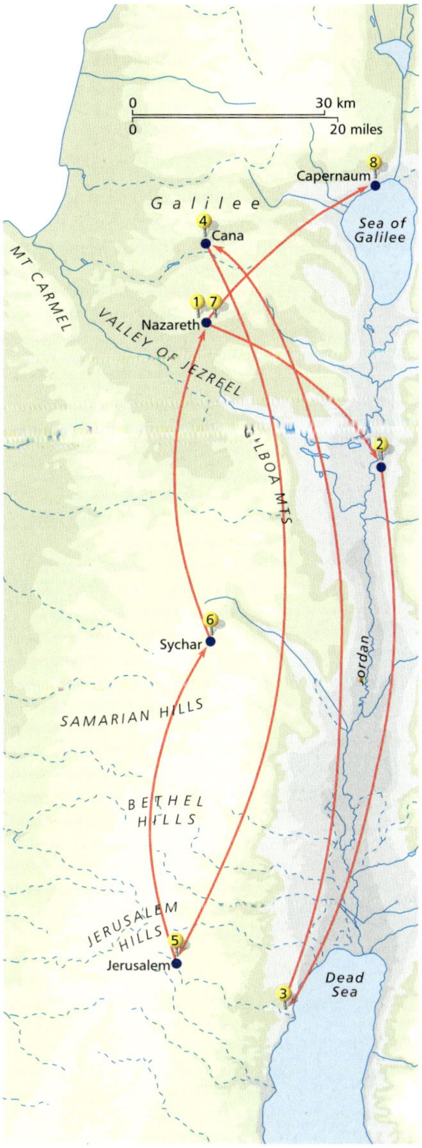

Capernaum

Rejected in Nazareth, Jesus moved to Capernaum (Kephar Nahum, "the village of Nahum"), a small town by the Sea of Galilee. The main north–south highway skirted the town, which lay close to the border with Gaulanitis, generating considerable commercial activity. So although relatively quiet, Capernaum was also relatively influential, making it an ideal base for Jesus' ministry and a place he often returned to, seeing it as "home".

His disciples

Jesus had already been teaching and healing for some time before he called his twelve disciples, which may explain their prompt abandonment of everything to follow him, as they had probably already seen him in action, or at least heard of him. The number twelve was no coincidence; it was Jesus' way of showing he was re-forming the people of God, a new Israel, whose tribes had numbered twelve. The men he chose, whom he designated "apostles" ("sent ones") (Mark 3:13–19), were a mixed bunch.

- Simon Peter: hot-headed fisherman from Capernaum;
- James: fisherman from Capernaum;
- John: fisherman and James's brother;
- Andrew: fisherman and Peter's brother;
- Philip: from Bethsaida, perhaps of Greek background;
- Bartholomew: also called Nathanael, a straightforward man;
- Matthew: tax collector;
- Thomas: famous for doubting the resurrection;
- James: son of Alphaeus, about whom little is known;
- Thaddaeus: also called Judas;
- Simon the Zealot: former nationalist freedom fighter;
- Judas Iscariot: group treasurer who would betray Jesus.

Jesus also had a wider group of followers (Luke 10:1), including women (highly unusual, if not scandalous), some of whom supported him financially (Luke 8:2–3).

Faith idea: Discipleship

Jesus didn't simply engage in God's mission himself, but drew others into it through discipleship – training them to produce a change of heart, attitude, vision, and fruitfulness. The importance of discipleship to Jesus is seen in its being the focus of his final command before his ascension (Matthew 28:18–20), with the implication that it still lies at the heart of being a Christian today.

His Teaching

Words that Worked

While the Greek philosophers Socrates, Plato, and Aristotle all taught for over forty years, Jesus taught for only three; yet his influence on the world was arguably far greater than theirs. The reason, Christians believe, is that his teaching gave people hope that things could be different, not through knowing more or trying harder, but simply through knowing God as Father.

God

While Jesus' view of God was completely orthodox, it was also utterly radical, transforming the scribes' and Pharisees' vision of a demanding God into one of a gracious, forgiving Father whose love reached everyone. Of course, they acknowledged this was true – but only for them and their kind: for those who kept the Jewish Law and so deserved it. But Jesus taught that God's love went much further, reaching out to those who *didn't* deserve it, as seen in his parables of the prodigal son (Luke 15:11–32) and the workers in the vineyard (Matthew 20:1–16).

Jesus' favourite term for God was "Father", used 168 times in the Gospels. For his opponents this wasn't simply over-familiar, but blasphemous (John 5:18). But Jesus took this intimacy even further, calling God *Abba*, the Aramaic for "daddy" (Mark 14:36), and teaching his followers to see God as their heavenly Father too (e.g. Matthew 6:9). So impacting was this that they retained this word "*Abba*" even when Christianity moved from the Jewish into the Greek-speaking world (Romans 8:15; Galatians 4:6).

God's kingdom

Much of Jesus' teaching focused on the kingdom of God (or the kingdom of heaven as Matthew calls it, since he was writing for Jews and wanted to respect their sensitivities by avoiding using God's name). While Jews believed in this kingdom, they weren't expecting it until the end of the age. But Jesus said it was here right now; it was "near" (Mark 1:15), "within you" (Luke 17:26), was "forcefully advancing" (Matthew 11:12), had "come upon you" (Matthew 12:28). And yet, it was at the same time hidden, like treasure in a field, waiting to be unearthed, but worth giving everything for (Matthew 13:34). But although this kingdom had small beginnings, it was destined for incredible growth. Just like a little yeast spreads through a whole batch of dough (Luke 13:20), so it too would one day permeate everything.

Jesus taught, and demonstrated, that this kingdom – this "rule of God", which is what the Greek word "kingdom" (*basileia*) really means – changes everything. That's why Mark opens his Gospel with a string of stories showing how that kingly rule can deal with every area of life: demons (1:21–28), disease (1:29–34), uncleanness (1:40–45), sin (2:1–12), social exclusion (2:13–17), religious tradition and rules (2:18 – 3:5) – everything changes when God rules.

Love and forgiveness

When asked what was the greatest commandment, Jesus replied, like any good Jew, "The most important one is this: 'Hear, O Israel, the Lord our God, the Lord is one. Love the Lord your God with all your heart and with all your soul and with all your mind and with all your strength'" (Mark 12:29–30). But then he added: "The second is this: 'Love your neighbour as yourself.' There is no commandment greater than these" (v. 31). Jesus was asked for the one greatest commandment, but in his reply he gave *two*, thereby inextricably linking love for God with love for one's neighbour. It is impossible to do the former unless you are doing the latter, he was saying.

For Jesus, a good test of love is one's ability to forgive – not just friends, but also enemies (Matthew 5:43–48; Luke 6:27–36). Unforgiveness is wrong, not just because it shows ingratitude (after all, God forgives us again and again), but because it is a prison that locks us up, as his parable of the unforgiving servant shows (Matthew 18:21–35).

See also
His Disciples p. 169
His Miracles pp. 174–75
His Parables pp. 172–73

Sermon on the Mount

The traditional location of "The Sermon on the Mount" (Matthew 5:1 – 7:29; Luke 6:17–49), as it was first called by St Augustine (AD 354–430), in which Jesus challenged traditional religious interpretations of the Jewish Law and outlined the ethics of God's kingdom. Visited by pilgrims since the fourth century, this site makes sense of Matthew's locating the sermon "on a mountainside" but Luke on a "level place"; Luke's level place was a plateau on Matthew's hillside.

Discipleship

Jesus didn't just teach his followers, he discipled them. Discipleship ("apprenticeship" or "mentoring") was common in Jesus' time. Someone wanting to learn the skills of another became his disciple, at first listening, watching, and learning, but then gradually doing it until the skills or knowledge were fully transferred. But whereas apprentices normally sought out a teacher, Jesus chose his apprentices. His discipleship involved encouraging them when they got things right (Matthew 16:13–20), correcting them when they got things wrong (Matthew 16:21–28), helping them when they failed (Matthew 17:14–21), and sending them out to "have a go" (Luke 9:1–6, 10). It covered every aspect of life, not just religious matters: things like character (Matthew 5:1–12), attitudes (Mark 10:35–45), fears (Matthew 6:25–34), behaviour (Matthew 6:1–4), money (Luke 16:10–12), and relationships (Matthew 18:15–35).

Jesus' teaching style

- *It provoked thinking.* Unlike his contemporaries, Jesus didn't want people simply to learn by rote but to think for themselves. So he asked questions, challenged thinking, used riddles, and told parables – anything to present truth in a fresh way that would get people thinking.
- *It reached everyone.* While Jesus could engage in scholarly debate at the highest level, he could also captivate ordinary people with his parables and stories from everyday life.
- *It had authority.* His teaching wasn't just based on "words", like that of most other teachers, but what he said was backed up by how he lived and what he did.

Faith idea: The Old Testament

Jesus took the Old Testament seriously, seeing it as God's word. He quoted from it at least forty times in the Gospels and made seventy other allusions, often appealing to it to settle issues. He never criticized it, only religious leaders' interpretations of it, and said he had not come "to abolish the Law or the Prophets… but to fulfil them" (Matthew 5:17) – that is, "to bring them to their full meaning". Attempts to drive a wedge between his teaching and the Old Testament, therefore, are quite unfounded.

His Parables

Mysteries of the Kingdom

At the very heart of Jesus' message lay the kingdom of God. While his miracles were a *demonstration* of God's kingdom, his parables were an *explanation* of it. Through simple stories from everyday life he sought to reveal, to all with open hearts and faith, profound and eternal truths about that kingdom and how it works. Yet these very same stories hid these truths from those who thought they already understood them. Such were the mysteries of the kingdom, he said.

The power of story

Rooted as it is in Greek philosophy, Western education is largely based on principles, ideas, and theories. But for much of the world, knowledge is communicated through story-telling; and that was certainly true of the Jews. Much of the Old Testament is story: God revealing his eternal truth through the story of Israel, which in turn was made up of many individual stories of people. So in using stories, Jesus was drawing on a long-practised Jewish method of communicating truth. One-third of his teaching was in some sort of parable – a story with a meaning. Parables generally have one key point, and searching for endless hidden meanings in every detail inevitably leads to missing that point. A parable is rather like a joke; trying to explain it ruins it.

Points about parables

- They generally have one main point.
- They are generally short, omitting unnecessary description.
- They are usually based on everyday life, though some use ridiculous exaggeration for impact.
- They can hide as much as they reveal.

Some well-known parables

Parables	Matthew	Mark	Luke
Wise and foolish builders	7:24-27		6:47-49
The good Samaritan			10:25-37
The rich fool			12:13-21
The sower	13:1-23	4:1-20	8:4-15
Mustard seed	13:31-32	4:30-32	13:18-19
The lost sheep	18:12-14		15:3-7
The lost (prodigal) son			15:11-32
The rich man and Lazarus			16:19-31
The unforgiving servant	18:23-35		
The wedding banquet	22:1-14		
The bridesmaids	25:1-13		
The talents	25:14-30		19:11-27
Sheep and goats	25:31-46		

The teaching of the parables

Many of Jesus' parables were told in order to describe what God's kingdom is like and how it operates. Matthew gathers a whole cluster of them in chapter 13 of his Gospel, each beginning with the words "The kingdom of heaven is like…". All portray how God's kingdom has small beginnings in this world yet is destined to triumph, described as a seed that will grow despite all hindrances (vv. 1–23), a harvest that is certain despite the weeds that try to choke it (vv. 24–30, 36–43), a tiny mustard seed that becomes the biggest of plants (vv. 31–32), a grain of yeast that permeates the whole batch of dough (v. 33), treasure worth selling everything for (vv. 44–46), and a net catching many fish that are sorted only at the end (vv. 47–50). But other parables cover wide-ranging topics, such as prayer (Luke 18:1–8), self-righteousness (Luke 18:9–14), forgiveness (Matthew 18:21–35), the dangers of money (Luke 12:13–21), and what God is really like (e.g. Luke 15:11–32).

End-time parables

As well as gathering together parables of the kingdom, Matthew also gathered together parables about the end-time:

- The faithful and unfaithful servants (24:45–51) – a challenge to be faithful in both our lives and responsibilities.
- The wise and foolish bridesmaids (25:1–13) – a challenge to always be ready for Jesus' return.
- The talents (25:14–30) – a challenge to use wisely what God has given us, knowing he will require an account one day.
- The sheep and goats (25:31–46) – a challenge to live caring lives in the light of the coming judgment.

See also
Communication pp. 120–21
God's Kingdom p. 170
Jesus' Teaching Style p. 171

Imagery in John

John's Gospel contains no parables, at least not in the usual sense of that word. Nevertheless it is packed with imagery, especially from the Old Testament. One example is the vine. Israel was full of vineyards, as Israel's spies had discovered when exploring the land centuries earlier (Numbers 13:17–24). Not surprisingly, therefore, the vine and vineyard became symbols of Israel, with God seen as their owner (Isaiah 5:1–4). Jesus picked up this imagery, claiming that he himself was now the new vineyard of God, "the true vine" (John 15:1), and that only through attachment to him could branches live and bear fruit (John 15:2–8).

Other key imagery used by Jesus in John's Gospel includes: light, which often symbolized God's presence and goodness in the Old Testament, but which Jesus now claimed to be, not just for Israel, but everyone (John 8:12); and water, which was an important image of God's provision, refreshing, and cleansing, and which frequently symbolized his Spirit (Isaiah 44:3; Ezekiel 36:25–27; 47:1–12). Jesus claimed that he was now the provider of that life-giving water (John 7:37–38).

The good Samaritan
The Jerusalem to Jericho road through the Judean wilderness, the setting for the parable of the good Samaritan (Luke 10:25–37), a story in which a Jewish traveller is robbed and left for dead. Ignored by his own religious leaders, it is a despised Samaritan who comes to his rescue.

This parable has often been over-analysed, with every detail given some hidden meaning. But its context makes its main point clear: Jesus had been asked by a religious scholar, "Who is my neighbour?" The parable's answer, told to people who detested Samaritans, was both simple and shocking: anyone who needs you or will help you. Of course, the parable would have been much more acceptable if it had been about a good Jew helping a wicked Samaritan. But that was a twist that Jesus was not prepared to give it.

Other imagery

Besides full-blown parables, Jesus' teaching was full of all sorts of imagery, normally drawn from everyday life, including:

- birth (John 3:3–7)
- marriage (Matthew 25:1–13)
- domestic life (Matthew 5:13–16)
- farming (John 4:35)
- building (Matthew 7:24–27)
- nature (Matthew 6:26–30).

Faith idea: Mystery

In biblical usage, a "mystery" is something known to God alone, but which he chooses to reveal, like when Daniel was given the interpretation of Nebuchadnezzar's dream (Daniel 2:19–23, 27–28, 47) or when people are given understanding of God's plan in Christ (e.g. Ephesians 1:8–10; 3:1–12). Jesus said he taught in parables both to reveal and hide the mysteries of God's kingdom (Matthew 13:10–17): those with humility and faith would understand them, while those who thought they understood them would remain blind.

His Miracles

Demonstrating the Kingdom

Miracles formed a significant part of Jesus' ministry. Thirty-five specific miracles are recorded in the Gospels, as well as many general references. These miracles weren't designed to attract followers, nor even primarily to express compassion; for Jesus they were demonstrations of God's kingdom, proclaiming, "This is what life is like when you let God in. Things change!"

Jesus' first miracle

Water jars, used for ceremonial washings, were central to Jesus' first miracle: turning the water in them into wine at a wedding (John 2:1–11). Weddings lasted a week, and the whole village of Cana was invited; but to the host's embarrassment, the wine ran out. Jesus rescued the situation by changing water into wine. But the wine now made the jars "unclean" for ritual purposes, something John sees as a "sign": a pointer to a deeper truth. Like the jars, Judaism itself had become useless and needed replacing. In its place was Jesus, the man with the "new wine" of God's kingdom, who was right there with them.

Healing

As it became known that healing was central to Jesus' ministry, crowds flocked to him to be healed (e.g. Mark 1:33–34; 3:9–10; 6:55–56). What is striking about the miracles is not so much *what* Jesus did, but *who* he did it for; for in the eyes of the religious leaders, he simply healed the wrong sort of people – lepers, outcasts, the unclean, non-Jews – people who didn't deserve it. But that, of course, was Jesus' point. For his healings showed what God is like – gracious to all – and were demonstrations of God's kingdom at work.

The blind and deaf

Many of Jesus' healings concerned the blind and deaf, something very significant to Jews, for Isaiah had prophesied that this would be a key feature of Messiah's work (Isaiah 29:18; 35:5–6). So when John the Baptist began to doubt whether Jesus was indeed the messiah, Jesus sent a message to him, saying, "The blind receive sight, the lame walk, those who have leprosy are cured, the deaf hear, the dead are raised, and the good news is preached to the poor" (Matthew 11:5).

Power over nature

If Jesus' miracles had been confined to just healings, they might be more easily understandable; after all, they might have simply been psychological or the result of advanced medical insights. But some went way beyond what might be explainable, shaping nature itself. Such nature miracles fall into four categories:

- controlling nature (e.g. calming storms);
- stretching nature (e.g. feeding 5,000);
- ruling nature (e.g. walking on water);
- conquering nature (e.g. raising the dead).

Of course, events like these are "impossible". But trying to look for rational explanations misses the point: their *impossibility*. Nobody could do this kind of thing – unless, of course, he were God; the God who created these things in the first place and who was now simply being served by his creation.

Power over death

Jesus showed his ultimate power by conquering mankind's last enemy, death, on at least three occasions:

The widow of Nain's son
(Luke 7:11–17)
Showing compassion on a widow who had nothing now that her means of support was gone, Jesus turned to her dead son in the open coffin and told him to get up, which he did. People were understandably amazed, saying, "A great prophet has appeared among us" (v. 16), perhaps remembering

See also
Health and Healing pp. 124–25
Resurrection pp. 184–85
The Supernatural pp. 144–45

A Byzantine mosaic at Tabgha, commemorating Jesus' feeding of 5,000, the only miracle recorded by all four Gospels (Matthew 14:13–21; Mark 6:30–44; Luke 9:10–17; John 6:1–15). Only John records that the five loaves and two fish came from a little boy (John 6:9), probably his lunch and so not substantial. But not only did Jesus feed the huge crowd from this – 5,000 men plus wives and children (Matthew 14:21) – there was enough left to fill twelve baskets. Since twelve was the number of Israel's tribes, this was meant to symbolize Jesus' ability to satisfy *all* God's people.

Elijah's similar miracle (1 Kings 17:8–24). They could only conclude: "God has come to help his people."

Jairus's daughter (Matthew 9:18–26; Mark 5:21–43; Luke 8:40–56)
The journey to Jairus's house was interrupted by a woman in need, so by the time Jesus arrived, Jairus's daughter was dead. When Jesus told the mourners she wasn't dead but sleeping, they laughed, for they recognized death well enough. But he put them outside and told the girl to get up. Mark's retention of Jesus' actual Aramaic words ("*talitha koum*", "Little girl, get up!") shows how profoundly this event stuck in their memories.

Lazarus (John 11:1–44)
By the time Jesus arrived, Lazarus had been dead four days (v. 17). Declaring he was "the resurrection and the life" (v. 25), Jesus had the stone rolled back and called Lazarus out. Lazarus came back to life and walked out, leaving everyone so shocked that they needed to be told to take off his grave clothes (v. 44).

All three of these would die again one day; but in the meantime they were powerful signs of Jesus' resurrection and of the future resurrection of all who believed.

Faith healing?

While miracles and faith are linked, it is important to note the following:

- Miracles didn't always depend on faith. Sometimes people had little faith (John 5:6–7); sometimes they had a lot (Matthew 9:21). It is not faith that heals, but God.
- Miracles didn't always produce faith. Ten lepers were healed, but only one came back to say thank you (Luke 17:11–19).

Why the secrecy?

Jesus often told people to keep his miracles secret (e.g. Mark 1:43–44). He didn't want to be misinterpreted as a messiah who would free Israel through miracles and force. His mission was quite different, he said, which is why he often commanded secrecy after performing miracles, though this wasn't always obeyed (e.g. Mark 1:45).

Faith idea: Signs

Some of Jesus' opponents constantly asked for a "sign" (e.g. Matthew 12:38–40; Mark 8:10–12; Luke 11:16) – some spectacular event in the sky to "prove" who he was. Jesus consistently refused to give such proofs, knowing they cannot produce real faith. In John's Gospel the word "sign" is used differently, however, describing Jesus' miracles (e.g. John 2:11), highlighting their significance, rather than the power itself, in pointing to who Jesus really was.

His Ethics and Lifestyle

Being Good, Doing Good

Many have admired Jesus' ethics, and the lifestyle and values they produced, while rejecting his religious message. However, it is quite impossible, Jesus said, to separate his ethics from his teaching about himself; to follow *them* without first following *him*. His challenge was, "Come, follow *me*" (Mark 1:17), not "Come, follow a system". It is in following him that true ethical living begins. Or to put it another way, *doing* good can only come out of *being* good, not vice-versa.

Principles, not a system

Many great teachers have developed coherent ethical systems. That's what the rabbis had done, applying the Jewish Law to the whole of life, creating countless rules for living. But Jesus was different; he had no "system", just two simple principles:

- Love God with all your being.
- Love your neighbour as yourself.

These two principles, he said, fulfil everything God wants (Matthew 22:36–40). For Jesus, systems and rules could never change a person's behaviour, as the Pharisees proved in his day. What truly changes behaviour is a change of heart, Jesus insisted.

The Golden Rule

Many religions and philosophies have taught "the Golden Rule" – "*Don't do* to others what you wouldn't want them to do to you." But Jesus turned this round, making it utterly positive: "*Do* to others what you would have them do to you" (Matthew 7:12; Luke 6:31). His ethics were proactive, not reactive.

Examples of Jesus' ethical teaching

Of the many ethical issues Jesus taught about, here are just some examples from Matthew's Gospel:

- values (5:3–11)
- anger (5:21–22)
- forgiveness (5:23–26)
- revenge (5:38–42)
- enemies (5:43–48)
- marriage (5:31–32; 19:1–12)
- sex (5:27–30)
- children (18:1–6)
- speech (5:33–37)
- giving (6:2–4)
- materialism (6:19–33)
- judging others (7:1–5)
- caring for the poor (19:21)
- social responsibilities (Matthew 22:15–21).

The Beatitudes

Jesus' famous Sermon on the Mount opens with what are called "the Beatitudes" or "Blessings" (Matthew 5:3–10), each beginning with the words "Blessed are...", or in today's language "Congratulations to...!" But each of them seems far from being something to be congratulated for, as Jesus turned traditional ethical and social values upside down. But this came out of his conviction that those who felt unblessed were about to experience God's blessing as his kingdom broke in and as they trusted in him.

The Franciscan Church of the Beatitudes, built on the site of fourth-century AD ruins. The chapel's octagonal shape represents the eight beatitudes.

See also
Essenes pp. 152–53
His New Community pp. 178–79
Sermon on the Mount p. 171

Care and education

Christians have always been at the forefront of education and caring for the needy, both of which have often antagonized their atheistic opponents. This is Mother Teresa (1910–97), an Albanian Roman Catholic nun who founded the Missionaries of Charity and who for over forty-five years cared for the poor, sick, orphaned, and dying of the streets of Calcutta, India, as an expression of her faith.

Ethical motivations

Some have seen Jesus' teaching about future rewards and punishments as an obstacle to his ethics, since acting out of hope of reward or fear of punishment hardly seems the highest motivation for doing good. But in fact, Jesus believed that disinterested goodness (Luke 14:12–14) is always the highest motive, and that the reward of simply knowing you have done God's will for which you will one day be commended (Matthew 25:23) should be sufficient. However, he also said that God rewards right behaviour (Matthew 6:4) and punishes bad or selfish behaviour (Matthew 25:41). He believed things are judged by their results: "Every good tree bears good fruit, but a bad tree bears bad fruit" (Matthew 7:17). Good trees are worth keeping; bad ones aren't (7:18–19). And so it is with people. Knowing this is how things are, yet not saying so, would surely be the most unethical thing of all.

Simple living

Jesus lived a simple lifestyle, uncluttered by "things" and utterly dependent on God. He had no means of transport, borrowing a donkey when he needed one (Matthew 21:1–5); "nowhere to lay his head" (Luke 9:58), accepting hospitality wherever it was given; no income, receiving support through friends (Luke 8:1–3) and miraculous provision (Matthew 17:27). Here was a man who believed in simple, faith-filled living. By contrast, he warned strongly of the dangers of materialism (Matthew 6:24; Luke 8:14; 12:13–21; 16:13–14), and some would-be followers turned away when he challenged their love of money (Luke 18:18–30). However, Jesus was no ascetic, glorifying poverty for its own sake. He could enjoy life, for example attending meals and weddings with all the enjoyment they brought. But such things weren't the goal of his life; he could live with them or without them, for his contentment was not in "things" but in God.

Self-denial

Jesus believed in self-denial, but not as an end in itself. For him, it was about controlling your desires rather than letting them control you (Matthew 5:29–30) and refraining from valid appetites sometimes to devote yourself to something better (Luke 4:1–13). Like him, his followers had to be ready for the ultimate act of self-denial: "If anyone would come after me, he must deny himself and take up his cross and follow me" (Matthew 16:24).

Ruins at Qumran, home to the monastic Essene community. Jesus rejected this sort of lifestyle, preferring engagement with a fallen world rather than retreat from it. He believed his followers should make a difference, telling them, "You are the salt of the earth… you are the light of the world" (Matthew 5:13–14). They were to be like salt that flavours and preserves, and light that reveals things for what they are and shows God's way forward.

Faith idea: Giving

Jesus encouraged giving to the poor (e.g. Matthew 6:2–4; 19:21; Luke 12:33; 14:13–14; John 13:29), something the early church prioritized (Acts 2:45; 4:34–35; 9:36; 24:17; Galatians 2:10). Jesus challenged those who could have helped the poor but didn't (Matthew 25:31–46; Luke 12:13–21) and said that how we care for those in need will be a significant factor at the last judgment that all must face (Matthew 25:31–46).

His New Community

Life Together with Jesus

One of Jesus' first acts was calling twelve disciples, "that they might *be with him*..." (Mark 3:14), indicating that from the beginning he intended to establish a new people, a new Israel, formed around himself. This building of community modelled what God's kingdom was like, as twelve very different men discovered God's transforming power to enable them to live together.

Israel, old and new

From the very beginning of Israel's history, the Bible shows that God's plan was to build a community, not simply to save individuals (Genesis 12:1–3). Jesus said he came to complete that plan, but also to give it a new twist. There was an expectation in his day that the twelve tribes of Israel would once again be re-assembled before the end time. So when Jesus called twelve disciples, he was making a deliberate reference to this, declaring he was re-forming Israel, around himself. *He* was the new Israel, "the true vine" (John 15:1), and all who committed to being his disciples could become part of that new Israel too. It was this new community that was now the true embodiment of God's people – a community open to all: men, women, old, young, outcasts, lepers, prostitutes, tax collectors, Jews, Samaritans, non-Jews. There were no religious hoops to be jumped through, no badges of allegiance to be attained; simply a willingness to follow him and to learn to do things his way.

After the resurrection, his followers increasingly realized the implications of this, coming to see that "there is neither Jew nor Greek, slave nor free, male nor female, for you are all one in Christ Jesus" (Galatians 3:28). This "new Israel" was at last becoming what the old Israel was always meant to be: a people showing what life is like with God as king, who are eager to share this with others.

Communal images

Jesus used a variety of images to describe this new community: family members (Mark 3:34–35), brothers (Matthew 23:8), a little flock (Luke 12:32), a city (Matthew 5:14), wedding guests (Mark 2:19).

Eating together

Being invited to share a meal was a mark of friendship and honour, so betrayal of someone you shared the table with was a dreadful thing (Luke 22:21–22). Normally separate tables were set for people of different ethnic backgrounds (Genesis 43:32) and places assigned according to rank (Luke 14:8–10). But Jesus broke all these cultural rules, happily sharing table fellowship with anyone, no matter what their background or status (e.g. Mark 2:15), thereby modelling the acceptance that lies at the heart of the new community in God's kingdom.

See also
Acceptance p. 153
Birth of the Church pp. 44–45
Discipleship p. 171

Israel's oldest church building

In 2005 this well-preserved mosaic was discovered in the grounds of a prison in Megiddo. Dating from the early third century AD, before Christianity was even legalized, the mosaic of two fish (an early Christian symbol) was accompanied by Greek inscriptions saying the octagonal building was dedicated to "the memory of the Lord Jesus Christ" and was paid for by a Roman officer called Gaianus. To date, this is the oldest church building ever discovered.

Characteristics of the new community

This new community wouldn't be characterized by external badges of belonging, like circumcision and sabbath-keeping in Judaism, but rather by attitudes and actions of commitment to one another and those outside the community. These included:

- acceptance (e.g. Luke 5:27–32)
- forgiveness (e.g. Matthew 18:21–35)
- love for one another (e.g. John 13:34–35)
- love for enemies (e.g. Luke 6:32–36)
- giving to others (e.g. Luke 12:33)
- trusting God (e.g. Matthew 6:25–34)
- serving one another (e.g. John 13:12–17)
- humility (e.g. Matthew 18:1–4)
- prayerful dependence on God as Father (e.g. Matthew 6:5–13).

Acceptance of all

While Jesus' ministry was primarily among the Jews, it's clear that those whom the religious leaders saw as "outsiders" were welcomed by him. His teaching, for example in the parable of the wedding banquet (Matthew 22:1–14), portrayed God as hugely welcoming of all, and Jesus' practice of happily eating with those the religious leaders saw as "sinners" (those who didn't live up to their high standards), despite being criticized for it (e.g. Luke 5:29–32), reinforced this. He was at ease with the traditionally despised Samaritans, among whom he found an openness to his message (e.g. John 4:1–42), and even Gentiles were welcomed and healed, like the Roman centurion's servant (Matthew 8:5–13) and the Syro-Phoenician woman's daughter (Mark 7:24–30). All of this modelled how, at the end, "many will come from the east and the west, and will take their places at the feast with Abraham, Isaac and Jacob in the kingdom of heaven" (Matthew 8:11).

Did Jesus plan the church?

The word "church" (*ekklēsia* in Greek) occurs only twice in the Gospels, both in Matthew's Gospel. In the first occurrence (16:18), Jesus promises he will build his *church* on the rock of Peter; in the second (18:17), he teaches his followers how to resolve disputes, first by dealing directly with the other party or through another's help if necessary, but if that didn't work, by taking it to the *church*. Some have suggested this lack of reference to "church" means that Jesus himself didn't teach about it and that Matthew put these words on Jesus' lips from his own later perspective. However, although the actual word "church" isn't common in the Gospels, the concept certainly is. Indeed the central idea of Jesus' message, the kingdom of God, is impossible without community – kingship cannot be exercised over *one person*, only over *one people*. God's concern throughout the Old Testament had been to establish a people, not to save individuals. It is therefore inconceivable that Jesus would suddenly have abandoned such a fundamental truth, especially when God's kingdom lay at the heart of his teaching.

Faith idea: Fellowship

Fellowship – the open sharing of hearts and lives – lay at the centre of the new community Jesus built with his disciples. After his ascension they continued meeting together (Acts 1:14), and post-Pentecost their life was characterized by four things: the apostles' teaching, fellowship, breaking bread, and prayer (Acts 2:42). They simply continued doing with one another what Jesus had done with them, living a life of community and fellowship with one another.

His Conflicts

Encountering Opposition

It is surprising that the man who came to establish God's kingdom on earth found himself in conflict, not with the representatives of earthly kingdoms who might have had cause to fear him, but with the religious leaders who felt they were the guardians of that very kingdom he had come to bring. They simply couldn't cope with Jesus teaching that this kingdom was coming in an utterly different way from what they believed, and so conflict was inevitable.

Conflict with religious leaders

Jesus often found himself in conflict with the religious leaders:

The scribes had taken on new significance during the Babylonian exile. With priests no longer needed because the Temple lay hundreds of miles away in ruins, the Law took on even more importance. Scribes began to interpret that Law for the new situation Jews found themselves in, and by New Testament times those interpretations had become as important as the Law itself. Conflict was inevitable when Jesus rejected their interpretations, saying they had become over-concerned with minute details to the exclusion of life's big issues (Matthew 15:1–20).

The Pharisees saw scrupulous obedience to God's Law as every Jew's duty, and they themselves led the way. Not only did they keep the 613 commandments identified by the rabbis, but also all the oral traditions built around them. It was the latter that brought conflict with Jesus, especially over their crucial identity markers (such as ritual washings, fasting, tithing, sabbath-keeping and avoiding anything, or anyone, defiling). But Jesus rejected their rituals and traditions as undermining the very heart of what God had intended (Matthew 5:21–48), berated their hypocrisy (Matthew 23:1–39), and went out of his way to mix with those the Pharisees saw as "sinners" (e.g. Matthew 9:10–13; Luke 15:1–7).

The Sadducees controlled the high priesthood and the Temple and were afraid of Jesus lest he upset the political status quo and cause them to lose influence. But they also had theological disagreements with him on issues like the resurrection of the dead (Mark 12:18–27) and attitudes to the Temple (Matthew 26:59–61). While they had little in common with Pharisees, either politically or theologically, they nevertheless joined them in opposing Jesus, and it was their man Caiaphas, the high priest, who pressed for Jesus' execution (John 18:14).

John's Gospel often groups these religious leaders together, describing them simply as "the Jews".

Conflict over the Temple

Because the Temple was the central symbol of Jewish life, Herod's rebuilding of it – an attempt to legitimize his kingship since he was Idumean not Jewish – met with mixed reactions. While the Sadducees approved of his rebuilding, others strongly disapproved:

The Essenes saw the Temple as the power base of the ruling elite, ritually impure because God's Law wasn't interpreted properly there, and flawed because it didn't match Ezekiel's vision of the restored Temple (Ezekiel 40–48).

The Pharisees didn't see the Temple as crucial since, for them, the blessing of visiting it could just as equally be gained by studying the Torah.

The common people saw the Temple as a symbol of all that oppressed them.

Jesus too was opposed to the Temple, but for completely different reasons. He believed it symbolized everything that was wrong with Israel, and that it had served its purpose, that its time had come, and that it would therefore be destroyed (Mark 13:1–2; 14:58). He himself was the new temple, the "place" where sin could be forgiven.

Conflict with political leaders

Perhaps surprisingly, Jesus had few conflicts with those in political power. This may have been because he kept a low profile in Galilee most of the time and because he made it clear he hadn't come to oppose Rome. Politics wasn't his concern; God's kingdom was. So he had no problem telling people to pay their Roman taxes (Mark 12:13–17) or to carry Roman soldiers' packs (Matthew 5:41). It was all simply irrelevant to his purpose.

King Herod responded to news about Jesus with a mixture of curiosity (Luke 9:7–9), opposition (Luke 13:3), and wanting a miracle (Luke 23:8); but he only ever met Jesus on the eve of his death (Luke 23:7–12), when Jesus refused to answer any of his questions.

The Herodians wanted Herod's rule restored in Judea, so were troubled by anyone who might cause Rome to tighten its direct control. They often tried to catch Jesus out, like over the issue of paying taxes to Caesar (Matthew 22:15–22).

The Romans never saw Jesus as a threat. In fact, Romans come out well in the Gospels: one centurion was commended by Jesus for his faith (Luke 7:1–10), and another esteemed him at the cross (Matthew 27:54; Luke 23:47). Even though Pilate sanctioned Jesus'

See also
Groups and Sects pp. 152–53
Herod's Temple p. 147
Jerusalem pp. 154–53

Herod the Great
Ruled 40–4 BC
Great builder, ruthless ruler
Ruled at birth of Jesus
(Matthew 2:1–19)

Archelaus
Governor of Judea, Idumea and Samaria (4 BC–AD 6)
Ruler when Jesus' family returned from Egypt (Matthew 2:19-23)
Brutal and inept ruler; replaced by a Roman Procurator

Herod Antipas
Tetrarch of Galilee and Perea (4 BC–AD 39)
Executed John the Baptist (Matthew 14:1–12)
Wanted to kill Jesus (Luke 13:31–32)
Involved in Jesus' trial (Luke 23:6–12)

Philip
Tetrarch of Trachonitis (4 BC–AD 34)
Rebuilt Caesarea Philippi and Bethsaida
Generally well-liked by his subjects

Aristobolus
Not mentioned in the Bible

Herod Agrippa I
King of Judea (AD 37–44)
Killed James
Imprisoned Peter
Killed by an angel (Acts 12:1–23)

Herod Agrippa II
King of Judea
Paul appeared before him (Acts 25:13–26:32)

Jerusalem

A 1:50 scale model of first-century AD Jerusalem showing how the Temple (top right) completely dominated the city. This physical domination mirrored its spiritual domination of peoples' lives by this period, because of the way it operated for the benefit of the few, the priestly families, not the many.

death, the Gospels show that it was the religious leaders who were primarily responsible for it, as Peter boldly declared at Pentecost (Acts 2:13–15).

The Herods

Rome had imposed the Herods as Israel's rulers in 40 BC. Coming from Idumea (Old Testament "Edom"), the Herods were non-Jews and therefore despised. Different members of the Herod dynasty appear in the New Testament, but always opposing Jesus and the church.

Conflict with his family

Sometimes Jesus faced conflict from unexpected quarters. This included his own family, as we see with his brothers who didn't believe in him (John 7:1–5) and who came to Capernaum to take him home (Mark 3:31–32). It also included Peter who, having been commended by Jesus for his insight, suddenly found himself being called Satan for attempting to deflect him from his chosen path (Matthew 16:22–23).

Faith idea: Conflict

While Jesus faced conflict, he never deliberately sought it, and he taught his followers to do all they could to avoid it. He said it was peacemakers who were blessed (Matthew 5:9) and that it was better to be sued or forced to carry a soldier's pack than to get into conflict (Matthew 5:40–41). But he also recognized the need to make a stand, even to your own cost (e.g. Matthew 16:24–28). Where personal conflicts do arise, Jesus gave a model for how to resolve them (Matthew 18:15–17).

His Final Week

Approaching the Goal

Three years of showing what God was really like, three years of kindness, miracles, and amazing teaching, suddenly came to a climax in one final action-packed week. Jesus had crossed the religious leaders once too often, so they conspired to get rid of him. And yet everything about this final week, called "Holy Week" in the church, spoke of Jesus being in control as he approached his goal.

Triumphal entry

The atmosphere was always electric when pilgrims saw Jerusalem; but it was even more so the day Jesus entered the city. Underlining how his messianic claims were different from those expected, he rode not a horse (an animal of war) but a donkey (an animal of peace), fulfilling Zechariah's prophecy of how Israel's king would come (Zechariah 9:9). The crowds waved palm branches (victory symbols), laying their cloaks on the road, welcoming the one who "comes in the name of the Lord", and shouting "Hosanna" ("Save!"). But to their surprise, he simply looked around before returning to Bethany (Mark 11:11).

1. Friday: Arrival in Bethany
Jesus arrived in the tiny hamlet of Bethany, staying with his friends Lazarus, Mary, and Martha. Mary anointed his feet with expensive perfume, which Jesus saw as preparation for his burial but which Judas resented as wasteful (John 12:1-8).

2. Saturday: Rest
While the Gospels give no details, Jesus probably spent his final sabbath relaxing in Bethany.

3. Sunday: Triumphal Entry
Borrowing a donkey from nearby Bethphage (Matthew 21:1), Jesus rode into Jerusalem, where the crowds welcomed him as their king (Matthew 21:1-11; Mark 11:1-11; Luke 19:28-44; John 12:12-16); but Jesus wept over Jerusalem's tragic destiny (Luke 19:41-44).

4. Monday: Cleansing the Temple
Jesus returned from Bethany, cursing a fruitless fig tree on the way (Mark 11:12-14). He was outraged to find the Temple's outer courtyard full of traders and moneychangers, throwing them out and overturning their tables (Matthew 21:12-17; Mark 11:15-19; Luke 19:45-46).

5/6. Tuesday and Wednesday: Teaching
Returning to the Temple, Jesus taught all who would listen, while the religious leaders challenged him (Matthew 21:23 - 23:39; Mark 11:27 - 12:44; Luke 20:1 - 21:4). Going to the Mount of Olives, he spoke of Jerusalem's destruction and his return (Matthew 24:1 - 25:46; Mark 13:1-37; Luke 21:5-38).

7. Thursday: Last Supper and Gethsemane
After washing his disciples' feet, Jesus celebrated Passover, one day early, knowing he wouldn't be alive the next day. Judas left to betray him, while the rest left for Gethsemane where Jesus predicted Peter's denial and spent time praying, waiting to be arrested (Matthew 26:31 -56; Mark 14:27-52; Luke 22:31-53; John 18:1-14).

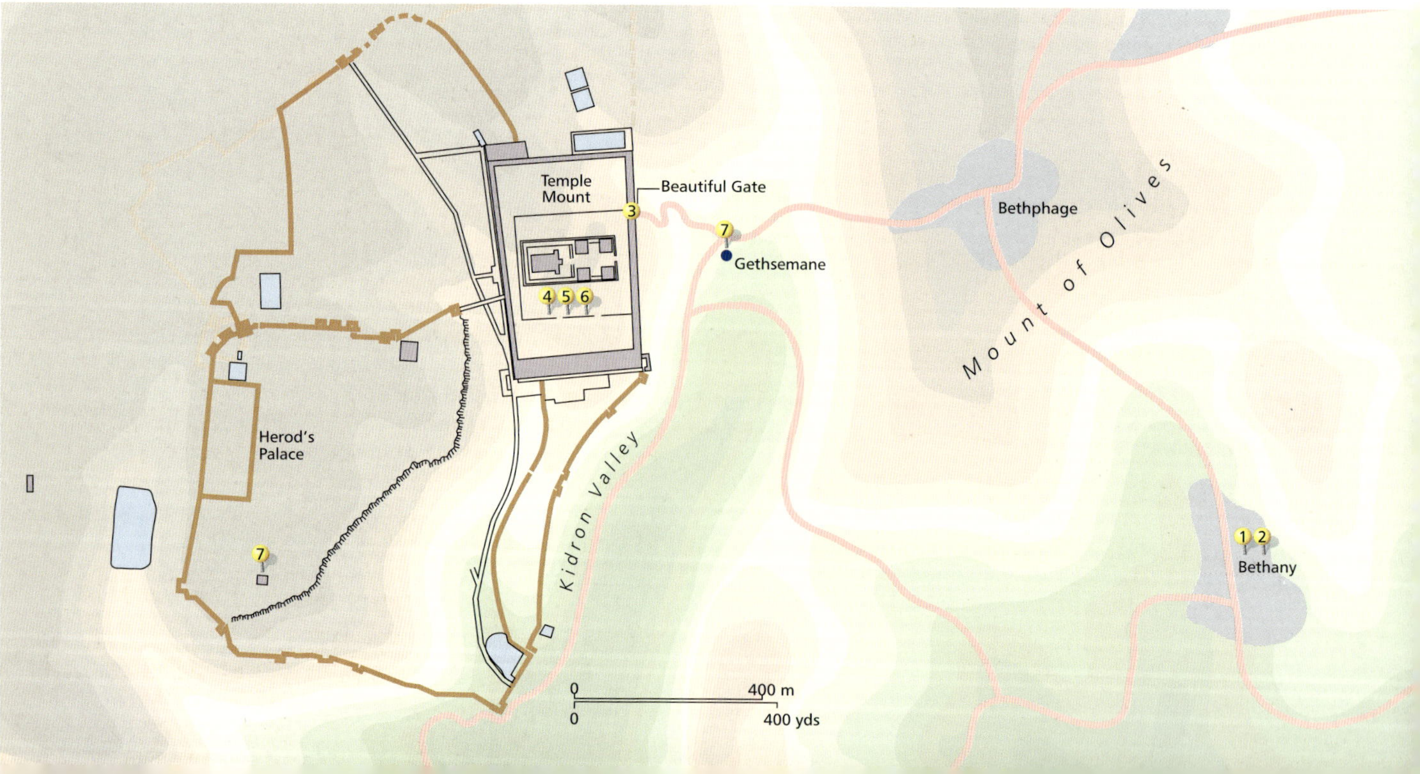

See also
His Conflicts pp. 180–81
His Death and Resurrection pp. 184–85
Passover pp. 138–39

Cleansing the Temple

On Monday Jesus drove out the merchants from the Temple and upturned the moneychangers' tables (Matthew 21:12–17; Mark 11:15–19; Luke 19:45–46), saying they had turned a house of prayer into a robbers' den. Not only was he showing concern for Gentiles, since this was the only area where they could pray, he was also declaring that the Temple's purpose and days were numbered.

John has a Temple cleansing at the beginning of Jesus' ministry (John 2:12–22), and some think he deliberately relocated this incident to underline that God's judgment was at work from the very beginning of Messiah's ministry. However, there are several different details in the two accounts, perhaps suggesting that separate incidents are being described. After all, vested interests frequently lead to malpractice creeping back, and three years had now passed, ample time to return to old ways.

The Last Supper

It was Thursday 14 Nisan, and the priests had been slaughtering Passover lambs all afternoon. Passover would be celebrated the next day, but since Jesus knew he wouldn't be around then, and since for Jews each day ended at sunset, he celebrated it the night before. Meeting in an upper room that he had previously organized (Matthew 26:17–19; Mark 14:12–16; Luke 22:7–13), he washed his disciples' feet (John 13:1–17) before celebrating Passover with them.

Passover was central to Jewish identity, looking back to celebrate God's deliverance of Israel from slavery in Egypt (Exodus 12), but also looking forward to his rescuing them again, this time from Rome. But Jesus was about to give Passover a new meaning. At first, everything followed the old traditions, but suddenly Jesus changed the wording over the bread and wine, placing his body and blood at the centre of Israel's story, thereby claiming he was about to bring the new exodus that Israel had been longing for. But not only would there be a new exodus, but also a new covenant, he said, established by him between God and people, that would bring forgiveness of sins (Matthew 26:28).

It was here that Jesus told his disciples to "do this in remembrance of me" (Luke 22:19), and this quickly became a key part of Christian worship, though initially in the context of a meal. Today, Christians still share bread and wine to remember Jesus' death, though calling it by different names: the Lord's Supper, Breaking of Bread, Holy Communion, and Mass.

Judas's betrayal

Judas had been seeking the right moment for several days (Matthew 26:14–16; Mark 10:2; Luke 22:1–6), ever since the anointing in Bethany that had so angered him, and Jesus knew his intentions (Matthew 26:20–25; Mark 14:17–21; Luke 22:22–23; John 13:18–30). Why he betrayed Jesus is hard to understand. While some suggest he was trying to force Jesus' hand into acting against the Romans, the only psychological insight the Gospels offer is that he simply did it for the money (Matthew 26:8–9, 14–16) – not that he gained much, as thirty pieces of silver was only the value of a slave, or about four months' wages. Later, troubled by his conscience, he tried to return the money, but when the religious leaders washed their hands of it, he committed suicide (Matthew 27:1–5).

Faith idea: Submission

Submission to God is doing what he wants rather than what we would choose. Jesus modelled this supremely in Gethsemane, where he didn't run but awaited arrest, praying for strength and committing himself anew to his Father's purpose above his own feelings or desires (Matthew 26:36–46; Mark 14:32–42; Luke 22:39–46). Christians are called to follow his example, submitting both to God (James 4:6–7) and one another (Ephesians 5:21).

Jerusalem as seen from the Mount of Olives where Jesus awaited his arrest.

His Death and Resurrection

God's Ransom

Jesus' death was inevitable, as vested interests conspired against him during that final week. And yet that inevitability had been there from the beginning; for this had been God's plan all along, Jesus claimed, as the only way to deal with human sin. The moment had arrived for God himself to "give his life as a ransom for many" (Mark 10:45).

Jesus was whipped with a flagrum, whose leather thongs were studded with metal or bone to inflict maximum damage.

Execution

Jesus was executed by crucifixion, the *titulus* above his head recording his crime in Aramaic, Latin, and Greek: "This is the King of the Jews", despite the religious leaders' objections. This was his darkest hour, feeling even God had abandoned him (Matthew 27:46). Darkness covered the land for three hours (Luke 23:44–45), until he finally cried out, "It is finished!" (John 19:30). His work completed, he yielded his life and entrusted himself to his heavenly Father (Luke 23:46). Roman soldiers, sent to hasten his death before sabbath at the religious leaders' request, found he was already dead. But to make sure, they thrust a spear into his body, causing blood and water to spurt out (John 19:31–37), probably from the rupturing of his heart. The man who claimed to be Messiah was dead.

Crucifixion

The Romans used crucifixion as a brutal means of execution to instil fear. The condemned man was flogged before carrying the crossbar to the execution place. Stripped naked, his wrists were nailed to the crossbar, which was then hoisted onto a stake. His legs were pushed up and sideways and his ankles nailed to the upright so his arms had to carry his weight. Death came slowly, as the hanging body put strain on the diaphragm. Prisoners could remain conscious for days, and soldiers sometimes shortened their suffering by breaking their legs so they couldn't push themselves up to breathe. The bodies were left for birds of prey.

For both Romans and Jews, crucifixion was shameful; for Romans, because it was reserved for the worst offenders; for Jews, because the Law said anyone hanging on a tree was under God's curse (Deuteronomy 21:23). Jesus therefore experienced not just death, but a despised death.

A heel bone with an iron nail, showing how feet were brutally nailed to the cross.

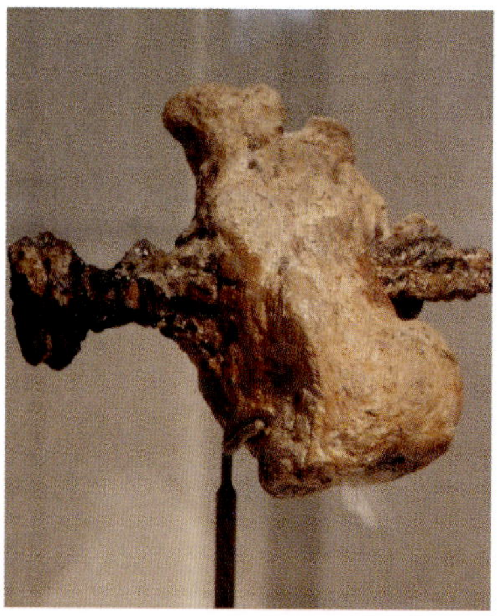

Jesus' final hours

1. Arrest in Gethsemane (Matthew 26:47–56; Mark 14:43–52; Luke 22:47–53; John 18:1–11).
2. Preliminary investigation by Annas, former high priest (John 18:12–13, 19–24).
3. Questioned by Caiaphas, the high priest, for evidence to bring to the Sanhedrin (Luke 22:54, 63–65).
4. Trial before the Sanhedrin, where he was questioned about opposition to the Temple and claims to be Messiah, culminating in an accusation of blasphemy (Matthew 26:57 – 27:1; Mark 14:53 – 15:1; Luke 22:66–71). Meanwhile, outside, Peter denied Jesus (Luke 22:54–65; John 18:15–18, 25–27).
5. Appearance before Pilate, the Roman governor (though some think this may have taken place in Herod's palace), where religious leaders accused him of opposing Roman taxes and claiming to be king of the Jews (Matthew 27:2, 11–14; Mark 15:1–5; Luke 23:1–5; John 18:28–40). Finding no basis for a charge (Luke 23:4) and discovering he was Galilean, Pilate sent Jesus to Herod.
6. Appearance before Herod Antipas, who mocked him (Luke 23:6–12). Refusing to answer Herod's questions, Jesus was returned to Pilate.
7. Trial before Pilate at "the Pavement", with demands for his death (Matthew 27:15–26; Mark 15:6–15; Luke 23:13–25; John 18:39 – 19:16). Pilate tried to release Jesus through the Passover amnesty, but the religious leaders rallied support for another prisoner, Barabbas, telling Pilate he was "no friend of Caesar" (John 19:12) if he released Jesus. Washing his hands of the case, Pilate handed him over for execution.
8. Mocked and flogged by Roman soldiers (Matthew 27:27–31; Mark 15:16–20).
9. Made to carry his cross to the execution place, but unable to continue. Simon of Cyrene was press-ganged into carrying it for him (Matthew 27:32; Mark 15:21; Luke 23:26).
10. Crucifixion outside the city between two criminals (Matthew 27:33–56; Mark 15:22–41; Luke 23:32–49; John 19:17–37).

See also
First-Century Burials p. 160
Jesus the Saviour p. 167
The Cross pp. 158–59

Resurrection

All four Gospels agree that when the women went to Jesus' tomb on Sunday, having had to rest on the sabbath, they found it empty (Matthew 28:1–10; Mark 16:1–8; Luke 1–12; John 20:1–9). Resurrection didn't occur to them – initially the women thought someone had moved the body (John 20:2, 15), while the men thought they were being hysterical (Luke 24:11). It was only gradually that the truth became clear, as further appearances occurred, first to Peter (Luke 24:34; 1 Corinthians 15:5), then to two unnamed disciples (Luke 24:13–35), then to all of them that evening as they sat behind locked doors (John 20:19–23).

What is clear from all this is that the disciples weren't gullible, waiting for the slightest thing to give them hope. Resurrection was the furthest thing from their minds, and none of them believed it at first. But gradually the truth dawned: Jesus had indeed risen, just as he said he would. Over the next thirty-nine days he continued to appear to his followers, on one occasion to more than 500 at once (1 Corinthians 15:6).

Celebrating resurrection

Easter became the greatest annual festival in the church as Christians celebrated Jesus' resurrection. But there was also a weekly celebration of it, for from earliest times they moved their day of corporate worship to "the first day of the week", Sunday (Acts 20:7; 1 Corinthians 16:2). Abandoning the long-established tradition of the sabbath (Saturday) shows just how important the resurrection was to them, and all mainstream churches have followed this practice ever since.

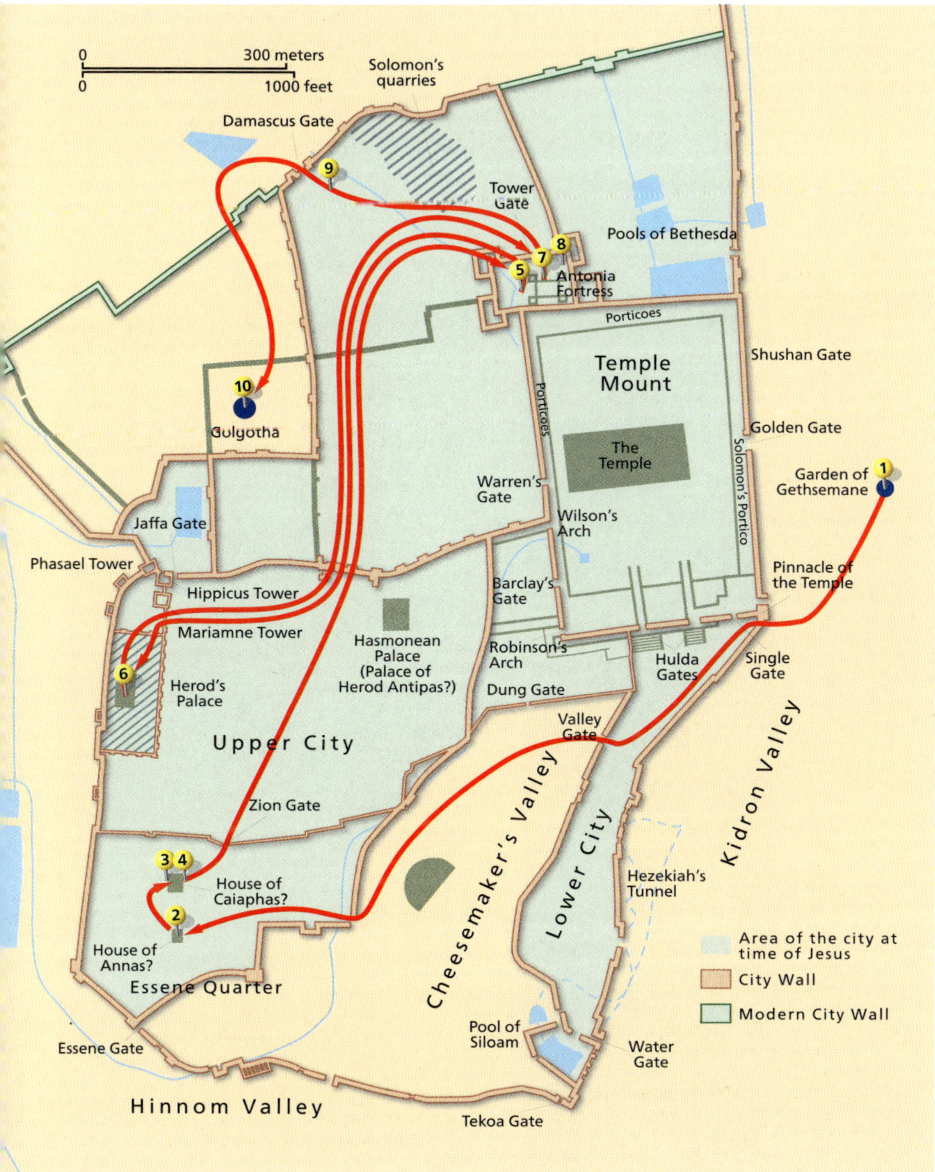

The Garden Tomb in Jerusalem which, though probably not the original one, is like the one where Joseph of Arimathea buried Jesus. A large millstone, set in a channel, was rolled across the entrance to seal the tomb (Matthew 27:57–61; Mark 15:42–47; Luke 23:50–56; John 19:38–42).

Faith idea: Belief

Belief in Jesus, and especially his resurrection, has always been foundational to Christianity. The earliest preaching included his resurrection as historical fact (e.g. Acts 2:23–24) and Paul said that if it had never really happened, then Christianity was meaningless and sin remained unforgiven (1 Corinthians 15:14–17). This belief is not just "blind faith", Christians claim, but is based on both the historical evidence of the Gospels and personal experience of the risen Jesus.

His Commission and Ascension

Time to Leave

In the weeks following the resurrection, Jesus gave his disciples "many convincing proofs that he was alive" and taught about God's kingdom (Acts 1:3). Had his appearances been confined to that first Sunday, they could perhaps be dismissed as mere hysteria or wishful thinking. But the claims persisted for forty days, and then suddenly stopped, never repeated again in that way. Jesus had commissioned his disciples to continue his work, so now he could leave them.

Ongoing appearances

Besides the Easter Sunday appearances, the New Testament records other appearances over the following weeks:

- **Thomas** (John 20:24–29)
  Thomas, not with the disciples when Jesus appeared to them, refused to believe their claims that he had risen. One week later Jesus appeared to him, inviting him to do what he had said would alone convince him: put his fingers in his wounds to prove it really was him. Thomas fell on his knees, saying what Christians have acknowledged ever since: "My Lord and my God!"
- **A group of 500** (1 Corinthians 15:6)
  In Paul's list of resurrection witnesses in 1 Corinthians 15:3–8 he records that Jesus "appeared to more than five hundred of the brothers at the same time, most of whom are still living" (15:6), the implication being that they could therefore be questioned by doubters.
- **James** (1 Corinthians 15:7)
  Listed separately to the apostles, this was James, Jesus' brother (Matthew 13:55), who didn't believe before the resurrection (John 7:5) but who became a leader in the Jerusalem church (Acts 15:13).
- **Disciples by the lake** (John 21:1–14)
  Jesus appeared to some disciples who had been fishing all night but had caught nothing. But following his direction, they had one of their biggest catches ever. Peter suddenly realized that the stranger on the beach was Jesus and rushed to him. After eating together, Jesus restored Peter, inviting him to cancel his threefold denial (Matthew 26:69–75) with a threefold declaration of love, commissioning him for his future work (John 21:15–19).

See also
God's Kingdom p. 170
His Gift of the Spirit pp. 188–89
Pentecost p. 188

The forty days

Besides convincing his disciples he really had risen from the dead – which understandably took more than one appearance – Jesus spent this period teaching the apostles about God's kingdom (Acts 1:3). Of course, he had done this throughout the previous three years; but the fact they hadn't fully understood is reflected in their question before his ascension: "Lord, are you at this time going to restore the kingdom to Israel?" (Acts 1:6). Clearly they were still thinking of God's kingdom in nationalistic terms, involving the removal of Rome and the re-establishment of Israel as a nation. But Jesus' answer showed he had a much bigger vision in mind, one that went back to God's promise to Abraham (Genesis 12:1–3): a vision not just for Israel, but for all the nations (Acts 1:7–8).

The resurrection body

While recognizably human, doing things like walking, talking, and eating, Jesus' post-resurrection body was also somehow different. Even his friends didn't recognize him immediately: Mary thought he was the gardener, until he spoke her name; the disciples on the Emmaus Road thought he was another traveller, until he broke bread. Something had obviously happened to his body, so much so that Mark's Gospel speaks of Jesus appearing "in a different form" (Mark 16:12) – what Paul called "the resurrection body". In 1 Corinthians 15:35–57 Paul explains how God will not leave believers as incorporeal spirits but will transform them, giving them "spiritual bodies", just like he gave Jesus after his resurrection, suited to life in the new creation.

The Nazareth Inscription

This marble tablet, dating from shortly after the resurrection, conveys Caesar's edict forbidding interference with tombs, on pain of death. It may simply have been a prohibition against tomb robbery; but its issue in Nazareth (an obscure town) rather than in major cities may be rooted in news of the disappearance of Jesus' body and claims of resurrection having reached the Roman authorities, who wanted to quell any further such stories.

The great commission

While in Galilee Jesus gave his disciples a key instruction, which Christians call "the great commission": to take his message to the whole world (Matthew 28:18–20; Acts 1:8). His own ministry had been confined to Israel; but in the light of the resurrection, the message could now go further, inviting all nations to become part of his "new Israel". This commission is rooted in the fact that "all authority in heaven and on earth has been given to me" (Matthew 28:18), a phrase reminiscent of Daniel's vision (Daniel 7:13–14), in which he saw the coming Son of Man; but Jesus was saying that the Son of Man was now here. In the light of that, he sent out his disciples to spread his rule over all the nations through making even more disciples. But they were not to settle for a superficial response; they were to require total commitment to Jesus, expressed in baptism and obedience to his teaching (Matthew 28:19). While they would face challenges, as the longer ending to Mark's Gospel notes, Jesus would not only be with them but would confirm their message with the sort of miracles he himself had done (Mark 16:15–20).

The ascension

Forty days after the resurrection, Jesus took his disciples to a spot near Bethany, from where he "ascended" to heaven (Luke 24:50–52; Acts 1:1–11), enveloped by a cloud, an Old Testament symbol of God's presence. The disciples were unable to believe their eyes, and it took two angels to jolt them into action.

The New Testament sees the ascension as God's final seal on Jesus' sacrifice, as he claimed his rightful place in heaven (Acts 2:33–36). But Jesus was different when he returned. At his incarnation he had become a real human being; now he was taking that same humanity back to heaven with him – the assurance that there is indeed a place for humanity in heaven.

Faith idea: Victory

The ascension convinced Christians that Jesus was victorious, exalted in heaven, reigning over his enemies (Acts 2:32–33; 5:30–31; Ephesians 4:7–10; Colossians 1:2; Hebrews 4:14; 1 Peter 3:22). Revelation, written under persecution, boldly declares that, despite the worst the devil can do, Jesus is always reigning on his throne, sharing his victory with all who trust in him (Revelation 1:17–18; 5:1–14; 7:9–17).

His Gift of the Spirit

God's Empowering Presence

During his earthly ministry Jesus had chosen twelve apostles, sending them out to preach God's kingdom (Mark 3:13–19). Before returning to his Father, he had repeated that commission, though with a significant difference: the goal was no longer Israel, but the whole world (Matthew 28:18–20; Acts 1:8). But for this they would need God's empowering presence.

Waiting

After Jesus' ascension, the disciples returned to Jerusalem. They sensed the need to replace Judas, who had committed suicide after betraying Jesus (Matthew 27:1–10; Acts 1:18–19), wanting to restore their number to twelve (reflecting the twelve patriarchs of Israel) as the foundation of Jesus' "new Israel". They resorted to the old Jewish method of seeking guidance: "casting lots" between two candidates who were eyewitnesses to Jesus' life, death, and resurrection, out of whom Matthias was chosen (Acts 1:21–26).

Pentecost

It was 9 a.m. and the disciples were waiting for the Pentecost celebrations to begin. Suddenly what seemed like wind and fire surrounded them, and they were filled with the Holy Spirit (Acts 2:1–4). Others thought they were drunk, but Peter explained to the crowd that it was too early for that; this was the work of the promised Holy Spirit, the Spirit sent by the very Jesus who had been crucified, but whom God had raised from the dead and exalted to heaven (Acts 2:14–36). Peter issued a call to repent, and 3,000 responded and were baptized (v. 41). The mission Jesus had given his disciples had exploded into action.

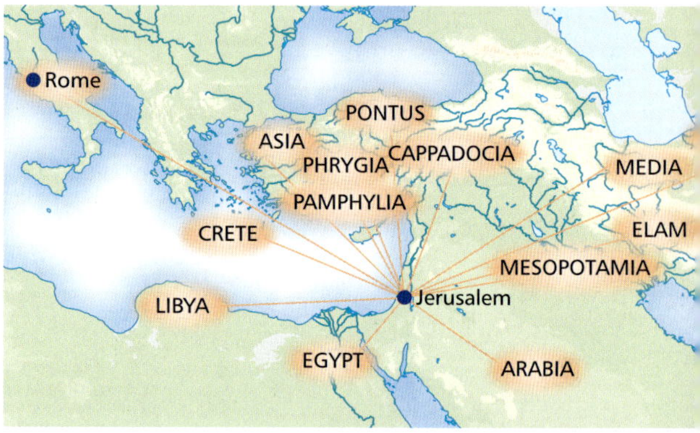

Peter's audience came from far and wide, as this map shows. As the converts returned home, they took the message with them, the first Christian missionaries.

The Royal Stoa

While it has been common to think that the Spirit came in the upper room, the Bible never says this. In fact it is far more likely to have happened here, at the Royal Stoa, a large colonnaded area at the southern end of the Court of the Gentiles in the Temple. In support of this:

- Pentecost was one of the three occasions when all Jewish men were required to visit the Temple, and it is unlikely the disciples would have ignored this.
- They numbered 120 (Acts 1:15), far too many for a home but easily accommodated in the huge courtyard.
- They attracted a large crowd quickly (Acts 2:6), impossible in an upper room or Jerusalem's narrow streets, but easy in this courtyard.
- The converts were baptized immediately (Acts 2:40–41), for which the Temple's ritual bathing tanks would have been ideal.
- The Spirit "filled the whole house" (Acts 2:2), and the Temple was often called "God's house".

Pentecost was a particularly suitable occasion for the gift of the Spirit, for it celebrated two things: the giving of the Law and the main harvest. It showed that, through the Spirit, there was now a new "law", written on people's hearts as the prophets predicted (Jeremiah 31:33; Ezekiel 36:26–27), and a new harvest, a harvest of people.

Speaking in tongues

As the Spirit came, the disciples began to "speak in other tongues" (Acts 2:4) – not gibberish or ecstasy, but languages ("tongues") that others understood (Acts 2:11), a reverse of Babel's curse (Genesis 11:1–9). However, its primary purpose was not evangelism, but worship: they were "declaring the mighty wonders of God" (Acts 2:11).

This gift wasn't restricted to Pentecost. In fact, every time the Spirit was given in Acts, speaking in tongues was evidenced, with one exception – though even there *something* so powerful happened that it shocked a former sorcerer (Acts 8:14–19). The gift was still being used in Corinth twenty-five years later, and many Christians today use this gift to help them praise or intercede.

Other spiritual gifts, called *charismata* ("grace gifts") and *pneumatika* ("spirituals"), were also practised in the early church (e.g. Romans 12:4–8; 1 Corinthians 12:7–11, 27–31; 14:1–39; Galatians 3:5; Ephesians 4:11–13; 1 Timothy 4:14).

Transformation

The Spirit's coming led to a transformation of lifestyle among the disciples, a broadening of the generous and communal life they had already experienced with Jesus, as they shared their possessions with one another and the needy (Acts 2:44–45) and even sold off surplus land (Acts 4:32–37). Luke links this generosity of lifestyle with the powerful impact made upon the community around the disciples (Acts 2:43, 47; 4:33). The Spirit was the unifying force of this Christian community, expressed in the word "fellowship" (*koinō nia*) (e.g. 2 Corinthians 13:14).

See also:
Ascension pp. 186–87
Birth of the Church pp. 44–45

Paul and the Spirit

As an ardent opponent of Christianity (Acts 8:1–3), Paul knew that if Christianity reached Damascus, situated on key trade routes, it could spread everywhere; so he resolved to stop it (Acts 9:1–2). But what he hadn't counted on was meeting the very man whose message he opposed. Blinded by a light on the Damascus Road, he discovered he had encountered the risen Jesus (Acts 9:3–5). Staggering into Damascus, he was prayed for by Ananias, whereupon he regained his sight, was filled with the Holy Spirit, and was baptized as a follower of Jesus (Acts 9:17–19).

Two things changed that day. First, the opponent became a follower, immediately preaching that Jesus was indeed the Son of God (Acts 9:20–22). Second, his experience of the Spirit became formative to his theology. He would write that it was the Spirit who raised Jesus from the dead (Romans 8:11), set people free (Romans 8:1–2), made them more like Jesus (2 Corinthians 3:18), sanctified them (1 Corinthians 6:11), helped develop Christ-like fruit in them (Galatians 5:22–23), made them his temple (1 Corinthians 6:19), gave gifts to them (1 Corinthians 12:7–11), empowered preaching (1 Corinthians 2:4), inspired mission (Acts 13:2–3), and guaranteed our future inheritance (2 Corinthians 1:22; 5:5). From start to finish, the Christian experience was all about the Spirit – so much so that he could say, "If anyone does not have the Spirit of Christ, he does not belong to Christ" (Romans 8:9).

Faith idea: Opposition

Being filled with the Spirit was no guarantee of an easy life; indeed, the Spirit's work quickly prompted opposition, as Acts shows: Peter and John were arrested for healing someone (3:1 – 4:21); the apostles were jailed and threatened (5:17–42); Stephen was martyred (6:8 – 8:1); church members were persecuted (8:1–3). But Jesus had promised that the Spirit would help them in such opposition (John 15:18 – 16:15), reinforcing the apostles' belief that "We cannot help speaking about what we have seen and heard" (4:20).

His Message

Ongoing Truth

The disciples' understanding of Jesus had been radically transformed by his death, resurrection, and ascension. So now, empowered by the Spirit, they began to preach – not just the message *of* Jesus but also the message *about* Jesus. Some have accused the early church, and especially Paul, of changing that message by turning Jesus into a pseudo-divine being. But such a conclusion is only possible by ignoring what Jesus actually taught, not least about himself. *Their* message was also *his* message.

Who Jesus was

While Jesus rarely spoke overtly about who he was, preferring veiled statements to provoke thinking, his claims are nevertheless clear. Things that point to his own self-understanding include: his forgiveness of sins (Matthew 9:2–6), his claim to be David's Lord (Luke 20:41–44), his divine claims (John 8:58), his acceptance of others' worship (Matthew 28:9–10), his actions compatible with divinity, like stilling storms (Matthew 8:23–27) and raising the dead (John 11:43–44), and his claim to have a role in the final judgment (Matthew 25:31–46) – all things that the Old Testament saw as God's prerogative alone. A more open claim came at the most unlikely and, frankly, most ridiculous point: when on trial for his life. Only now, under an oath, did he at last openly acknowledge that he was "the Christ, the Son of God" who would one day come on the clouds in glory, which Caiaphas saw as blasphemy (Matthew 26:62–66).

It isn't surprising, therefore, that the rest of the New Testament continued to express this theme of Jesus' divinity. Paul described him as "Christ, who is God over all" (Romans 9:5), "our great God and Saviour, Jesus Christ" (Titus 2:13), and said that "he is the image of the invisible God" (Colossians 1:15) and that "in Christ all the fulness of the Deity lives in bodily form" (Colossians 2:9). Great claims indeed; but no greater than those Jesus himself had made. The Christian message is a message of God loving people enough to come into the world himself to save them.

Jesus, the way

"I am the way and the truth and the life. No-one comes to the Father except through me" (John 14:6). In multi-faith societies it isn't fashionable to claim your religion is the only way to God; but that's exactly what Jesus did, claiming to be the *only* way to God because of his unique relationship with him.

What Jesus did

At the heart of Christianity lies Jesus' death on the cross. This wasn't something reinterpreted by the church after the event, for Jesus himself spoke about it, prophesying with increasing clarity and detail the death he knew awaited him. (See for example the increasing detail revealed in Matthew 12:38–40; 16:21; 17:22–23; 20:17–19). But he didn't see that death as merely inevitable. Rather he said he had "come to give his life as a ransom for many" (Matthew 20:29), that the good shepherd "lays down his life for the sheep" (John 10:11), that his blood was "the blood of the covenant, which is poured out for many for the forgiveness of sins" (Matthew 26:28) – all thoroughly sacrificial imagery.

The resurrection helped the first Christians to understand the full implications of what Jesus had done at the cross. And with his lifelong study of the Old Testament, Paul in particular was able to explain better than anyone how the Old Testament sacrifices pointed to Jesus. He saw his death as:

- **a sacrifice** – his death in place of humankind, the fulfilment of all the Old Testament sacrifices, to cleanse people from sin (e.g. Romans 3:25; 5:6–7);
- **a redemption** – his paying the price to free people from slavery to sin, as surely as Israel had been redeemed from slavery in Egypt (Romans 3:24; Ephesians 1:7–8);
- **a verdict** – God's declaration that people can be "not guilty", not because of anything they have done, but because Jesus paid for their sins so no charge remains against them (Romans 3:21–26; 5:1–2; 8:1–2);
- **a reconciliation** – his breaking of the barriers that separated people from God and one another (Romans 5:9–11; Ephesians 2:14–22);
- **a victory** – his overcoming of the devil and evil forces, stripping them of the power they held over people through their sin (e.g. Colossians 2:15).

See also:
His Death and Resurrection pp. 184–85
His Teaching pp. 170–71
Jesus the Saviour p. 167

Stained-glass window portraying open-air preacher John Wesley (1703–91). Wesley was an Anglican clergyman who took the message of Jesus into the fields and streets across the United Kingdom, seeing tens of thousands turn to faith.

What Jesus offers and demands

The New Testament expresses, through a variety of language, the blessing that Jesus came to bring. Jesus himself described it as eternal life (John 3:16), salvation (Luke 19:9), freedom (Luke 4:18), forgiveness (Matthew 26:28), new birth (John 3:3), rescue (Mark 10:45), and becoming the Father's sons (Matthew 5:45) – all images picked up by the early church as part of its message.

The door to this blessing, in both the preaching of Jesus and the early church, was "repentance" – a complete change of heart and mind. This was how Jesus' ministry began, telling people, "The kingdom of God is near. Repent and believe the good news!" (Mark 1:15). So, when he forgave the adulteress, he told her to "go now and leave your life of sin" (John 8:11). His was no comfortable message, then; and yet, those who felt uncomfortable with the Jewish religious leaders felt comfortable in his presence, despite these challenging words.

The early church continued this challenge to change. At Pentecost Peter told his audience, "Repent, and be baptised every one of you in the name of Jesus Christ for the forgiveness of your sins" (Acts 2:38). Very soon after his conversion Paul was telling people "that they should repent and turn to God and prove their repentance by their deeds" (Acts 26:20). Repentance – facing up to sin and being willing to turn from it – has always been at the heart of the Christian message.

Faith idea: Salvation

The Hebrew for "salvation" meant "brought into a spacious place" – freedom from that which restricts and confines. Being saved is about becoming free to be what God designed us to be, the Bible says; being rescued from an old way of living and being given a brand new start through Jesus, with a new inner impetus through the Holy Spirit so we can live "spaciously" and in a way that is pleasing to God. Salvation lies at the heart of the Christian message.

His Followers

God's New People

After Pentecost, the new community Jesus came to establish – variously called "followers of the Way" (Acts 9:1–2), "the believers" (Acts 2:44), "the church" (Acts 8:1–3) – surged ahead. Within a generation his followers could be found in every key city in the Roman empire. Despite fierce opposition nothing could stop them, and today his followers number over two billion, one-third of the world's population, who can be found all around the world.

Nero

In AD 64 much of Rome was destroyed by fire, reputedly started on Nero's instructions, furious that his plans for remodelling the city had been blocked by the Senate. Nero made Christians the scapegoat and thousands were crucified, thrown to lions, made to fight gladiators, or set alight as human torches in his gardens. But the church simply kept growing.

Church is people

Those who responded to Peter's message at Pentecost weren't left as individual believers but "were added to their number" (Acts 2:41), becoming part of the church. We tend to use the word "church" to mean a religious building, and they come in all sorts of shapes and sizes; but that's not how the New Testament used the word. "Church" always meant the people, never the place. Indeed church buildings didn't develop until after the emperor Constantine's conversion in AD 312 and his legalization of Christianity the following year. At its very heart, "church" is "God's people" – those seeking to follow Jesus and share his good news with others.

Images of the church

The different images used in the New Testament to describe the church all underline its corporate nature in some way or other. These include:

- family (1 Timothy 3:15; Hebrews 2:11)
- people (1 Peter 2:9–10; Revelation 7:9)
- priesthood (1 Peter 2:4–5, 9–10; Revelation 5:9–10)
- flock (Acts 20:28; 1 Peter 5:2)
- body (Romans 12:4–5; 1 Corinthians 12:27)
- God's house (Hebrews 3:6)
- temple (1 Corinthians 3:16; Ephesians 2:19–22).

Early expansion

In the decades following the ascension, the church expanded rapidly. Nothing could stop Jesus' followers, neither the opposition of Jewish authorities who persecuted (e.g. Acts 5:17–40) and even killed them (e.g. Acts 6:8 – 7:60), nor the might of the Roman emperor, whose claim to divinity brought them into direct conflict with him. Their message simply kept spreading and their numbers kept growing.

Probably more than any other individual, it was Paul who was responsible for extending the reach of the gospel. Through four missionary journeys, and many trials along the way (2 Corinthians 6:3–10; 11:23–29), he finally ended up in Rome under house arrest, awaiting a hearing before Caesar (Acts 28:30–31). His letters indicate he was released and returned to his mission; but his final words show him back in prison again, awaiting the death penalty (2 Timothy 4:6–8). He was martyred around AD 67, probably, as a Roman citizen, by being beheaded.

Christian impact

Over the past 2,000 years Jesus' followers have made a huge impact on the world, touching every area of life, including:

- **Music**
  Christian faith has inspired all kinds of music – classical anthems, Gregorian plainchant, requiem masses, gospel, country and western, hymns, pop – as composers expressed their faith for their time and culture. One of the most magnificent works is Handel's *Messiah*, a wonderful portrayal of Jesus' life and significance.

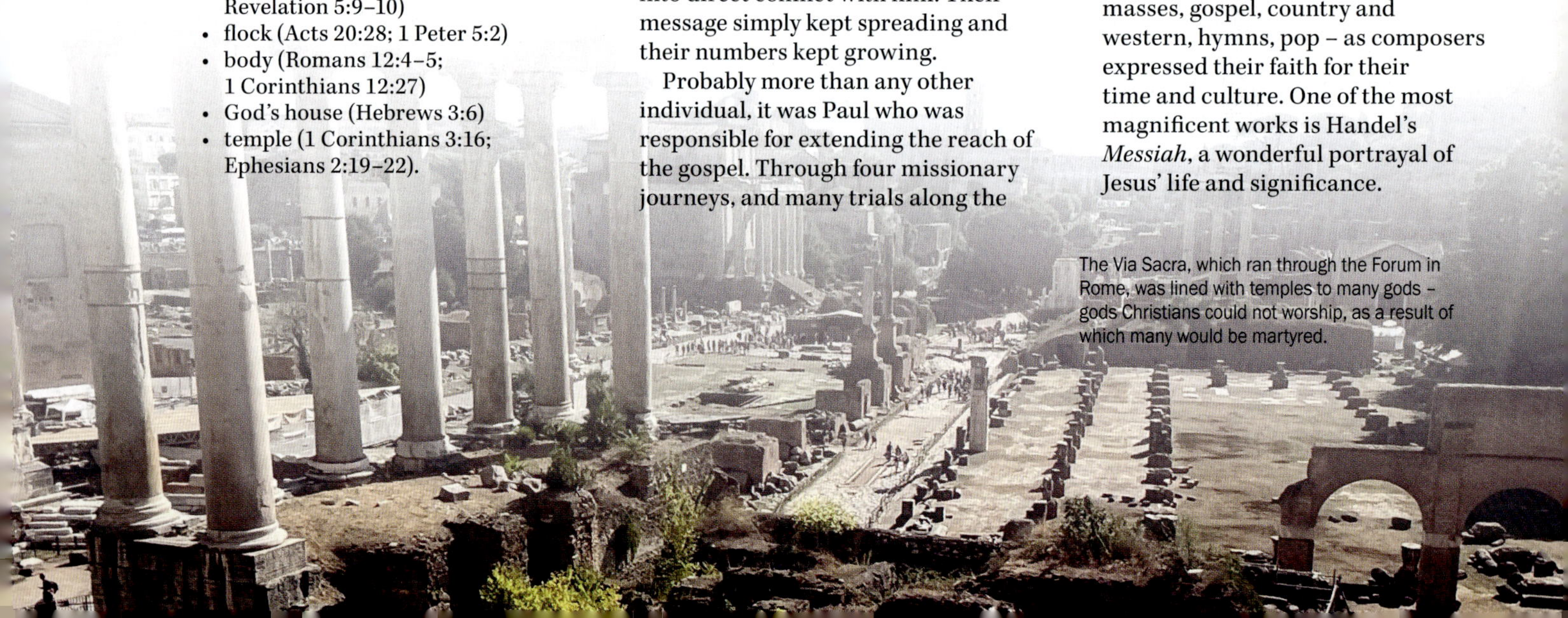

The Via Sacra, which ran through the Forum in Rome, was lined with temples to many gods – gods Christians could not worship, as a result of which many would be martyred.

See also:
Growth of the Church pp. 46–47
The Christian Faith pp. 158–59
His New Community pp. 178–79

- **Art**
Artists through the ages have sought to express something of Jesus' humanity and divinity, sufferings and glory, creating countless masterpieces of paintings, frescos, icons, and sculptures, all reflecting their vision of Jesus their Saviour.

- **Literature**
Christianity has been a huge inspiration for poetry, fiction, and drama, as well as more directly spiritual writings. Some of the best-known examples include Christian fiction like Dante's *Divine Comedy* (1308–21), Milton's *Paradise Lost* (1667), and Bunyan's *Pilgrim's Progress* (1678).

- **Architecture**
In the twelfth century AD Gothic architecture gave churches a sense of grandeur through flying buttresses and large windows with stained glass portraying Bible stories. Masons spent their whole life creating masterpieces, prompted by their faith.

- **Education**
Universities developed from religious orders, providing education in Paris, Oxford, and Cambridge. The Czech Jan Comenius (1592–1670) championed universal education, while Robert Raikes (1736–1811) pioneered Sunday Schools in Britain, convinced that education was the key to helping people out of poverty.

- **Social justice**
Elizabeth Fry (see left; 1780–1845), a Quaker, worked tirelessly to reform prison conditions in the UK; William Wilberforce (1759–1833) devoted his life to the abolition of slavery in the British empire; Martin Luther King (1929–68) played a leading role in the USA non-violet civil rights movement; Helder Camara (1909–99), a Latin American Roman Catholic archbishop, defended the rights of the poor and challenged unjust social structures – all prompted by their Christian faith.

- **Social improvement**
John Cadbury (1801–89), a British Quaker, believed alcohol was a major cause of social ills, so began to produce drinking chocolate and cocoa as wholesome alternatives. He built not just a factory to produce it but a whole "model village" for his workers. Lord Shaftesbury (1801–85), a British politician, was responsible for introducing better working conditions in factories and mines, for reforms to mental health and education and limiting child labour. Thomas Cook (1808–92), a Baptist minister, chartered trains to take people away on day-trips and was soon offering holiday tours of Europe, Egypt, and the USA.

- **Caring for the poor**
Albert Schweitzer (see above; 1875–1965), a German theologian, philosopher, musician, and missionary doctor, won the Nobel Peace Prize for his philosophy of "Reverence for Life", expressed practically through the hospital he founded in French Equatorial Africa (Gabon). Mother Teresa (1910–97), an Albanian Roman Catholic nun, founded the Missionaries of Charity in Calcutta to care for India's poor, sick, orphaned, and dying. By her death the mission had 610 bases in 123 countries.

- **Healthcare**
Florence Nightingale (1820–1910) studied public health and started caring for the sick, despite her wealthy family's opposition. In 1854 she was sent to the war zone in Turkey and given responsibility for hygiene and patient care. On returning home she met Queen Victoria, who established a Royal Commission on hospital procedures in which Florence played a key part.

Faith idea: Christian values

Christian values – like freedom, dignity, equality, forgiveness, tolerance, the value of the individual, the right to act according to conscience – are fundamental liberties that we would not enjoy today in Western civilization had followers of Jesus not taken his message and principles and grafted them into the very fabric of society. Without Jesus and his influence, society would have been very different, Christians believe.

His Return

Hope for the Future

The first Christians believed Jesus would return soon, and persecution only increased that expectancy. Gradually they realized this wouldn't happen in their lifetime, for God wanted many more to be saved (2 Peter 3:9). Although that return still hasn't happened, the Bible affirms its certainty, bringing God's plan to completion: the restoration of humanity and the whole of creation. The study of these end-time events is known as *eschatology*.

Future hope

Many of Jesus' parables – the tenants, the wedding banquet, the servants, the ten virgins, the talents, the sheep and goats – spoke of future hope for his followers, as well as future judgment for unbelievers. He repeated this hope the night before his crucifixion when, sensing his disciples' anxiety, he promised, "In my Father's house are many rooms; if it were not so, I would have told you. I am going there to prepare a place for you. And if I go and prepare a place for you, I will come back and take you to be with me that you also may be where I am" (John 14:2–3). Jesus was confident, not only of his own destiny, but of that of all who believed in him.

Jesus' return

Jesus promised that one day God will destroy evil, judge sinners, save his people, and establish the new creation. He prophesied two key stages to this: first, the destruction of the Temple (Mark 13:1–23), now irrelevant to God's purposes (Rome destroyed it in AD 70), and second his own return (Mark 13:24–37). The disciples assumed these events would occur simultaneously, though gradually came to see they wouldn't. In Mark 13 Jesus gives four characteristics of his return, saying it would be:

- **personal** (v. 26) – not a metaphor for death, but Jesus himself returning to earth just as he left (Acts 1:11);
- **public** (vv. 24–27) – not secret like his first coming, but glaringly obvious;
- **triumphant** (v. 26) – not modest, but splendid and victorious (see also 1 Thessalonians 4:13–18);
- **unexpected** (vv. 32–37) – its timing known only by the Father (v. 32), it was essential to be constantly ready, for life would be continuing as normal when it happened (Matthew 24:36–44).

While often called "the second coming", the New Testament itself never uses this expression, but rather three Greek words:

- ***Parousia*** = "arrival" (James 5:7–8; 2 Peter 3:4) – used of royal visits when everyone turned out to greet the king.
- ***Apokalypsis*** = "revelation" (Luke 17:30; 2 Thessalonians 1:7) – used of lifting the curtain at the theatre. Jesus' coming will "lift the curtain" to show things and people as they really are.
- ***Epiphaneia*** = "appearance" (2 Thessalonians 2:8; Titus 2:13) – literally, "a glorious manifestation", with Jesus seen in all his glory.

Hell

Jesus used the traditional imagery of Jerusalem's garbage dump, "Gehenna" (usually translated "hell"), to describe the destiny of the godless (e.g. Matthew 5:29–30; Luke 12:5). Some see it as a place of eternal punishment, while others a place of utter destruction. Whichever it is, Jesus said it was fearsome and to be avoided at all costs.

"Christ has indeed been raised from the dead, the firstfruits of those who have fallen asleep" (1 Corinthians 15:20).

The "firstfruits" was the first sheaf of harvest given to God (Leviticus 23:10–20), a token that it all belonged to him. Jesus' resurrection is God's token that the rest of the "resurrection harvest" (believers in Jesus) will surely follow.

See also:
Hope for the Future p. 161
The Resurrection Body p. 187
What Happens After Death? pp. 160–61

Christ's return

"The Lord himself will come down from heaven, with a loud command, with the voice of the archangel and with the trumpet call of God, and the dead in Christ will rise first. After that, we who are still alive and are left will be caught up together with them in the clouds to meet the Lord in the air. And so we will be with the Lord for ever" (1 Thessalonians 4:16–17).

The last days

The Bible says that the end of human history will be preceded by great troubles (Matthew 24:29; 2 Timothy 3:1–5), which is why Christians have often thought they were in "the last days", especially during persecution or crisis. But in fact the Bible sees the whole period between Jesus' ascension and return as "the last days". Rather than being an "end" we walk *towards*, "the last days" are an end we constantly walk *along*, like walking along a cliff edge over which we could be pushed at any moment – hence the challenge to always be ready.

While some things will characterize this whole "last days" period – apostasy, false religion, godlessness, persecution, increasing catastrophes – the Bible prophesies one final opponent appearing prior to Jesus' return, variously called "Antichrist" (1 John 2:18–22; 4:3; 2 John 7), "the man of lawlessness" (2 Thessalonians 2:3), and (for some interpreters) "the beast" (Revelation 13:1–10); but Christ's victory over him is absolutely assured (Revelation 19:19–20; 21:10).

Heaven: not our final home!

While Christians often speak of "spending eternity in heaven", that's not actually what the Bible promises. It says the goal is spending eternity with God *on earth*. Heaven is simply God's magnificent waiting room where believers are safe, with Jesus, until he returns. At that point they will accompany him, given "resurrection bodies" (Romans 8:23; 1 Corinthians 15:35–57) for their life on a renewed earth (Revelation 21:1 – 22:5).

The millennium

Revelation 20:1–7 describes a 1,000-year reign of Jesus. Three different views of this "millennium" are held by Christians today:

The post-millennial view sees it as a literal 1,000 years that will *climax* in Jesus' return.	**The pre-millennial** view sees it as a literal 1,000 years that will *begin* when Jesus returns, binding Satan, but not overthrowing him until the end of that period before the final judgment.	**The a-millennial** view sees it as a symbolic period, since Revelation uses all other numbers symbolically, signifying the time between Jesus' first and second comings.

The fact that it is only mentioned here in the whole Bible suggests this is not a crucial point of belief, despite many Christians making it so.

Faith idea: Being ready

"Be prepared, because you don't know what day your Lord is coming" (Matthew 24:42). The Bible calls everyone to be ready, living in the light of Jesus' return, for this life is the only opportunity to prepare for eternity. Through faith in Jesus, however, it affirms that it really is possible to be confident of our eternal destiny.

Index and Fast Fact Finder

This section is both an index to the Encyclopedia and a Fast Fact Finder for use with the Bible, providing both biblical references and page references to articles in the Encyclopedia.

Words in italics are explained at their own entry.

A

Aaron
Moses' elder brother and spokesman (Exodus 4:14–16; 6:28 – 7:7), *Israel*'s first *high priest* (Exodus 28:1; Leviticus 8) who, when Israel wanted another god when Moses didn't return from *Mount Sinai*, made a golden *idol* (Exodus 32). Sharing Moses' anger, he forfeited his right to enter the *Promised Land* (Numbers 20:1–12, 22–29). pp. 56, 133, 146, 148

Abba
Aramaic for "daddy", used of God by *Jesus* (Mark 14:36) and subsequently by the early *church* (Romans 8:15; Galatians 4:6).

Abel
Adam's second son, killed by his brother *Cain* (Genesis 4:1–16). p. 22

Abihu
See *Nadab*

Abimelech
1. Philistine king to whom *Abraham* pretended *Sarah* was his sister (Genesis 20).
2. Son of *Gideon*, the judge who killed his seventy brothers to clear the way for proclaiming himself king (Judges 9).

Abortion
Deliberate termination of pregnancy. p. 89

Abram (Abraham)
Israel's founding father. Originally from *Mesopotamia*, Abram ("exalted father") responded to God's call to move to *Canaan* (Genesis 12:1–3). God made a *covenant* with him, promising him a son and a nation (Genesis 15:1–21), giving *circumcision* as the covenant's sign, and naming him Abraham ("father of many") (Genesis 17:1–27). Abraham is noted for putting his *faith* in God (Genesis 15:6), and the *New Testament* sees him as "the father of all who believe" (Romans 4:11). pp. 15, 19, **24**, 28, 31, 34, 36, 42, 44, 46–47, 49, 52–53, 57, 63, 64, 66–69, 71, 118, 128, 132–33, 137, 139, 160–61, 179, 187

Absalom
Third of *David*'s six sons, who murdered his brother *Amnon* for raping his sister Tamar (2 Samuel 13). Subverted his father's rule, climaxing in rebellion (2 Samuel 15–18).

Acceptance pp. **153**, 178–79

Achan
Responsible for *Israel*'s defeat at *Ai* through stealing items devoted to God after the victory at *Jericho* (Joshua 7–8). pp. 28, 115

Acts (of the Apostles)
Account of the life and growth of the early *church*. pp. 12, 18, 135

Adam
Hebrew word meaning both "mankind" and "man", first occurring in Genesis 1:26–27. Though created on the same day as animals, Adam and his female counterpart *Eve* were made "in the image of God", lifting them above the animal world. His disobedience led to their expulsion from the Garden of *Eden* and brought *sin* and *judgment* into the human race (Genesis 3; Romans 5:12–21), something the *New Testament* says only *Jesus*, "the last Adam", can redeem humanity from. pp. 22, 56, 140, 148

Adoption p. 26

Agabus
Christian *prophet* from *Jerusalem* who prophesied a famine (Acts 11:27–30) and *Paul*'s imprisonment (Acts 21:10–14).

Agricultural year pp. 138–39

Agriculture
See *Farming*

Agrippa
1. Herod Agrippa I, grandson of Herod the Great, who ruled *Judea* (AD 37–44). Killed *James*, imprisoned *Peter*, struck down by an angel (Acts 12:1–23).
2. Herod Agrippa II, before whom *Paul* appeared at *Caesarea* (Acts 25:13–26).
See *The Herods*, pp. 181–82

Ahab
Wicked king of *Israel* (874–853 BC) who, influenced by his wife *Jezebel*, led Israel into *Baal* worship (1 Kings 16:29–33), bringing conflict with *Elijah* (1 Kings 18:16 – 19:5; 21:1–28). Killed in battle against the *Arameans* despite elaborate deception, his blood licked by dogs as prophesied (1 Kings 21:19). pp. 33–36, 52, 69, 73

Ai
Canaanite town, where *Israel* experienced its first defeat (Joshua 7:1–5) because of *Achan*'s *sin* of taking booty from *Jericho*. Once the *sin* was exposed (Joshua 7:6–27), Ai was taken (Joshua 8:1–29).

Akkad, Akkadian(s)
Mesopotamian people group whose empire grew under King *Sargon* in the third millennium BC, ruling from his capital of Akkad, later called *Babylon*. Akkadian became the unifying language of the region. pp. 48, 63, 120

Alexander the Great
Founder of the huge Greek empire and fierce promoter of *Hellenization*. pp. **40–41**, 49, 64, 76, 78–79, 123, 128, 152, 162

Alexandria
Major *Egyptian* port founded by *Alexander the Great*. Capital of *Egypt* under the *Ptolemies* and second city of the *Roman empire*. Home to the largest community of *Jews*, it was here that the *Septuagint* was translated. pp. 15, 18, 40, 46, 64, 110, 113, 121

Almighty
One of God's names, in *Hebrew* El Shaddai, "the all-powerful one"or "the all-sufficient one". pp. **130–31**

Alpha and omega
First and last letters of the *Greek* alphabet, signifying beginning and end, used as a title by God himself (Revelation 1:8; 21:6) and by Christ (Revelation 22:13).

Altar
A place of *sacrifice*. pp. 28, 36, 40, 52, 78, 139–140, 146–48, 167

Amalekites
Descendants of Amalek, *Esau*'s grandson, who lived as *nomads* in *Sinai* and the *Negev*. Attacked the *Israelites* at the time of the *exodus*, for which they were put under a permanent *vow* of destruction (Exodus 17:8–16). p. 82

Ammonites
Descended from *Lot*'s daughters (Genesis 19:36–38) and living in *Transjordan*, the *Israelites* were forbidden to conquer them because of family ties (Deuteronomy 2:19). They still attacked *Israel*, however (Judges 2:12–13; 10:6–18; 1 Samuel 11:1–14; 2 Samuel 10:1–19), but *David* defeated them (2 Samuel 11:1; 12:26–31). pp. 36, 82, 89

Amnon
King *David*'s firstborn son (2 Samuel 3:2), killed by his brother *Absalom* for raping Tamar (2 Samuel 13). p. 31

Amorites
Nomadic people from *Mesopotamia* who spread to *Syria* and *Canaan*. The *Israelites* defeated their kings Sihon and *Og*, who controlled most of the land east of the *Jordan*. Gradually absorbed by *Reuben*, *Gad*, and *Manasseh* (Joshua 12:1–6).

Amos
Eighth-century BC *prophet* from *Judah* who prophesied mainly in *Israel*, challenging its lack of justice and godliness, denouncing the *sanctuary* at *Bethel*, and warning of coming *judgment*. pp. 34–35, 51, 57, 73, 151

Amulet
Object worn as a charm or protection against *evil* in the form of a bracelet, pendant, statue, or engraved gem. pp. 65, 75, 120, 145

Ananias
1. Jerusalem *Christian* struck dead, with his wife Sapphira, for trying to deceive the *church* (Acts 5:1–11). p. 44
2. Christian in *Damascus* who played a significant role in *Saul*'s conversion (Acts 9:1–19). p. 189

Andrew
Simon Peter's brother, fisherman, one of *Jesus*' twelve *disciples*, who introduced Peter to Jesus (John 1:35–42) and brought the boy with five loaves and two fish with which Jesus fed 5,000 (John 6:8–9). p. 169

Angels
Spirit messengers, often appearing in human form, who brought God's word, provision, or protection. pp. 16, 28, 43, 45, 141, 144–45, 164–65, 167

Anger pp. 14, 25, 27, 35, 37, 46, 67, 72–73, 130, 157, 176

Animals pp. 22–23, 50, 56, **58–61**, 67, 69, 73, 75, 77, 81, 85, 93–94, 96, 100, 104–105, 108, 111, 113–114, 123, 125, 132, 136, 145, 148–49, 160, 166, 182

Animal welfare p. **59**

Anna
Prophetess who foretold *Jesus*' messianic work when his parents presented him in the *Temple*.

Annunciation
The angel *Gabriel*'s message to *Mary*, announcing she would conceive and give birth to God's Son. p. 164

Anointing
The pouring of oil over the head to set someone apart for God's service, symbolic of the outpouring of the *Holy Spirit*. pp. 42, 54–55, 57, 99

Antichrist
Final major opponent of Christ appearing before his return, called "Antichrist" (1 John 2:18–22; 4:3; 2 John 7), "the man of lawlessness" (2 Thessalonians 2:3), and (for some interpreters) "the beast" (Revelation 13:1–10). p. 195

Antioch
Key city on the Orontes River in *Syria* where the *church* was established by *Christians* fleeing *Jerusalem* after *Stephen*'s *martyrdom* and which became a significant base for Christian *mission*. pp. 40, 45–47

Antiochus IV Epiphanes
Seleucid ruler (175–164 BC) who sought to impose Greek culture on the *Jews* and whose actions provoked the *Maccabean* revolt. pp. 17, 40, 136

Anxiety pp. **101**, 194

Apocalyptic
Genre of literature concerned with God's end-time intervention, rich in symbolism rooted in *Old Testament* stories and imagery. *Revelation* and much of Daniel are written in this style.

Apocrypha
See *Deuterocanonicals*.

Apollos
Jew from *Alexandria* who became a *Christian* in *Ephesus* through the teaching of *Aquila* and *Priscilla*. Went to *Corinth* where he became a teacher and apologist (Acts 18:24–28).

Apostles
1. The foundational "*twelve*" appointed and sent out ("apostle" means "someone sent") by *Jesus* to preach the *kingdom of God* (Mark 3:13–19). Being an eyewitness to the *resurrection* was later seen as key to being recognized as such an apostle (Acts 1:15–26; Galatians 1:1, 15–16).
2. A "messenger" from one church to another, like *Epaphroditus* whom *Paul* describes as "your messenger" (literally, "apostle") (Philippians 2:25).
3. Those engaged in wider church-planting (e.g. Acts 14:14) or church-strengthening ministry (e.g. Ephesians 4:11–13).
4. Jesus is described as God's apostle (Hebrews 3:1).

Aquila
Jewish *Christian* who, with his wife Priscilla, had to leave *Rome* when the emperor Claudius expelled the *Jews* (AD 48). As tentmakers they befriended *Paul* (Acts 18:1–3), accompanied him on some travels (Acts 18:18–19), and used their home for Christian meetings (1 Corinthians 16:19). p. 46

Arabah
The rift valley of the River *Jordan*, running from Lake *Galilee* in the north to the *Dead Sea* (the "Sea of Arabah") in the south and on to the Gulf of Aqaba. pp. 50, 56

Arabia
Land between the *Red Sea* and the Gulf of Aqaba. pp. 45–46, 49, 51, 54–55, 60, 111, 167

Aram, Arameans
Semi-nomadic tribe from *Mesopotamia*, descendants of the *patriarchs* (Deuteronomy 26:5). Arameans in *Syria* (Aram) became powerful city-states during the eleventh to eighth centuries BC with whom *Israel* had mixed relationships. pp. 31–32, 34–35, 62, 72, 82, 196–97

Aramaic
Language of the *Arameans* that became the international language of the Middle East from 750 BC until *Greek* replaced it, though it remained the daily language of the *Jews*. pp. 15, 21, 38, 77, 82, 116, 120, 131, 170, 184

Ararat
Mountain on which *Noah*'s *ark* grounded after the *flood* in southern Urartu, east of modern Turkey (Genesis 8:3–4). p. 23

Ark
See *Flood*

Ark of the covenant
Israel's most holy artefact, a gold-covered acacia-wood box, 4x2x2 feet (1.2x0.6x0.6 m), containing the *Ten Commandments* (Exodus 40:20; Deuteronomy 10:5) and symbolizing God's presence. Rings at its corners enabled the *Levites* to carry it whenever Israel moved camp. pp. 26, 28, 31, 37, 37–38, 52, 56, 71, 128, 133–35, **146–47**, 154

Armageddon
Focal point of the gathering of God's enemies on the *Day of the Lord*, mentioned only in Revelation 16:16.

Armour pp. 128–29, 145

Artemis
Greek goddess whose silversmiths felt threatened by *Paul*'s preaching. p. 81

Ascension
Jesus' return to *heaven* forty days after his *resurrection*. pp. 44–45, 158, 161, 169, 179, **186–89**

Asher
1. *Jacob*'s eighth son, born through *Leah*'s servant, *Zilpah* (Genesis 30:12–13), whose name means "happy".
2. One of the twelve *tribes of Israel* that settled in the coastal area between *Sidon* and *Mount Carmel* (Joshua 19:24–31).

Asherah
Canaanite mother-goddess, consort of *El*, but often associated with *Baal* in the *Old Testament*, which frequently refers to Asherah poles, poles carved in her image for worship. p. 68

Ashtoreth (Astarte)
Mother-goddess in *Mesopotamia*, *Sidon*, and *Phoenicia* associated with fertility, *love*, and war. Consort of the *Canaanite* god *Baal*. pp. 68, 71

Asia Minor
Western protrusion of Asia, roughly modern Turkey. pp. 40–41, 45–46, 49, 66, 79, 81, 112

Assyria, Assyrians
Semitic people from northern *Mesopotamia* who developed from independent city-states into a powerful nation dominating the region in the ninth and eighth centuries BC. Assyria conquered and deported *Israel* in 722/721 BC (2 Kings 17:5–6; Isaiah 10:5). pp. 14, 16, 20, 24, 32–33, **34–38**, 41, 49, 52–53, 60–64, 70, **72–74**, 82–83, 85, 116, 118, 127–29, 145, 154

Astrology
Attempt to establish omens from the movement of the stars, forbidden in the *Bible*. pp. 75, 145, 167

Athens
Capital of Greece and intellectual centre of the Roman empire where *Paul* preached on his second *missionary* journey (Acts 17:15–34). pp. 41, 46, 78–79, 103, 110, 119

Atonement
The restoration of relationship with God through the "covering" (which is the root meaning of the *Hebrew* word) of *sin* through sacrifice. The *New Testament* sees *Old Testament* sacrifices as merely a foreshadowing of the sacrifice of *Jesus*. pp. 96, 138, 143, 146, 149

Atonement, Day of
Annual festival when Israel's *high priest* undertook elaborate sacrificial rituals and entered the *Holy of Holies*, the only occasion he could do this, to offer *sacrifice* for Israel's *sin* (Leviticus 16:1–34; 23:26–32; Numbers 29:7–11). pp. **138**, 143, 146

Atraharsis Epic
Early second millennium BC *Mesopotamian* myth depicting creation, early human history, and a great flood. p. 23

Augustus
First Roman emperor, under whose reign (31 BC – AD 14) *Jesus* was born (Luke 2:1).

Authorities, Christian response to p. **81**

Azariah
Also called Uzziah, king under whose reign (791–739 BC) *Judah* prospered and whose death led to *Isaiah*'s vision and call (Isaiah 6). pp. 17, 33, 36

B

Baal
Canaanite fertility god whose *worship* proved an ongoing snare to *Israel* because of its highly sexualized nature. pp. 20, 28, 34, 36, 51–52, 68–69, 71, 144, 151

Babel
Site of the great tower (ziggurat), seen in the Bible as a symbol of human pride and ambition

thwarted by God (Genesis 11:1–9). pp. **23**, 63, 75, 189

Babylon
Capital of Babylonia, whose name means "gate of the gods". Through a series of powerful rulers, it conquered its *Assyrian* masters, swallowing up and expanding their empire, including *Judah* whom it exiled and whose *Temple* it destroyed in 586 BC. It fell to *Persia* in 539 BC. pp. 14–15, 17, 20, 23–24, 33, 35, **36–37**, 38–41, 48–49, 53, 60, 62–63, 66, 70, 72–73, **74–75**, 76, 82–83, 91, 97, 103–104, 108, 110, 114, 116, 118, 122, 127–28, 145, 147, 151, 154–55, 157, 167, 180

Balaam
Mesopotamian prophet hired by *Moabite* king Balak to curse *Israel* during its journey to the *Promised Land* but who could only bless them (Numbers 22–24). p. 27

Balak
See *Balaam*

Baptism
Immersion in water to symbolize the beginning of the Christian life, recalling *Jesus*' death, burial, and *resurrection* and his washing the sinner clean (Acts 2:38–41; Romans 6:1–11; Titus 3:5). pp. 19, 60, 132, 141, 159, 168–69, 187, 191

Baptism in the Spirit
See *Filling with the Spirit*

Bar Mitzvah
Jewish ceremony marking a boy's reaching of adulthood. pp. 15, 89

Barabbas
Prisoner released by *Pilate* in the *Passover* amnesty when the crowd demanded him rather than *Jesus* (Matthew 27:15–26).

Barnabas
Nickname of a Jewish Cypriot *Christian* called *Joseph* (Acts 4:36), meaning "son of encouragement". He welcomed the newly converted *Paul* when others were afraid of him (Acts 9:26–27), introduced him to the *Antioch* church (Acts 11:25–26), and shared in his *mission* (e.g. Acts 13:1–3). pp. 46, 83

Bashan
Fertile region east of *Galilee*, famous for cattle. pp. 59, 93

Bathsheba
Wife of *Uriah*, with whom *David* committed adultery, then conspired to have Uriah killed, a *sin* exposed by *Nathan* (2 Samuel 11–12). After David's *repentance*, Bathsheba bore *Solomon*. p. 31

Beatitudes
Blessings that begin the *Sermon on the Mount* (Matthew 5:3–10). pp. 19, **176**

Beersheba
Israel's southernmost town, on a trade route to *Egypt*. Its importance in patriarchal history (e.g. Genesis 21:22–34; 26:23–33; 46:1–4) led to it becoming a centre of pilgrimage (Amos 5:5). "From *Dan* to Beersheba" became a common expression for "from north to south". pp. 24–25, 32, 53, 57, 102, 110, 148

Benjamin
Jacob's twelfth son, born to his second wife, *Rachel* (Genesis 35:16–18), founder of the tribe of Benjamin whose descendants included *Saul* (1 Samuel 9:1), *Esther* (Esther 2:5), and *Paul* (Philippians 3:5). pp. 25, 84

Bethany
Hamlet 2 miles (3 km) east of *Jerusalem*, home to *Mary*, *Martha*, and *Lazarus*, and a favourite retreat of *Jesus* (e.g. Matthew 26:6–13; Luke 10:38–42; John 11:1 – 12:11). pp. 55, 154, 182–83, 187

Bethel
Town whose name means "House of God", named after *Jacob*'s dream of the heavenly staircase (Genesis 28:10–22). Home to the *ark of the covenant* (Judges 20:26–27) and a place of seeking God (Judges 21:2–3), leading *Jeroboam* to establish a shrine here after the kingdom divided (1 Kings 12:26–33) – what became known as "the sin of Jeroboam". pp. 32, 50, 52, 146

Bethlehem
Town whose name means "House of bread", 5 miles (8 km) southwest of *Jerusalem*, location of *Rachel*'s tomb (Genesis 35:19) and *David*'s home (1 Samuel 16). *Micah* prophesied *Messiah* would come from here (Micah 5:2; Matthew 2:1–6). pp. 43, 53, 81, 102, 154, 166–67

Bethsaida
Fishing town on Lake *Galilee*'s northern shore, whose name means "House of fish", home to *Philip*, *Andrew*, and *Peter* (John 1:44), and possibly *James* and *John* (Luke 5:10). Rebuilt by Philip the Tetrarch and renamed Julias.

Beth Shan
City in *Manasseh* whose *Canaanite* culture resisted *Israelite* influence. *Saul* and *Jonathan*'s bodies were attached to its walls after their defeat by *Philistines* (1 Samuel 31). pp. 32, 49, 71

Betrayal of Jesus pp. 178, 183

Betrothal p. **86**

Bible
Name *Christians* give to the combined Old and New Testaments, from the Greek and Latin *biblia* ("books"). pp. **10–13**

Birds pp. 59–61, 75, 98–99, 104, 136, 145, 184

Birth p. 88

Birth rituals p. **88**

Blasphemy
Dishonouring God by word or deed, for which the *Old Testament* penalty was death (Leviticus 24:10–23). *Caiaphas* saw *Jesus*' words at his trial as blasphemy, seeing them as claiming equality with God (Matthew 26:62–66). pp. 81, 170, 184

Blood
Symbolic of life in the *Bible*. Animal blood was shed in *sacrifice* and represented the animal's life poured out in death, foreshadowing "the blood of Christ", a common *New Testament* image for the sacrificial death of *Jesus*. pp. 34–35, 54, 86, 123, 132–33, 135–36, 139, 147–49, 155, 183–84, 190

Boaz
Landowner in *Bethlehem* who, as *kinsman-redeemer*, married *Ruth*, becoming an ancestor of *David* and *Jesus*.

Bread
Staple of the *Israelite* diet. pp. 50, 54, 96, **98–99**, 117, 132, 138–41, 143, 147, 159, 179, 183, 187

Bread of life
Title *Jesus* used of himself to declare his ability to sustain people's lives. p. 99

Breastpiece
Pouch on the *high priest*'s ephod, containing the *Urim and Thummim*, used to seek God's *guidance*. p. 149

Bride pp. 25, 71, 84, 86–87, 155, 172

Bride of Christ p. 87

Building pp. 24, 31–32, 37, 39, 51, 56–57, 62, 64–65, 67, 74–76, 81, 97, 102–103, **109**, 113, 129, 147, 155, 159, 167, 173, 179–80, 192

Burial pp. 53–55, 67, 157, **160–61**, 182, 185

Burning bush
Setting for *Moses*' encounter with God in the desert where God revealed his personal name, *Yahweh* ("the LORD"), and called him to lead the *Israelites* out of slavery (Exodus 3:1 – 4:17). pp. 131, 140

Byblos
Phoenician port. pp. 12, 24, 35, 39, 48, 82

C

Caesar
Title of Roman emperors in *New Testament* times: *Augustus* and *Tiberius* in the *Gospels*, Claudius in *Acts*, *Nero* at the time of Peter and Paul's *martyrdoms*. The practice of honouring Caesar as a god spread rapidly, and many *Christians* lost their lives because they refused to declare the oath of allegiance, "Caesar is Lord". pp. 21, 41, 47, 80–81, 103, 117, 123, 153, 180, 184, 187, 192

Caesarea
Mediterranean port built by Herod the Great in honour of Caesar *Augustus*, base of *Judea*'s Roman governors. Home of *Philip* the evangelist (Acts 8:40; 21:8) and the Roman *centurion* Cornelius, who was among the first *Gentile* converts (Acts 10). *Paul* spent two years in prison here (Acts 23:23 – 26:32). pp. 45–46, 52–53, 95, 103

Caesarea Philippi
Town at the foot of *Mount Hermon* by the source of the *Jordan*, rebuilt by Herod Philip, renowned for its shrines to the nature god Pan and its temple honouring Caesar *Augustus*. It was here that *Jesus* asked his *disciples* who they believed him to be (Matthew 16:13–28).

Caiaphas
High priest from AD 18 to 36, responsible for *Jesus*' execution (John 18:14). pp. 153–54, 180, 184–85, 190

Cain
Eldest son of *Adam* and *Eve* who killed his brother *Abel*, the

first example of *sin*'s effects on humanity (Genesis 4). pp. 22, 103, 108

Caleb
One of twelve spies sent into the *Promised Land* by *Moses*. Only he and *Joshua* brought back a positive report, for which their reward was settling there one day (Numbers 13–14; Joshua 14:6–14). pp. 27, 53

Calendar pp. **97**, 105, 117, 138, 166

Calf, Golden
See *Golden calf*

Calvary
Place of Jesus' *crucifixion*, from the *Latin* "calvaria", a translation of the *Greek* "kranion" ("skull") in Luke 23:33. Called *Golgotha* in *Aramaic* ("the Place of the Skull") in Matthew 27:33, perhaps because it was a place of execution.

Camel pp. 20, **58**, 63, 111

Cana
Galilean village where *Jesus* turned water into *wine* (John 2:1–11) and healed a royal official's son (John 4:46–54). pp. 96, 169, 174

Canaan, Canaanites
Region between the River *Jordan* and the Mediterranean, originally occupied by descendants of Canaan, *Noah*'s grandson, whose line was cursed for disrespect (Genesis 9:18–27). Canaan was Israel's *Promised Land* (Genesis 15:12–16; 17:8), but its fertility religions proved a constant snare. pp. 24–29, 31–32, 34–35, 38, 48–53, 55, 57, 59, 66–67, **68–69**, 70–71, 82–83, 92, 96–97, 101, 104, 112, 118–119, 131–33, 147, 168

Canaanite religion pp. 29, 32, 35, **68**, 131

Canon
From a *Greek* word meaning "measuring rod", the agreed list of books in the *Bible*. pp. **12**, 13–19, 41, 75, 79, 150

Capernaum
Town on the northwest shore of Lake *Galilee*, home of *Peter* and *Matthew*, which became *Jesus*' base after his rejection by *Nazareth* (Luke 4:31). pp. 52, 93, 112, 169, 181

Caravans
Convoys of donkeys and camels used by traders. pp. 54, 59, 83, **111**, 113

Carchemish
City on the *Euphrates* in northern *Syria*, site of *Babylon*'s defeat of *Egypt* in 605 BC. pp. 24, 35, 37, 39, 67, 72, 74

Carmel
Mountain range jutting into the Mediterranean, scene of *Elijah*'s contest with *Baal*'s prophets (1 Kings 18) and *Elisha*'s base (2 Kings 4:25). pp. 34, 50, **69**, 151

Carpenter, carpentry
pp. 103, **109**, 167

Casting lots
A common means of decision-making, involving random choice of marked sticks or stones from a container into which they had been "cast". The sailors on *Jonah*'s ship cast lots to see who had caused the storm (Jonah 1:7), and the soldiers cast lots to divide up *Jesus*' clothing (John 19:23–24). The Jewish *Law* adapted the practice through the priest's use of *Urim and Thummim* to seek God's will. Only one example occurs in the *New Testament* (Acts 1:21–26), but after *Pentecost* the practice wasn't used again.

Census
1. Taken at the beginning and end of the *wilderness* wanderings (Numbers 1, 26) to number the men of military age (over twenty).
2. Taken by *David*, resulting in *judgment* on the nation through a plague (2 Samuel 24; 1 Chronicles 21), perhaps the consequence of their supporting the rebellions of *Absalom* and Sheba.
3. Called by Caesar *Augustus*, causing *Mary* and *Joseph* to return to *Bethlehem* where *Jesus* was born (Luke 2:1–2).
4. Taken in AD 6 when *Judea* became a Roman province, provoking the rebellion of *Judas* of *Galilee* (Acts 5:37).

Centurion
Roman army officer, in charge of between 80 and 100 men. pp. 45, 81, 103, 178–80

Chaldea
Region in southern *Mesopotamia*, *Abraham*'s ancestral home (Genesis 11:28–31). Often used in the *Old Testament* to refer to the whole of *Babylonia*. pp. 49, 62–63

Chariots pp. 27, 58, 66, 73, 75, **112**, 123, 128

Charismatic
Someone or something characterized by the working of God's *Holy Spirit*. Scholars describe the *Judges* as "charismatic leaders", meaning they were called and empowered by the spontaneous operation of God's Spirit, thus enabling them to deliver God's people from enemies. In the *New Testament* the *Greek* word "charisma" (meaning "grace gift"), plural "charismata", describes the spontaneous gifts of the Holy Spirit to believers (e.g. 1 Corinthians 12:7–11; 14:1).

Chemosh
"The detestable God of *Moab*" (1 Kings 11:7), to whom children were sacrificed (e.g. 2 Kings 3:26–27).

Child sacrifice pp. 34, 89, 128

Childlessness pp. 88, **89**

Children pp. 26, 84–87, **88–89**, 90–92, 96–97, 109, 122, 126, 129, 145, 153, 175–76

Chinnereth
Alternative name for the Sea of *Galilee*, probably from the *Hebrew* "kinnôr" ("harp") because of its harp-like shape. pp. 32, 50

Christ
See *Messiah*

Christian
Name given to followers of *Jesus*, first used in *Antioch* (Acts 11:26). p. **47**

Christian beliefs/faith
pp. **158–59**

Christian practices p. **159**

Chronicles (1 & 2)
Post-exilic retelling of *Israel*'s history to assure the restored community of God's ongoing presence and blessing.

Church
New Testament term for God's people gathered around *Jesus*. pp. 179, 192

Circumcision
Removal of the male foreskin as a *covenant* sign of belonging to God's people in the *Old Testament* (e.g. Genesis 17; Joshua 5:1–9), resisted by *Paul* as necessary for *Gentile* converts to Christianity. pp. 24–25, 28, 40, 45, 88, 133, 135–37, 152, 159, 167, 179

Cistern
Underground reservoir for storing water from *rainfall* or springs. pp. 51, 94, 104

Cities pp. **102–103**

Cities of refuge
Places of asylum for unintentional murderers, to avoid revenge and ensure a fair trial (Numbers 35: 6–34; Joshua 21).

Clan
Family groupings that made up *tribes*. pp. 84–86, 118–119

Clean and unclean
Designations in the Jewish *Law* of what was permissible and not permissible, both to safeguard *sanitation* and mark *Israel* out as holy. pp. 40, 41, 61, 88, **94**, 108, 136–37, 152, 160, 167, 170, 174

Clothing pp. 54, 58–59, 96–97, **100–101**, 115

Colossae
Town in southwest Turkey, recipients of one of *Paul*'s letters, Colossians. p. 46

Communion
See *Lord's Supper*

Community pp. 19, 38, 43, 45, 91–92, 102–103, 119, 127, 152–53, 157, 163, 177–79, 189, 192–93

Compassion
Feeling of pity and demonstration of *mercy*, a fundamental characteristic of God's nature in the *Bible* (Exodus 33:6; 2 Corinthians 1:3), reflected in *Jesus*' ministry (Matthew 9:36), which *Christians* are to emulate (Ephesians 4:32). pp. 76, 130, 144, 155, 163, 174

Concubine
Slave taken as a secondary wife. p. 87

Confession
1. Public declaration of *faith*.
2. Acknowledgment of *sin* before God.

Conquest
Taking by force of arms, like *Assyria*'s annexation of *Israel* and *Babylon*'s of *Judah*. The term "the conquest" is used to refer to *Joshua*'s taking of the *Promised Land*. pp. 28, 38, 48, 80, 95, 110, 126

Corinth, Corinthians
City on the isthmus joining the Greek mainland and its southern peninsula between the Aegean and Adriatic. With harbours on both sides it was an important trading centre with a mixed population and thousands of temple prostitutes. *Paul* spent

eighteen months here, and two of his letters (1 & 2 Corinthians) written to the *church* here are included in the *New Testament*. pp. 18, 21, 40–41, 46–47, 79–80, 83, 86–87, 99, 101, 103, 109, 113, 115, 123, 125, 127, 131, 133, 140–41, 144, 150–51, 155, 158–59, 161, 185–87, 189, 192, 194–95

Cosmetics pp. **100–101**

Council of Jerusalem
Meeting of church delegates from *Antioch* with *apostles* and *elders* from *Jerusalem* (c. AD 49/50) to resolve problems from the influx of *Gentile* converts, where it was agreed the latter didn't need to embrace traditional Jewish *identity markers* to be saved (Acts 15). p. 45

Covenant
Binding contract between two parties, a foundational expression of relationship in Bible times. pp. 13–14, 18, 23–24, 26–28, 30–31, 36–38, 52, 56, 71, 84, 88, 119, 128, **132–33**, 134–35, 137, 141, 147, 150, 154, 183, 190

Covenant, new
The relationship between God and humanity promised by the *prophets* (Jeremiah 31:31–34; Ezekiel 36:25–27) and established by *Jesus* through his death on the *cross* (Matthew 26:27–28). pp. **133**, 141, 183

Crafts pp. 48, 63, 69, 77, 96–97, **108–109**, 110

Creation
The bringing into being of everything that exists out of nothing by God's activity (e.g. Genesis 1–2; Job 38–42; Hebrews 11:3), though the *Bible* makes no attempt to explain how. pp. 14, 19, **22–23**, 46, 54, 56, 59–61, 63, 67, 75, 77, 117, 130, 138, 174, 187, 194

Creeds p. **141**

Crete
Mediterranean island, home to the Minoans in ancient times, called Caphtor in the *Old Testament*. In *New Testament* times *Titus* led a church here (Titus 1:5). pp. 40, 57, 70–71, 78, 83

Crime and punishment
pp. **119**, 126, 184

Cross, Crucifixion
Brutal means of execution invented by *Phoenicians* and used by Romans, involving the nailing of criminals to wooden posts. This is how *Jesus* was killed. pp. 42–43, 54–55, 127, 129, 132, 137, 139, **158–59**, 161, 165, 177, 180, 184

Cuneiform
Wedge-like script of ancient *Mesopotamia*. pp. 62, 68–69, 73, 120, 127, 135

Cush
The region south of *Egypt*. pp. 36, 64, 82

Cyprus
Mediterranean island, home of *Barnabas*, visited by *Paul* on his first *missionary* journey (Acts 13:4–12). pp. 40, 71, 83

Cyrene
Greek city on North African coast (in modern Libya), home of Simon, who was press-ganged into carrying Jesus' *cross* (Matthew 27:32). p. 184

Cyrus the Great
King of *Persia* (ruled 559–530 BC) who overthrew *Babylon* and allowed the exiled *Jews* to return home (Ezra 1:1). pp. 76–77, 83

D

Dagon
Philistine god whose statue kept falling on its face when the captured *ark of the covenant* was placed before it at Ashdod (1 Samuel 5:1–5). pp. 68, 71

Daily life pp. **96–97**

Damascus
Capital of *Aram* (Syria) to *Israel*'s north, frequently denounced by the *prophets* (e.g. Isaiah 17:1–3; Amos 1:3–5). Its strategic location dominated the main trade routes between *Mesopotamia*, *Egypt*, and *Arabia*, which was why *Paul* was so determined to stop Christianity reaching there; but it was on the road to *Damascus* that he encountered the risen *Jesus* (Acts 9:1–25). pp. 24, 31–32, 35, 37, 39–40, 46, 48, 82–83, 112, 185, 189

Dan
1. *Jacob*'s fifth son, born of *Rachel*'s servant Bilhah, whose name means "he has vindicated" (Genesis 30:4–6).
2. *Tribe* founded by Dan. Unable to fully possess their assigned territory along the coastal plain, some were absorbed into *Judah* while many migrated north, taking over Laish (Leshem) and renaming it Dan (Joshua 19:47).
3. *Israel*'s northernmost town. The expression "from Dan to *Beersheba*" meant "from north to south".

Daniel
Member of the Jewish nobility exiled to *Babylon* in the first deportation (605 BC), where he served at court under *Nebuchadnezzar*, Belshazzar, and *Darius*. He came to prominence through his ability to interpret *dreams* (Daniel 2 and 4), but also received *revelation* about the destiny of empires (chs 7–8) and *Messiah*'s coming and the end times (chs 10–12). pp. 14, 16–17, 38–40, 42, 60, 63, 74–75, 77, 79, 91, 116, 121, 143–44, 151, 154–55, 161, 167, 173, 187

Darius
1. Darius the Mede, king of *Babylon* (Daniel 5:31).
2. Darius the Great, king of *Persia*, who revived *Cyrus*'s edict allowing the *Temple* restoration to be completed (Haggai 1:1; Zechariah 1:1).
3. Darius II, king of *Persia* (Nehemiah 12:22). See *Persia*

David
Israel's second king (1010–1002 BC ruling over *Judah*; 1002–970 BC ruling over a united kingdom of Judah and *Israel*). He established *Jerusalem* as his capital, where he installed the *ark of the covenant* (2 Samuel 5–6). He wanted to build a temple for God, but God said he would build a "house" for David instead, a house of everlasting descendants on the throne, a promise known as "the Davidic Covenant" (2 Samuel 7: 1–29). Under David's reign Israel's enemies were at last defeated and its borders consolidated. pp. 17, 20, 30–34, 36, 42, 53–54, 56, 60, 67, 70–71, 82, 85, 96, 109, 118, 121–22, 128–29, 133, 140–41, 154, 163, 190

Day of Atonement pp. **138**, 143, 146

Day of the LORD
Old Testament term for the final Day of *Judgment* when sinners will be punished and God's promises will be at last fulfilled. pp. 39, **75**

Dead Sea
Inland sea (also called the *Salt Sea*, Eastern Sea, and Sea of *Arabah*) into which the *Jordan* flows, comprising 25 per cent salt, rendering it useless. *Ezekiel*'s vision of restoration saw life brought to it by water flowing from the *Temple* (Ezekiel 47). pp. 21, 24, 50–51, 68, 82, 106, 112, 152–53, 163, 169

Dead Sea Scrolls
Manuscripts of the *Qumran* community. pp. **21**, 152–53

Death
Seen in the *Bible* not merely as a biological inevitability, but as the consequence of *sin* (Romans 6:23), leading to *judgment* (Romans 5:12–21). Yet through Christ, the *New Testament* says, there is *hope* of life after death. pp. 18, 25–26, 29–30, 32–33, 36, 40–41, 43, 47, 64–65, 68–69, 72, 74, 77–78, 80–81, 86–87, 106, 109, 118–119, 124, 126–27, 129, 132, 135–37, 139, 144, 147, 149, 155, 157–58, **160–61**, 163, 165, 167, 174–75, 180, 183–85, 187–88, 190–95

Death of Jesus pp. 18, 77, 139, 144, 147, 149, 160–61, 163, 165, 174, 180, 183, **184–85**, 188, 190

Deborah
Prophetess and *judge* in the time of the *Judges* (Judges 4–5). p. 29

Debt
While warning against the dangers of debt, the *Bible* also urges help for those ensnared by it. The *Law* sought to minimize debt by commanding alms-giving and generous lending, and by preventing the exploitation of those in debt. Remembering the poor was a foundational apostolic principle (Galatians 2:9–10). pp. 16, 115, 126–27, 143

Decapolis
Association of ten free Greek cities south of Lake *Galilee* and east of the *Jordan*, home largely to non-Jews, many of whom were attracted by *Jesus*' teaching (e.g. Matthew 4:25; Mark 5:1–20). Jewish *Christians* fled to one of these cities, Pella, before *Jerusalem*'s fall in AD 70.

Delilah
Philistine woman who betrayed *Samson* (Judges 16). p. 71

Demons
Seen in the *Bible* as fallen *angels* who rebelled with *Satan*, whose power and influence are real but limited. Christ's deliverance *miracles* demonstrate a foretaste of God's ultimate victory over both them and the devil. pp. 16, **75**, 135, **144–145**, 156, 170

Dentistry pp. **125**

Deuterocanonical books
Jewish writings from the inter-testamental period (also called *Apocrypha*) that never formed part of the original Hebrew *Scriptures* but were added to its *Greek* translation (the *Septuagint*). While some branches of the church accept these as Scripture, others do not, merely seeing them as helpful insights into Jewish inter-testamental beliefs.

Devil
See *Satan*

Diaspora
Greek for "scattering"; the dispersion of *Jews* after the *exile*, resulting in more of them living outside *Judea* than inside it. The scattered Jewish *synagogues* became the favourite starting point for the Christian *mission*. pp. 41, 113

Dietary laws p. **136**

Disciples
Followers of *Jesus*, in the *Gospels* especially the *twelve* who became *apostles*. pp. 29, 43–44, 46–47, 87, 89, 90, 103, 106–107, 123, 139, 141, 153, 155, 159, 161, 163, 169, 171, 178–79, 182–83, 185–90, 194

Discipleship pp. 163, 169, **171**, 179

Discipline pp. 29, 72, **89**, 125, 156

Disease pp. 94, **124–25**, 160, 170

Divination pp. 36, 71, **75**, 145

Division of the kingdom
Israel's split into *Israel* in the north and *Judah* in the south after *Solomon*'s death, the result of *Rehoboam*'s foolishness, never to be united again. pp. 37, 52

Divorce
Termination of *marriage*, not banned in *Old Testament* times but regulated (Deuteronomy 24:1–4). By *New Testament* times *Judaism* had two main approaches to it, one easier, one harder. *Jesus* not only took the harder line but went further, saying remarriage after *divorce* on any grounds except marital unfaithfulness was adultery (Matthew 19:1–12). pp. 83, 86–87

Doctors pp. **124**, 163, 193

Dorcas
Christian noted for her good *works*, whom *Peter* raised from the dead (Acts 9:36–42).

Dreams
Common means of God communicating with people in the *Bible*, bringing direction, warning, and *revelation*. *Visions* are similar but occur while the recipient is awake. pp. 25, 40, 52, 65, 80, 94, 125, **144**, 150, 164–65, 167, 173

Dress pp. 61, 71, 86, 148, 155

Drink pp. 63, 67, 77, 95–96, **98–99**, 135, 193

E

Easter
Central festival of the Christian year, celebrating Jesus' *resurrection*. pp. 185–86

Ebal
Mountain near *Shechem* where six *tribes* of *Israel* proclaimed curses for breaking God's *covenant*, while opposite it on Mount *Gerizim* six tribes proclaimed blessings for obeying it (Deuteronomy 11:29; 27:1 – 28:6; Joshua 8:30–35). p. **28**

Ecbatana
Capital of the *Medes*, conquered by *Cyrus the Great* in 550 BC. Referred to in Ezra 6:1–2 and the *Deuterocanonical books* of Tobit and Judith.

Ecclesiastes
Septuagint translation of the *Hebrew* "qoheleth" ("Teacher", Ecclesiastes 1:1), whose writings see life as but "a breath" so it should be enjoyed while we have the opportunity. pp. 14, 31, 123, 156–57, 160

Ecstasy, ecstatic
An altered state of consciousness enabling the recipient to focus on the object of adoration or inspiration, expressed in emotions ranging from frenzied actions to trance-like stillness.

Eden
Area between the *Euphrates* and *Tigris* where the *Bible* says human life began. *Eden* (meaning "delight" or "pleasure") contained an idyllic garden where God placed *Adam* and *Eve* to enjoy his special presence (Genesis 2) but from which they were expelled when they sinned (Genesis 3). In the *Septuagint*, "garden" was translated by the *Greek* word "paradeisos" ("garden" or "park"), from which the idea of Eden as "Paradise" arose. pp. 22, 100, 140, 145

Edom, Edomites
Descendants of *Esau* living in the mountains south of the *Dead Sea* who, despite their common ancestry, refused *Israel* passage on their way to the *Promised Land* (Numbers 20:14–21). Many Edomites migrated to southern *Judah* after *Jerusalem*'s fall in 586 BC and again in the third century BC when Edom was conquered by the *Nabataeans*, the area becoming known as *Idumea* and its inhabitants *Idumeans*. pp. 27, 70, **82–83**, 181

Education pp. 78, 80, 89, **90–91**, 121, 127, 172, 177

Egypt, Egyptians
Nation southwest of *Palestine*, habitable only along the banks of the *Nile*. At times a refuge (Genesis 12:10–20; Matthew 2:13–15), at times an enemy (Genesis 1:1–22; Exodus 1–11), *Israel* was often tempted to look to Egypt for security (Numbers 14:1–4; Isaiah 30:1–5). God's deliverance of Israel from slavery in Egypt (the *exodus*) was seen as the greatest turning point in their history. pp. 15, 17, 20, 24–27, 34–37, 40, 42, 48–51, 54, 59, 61, **64–65**, 67–68, 70, 72, 74–76, 78, 88, 97–98, 100–101, 104, 106, 108, 111–113, 117, 120–27, 131, 134, 136, 138–40, 144, 151, 161, 167, 183, 190, 193

Ekron
One of five *Philistine* cities along the coastal plain and where the captured *ark of the covenant* was held for a period (1 Samuel 5). pp. 70–71

Elam/Elamites
Country east of the *Tigris*, whose capital *Susa* came to importance under the *Persians*. pp. 24, 37, 63, 83, 87, 120

Elders pp. 32, 45, 118–119, 137, 152

Eli
Priest and *judge* at *Shiloh* who trained the young *Samuel* (1 Samuel 1–3).

Elihu
Angry young man in the story of *Job* who thought he knew all the answers.

Elijah
Israelite *prophet* (875–848 BC) whose name ("the LORD is God") summed up his message to those who wanted to *worship* both *Yahweh* (the LORD) and *Baal* but whom he called to choose between them (1 Kings 18:21). Noted especially for his *miracles* (1 Kings 17), his contest with Baal's prophets (1 Kings 18), and being taken to *heaven* in a fiery chariot (2 Kings 2). He appeared at Jesus' *transfiguration* along with *Moses*, together symbolizing the *Law* and the prophets that witnessed to him. pp. **34–35**, 51, 61, 68–69, 85, 88, 144, 150–51, 168, 175

Elisha
Disciple of *Elijah* who continued his ministry, performing numerous *miracles* of *compassion* (2 Kings 4) and responsible for the defeat of the *Arameans* (2 Kings 6:8 – 7:20). His name means "My God saves". pp. **34–35**, 68, 85, 92–93, 144, 151

Elizabeth
Wife of *Zechariah* the *priest* and mother of *John the Baptist* (Luke 1). pp. 89, 164, 168

Emmaus
Village 7 miles (11 km) from *Jerusalem* on the road to which *Jesus* appeared to two *disciples* on *Easter* Sunday, explaining his death and *resurrection* in the light of Old Testament *Scriptures* (Luke 24:13–35). p. 187

Emperor worship p. **81**

Enjoyment pp. 51, 59

Enoch
Descendant of *Adam*'s son, Seth, who "walked with God" and was taken to *heaven* without dying (Genesis 5:24).

Enuma Elish Epic
Early-second millennium BC *Mesopotamian* myth recounting on seven stone tablets their story of *creation*. *See* pp. 22–23, 75

Epaphroditus
Christian from *Philippi* who helped *Paul* and risked his life for him (Philippians 2:25–30).

Ephesus
Capital of the Roman province of Asia, population c. 300,000; important port at the mouth of the River Cayster on a major trade route; renowned for its temple to *Artemis*, one of the seven wonders of the *world*. *Paul* understood the city's significance, visiting it twice and spending over two years there (Acts 19:8–10), and experiencing a riot when craftsmen producing shrines to Artemis felt their business was threatened by his *preaching* (Acts 19:23–41). The letter to the Ephesians and one of *John*'s seven letters to the churches

(Revelation 2:1–7) were addressed to the church here. An ancient tradition says the apostle *John* settled here. pp. 40, 46, 95, 103, 109, 119, 121.

Ephraim
1. *Joseph*'s younger son, born in *Egypt* (Genesis 41:50–52), blessed by *Jacob* (Genesis 48:12–20).
2. *Tribe* descended from Ephraim, which acquired considerable significance (Judges 8:1–3).
3. Territory west of the *Jordan*, between *Benjamin* and *Manasseh*, renowned for its beauty and fertility, but which the tribe couldn't fully possess (Joshua 16:10).
4. Synonym for the northern kingdom of *Israel* after the *division of the kingdom* (Isaiah 7:1–17; Jeremiah 7:15).

Ephrathah
The region around *Bethlehem*.

Epicurean
Greek philosophical school, established by Epicurus, who taught that the greatest good was to pursue modest pleasure in order to achieve tranquillity and *freedom* from pain and fear, thus finding happiness.

Esau
Elder twin of *Jacob*, son of *Isaac* and *Rebekah*, who sold his birthright to Jacob (Genesis 25:19–34). Jacob tricked him out of Isaac's blessing (Genesis 27:1 – 28:5), though the brothers were later reconciled (Genesis 33). Esau moved to Seir, south of the *Dead Sea*, where he became the ancestor of the *Edomites* (Genesis 36:6–40). The *Bible* sees Esau's rejection as an example of "election" (God's free choice), symbolizing those God had not elected for his purpose, while Jacob symbolized those he had (Malachi 1:2–3; Romans 9:10–16). pp. 25, 27, 67, 82, 98

Eschatology
Doctrine of the end times, from the *Greek* "eschatos" ("last"). p. 194

Eshcol
Valley from which the spies sent to explore the *Promised Land* brought back a branch heavy with grapes requiring two men to carry it to prove *Canaan*'s fruitfulness (Numbers 13:21–25).

Essenes
Exclusive Jewish sect committed to radical obedience to the *Law*, mainly living in monastic communities like the one at *Qumran*. pp. **152–53**, 154, 177, 180, 185

Esther
Jewish orphan in *exile* in *Persia* whose story is told in the book of Esther. Chosen to marry King *Xerxes I* (486–465 BC), she was able to play a key role in foiling *Haman*'s plot to exterminate the *Jews* (chs 5–9), an event remembered in the Jewish festival of *Purim*. The story, unique in the *Bible* for not mentioning God, is nevertheless full of examples of God's *sovereignty*. pp. 14, 16, 21, 39, 76–77, 83, 99, 122, 132, 139, 143, 157

Ethics of Jesus pp. **176–77**

Ethiopia
See *Cush*

Euphrates
Largest of *Mesopotamia*'s two great rivers (the other being the *Tigris*), often simply called "the river" in the *Old Testament*, along which most of the region's important cities were situated and which marked the boundary between *Israel* and its enemies (e.g. Genesis 15:18; Joshua 1:4; Revelation 9:14). It is by the Euphrates that Genesis locates *Eden* (Genesis 2:10–14). pp. 24, 38, 48–49, 62, 72, 75, 77

Evangelism, evangelist
Sharing the message of *Jesus* with others. Evangelist: one who shares this message.

Eve
Adam's wife, whom the *serpent* deceived into taking the fruit God had forbidden them to eat (Genesis 3:1–6). While often blamed for the deception, even within the *New Testament* (2 Corinthians 11:3; 1 Timothy 2:14), the text shows that Adam was "with her" when she took the fruit yet did not intervene (Genesis 3:6). Since, as her husband, he had responsibility for her, this is perhaps why the disobedience is called Adam's *sin* rather than Eve's (e.g. Romans 5:12–19). pp. 22, 56, 100, 140, 148

Evil
Opposite of good, from a *Hebrew* root meaning "spoil" or "break in pieces". Something evil is therefore ruined, worthless, unpleasant, offensive. The *Bible* says evil exists at moral, spiritual, and physical levels, and the *New Testament* sees it as the work of the *devil*, often called "the evil one". *Jesus* opposed every expression of evil, triumphing over it through his death on the *cross* (e.g. Colossians 2:15; 1 John 3:8), thereby ensuring God's end-time creation will be characterized by a total lack of evil (Revelation 21:1–8). pp. 21–22, 33, 77, 114, 120, 129, 137, 143, **156**, 161, 163, 190, 194

Exile
The period *Judah* spent in *Babylon* after *Jerusalem*'s destruction in 586 BC, though the first group was exiled as early as 597 BC. Unlike *Assyria*, which had scattered the *Israelites* across its empire, Babylon allowed the *Jews* to stay together, enabling them to maintain their identity. This seventy-year period, prophesied by *Jeremiah* (29:10), proved to be one of the most formative periods of Jewish life. They remained here until *Cyrus* of *Persia* conquered Babylon and allowed them to go home in 538 BC, though returns were spasmodic and many chose to stay. pp. 15, 17, 31, 33, 36, **38–39**, 41–42, 52, 77, 90, 97, 128, 131, 141–43, 147–48, 151, 154, 167, 180

Exodus
Israel's miraculous escape from slavery in *Egypt* under the leadership of *Moses*, looked back upon as the most significant event in their history. pp. 13–14, **26–27**, 29, 34, 50, 54–57, 59–61, 64, 66–67, 69, 82, 88, 90, 97, 99–101, 105–106, 108, 112, 114, 117–119, 121–22, 124–27, 130–43, 146, 148–49, 157, 161, 183

Ezekiel
Member of a priestly *family* deported to *Babylon* in 597 BC. Unable to work as a priest, God called him to become a *prophet* (Ezekiel 1–3). Until *Jerusalem*'s destruction (586 BC) his focus was calling *Jews* to *repentance*, but his message then changed to one of *hope* and restoration, seeing them as dry bones that would be re-formed into an army (ch. 37), and foreseeing a day when life-giving waters would flow from a rebuilt *Temple* (ch. 47). pp. 14, 54, 56–57, 60, 75, 89, 102, 104–106, 110–111, 113, 117, 121, 129, 131–33, 144–45, 150–51, 161, 173, 180, 189

Ezion Geber
City at the northern end of the Gulf of Aqaba where *Solomon* based his fleet (1 Kings 9:26). pp. 27, 110, 113

Ezra
Priest and *scribe* sent to *Jerusalem* by Artaxerxes I in 458 BC to enforce observance of the Jewish *Law* (Ezra 7–10). He found a rebuilt *Temple* but little enthusiasm for maintaining the *faith*; so he ended mixed marriages, which threatened *Judaism*'s very existence. He may then have returned to report to the king, as we don't hear of him again until his public reading of the *Law* in 444 BC (Nehemiah 8–10). Jewish tradition sees him as involved in the final editing of the *Old Testament* books. pp. 14–15, 18, 39, 76–77, 90, 142, 147

F

Faith
The *Bible* sees faith not as mere assent to doctrine, but as a personal relationship of trust in God based on conviction that he not only exists but is good and keeps his promises. The *New Testament* speaks of "the faith", meaning the basic teachings about *Jesus* and the way of life this leads to. pp. 24–25, 38, 47, 55, 79–80, 85–86, 89, 112–113, 127, 130–31, 136, 138, 141, 143–44, 147, 150, **158–59**, 161, 167, 172, 173, 175, 177, 180, 185, 191, 193, 196

Faithfulness
A fundamental aspect of God's nature (Exodus 34:6), his commitment to remain true to himself, his purposes, and his people. God's people are called to respond through being faithful to him and one another.

Fall
The disobedience of humanity first expressed in the *sin* of *Adam* and *Eve* that led them to "fall" from the perfect state God intended for them and to lose the sense of God's intimate presence (Genesis 3). This fallenness has been passed on through the human race, reflected in its deterioration (Romans 1:18–32), and even *creation* itself has been affected (Romans 8:20–21). Only through the death of Christ, the *New Testament* says, can its effects be undone.

False prophets p. 151

False teachers
Proponents of wrong or imbalanced teaching, who want to gather followers (Acts 20:30), impose Jewishness on converted *Gentiles* (Acts 15:1; Galatians 2:11–14; Colossians 2:16–23), share supposed spiritual insights unseen by others (Colossians 2:18–19), or respond to those who want only pleasant truths (2

Timothy 4:3). *Paul* often warned the church to watch out for such people.

Family
Basic unit of human existence and relationships, but wider than just parents and their children.
pp. 15, 22–25, 27, 29, 31, 45–47, 63, 67, 70, 79–80, 82, **84–85**, 86–94, 96–100, 102, 108, 110, 112, 115, 118–119, 138, 153, 156, 160, 166–67, 170, 178, 181, 192–93

Farming pp. 22, 51, 57, 59, 61, 96–97, 99, 102, **104–105**, 109, 111, 139, 173

Farming yearly cycle p. 96

Fasting
Abstaining from food, partially or totally, for a period of time to devote oneself more fully to God and seek him in *prayer*. pp. 19, 137–38, 140, **143**, 161, 168–69, 180

Fatherhood of God
Jesus taught that God is a loving heavenly Father, not as an anthropomorphic description (he is not *like* a father) but as a description of reality (he *is* a father), not in human terms of procreation, but in terms of his *love*, provision, and protection. pp. 84, **143**

Feasts
See *Festivals*

Felix
Roman procurator who imprisoned *Paul* at *Caesarea* for two years (Acts 23:23 – 24:27).

Fellowship
Key characteristic of early church life, involving not just membership but participation in life for mutual benefit and the blessing of others (Acts 2:42–47), thus excluding the notion of solitary Christianity. pp. 47, 99, 141, 147–49, 178, **179**, 189

Fertile Crescent p. 48

Festivals
Opportunities for God's people to remember his past actions and enjoy his present blessings. pp. 39–40, 44, 57, 65, 67, 72, 75, 90, 97, 99, 114–115, 122, **138–39**, 141, 152, 155, 166, 185

Filling with the Spirit
The experience of receiving the *Holy Spirit* to transform and empower believers for the Christian life, available to all who *repent* (Acts 2:37–39). Also called "receiving the Spirit" and "baptism in the Spirit". *Paul* said this was not just a one-off experience but an ongoing characteristic of the Christian life (the *Greek* in Ephesians 5:18 means "Go on being filled with the Spirit"). pp. 44, **45**, 188–89

Fish, fishing pp. 16, 50, 99, **106–107**, 136, 154, 158, 172, 175, 179, 186

Fishers of men pp. 106–107

Flesh
1. Flesh and *blood* – e.g. "The Word became flesh" (John 1:14).
2. Mortal humanity – e.g. "My spirit shall not abide in mortals for ever, for they are flesh" (Genesis 6:3, NRSV).
3. The sinful self – e.g. "do not gratify the desires of the flesh. For what the flesh desires is opposed to the Spirit" (Galatians 5:16–17, NRSV).

Flood
Great deluge sent on the earth when human *sin* became so great that God decided to start all over again (Genesis 6:1–7). Only the godly *Noah*, his *family*, and pairs of all animal life escaped as Noah obeyed God and built an *ark* – a huge, three-decked floating box – where they stayed until the waters receded (6:8 – 8:22). God then made a *covenant* with Noah, making the *rainbow* its outward *sign*, promising that the seasons would henceforth be consistent (8:22) and the earth would never again be flooded in that way (9:1–17). pp. 22, **23**, 28, 60, 64–65, 99, 133

Flowers pp. **54–55**, 56–57, 101

Food pp. 34, 54–56, 58–61, 64, 67, 69, 75, 94–97, **98–99**, 101, 104–105, 107, 115, 125, 129, 135–38, 143, 152

Food laws
A crucial expression of Jewish identity, the *Law* contained lists of "clean" (permitted) or "unclean" (forbidden) animals (Leviticus 11:1–47; Deuteronomy 14:3–21), not only for health reasons but to mark *Israel* out as "holy". The early church struggled with whether such laws were binding on *Christians*, though eventually came to see they weren't (Acts 10:1 – 11:18; Romans 14:1 – 15:13). pp. 94, 99, **136**

Footwear pp. 101, 108

Forgiveness
Seen in the *Bible* as a fundamental aspect of God's nature (Exodus 34:6–7) that can be experienced through *confession* and *repentance*, gained through the death of *Jesus* (Matthew 26:28; Ephesians 1:7–8; Hebrews 9:13–14). The forgiveness that characterizes God is to characterize *Christians* too (Matthew 6:14–15; 18:21–35; Ephesians 4:32). pp. 35, 43, 73, 127, 133, 141, 158, 165, 168, **170**, 172, 176, 179, 183

Foundations p. **109**

Frankincense
Aromatic resin used to make *incense*, one of the *Magi*'s gifts to *Jesus*. pp. **54**, 167

Freedom
One of the experiences *Jesus* said he came to bring (Luke 4:16–30), in fulfilment of *Isaiah*'s prophecy (Isaiah 61:1–2). His countrymen interpreted this narrowly as freedom for *Jews* from *Rome*'s oppression; but Jesus was thinking of a bigger freedom: freedom from *sin*. He claimed it was only through knowing him and his truth that people could truly be set free (John 8:32). pp. 87, 93, 101, 123, 126–27, 155, **159**, 169

Fruit pp. 51, 56–57, 68, 96–98, 101, 104, 138, 169, 173, 177, 182, 189, 194

Fruit of the Spirit
The qualities of someone who is truly filled with God's *Holy Spirit*, which can only be experienced, not in solitude, but in relationship with others (Galatians 5:22–25).

Furniture pp. **93**, 109

Future destiny
While the *Old Testament* expresses little *hope* for the individual's future, seeing good and bad alike as destined for *Sheol*, the *New Testament* confidently proclaims, in the light of Christ's *resurrection*, that when *Christians* die they go to be with *Jesus* in *heaven*, awaiting his return to earth (1 Thessalonians 4:13–18) when they will be given *resurrection bodies*, suited to life in God's new creation (1 Corinthians 15:35–58; Revelation 21:1 – 22:5). pp. **160**, 194–95

G

Gabbatha
Aramaic name for "the Pavement", where *Jesus* was tried by *Pilate* (John 19:13). It means "height" or "eminence", suggesting it was a raised terrace, either in the Fortress of Antonia or, as some scholars think, in Herod's palace. See *Pavement*

Gabriel
A leading *angel* in Jewish thinking. In the *Old Testament* he appears twice to *Daniel*, first to interpret a *vision* (Daniel 8:15–27) and later to predict *Jerusalem*'s future and *Israel*'s coming *messiah* (Daniel 9:20–27). In the *New Testament* he announces the birth of *John the Baptist* to *Zechariah* (Luke 1:9–20) and the birth of *Jesus* to *Mary* (Luke 1:26–38). p. 164

Gad
1. *Jacob*'s seventh son, through *Leah*'s maid, *Zilpah* (Genesis 30:9–11). His name means "good fortune".
2. *Tribe* founded by Gad. Along with *Reuben* and half of *Manasseh*, they asked to settle in *Transjordan* east of the *Jordan* because the land was suitable for their livestock. *Moses* agreed, but on condition they helped their fellow-*Israelites* take the *Promised Land* first (Numbers 32).

Galatia, Galatians
Ancient kingdom settled in the third century BC by the Gauls in northern *Asia Minor* along the Black Sea coast. It became part of the larger province of Roman Galatia that stretched further south and included cities like Pisidian Antioch, Iconium, *Lystra*, and Derbe, cities where *Paul* planted churches on his first *missionary* journey (Acts 13–14). Although a subject of debate, Paul's letter to the Galatians was probably written to these churches, as *Acts* doesn't mention *Paul* visiting churches further north. pp. 18, 45–47, 84–85, 89, 99, 115, 127, 131, 133, 135, 155, 159, 164, 170, 177–78, 189

Galilee
1. Lake in northern *Israel*, known in *New Testament* times as the Sea of Galilee, Sea of Tiberius, or Lake Gennesaret, and in *Old Testament* times as the Sea of *Chinnereth*. Rich in fish, it was here that several of Jesus' *disciples* had worked as fishermen. pp. 50, 59, 106–107, 119, 169
2. Region between this lake and the Mediterranean where several major roads crossed and where *Jesus* spent most of his life, becoming known as "Jesus of Galilee" (Matthew 26:69). After the *Assyrian* invasion in the eighth century BC it was settled by non-Jewish immigrants (2 Kings 17) so became known as "Galilee

of the *Gentiles*" (Matthew 4:15), and people there were familiar with *Greek* as well as *Hebrew* and *Aramaic*. pp. 51–52, 78, 99, 103, 106, 119, 167–69, 180, 187

Gamaliel
Leading Jewish *rabbi* who trained *Paul* (Acts 22:3) and who, as a *Sanhedrin* member, advised a "wait-and-see" approach to *Christians* (Acts 5:33–40).

Games pp. **79**, 122–23

Garden of Eden
See *Eden*

Gates pp. 66, 74–75, 102–103, 110–111, 118–119, 185

Gath
One of the five *Philistine* cities, home of *Goliath*, the Philistine champion defeated by *David* (1 Samuel 17). David fled here for refuge from King *Saul* (1 Samuel 22:10–15). pp. 32, 70–71

Gaza
One of the five *Philistine* cities, home of *Delilah*, who persuaded *Samson* to share the secret of his strength that led to his capture (Judges 16). pp. 24, 32, 37, 40, 48, 53, 70–71

Genealogies
Family records, common in the *Bible*, important for establishing identity and property rights. p. **85**

Generosity pp. 57, **115**

Gentiles
All non-*Israelite* peoples.

Gerizim
See *Ebal*

Gershon, Gershonites
One of *Levi*'s three sons whose *family* and descendants were responsible for the curtains, coverings, and cords of the *tabernacle* (Numbers 3:21–26). p. 148

Gethsemane
Garden on the slopes of the *Mount of Olives*, overlooking *Jerusalem*, a favourite retreat of *Jesus* and his *disciples* (John 18:1–2) and site of his betrayal (Matthew 26:36–56). pp. 154, 182–85

Gezer
Canaanite town strategically located on the *Joppa* to *Jerusalem* road, conquered by *Egypt* in 1468 BC, and a pocket of resistance in *Ephraim*'s territory (Judges 1:27). Egypt gave it as a wedding gift to *Solomon*, who fortified it, along with *Hazor* and *Megiddo* (1 Kings 9:15–17). It retained military significance throughout the *Old Testament* period. It was here that the Gezer Calendar was discovered. pp. 32, 50, 97, 105

Gibeon
Town 6 miles (10 km) northwest of *Jerusalem* whose inhabitants tricked *Joshua* into making a treaty with them (Joshua 9). Assigned to the tribe of *Benjamin* and set apart for the *Levites* (Joshua 18:25; 21:17). As home to the *tabernacle* it was "the most important high place" (1 Kings 3:4), and it was here that God appeared to *Solomon* in a *dream* (1 Kings 3:4–15). pp. 28, 32

Gideon
Israelite *judge*, called to deliver *Israel* from the *Midianites*. Having destroyed his household's *altar* to *Baal* (Judges 6:1–32), he asked God to confirm his call through a *sign* (6:33–40). With his army drastically reduced by God, he approached them by night, blowing trumpets and smashing jars containing torches, producing panic that led them to flee (Judges 7). Israel then wanted to make him king, but he refused (8:22–23). pp. 29, 83

Gilboa
Mountain range between the Plain of *Jezreel* and the *Jordan* where *Saul* and *Jonathan* died in the battle against the *Philistines* (1 Samuel 31). p. 70

Gilead
Region east of the *Jordan* between Lake *Galilee* and the *Dead Sea*, renowned for its flocks and spices, settled by *Reuben*, *Gad*, and half the tribe of *Manasseh*. *Elijah* came from here (1 Kings 17:1).

Gilgal
Place where the *Israelites* marked entering the *Promised Land* and where *Joshua* reinstituted the *covenant* sign of *circumcision* and celebrated *Passover* (Joshua 4–5). It later became a *sanctuary*, where *Saul* was both confirmed as king (1 Samuel 11:15) and rejected as king (1 Samuel 13). By the eighth century BC the shrine had become idolatrous and was rejected by the prophets *Hosea* (9:15) and *Amos* (4:4). p. 28

Gilgamesh Epic
Early second-millennium BC *Mesopotamian* story telling the adventures of Gilgamesh, ruler of Uruk, including his meeting Utnapishtim, the great flood's only survivor. p. 23

Giving pp. 97, 100, 115, 176, **177**, 179

Gladiators pp. 81, 123, 192

Gleaning
Harvesting by the poor of crops left at the edges of fields (Deuteronomy 24:19–22). pp. 100, 105

Gnosticism
A range of dualistic beliefs that saw matter and spirit as utterly opposed, meaning that God, who dwelt in the spirit-world, could only engage with this world through a series of intermediaries. Humans therefore needed special knowledge (*Greek*, "gnōsis") to understand their spiritual condition and find the pathway out of it, and Gnostic cults claimed to have those secrets. Gnostic-like beliefs proved challenging to the early church. pp. 19, 145

Goats pp. 59–60, 63, 92, 96, 99–100, **105**, 139, 149, 172, 192, 194

God pp. **130–31**

God's kingdom
See *Kingdom of God*

Gods, Greek and Roman
pp. 80–81

Golden calf
Idol made by the *Israelites* when they thought *Moses* wasn't returning from *Mount Sinai* (Exodus 32), based on the bull cults they knew in *Egypt*. pp. 26, 148

Golgotha
See *Calvary*

Goliath
Philistine giant, 9 feet (3 m) tall, who had a spear with an iron tip weighing 600 shekels (15 lb/7 kg) but whom the young *David* killed by trusting in *Yahweh* (1 Samuel 17). pp. 17, 30, 70–71, 129

Gomorrah
City which, with its neighbour Sodom, experienced violent destruction as God's *judgment* for its gross *sin* (Genesis 18–19), now lying beneath the southern end of the *Dead Sea*. The two cities were often cited as examples of human depravity and God's inevitable judgment (e.g. Jeremiah 23:14; Matthew 10:15; Romans 9:29; 2 Peter 2:6). p. 24

Good Samaritan
Parable told by *Jesus* to answer the question, "Who is my neighbour?", whose reply is: anyone who needs you or will help you. pp. 113, 172, **173**

Good Shepherd
Title used of, and by, both God and *Jesus* to underline their caring nature. pp. 105, 190

Goodness pp. 23, 47, 50, 57, **77**, 135, 138, 141, 149, 156, 173, 177

Goshen
Nile Delta region where *Joseph* settled his *family* to avoid *Canaan*'s famine (Genesis 45:9–11; 46:28 – 47:11). They were still there 400 years later (Exodus 8:22). p. 27

Gospel
Greek word meaning "good news", originally announced by imperial messengers in town squares, but used by the early church to describe their message of who *Jesus* was and what he taught and did. The four Gospels are records of this. pp. 17–19, 21, 42–44, 46, 49, 78–80, 83, 103, 105, 112, 115, 131, 135, 153, **162–64**, 170–76, 179–80, 182–83, 185, 187, 192

Government pp. 77, 81, **118–119**

Grace
God's undeserved *love* and kindness towards sinners, seen in Old and New Testaments alike, but especially in his sending his Son *Jesus* to be mankind's *Saviour*. Even at *Mount Sinai*, where the *Law* was given, God revealed his *grace*, describing himself as "the LORD, the LORD, the compassionate and gracious God..." (Exodus 34:6). This became a consistent theme of *Scripture* (e.g. Psalm 86:15; 103:7–18; Joel 2:13). pp. **73**, 143, 159, 189

Great commission
Jesus' final command to his *disciples* to preach his message to the whole *world* (Matthew 28:18–20; Acts 1:8). p. **187**

Great Sea
Old Testament name for the Mediterranean.

Greece, Greeks pp. 12–13, 15–19, 21, 26, 40–42, 45–46, 49, 59, 62, 64, 70–71, 75–76, 78–82, 84–85, 87, 90, 93, 97, 103, 107, 110–111, 114, 119–120, 122–25, 127, 131, 136, 138, 141, 147, 158–60, 162–64, 166–67, 169, 170, 172, 178–79, 184, 194

Greed
The insatiable desire for more, consistently condemned in the *Bible* and seen as the greatest cause of *poverty* in society. The *prophets* denounced those who deprived, cheated, and oppressed the poor (e.g. Isaiah 3:13–15; Amos 4:1; 8:4). pp. 115, 157

Greek
Language in which the *New Testament* was written.

Guidance
The *Bible* has many examples of God guiding people, out of his *love* and resolve to see his purposes fulfilled. At times that guidance is obvious (Acts 16:9–10), at times seen only with hindsight (Genesis 50:20). Biblical ways of guidance include *prophecy* (1 Samuel 10:1–9), God's *word* (Psalm 119:105), *prayer* (Acts 13:1–3), *dreams* and *visions* (Acts 10:9–20), circumstances (Acts 16:6–8), inner conviction (Luke 2:27), and the counsel of godly friends (Proverbs 15:22).

Guilt
The realization that you have violated God's standards and bear responsibility for your actions. The way out of guilt is through *repentance*, acknowledging *sin* rather than explaining it away or blaming others, as *Saul* did (1 Samuel 13 and 15), and resolving to change your thinking and behaviour from now on. Psalm 32 contrasts the heaviness of hiding *sin* with the *freedom* found through *confessing* it.

H

Habakkuk
Prophet to *Judah*, who prophesied c. 605 BC, puzzled over why God would use the godless *Chaldeans* to punish his people. pp. 37, 61, 151, 157

Hades
See *Sheol*

Hagar
Sarah's Egyptian maidservant who, following contemporary custom, was given to *Abraham* for him to father a child through since Sarah was barren (Genesis 16:1–4). But when Hagar became pregnant, Sarah so ill-treated her that she fled into the desert. Here she received angelic reassurance that her son would be blessed, recalled in his name, *Ishmael*, meaning "God hears" (16:5–16). When Sarah eventually bore her own son, *Isaac*, a new bout of rivalry led to Hagar and Ishmael being sent away. But God reassured them he would make Ishmael into a great nation (21:8–20), and he became the ancestor of the Arab peoples.

Haggai
Prophet who returned to *Jerusalem* from *exile* in *Babylon* and encouraged God's people to complete the rebuilding of the *Temple* in 520 BC when enthusiasm had lapsed. pp. 39, 77, 151

Hair pp. 58–59, 66–67, 92, **101**, 108

Ham
Noah's second son (Genesis 5:32), ancestor of the Hamites who settled in *Cush*, *Egypt*, Libya, and *Canaan* (Genesis 10:6–20).

Haman
Villain of the book of *Esther* who, as chief minister of King Ahasuerus of *Persia*, tried to use his position to exterminate the *Jews*. Through Queen Esther the plot was exposed and the Jews were spared, an event recalled in the Festival of *Purim*. p. 39

Hannah
Barren woman who prayed for a child and whose *faith* was rewarded with the birth of *Samuel*, one of *Israel*'s greatest *prophets* (1 Samuel 1–3).

Hanukkah
Jewish festival celebrating the rededication of the *Temple* by *Judas Maccabeus* in 165 BC. pp. 40–41, **139**

Haran
City in northern *Mesopotamia* to which *Abraham*'s father and *family* migrated and from where Abraham moved to *Canaan* in response to God's call (Genesis 11:31 – 12:5; Acts 7:2–4). pp. 24–25, 35, 37, 39

Hasidim
Pious *Jews* who resisted the *Hellenization* of *Alexander the Great* and his successors. p. 152

Hasmoneans
Jewish priestly *family* (named after Hasmon, the father of Mattathias who sparked off the *Maccabean revolt*), instrumental in freeing *Judea* from *Seleucid* rule in the second century BC. They served as *high priests*, governors, and kings until the Roman *conquest* in 63 BC and until Herod the Great ousted them from office in 37 BC.

Hazor
Canaanite city in northern *Israel*, defeated by *Joshua* (Joshua 11) and again later by *Deborah* and Barak (Judges 4). *Solomon* fortified the city in the tenth century BC along with *Megiddo* and *Gezer* (1 Kings 9:15). Archaeology has revealed a casement-walled city that could accommodate 40,000 people, with the gates of all three cities following a common plan. pp. 24, 28, 32, 92

Headwear p. 101

Health and healing
pp. 43–44, 77, 94–95, **124–26**, 136, 138, 145, 148, 156–57, 163, 169, 174–75, 189, 193

Heart pp. 10, 26, 30–31, 33, 35, 39, 44, 50, 74, 90, 92, 97, 115, 130, 132–35, 137, 140–41, 143, 146–47, 154, 158–59, 161, 165, 169–70, 172, 176, 178–80, 184, 189–92

Heaven
1. "The sky" (e.g. Nehemiah 9:6). The expression "the heaven(s) and the earth" meant the universe; "a new heaven and a new earth" (Revelation 21:1) is a total new creation.
2. God's dwelling place (e.g. Deuteronomy 26:15). Hence *Jesus* taught his *disciples* to pray, "Our Father in heaven..." (Matthew 6:9).
3. The place where believers in Jesus go after death to await his return to earth (e.g. John 14:1–6; Philippians 1:1–23; 3:12–14; 1 Thessalonians 4:13–14; 1 Peter 1:3–5; Revelation 4–5; 21–22).
4. Jewish periphrasis for "God". Despite God revealing his personal name, *Yahweh* (the LORD), as the name by which he was forever to be known (Exodus 3:15), later *Judaism* began to see God as more and more transcendent, too holy to even be called by name; so they substituted the word "heaven" instead. Hence *Matthew*, writing for Jewish *Christians*, speaks of "the kingdom of heaven" rather than "the kingdom of God". pp. 14, 22–24, 34, 56, 63, 74, 98, 101, 122–23, 140, 143, 145–46, 155, 157–58, 163, 168, 170, 172, 179, 184, 187–88, 195

Hebrew
The historic language of the Jewish people in which their *Scriptures* are written. pp. 12–13, 15–18, 22, 26–27, 41–42, 52, 59, 61, 69, 84, 87, 90, 97–99, 106, 109, 114, 120, 122, 131–34, 138, 141, 143, 149, 152, 157, 164, 191

Hebrews
1. Term used to describe God's people in parts of the *Old Testament*, generally by foreigners in a disparaging way: e.g. of *Joseph* in *Egypt* (Genesis 39:13–17), of *Israelite* slaves by Egyptians (Exodus 2:11), *Jonah* in identifying himself to pagan sailors (Jonah 1:9), of Israelites by the *Philistines* (1 Samuel 4:5–9). Some scholars see it as a variant of the Habiru/Apiru, referred to in many ancient texts, who were a propertyless, immigrant social class. pp. 26, 29
2. *New Testament* letter of unknown authorship, but almost certainly not by *Paul*, as its style is so different from his letters. Written to encourage Jewish *Christians* under pressure to return to *Judaism*, urging them to persevere in their Christian *faith* because *Jesus* was the fulfilment of, and better than, everything from the Old Testament.

Hebron
City in the *Judean* hills, originally called Kiriath Arba (Genesis 23:2). Base for the *patriarchs* (Genesis 13:18; 35:27), taken by *Caleb* during the *conquest* (Joshua 14:6–15), *David*'s capital during his first seven years as king (2 Samuel 5:1–5). pp. 24, 28, 30–32, 50, 53, 154, 160

Hell
Usual translation of the *Greek* "Gehenna", meaning "the Valley of Hinnom", where children were sacrificed by fire to pagan gods in *Old Testament* times (e.g. 2 Kings 23:10) and which by *New Testament* times was *Jerusalem*'s garbage dump. In later Jewish writings it symbolized the place of punishment of sinners, a belief affirmed by *Jesus*, who described its fire as eternal (Matthew 18:8) and unquenchable (Mark 9:43). This may be intended metaphorically rather than literally, as the New Testament uses a range of imagery to describe hell: a place of darkness and misery (Matthew 25:30), everlasting destruction and exclusion from God's presence (2 Thessalonians 1:9), the second death (Revelation 2:11), a lake of fire (Revelation 20:15). Whatever its reality, Jesus said it was to be avoided at all costs. p. **194**

Hellenization
Imposition of Greek culture and ideas whose man-centredness led to fierce clashes with *Judaism*. pp. 40, 78, 136, 152

Herbs pp. **54**, 99, 101, 135, 138

Hermon, Mount
Mountain on the *Lebanon/Syria* border, 9,232 feet (2,814 m) high, whose melting snows form part of the source of the *Jordan*. Probably the mountain in Jesus' *transfiguration*. p. 28

Herod
See "The Herods" pp. 181–82

Herodians
Supporters of King Herod who wanted his rule restored in *Judea*. pp. **153–54**, 180

Herodias
Wife of Herod Antipas who instigated *John the Baptist*'s execution (Matthew 14:1–12).

Hezekiah
One of *Judah*'s best kings (715–686 BC), who removed paganism, re-organized the *Temple* and its *worship*, fortified cities, strengthened the army, withheld taxes from *Assyria*, and built a tunnel to secure *Jerusalem*'s water supply. Noted for how he resisted Assyria's assault on *Jerusalem* by trusting God (2 Kings 18–19; Isaiah 36–37). pp. 33, 36–37, 53, 72–73, 94, 154, 185

Hezekiah's tunnel pp. 37, 94, 185

Hierapolis
City in the Roman province of Asia (modern western Turkey), 6 miles (9.5 km) from *Laodicea*, renowned for its hot springs rich in minerals. See photo p. 125

High priest
See *Priest*

Hinnom Valley
Valley outside *Jerusalem*. See *Hell*.

Hiram
King of *Tyre* who provided cedar wood and craftsmen for *David*'s palace (2 Samuel 5:11) and Solomon's *Temple* (1 Kings 5).

Hittites
Originally from *Asia Minor*, founders of a great empire between 1400 and 1200 BC. pp. 49, 66–68, 70, 82, 120

Holiness
That aspect of God's nature that separates him from anything imperfect or impure, and that was to be reflected in both the *worship* and lifestyle of God's people. pp. 23, **53**, 94, 130, 135–36, 148

Holy of Holies
The most sacred part of the *tabernacle* and *Temple* containing the *ark of the covenant*, which only the *high priest* could enter on the annual *Day of Atonement*.

Holy Land
Term found only once in the *Bible* to describe *Israel* (Zechariah 2:12), the more common designation being "*the Promised Land*" or simply "the land". The term only came into common Christian usage in the Middle Ages. pp. 29, **52–53**

Holy Spirit
God at work in the world, which Christian theology came to understand not just as God's power but as God himself, the third person of the *Trinity*. In *Old Testament* times experience of the Spirit was limited to people like *prophets*, *priests*, and kings, and his presence was always temporary. But *Joel* foresaw a day when all God's people would receive his Spirit (Joel 2:28–32), a day *Peter* declared had arrived at *Pentecost* (Acts 2:16–21).

Holy War p. 128

Homes pp. 38, 67, 81, 85, 87, 92, **93–94**, 95, 97, 102–103, 109, 137, 141, 147, 155, 166

Honesty pp. 111, 116–117

Honey
Used as a sweetener and food (Judges 14:8–9; Matthew 3:4). pp. 50–51, 60, **61**, 99, 110

Hope
Confident expectation of God's intervention, now and for the life to come, rooted in his *faithfulness* and promises. pp. 10, 17, 21, 33, 43, 47, 88, 129, 138, 151, 153, 158–60, **161**, 163, 169–70, 177, 185, 194–95

Horeb, Mount
Alternative name for *Mount Sinai*. pp. 27, 34

Horn
1. Wind instrument used in *worship* and battle. p. 140
2. Protuberances on the corners of *altars* where the *blood* of *sacrifices* was smeared (e.g. Exodus 29:12).
3. Used metaphorically as a symbol of strength (e.g. Psalm 18:2; Zechariah 1:18–19; Luke 1:69; Revelation 13:1).

Hosea
Prophet to *Israel* during its final years when it was falling into decline politically and spiritually. Hosea used his unhappy *marriage* to a faithless wife to picture the sadness God felt towards his unfaithful people. When they failed to respond, *judgment* at the hands of *Assyria* was inevitable. pp. 34–35, 68, 73, 151

Hospitality
Not merely an ancient social custom, but a requirement for God's people in both the Old and New Testaments as an expression of God's own *compassion* (Deuteronomy 10:17–18) and grateful response to his provision (Deuteronomy 24:17–19). The *New Testament* frequently underlines its importance (e.g. Romans 12:13; Hebrews 13:2; 1 Peter 4:9). pp. 84, 97, **113**, 177

Houses pp. **92–93**, 95, 102–103, 106, 127

Humility pp. **165**, 173, 179

Hurrians pp. 66, 82, 120

Hypocrite, hypocrisy
From the *Greek* word "hypokritēs", meaning "play-actor". Used by *Jesus* of the *scribes* and *Pharisees* because of their saying one thing but doing another and trying to find ways round the *Law*'s demands while claiming to keep it (Matthew 23:1–39). *Peter* said hypocrisy was incompatible with Christian living (1 Peter 2:1). pp. 152, 180

I

Ichabod
Name meaning "No glory", given to her newborn son by the wife of Phineas the *priest* on hearing the *Philistines* had captured the *ark of the covenant* (1 Samuel 4:19–22).

Identity markers, Jewish pp. 136–37, 152, 180

Idols, idolatry
Representations of gods, common in ancient times but forbidden to *Israel* in the *Ten Commandments*, for it was impossible to represent God in any meaningful way (Exodus 20:3–6). Idolatry, the *worship* of idols, was consistently opposed in both the Old and New Testaments, though the northern territory of Israel, founded on idolatry (1 Kings 12:25–33), became strongly influenced by it. pp. 17, 34, 40, 57, 59, 68–69, 89, 131, 135, 150

Idumea
Greek name for *Edom*, in particular the southern part of *Judea* to which *Edomites* had migrated. The *Herods* were Idumeans, which is why they were so despised by *Jews*. pp. 147, 180–81

Immanuel
"God with us", name of a child promised by *Isaiah* as a *sign* in the face of *Assyria*'s increasing power (Isaiah 7:14; 8:8), seen in the *New Testament* as a prophetic anticipation of the birth of *Jesus* (Matthew 1:23). pp. 73, 165

Incarnation
Foundational Christian doctrine that believes God became a human being in the person of *Jesus* of *Nazareth* (from the *Latin* "in carne", meaning "in the flesh"). pp. 42, 141, 158, 161, 165

Incense
Costly aromatic resin (like *frankincense*) that was burned on the *altar* by *priests* (Exodus 30:7–8). Also used symbolically of *prayer* (Psalm 141:2; Revelation 8:3–4). pp. 54, 146–47, 149, 167

Inheritance pp. 25, 28, 84, **85**, 189

Injustice
Failure to live up to God's righteous standards, whether ethically, legally, or morally. God's people are called to "act justly and love mercy" (Micah 6:8), and injustice was consistently condemned by the *prophets* (e.g. 1 Kings 21:1–29; Jeremiah 22:13). The *Bible* warns that on *Judgment* Day every act of injustice will be called to account (e.g. Romans 2:5–11; 2 Peter 2:4–12; Revelation 20:11–15). pp. 35, 111, 150, **157**

Inns p. **113**

Insects p. **61**

Isaac
Son of *Abraham* and *Sarah*, born when both were too old to have children, through whom God's promises to Abraham would be fulfilled (Genesis 17:19–21; 21:12; 26:1–5), though God's testing of Abraham seemed to throw this into jeopardy (Genesis 22). Married *Rebekah* (Genesis 24) through whom the twins *Esau* and *Jacob* were born (Genesis 25:19–26). Tricked in his old age into giving Jacob his inheritance blessing (Genesis 27). pp. 24–25, 53, 82, 89, 118, 160, 179

Isaiah
Prophet called through a *vision* of God in his *holiness* (Isaiah 6) when *Judah* was in constant

danger of attack from *Assyria*. He called people to *repent* of *sin* and warned of coming defeat if they didn't. But he also offered *hope*, seeing not only a return from future *exile* (Isaiah chs 40ff.) and even prophesying by name *Cyrus*'s involvement in this (43:28 – 45:1,13), but also prophesying much about the coming *messiah* (e.g. 9:1–7; 11:1–9; 32:1–20; 42:1–4; 52:13 – 53:12; 61:1–11). Author of the book Isaiah, though some, doubtful of long-term *prophecy*, think his followers wrote chapter 40 onwards. pp. 35–37, 42–43, 56–58, 60–61, 64, 69, 71–73, 76, 82–83, 88–90, 97, 99–101, 104–105, 109–110, 112, 115, 120–21, 124–25, 130, 144–45, 150–51, 154, 156–57, 161, 166, 168–69, 173–74

Ishbosheth
Saul's son, whose name means "man of shame", crowned after Saul's death in battle. He reigned over the northern tribes for just two years before being murdered by two of his own commanders, clearing the way for *David* to become king over a united kingdom (2 Samuel 2–4).

Ishmael
Abraham's son through *Hagar*, *Sarah*'s maidservant (Genesis 16). Although the object of Sarah's resentment, God blessed him, promising to make him a great nation (Genesis 21:8–20). He became the ancestor of the Arabs. pp. 111, 137

Islands, the
Term for the Mediterranean coastal area. p. 83

Israel, Israelites
Name given to *Jacob*, after wrestling all night with God (Genesis 32:22–32; 35:9–10), meaning "he struggles with God". The *tribes* tracing their descent from him became known as "the twelve tribes of Israel" (Genesis 49:28) or "Israelites", and the land where they settled as Israel. pp. 14, 16–17, 20–21, 24–36, 41–42, 44, 49–54, 56–62, 64, 67–73, 82–90, 92–94, 96–98, 102, 104, 106, 108–115, 117–120, 122–26, 128–39, 141, 144, 146–55, 160–61, 163–64, 167–70, 172–73, 175, 178–83, 187–88, 190

Issachar
1. Ninth son of *Jacob*, born through *Leah* (Genesis 30:17–18), whose name probably means "hired worker".
2. *Tribe* named after him that settled in northern *Canaan*, southwest of the *Sea of Galilee* and west into the *Jezreel* Valley (Joshua 19:17–23). By *David*'s time, the tribe had gained a reputation for *wisdom* (1 Chronicles 12:32), something emphasized in the *Talmud*, which said the wisest members of the *Sanhedrin* came from Issachar.

Italy
See *Rome*

J

Jabbok
Tributary of the *Jordan* marking the boundary between *Ammon* and *Gad* (Deuteronomy 3:16), forded by *Jacob* on the occasion of his heavenly wrestling match (Genesis 32:22–32).

Jabesh-Gilead
Town east of the *Jordan* in *Gilead* that wouldn't join *Israel*'s campaign against *Benjamin* and suffered reprisals (Judges 21). *Saul* proved his kingship by rescuing the city from the *Ammonites* (1 Samuel 11:1–11). Its citizens repaid the kindness by rescuing his mutilated body and burying it (1 Samuel 31:11–13).

Jacob
Patriarch of *Israel*, who fled to *Haran* after tricking *Esau* out of his birthright (Genesis 27:1–45), where he fathered eleven of his twelve sons (Genesis 30:1–24) who became the founders of Israel's tribes. His name was changed to *Israel* after a supernatural wrestling match (Genesis 32:22–32). His twelfth son, *Benjamin*, was born on the journey back to *Canaan*, though *Rachel* died during his delivery (Genesis 35:16–20). pp. 24–25, 27, 52–53, 65, 82, 84, 86–87, 105, 118, 123, 146, 160, 179

Jairus
Synagogue official whose daughter was restored to life by *Jesus* (Matthew 9:18–26; Mark 5:21–43; Luke 8:40–56). p. 175

James
1. Son of Zebedee, brother of *John*, a fisherman, one of *Jesus*' twelve *disciples* (Matthew 4:21–22). Jesus named the brothers "sons of thunder" (Mark 3:17), suggesting they had fiery temperaments, and together with *Peter* they formed Jesus' inner circle (e.g. Matthew 17:1; 26:37; Mark 5:37). He was *martyred* by Herod *Agrippa I* (Acts 12:1–2).
2. Son of Alphaeus, also called James the younger, another disciple of Jesus about whom nothing is known (Matthew 10:3; Mark 15:40).
3. Brother of Jesus (Matthew 13:55), who became a disciple only after Jesus personally appeared to him after the *resurrection* (1 Corinthians 15:7). Became leader of the *Jerusalem* church (Acts 12:17; 15:13–19) and wrote the *New Testament* letter bearing his name.

Japheth
One of *Noah*'s three sons, seen as the ancestor of the Indo-European peoples.

Jebus, Jebusites
Early name for *Jerusalem* and its inhabitants (2 Samuel 5:6–7).

Jehoahaz
1. Son of *Jehu*, king of *Israel*, who ruled 814–798 BC (2 Kings 13:1–9).
2. Son of *Josiah*, king of *Judah*, who reigned for just three months in 609 BC before being deposed by Pharaoh *Neco*.

Jehoiachin
Eighteen-year-old king of *Judah* who reigned for just three months in 597 BC before being exiled to *Babylon* by *Nebuchadnezzar* (2 Kings 24:8–17). Imprisoned until his thirty-seventh year of *exile*, when he was granted more freedom, with a privileged place at court (2 Kings 25:27–30). pp. 33, 37, 39, 75

Jehoiada
Chief *priest* who thwarted the attempts of Athaliah, the Queen Mother, to destroy the royal *family* by hiding the young *Joash* in the *Temple* for six years then bringing him out of hiding in a coup d'état and establishing him as rightful king (2 Kings 11).

Jehoiakim
Son of *Josiah*, godless king of *Judah* (609–598 BC) who "filled *Jerusalem* with innocent blood" (2 Kings 24:4), killed the *prophet* Uriah for opposing him (Jeremiah 26:20–23), and burned *Jeremiah*'s prophecies (Jeremiah 36). In 605 BC *Babylon* forced him to submit as a vassal. When he rebelled three years later Babylon sent forces against him (2 Kings 24:1–2) and took him into exile (2 Chronicles 36:6). pp. 33, 37

Jehoshaphat
King of *Judah* (872–848 BC), a good king who rejected foreign gods, taught God's *Law*, reformed the legal system, strengthened the army and defences, and defeated *Moab* and *Ammon* through a praise march (2 Chronicles 17–21). His alliance with *Ahab* was a mistake, however, since it drew him into *Israel*'s wars. pp. 33, 36, 82, 141

Jehovah
Older rendering of God's name, *Yahweh*.

Jehu
Anointed by *Elijah* to destroy *Ahab*'s line and become *Israel*'s king in his place (841–814 BC) (1 Kings 19:15–17; 2 Kings 9–10). pp. 20, 33–35

Jephthah
Judge whose careless vow led to the death of his own daughter (Judges 11).

Jeremiah
Prophet to *Judah* (c. 627–590 BC), whose *work* and prophecies are recorded in the book of his name. Called while still young (Jeremiah 1), he warned that unless God's people changed their ways, their land would be captured and the people exiled; but he was plotted against (11:18–23; 12:6; 18:18), put in the stocks (20:1–2), threatened with death (26), imprisoned (37), thrown into a *cistern* (38), and his words burned (36). Despite this he continued to prophesy, promising that restoration would come (30; 32; 33) and that God would one day make a new *covenant* with his people (31:29–34). He was eventually dragged to *Egypt* with the fleeing *remnant* where he probably died (43). pp. 14, 6–17, 37–38, 42, 51–52, 60, 64, 71, 75, 89, 114, 121, 125, 130–31, 133, 140, 150–51, 155, 157, 160, 189

Jericho
Oasis north of the *Dead Sea*, also called the City of Palms (2 Chronicles 28:15), a fortress city guarding the ford at the *Jordan* and the road linking the *King's Highway* with the *Way of the Sea*. First city captured by *Joshua* when *Israel* entered the *Promised Land* (Joshua 5:1 – 6:27). In *New Testament* times *Jesus* healed blind Bartimaeus here (Mark 10:46–52) and met *Zacchaeus* (Luke 19:1–10). pp. 28, 51, 53, 92–93, 102, 112, 128, 141, 154, 173

Jeroboam I
First king of the northern kingdom of *Israel*, who led a rebellion against *Rehoboam* (1 Kings 12:1–22). His establishment of shrines at *Dan* and *Bethel*, to discourage people from making pilgrimages to *Jerusalem*, and his appointing

unauthorized *priests* (1 Kings 12:25–33) set an evil example his successors followed and that was known thereafter as "the sin of Jeroboam". pp. 32–33, 52

Jeroboam II
King of *Israel* (782–753 BC) (co-regent from 793) who restored Israel's boundaries and brought economic prosperity (2 Kings 14:23–29), but at the cost of spiritual decline, despite warnings from *Amos* and *Hosea*. pp. 33–35

Jerusalem
Capital of the united nation of *Israel* after its *conquest* by *David*. pp. 12, 15, 17, 20, 30–33, 35–42, 44–47, 49–51, 53, 56, 58, 73, 75, 81, 89–90, 93–95, 103, 106, 110, 113, 116, 119–120, 122,–23, 129, 135, 137, 140–41, 143, 147, 151, 153–54, **155–56**, 166–67, 169, 173, 181–82, 185–86, 188, 194

Jerusalem, fall/destruction of pp. 12, **37**, 75, 106, 143, 153, 155, 182

Jerusalem, the New
Image used in Revelation 21 of God's eternal home for his people. pp. 103, **155**

Jesse
Grandson of *Ruth* and *Boaz* (Ruth 4:21–22), father of King *David* (1 Samuel 16:1; 17:12–15).

Jesus Christ
Jesus: a form of the *Old Testament* name *Joshua* ("Yahweh saves"); Christ: the *Greek* translation of the *Hebrew* word "*messiah*" (meaning "anointed one").

- **Ascension** pp. 44–45, 158, 161, 169, 179, **186–87**, 188–90, 192, 195
- **Attitude to money** pp. **114–115**, 171–72, 177
- **Baptism** p. 168
- **Betrayal by Judas** pp. 169, 178, 182–83
- **Birth** pp. 43, 144, 166–67
- **Cleansing of Temple** pp. 182–83
- **Community** pp. 153, 163, **178–99**
- **Conflicts** pp. **180–81**
- **Crucifixion** pp. 43, 49, 55, 119, 158, **184–85**, 194
- **Death, explanations of** pp. **184–85**
- **Disciples** p. **171**
- **Ethics** p. **176**
- **Final week** pp. **182–83**
- **Followers** pp. 18, 34, 44–45, 55, 95–96, 101, 107, 121, 129, 143–44, 156, 158, 161, 168–71, 174, 177–79, 181, 185, **192–93**
- **Gift of the Spirit** pp. 188–89
- **Great commission** p. 187
- **Healings** pp. 44, 124, 145, **174**
- **Last Supper** pp. 159, 182–83
- **Ministry** pp. 43–44, 52, 84–85, 103, 122, 124, 150, 153, 167–69, 174, 179, 183, 187–88, 191
- **Miracles** pp. 21, 34, 43, 53, 144–45, 162, **174–75**, 182, 187
- **Parables** pp. 12, 43, 171–72, **173–74**, 194
- **Power over death** p. 174
- **Power over nature** p. 174
- **Prayer** pp. 19, 93, **142–43**
- **Rejection** pp. 53, 151, 157, 169
- **Resurrection** pp. 18–19, **43–44**, 106, 139, 144–45, 158, 160–61, 169, 175, 178, 180, **184–85**, 186–88, 190–91, 194–95, 197
- **Resurrection appearances** pp. 185–87
- **Return** pp. 47, 172, 194–95
- **Saviour** pp. 81, 107, 158, 164, 167, 185, 190–91, 193
- **Sermon on the Mount** pp. **171**, 176–77, 198
- **Teaching** pp. 19, 21, 43–44, 47, 87, 143, **170–71**, 172–73, 176–77, 180, 182, 187, 191
- **Temptations** pp. 143, **168**
- **Triumphal entry** p. 182
- **Victory** pp. 182, **187**, 190, 195
- **Virgin birth** pp. 42, 165
- **Who was Jesus?** p. 42

Jethro
Midianite priest and father-in-law of *Moses* (Exodus 2:11–22) whose wise counsel led Moses to delegate leadership responsibilities to others (Exodus 18). p. 119

Jewellery pp. 63, 73, 77, 86, **101**, 109

Jewish Revolt
Jewish resistance against *Rome*, sparked in AD 66 by tensions which grew into anti-taxation protests and attacks upon Roman citizens. A war dragged on between AD 66 and 73, resulting in Rome's sacking of *Jerusalem* in AD 70 and the *Temple*'s final destruction. Some *Zealots* fled to *Masada*, a fortress palace in the *Judean* desert, where they held out until AD 73. pp. 17, **47**, 79, 103

Jews
Originally, members of the state of *Judah*, a term used from post-exilic times. Also called *Hebrews* and *Israelites* in earlier history. Used in the *New Testament* of members of the Jewish *faith*, and especially by *John* in the sense of Jewish religious leaders. pp. 13–17, 21, 35, 37–41, 43–47, 49, 54–55, 58, 61, 68, 76–78, 80, 82, 86, 88–90, 93–95, 97, 101, 108, 113–114, 117, 119–20, 122–23, 131, 135–36, 139, 142, 147, 152–53, 155, 158, 163, 167–70, 172, 174, 178–81, 183–84

Jezebel
Phoenician wife of King *Ahab* who enticed him into *Baal* worship (1 Kings 16:30–33) and who became the manipulative power behind the throne (1 Kings 21:1–14). She outlived Ahab but experienced a violent death, as *Elijah* had prophesied (2 Kings 9:3–37), during a revolt led by *Jehu*. pp. 34, 36

Jezreel
Town and valley in northern *Israel* where *Ahab* had his palace and where *Jezebel* died.

Joab
King *David*'s nephew and military commander, a courageous yet violent man who stayed loyal to David.

Joanna
Wife of the manager of Herod Antipas's household who became a *Christian* after being healed by *Jesus* and who supported him financially (Luke 8:1–3). She was a witness to Jesus' empty tomb (Luke 24:10).

Joash
Young king of *Judah* (835–796 BC) rescued by *Jehoiada* from the Queen Mother Athaliah's attempts to wipe out the royal family, and hidden in the *Temple* for six years until a coup d'état established him as rightful king (2 Kings 11). During Jehoiada's lifetime he pursued a godly path, refurbishing the Temple (2 Kings 12), but after his death he returned to *idolatry* (2 Chronicles 24:17–25).

Job
Central figure of the book named after him, a wealthy and godly man whose *faith* and integrity were tested by *Satan* (Job 1–2). The book narrates conversations with friends who seek to answer his situation according to the accepted wisdom of the day: that great *suffering* must be the result of great *sin*. But not only did Job know this was untrue, it also brought him no relief from his suffering. His answer finally came, not through debate, but through a fresh *revelation* of God's presence, power, and justice (Job 42:4–6). pp. 14, 31, 51, 55–56, 60–61, 63, 106–107, 120, 124, 130, 145, 156–57, 160

Joel
Prophet of unknown background and setting who prophesied in response to a devastating locust plague, which he saw as a picture of God's *judgment* (Joel 1:2 – 2:11). He called people to *repent* (Joel 2:12–17), assuring them of a day of restoration (Joel 2:18–32) and of the coming *Day of the LORD* when *the nations* would be judged (ch. 3). He is best known for his *prophecy* of the coming of the *Holy Spirit* on all of God's people (Joel 2:28–32), a promise picked up by *Peter* on the Day of *Pentecost* (Acts 2:14–21). pp. 44–45, 65, 73, 105, 130, 150–51, 154

John
Son of Zebedee, brother of *James*, fisherman, one of *Jesus'* twelve *disciples* (Matthew 4:21–22). Together with *Peter* the brothers formed Jesus' inner circle (e.g. Matthew 17:1; 26:37; Mark 5:37), though John held a place of special affection, known as "the disciple whom Jesus loved" (John 13:23), to whom Jesus revealed his betrayer (John 13:21–27) and entrusted his mother (John 19:25–27). Became one of the leaders of the *Jerusalem* church (Galatians 2:9), though tradition sees him eventually living in *Ephesus* to a great age. Author of the *Gospel* and three *New Testament* letters that bear his name and the book of *Revelation*. pp. 46–47, 81, 95, 106, 117, 127, 145, 153, 155, 162–63, 165, 173–75, 180, 183, 189

John the Baptist
Messenger promised by the Old Testament *prophets* (e.g. Malachi 4:5–6; see Luke 1:13–17), whose *preaching* prepared the way for *Jesus* and who reluctantly gave him *baptism* (Matthew 3:1–17; Mark 1:1–8; Luke 3:1–22; John 1:1–34). His preaching won many common people but offended the religious leaders, and his opposition to Herod's *marriage* to *Herodias* led to his imprisonment

(Matthew 14:3–5) where Jesus had to calm his doubts (Matthew 11:2–6). He was eventually beheaded by Herod Antipas (Matthew 14:1–12). pp. 39, 42, 58–59, 61, 83, 89, 150, 153, 168–69

Jonah
Prophet in *Israel* under *Jeroboam II* (2 Kings 14:25) at the time of *Assyria*'s rise to power. God sent him to preach to *Nineveh*, Assyria's capital, but Jonah ran in the opposite direction. Through a *sign* involving a great fish (1:4 – 2:10) Jonah realized God indeed wanted him to preach to Nineveh – though when he obeyed and Nineveh *repented* (ch. 3), he was angry that God could so easily forgive Israel's enemy (ch. 4). *Jesus* referred to the story as a sign of his own death and *resurrection* (Matthew 12:39–41).

Jonathan
Eldest son of King *Saul* who became *David*'s closest friend (1 Samuel 18:1–4) and helped him avoid his father's jealousy (1 Samuel 19–20), even though he knew David might replace him as future king. He was killed with Saul on *Mount Gilboa* in battle against the *Philistines* (1 Samuel 31:1–2), deeply mourned by David (2 Samuel 1:17–27).

Joppa
Mediterranean seaport in *Israel* (modern Jaffa), the port for *Jerusalem* that was 35 miles (56 km) away. Used by *Solomon* for importing building materials for the *Temple* (2 Chronicles 2:16) and by *Jonah* when he ran from God's call (Jonah 1:3). *Peter* restored Tabitha to life here (Acts 9:36–43) and received the *vision* that took him to preach to *Gentiles* (Acts 10).

Jordan
Israel's main river that flows south from *Mount Hermon*, through Lake Hulah and the *Sea of Galilee*, and down to the *Dead Sea*. Its name means "the descender", from the fact that it drops 2,380 feet (725 m) along its course. It features in many key *Bible* stories, like Israel's miraculous crossing of it into the *Promised Land* (Joshua 3–4), *Elijah* and *Elisha*'s crossing of it at a strategic moment of hand-over (2 Kings 2:7–14), and *John the Baptist*'s baptizing there (Matthew 3). pp. 28–29, 32, 50–53, 60, 68, 82, 104, 112, 118, 168

Joseph
1. Eleventh son of *Jacob* by *Rachel* (Genesis 30:22–24), whose name means "may he add". His father's favouritism and his gift of interpreting *dreams* provoked his brothers' hostility and they sold him into slavery (Genesis 37). He ended up in *Egypt* where, after many setbacks, he finally rose to become *Pharaoh*'s right-hand man (Genesis 39–41), enabling him to bring his *family* there to avoid the famine in *Canaan* (chs 42–47). Although his brothers feared for their lives after Jacob's death, Joseph understood that God's *sovereignty* had been at work through everything (Genesis 50:20). There was no tribe called Joseph since Jacob adopted Joseph's two sons *Ephraim* and *Manasseh* (Genesis 48), who took the place of Joseph and [illegible] apart as *Israel*'s priesthood. pp. 25–26, 64–65, 100, 111, 127
2. Husband of *Mary* the mother of *Jesus* (Matthew 1:18–25), descendant of *David* (Luke 2:4). Apart from Jesus' birth stories the only occasion we encounter Joseph is during a visit to *Jerusalem* when Jesus was twelve (Luke 2:41–50), so it is likely he died while Jesus was young. This could explain why Jesus, as eldest child, waited until he was thirty before beginning his ministry so he could fulfil his family responsibilities as head of the household. pp. 43, 80–82, 84, 86, 103, 144, 164–67
3. Joseph of Arimathea, member of the *Sanhedrin*, who arranged for Jesus' burial, and whom *John*'s Gospel describes as a secret *disciple* (Matthew 27:57–60; Mark 15:42–46; Luke 23:50–54; John 19:38–42). pp. 160, 185

Josephus
(c. AD 37–100) Former Jewish governor of *Galilee* who abandoned his opposition to *Rome* and became a Roman historian. His writings illuminate Jewish history and the beliefs of Second-Temple *Judaism*. He mentions *Jesus* in two of his works, noting his teaching, *miracles*, *crucifixion*, and the claims of *resurrection*. pp. 21, 38, 45, 103, 137, 153

Joshua
1. *Moses*' assistant, with him on *Mount Sinai* (Exodus 24:13) and in the *tabernacle* (Exodus 33:7–11). Of the twelve spies sent to explore *Canaan*, only he and *Caleb* brought a positive report (Numbers 14:5–9), for which they were allowed to enter the *Promised Land* (14:26–38). Appointed as Moses' successor (Deuteronomy 1:38; 3:28; 31:7–8; 34:9), he led *Israel* in its *conquest* of Canaan, recorded in the book of Joshua. pp. 14, 27–29, 38, 48, 51–53, 68–69, 71, 82, 97, 102, 115, 121, 128, 131–32, 141–42, 148
2. *High priest* at the time of the *return from exile*, encouraged by *Haggai* to complete work on the *Temple* (Haggai 1:12 – 2:9) and seen by *Zechariah* as prefiguring the *messiah* (Zechariah 7:9–15).

Josiah
King of *Judah* (640–609 BC) who undertook thorough religious reforms after the discovery of "the book of the Law" (almost certainly Deuteronomy) during *Temple* restorations (2 Kings 22–23). Killed at *Megiddo* fighting Pharaoh *Neco*, who was marching to *Assyria*'s aid (2 Kings 23:29). pp. 17, 33, 36–37, 89

Jubilee Year
A year of freedom occurring every fiftieth year (seven *sabbath* years plus one) when *debts* were to be cancelled, slaves freed, and land returned to its original owners (Leviticus 25:8–17, 23–34). This ensured that land, God's gift to his people, could only be sold leasehold, the lease expiring either when the owner or *kinsman-redeemer* could buy it back, or at Jubilee when it was automatically returned, thereby preventing generational *poverty*. It is uncertain, however, whether this was actually practised, as we have no historical evidence for it.
The image of Jubilee was taken up by *Isaiah* (chs 58 and 61), who pictured the forthcoming release from *exile* in *Babylon* as "the year of the Lord's favour" (61:2), and by *Jesus*, who proclaimed himself to be the herald of God's long-awaited Jubilee Year (Luke 4:18–21). pp. 52, 93, 96, 127

Judah
1. *Jacob*'s fourth son, born to *Leah* (Genesis 29:31), whose name means "Praise". He urged his brothers not to kill *Joseph* (Genesis 37:26–27) and offered himself as a hostage in place of *Benjamin* (Genesis 44).
2. *Tribe* descended from Judah, whose territory included the hills south of *Jerusalem* and the desert bordering the *Dead Sea*. *Jesus* came from this tribe (Matthew 1:1–16).
3. Name of the southern kingdom that remained loyal to *David*'s descendants after the nation split in two after *Solomon*'s death (1 Kings 12:20). It experienced 200 years of conflict with its breakaway northern neighbour, *Israel* (1 Kings 12 – 2 Kings 17) until Israel fell to *Assyria* in 721 BC. Judah survived until its fall to *Babylon* in 586 BC (2 Kings 25) when its people were exiled, its *Temple* destroyed, and its territory annexed. After a brief period of independence from 128 BC, secured by the *Maccabees*, it fell to *Rome* in 63 BC, becoming part of the Roman province of *Syria* and known as *Judea*. pp. 14–15, 17, 20, 30–40, 49, 52, 60, 72, 75, 84, 105, 110, 114, 118, 128, 143, 151, 155

Judaism
The religion and way of life of the Jewish people. Its key biblical periods are often characterized as: patriarchal, Mosaic, *conquest*, monarchy, division, *exile* and restoration. The period from 168 BC (when the *Temple* was desecrated) is often known today as "early Judaism", a time of considerable diversification of beliefs and practices, rooted in a lack of unity that went back to the *return from exile* and that had many expressions by Jesus' day.

Judas
1. Brother of *Jesus* (Matthew 13:55), possibly the author of *Jude* (an alternative spelling).
2. *Apostle*, son of *James* (Luke 6:16).
3. Judas Iscariot, who betrayed Jesus for thirty silver coins, the price of a slave (Matthew 10:4; 26:14–16, 47–55; John 13:18–30; 18:1–11) and who later committed suicide (Matthew 27:3–10; Acts 1:16–19). pp. 169, 182–83, 188
4. Judas Maccabeus, See *Maccabees*

Jude
New Testament book, written either by *Judas* the apostle or, more likely, Judas the brother of Jesus, to safeguard the church against *false teachers* and encourage his readers to "contend for the *faith* that was once for all entrusted to the saints" (v. 3).

Judea
Greek and Roman name for *Judah*. It usually refers to the southern part of the country, though sometimes the whole land, including *Galilee* and *Samaria*.

Judges
1. Provided by the Jewish *Law* to dispense justice (e.g. Exodus 18:13–27; Deuteronomy 1:16–19). p. 119
2. Spirit-empowered leaders given by God to rescue his people in the dark period prior to the

monarchy (e.g. Judges 2:16). pp. 29, 70–71, 82
3. Book recording *Israelite* history between the death of *Joshua* and the rise of the monarchy.

Judgment
The expression of God's justice and fairness which calls everyone to account for their beliefs and behaviour, whether in this life or on "the Last Day". The *New Testament* teaches that only through *faith* in *Jesus* can this judgment be avoided (e.g. John 3:18) and God's *righteousness* be declared over us (e.g. Romans 3:21–26; 8:1–4).

Justice pp. 35, 47, 111, 118–119, 135, 150, 156–57, 193, 196

Justification
God's declaring someone to be righteous or "not guilty" through their *faith* in *Jesus Christ* and his *sacrifice* on the *cross*, the heart of *Paul*'s letter to the *Romans* (e.g. Romans 3:21–24; 5:1, 9; 8:1–4) – though Paul sees that even faith is God's gift (Ephesians 2:8). It was Paul's contention that *righteousness* comes through faith alone, as *Abraham*'s example reveals (Romans 4), not through keeping the *Law*, and that it comes while we are still ungodly, which brought him into conflict with the *Jews*.

K

Kadesh Barnea
Oasis in the desert south of *Beersheba* near which much of *Israel*'s desert wanderings occurred (Numbers 13:26; 20: 1–13; 33:36).

Kidron Valley
Valley between *Jerusalem* and the *Mount of Olives* to its east. On its western slope lies the Gihon Spring whose waters *Hezekiah* brought into the city through a tunnel (2 Kings 20:20). Reforming kings destroyed *idols* in this valley (e.g. 1 Kings 15:13; 2 Kings 23:4–14), and *Jesus* crossed it on the way to the Garden of *Gethsemane* from where he would easily have seen his captors approaching, yet chose to await them (John 18:1).

Kingdom of God/heaven
The rule of God, the central theme of *Jesus'* message. *Matthew*, out of respect for his Jewish-background readers, calls it "the kingdom of *heaven*". pp. 163, 170–72, 179, 191, 197

King's Highway
The main north–south route between *Damascus* and the Gulf of Aqaba running east of the *Jordan*. pp. 24, 82, 112

Kings of Israel and Judah
See chart p. 33

Kinsman-redeemer
Closest family member responsible for protecting any member of the wider *family* in need. *Redemption* from their need included providing an heir where a brother had died childless (Deuteronomy 25:5–10), buying back land sold to someone outside the family (Leviticus 25:25–28), or a family member who had sold themselves into slavery (Leviticus 25:47–53), and avenging a relative's *murder* (Numbers 35:16–21). The book of *Ruth* is full of themes of redemption.

Kiriath-Arba
Alternative name for *Hebron*.

Kiriath-Jearim
Chief *Gibeonite* town where the *ark of the covenant* stayed for twenty years after the *Philistines* returned it until *David* relocated it to *Jerusalem* (1 Samuel 6:21 – 7:2).

Kohath, Kohathites
Son of *Levi*, grandfather of *Moses* (Exodus 6:16–20), whose descendants formed one of the three Levitical families responsible for caring for the *tabernacle* (Numbers 3:27–32).

Korah
Levite who led a rebellion against *Moses* and *Aaron*, jealous of their leadership and angry at their apparent failure to lead them to the *Promised Land* (Numbers 16).

L

Laban
Rebekah's brother who tricked his nephew *Jacob* into marrying his first daughter *Leah* before giving him his chosen bride *Rachel* (Genesis 29), and whom Jacob tricked in return (Genesis 30:25 – 31:55). p. 25

Lachish
Canaanite fortified city southwest of *Jerusalem* whose king was defeated by *Joshua* on the day when the sun's setting was said to be delayed (Joshua 10). Rebuilt by *Rehoboam* as a defence against the *Philistines* and *Egyptians* (2 Chronicles 11:5–12). Its siege by *Assyria* (2 Kings 8:13–16) was depicted in a relief in *Sennacherib*'s palace. It was finally destroyed by *Babylon* in 587 BC. pp. 20, 28, 36, 50, 53, 94, 129

Lamb of God
Title given to *Jesus* by *John the Baptist* (John 1:29, 36), a reference to the lambs offered as *sacrifices* and therefore to Jesus' death as an *atonement*, the lamb provided by God himself. *Peter* described him as "a lamb without blemish or defect" (1 Peter 1:19).

Lamech
1. Descendant of *Cain*, the first murderer (Genesis 4:3–16), who not only committed *murder* himself but boasted of it (Genesis 4:23–24).
2. *Noah*'s father (Genesis 5:28–29).

Laodicea
City in the Lychus Valley in modern Turkey, modern Pamukkale, that grew wealthy from trade, banking, and producing textiles and medicines, especially eye ointments, but whose water supply was poor. All these images are picked up in one of the rebukes in the Letters to the Seven Churches in *Revelation* (3:14–22). p. 125

Last Days p. **195**

Last Supper
Jesus' final meal with his *disciples* in which he reinterpreted the *Passover* meal in the light of his impending death, declaring that God was about to establish a new *covenant* through him that would bring *forgiveness* of *sin* (Matthew 26:28). Having told them to "do this in remembrance of me" (Luke 22:19), sharing *bread* and *wine* quickly became a key part of Christian *worship*, initially in the context of a meal. Today it is called by different names: the Lord's Supper, Breaking of Bread, Holy Communion, and Mass. pp. 159, **182–83**

Latin
Language of the Romans, one of the languages in which *Jesus'* supposed crime was written on the sign (the "titulus") above his head (John 19:19–20). In the fourth century AD the *Bible* was translated into Latin by Jerome, called "*The Vulgate*", because it was written in the common or "vulgate" language.

Law (Torah)
Hebrew word meaning "instruction" or "guidance", God's gift to *Israel* through *Moses* and their guide for life. It included accounts of Israel's early history, as well as the *Ten Commandments* and laws expounding and applying them. *Jesus* affirmed the *Law* (e.g. Matthew 5:17–20) yet challenged its interpretations by the religious leaders (Matthew 5:21–48). The *New Testament* argues that Jesus' death both fulfilled and replaced the Law, and that keeping it cannot save anyone. pp. 12, 14, 17, 27, 30, 32, 36, 38, 39, 44, 47, 58–59, 61, 67, 74, 86, 88–92, 94–95, 99–101, 105, 108, 110–111, 114–115, 117–119, 121, 124, 126–27, 133–38, 148, 152–53, 170–71, 176, 180, 184, 189

Lazarus
1. Friend of *Jesus*, brother of *Mary* and *Martha*, who was raised to life by Jesus (John 11). pp. 144, 160–61, 175, 182
2. Beggar in one of Jesus' *parables*, whose eternal destiny was contrasted with that of an uncaring rich man (Luke 16:19–31).

Leah
Elder daughter of *Laban* whose father tricked *Jacob* into marrying her and who bore four of Jacob's sons: *Reuben*, *Simeon*, *Levi*, and *Judah* (Genesis 29). pp. 25, 84, 87, 89, 125, 160

Leather-working p. **108**

Lebanon
Fertile mountainous region north of *Palestine* sweeping down to the Mediterranean coast, famous for its forests (especially cedars) in *Old Testament* times as well as many kinds of fruit. Its great ports of *Tyre*, *Sidon*, and *Byblos* made it a prosperous trading nation.

Legalism
Belief that God's favour is dependent on detailed obedience to the *Law*, which frequently degenerates into punctilious rule-keeping while losing the spirit behind it, something that *Jesus* accused the *scribes* and *Pharisees* of and that *Paul* warned the early church to beware of. p. **135**

Leisure pp. 72, **122–23**

Leprosy
Various chronic skin diseases,

common in Bible times. pp. 34, 44, 124, 136, 174

Letters, New Testament
pp. 21, 45, 47, 121

Letter-writing p. 121

Levi, Levites
1. Third son of *Jacob*, born through *Leah* (Genesis 29:34).
2. *Tribe* descended from Levi, dedicated to God in place of the firstborn (Numbers 3:11–13), appointed to care for the *tabernacle* and assist the *priests* in their *work* (Numbers 1:47–53; 3:1–39). pp. 29, 32, 67, 84, 140, 146, 148

Leviticus
Third book of the *Law* giving detailed directions for the *work* of the *priests*.

Light pp. 12, 47, 91, **95**, 177, 189

Lighting pp. **94–95**

Lights, Festival of
See *Hanukkah*

Locusts
Swarming insects that can devastate crops within minutes, like those that afflicted *Judah* (Joel 1:1 – 2:11). Designated as a clean food in the *Law* (Leviticus 11:20–23), they formed part of *John the Baptist*'s diet in the *wilderness* (Matthew 3:4). pp. 61, **105**

Lord's Day
Occurring only in *Revelation* 1:10, an early Christian term for Sunday, "the first day of the week" (Acts 20:7; 1 Corinthians 16:22), when *Christians* met to *worship* in celebration of the *resurrection*. The name may have been a play on "Emperor's Day", the term Romans used in pre-Christian times for the first day of each month, as a way of declaring that *Jesus*, through his resurrection, had been shown to be the greatest emperor of all. For the first Christians, who were from a Jewish background, to change their special day from *sabbath* (Saturday) to Sunday shows how crucial and central they understood the resurrection to be.

Lord's Prayer
Name given to a prayer *Jesus* taught his *disciples*, recorded in slightly different forms (Matthew 6:9–13; Luke 11:2–4), perhaps reflecting different occasions when Jesus taught it. *Matthew*'s version is a pattern ("This then is how you should pray"), while Luke's is a prayer ("When you pray, say..."). Both approaches have been followed by *Christians*. pp. 19, **143**

Lord's Supper
See *Last Supper*

Lordship
Absolute supremacy. The earliest Christian *confession* was "Jesus is Lord" (1 Corinthians 12:3; Philippians 2:11). p. **145**

Lot
Abraham's nephew who accompanied him from *Haran* (Genesis 12:5). When increasing livestock numbers led them to separate, Lot chose land near *Sodom*, south of the *Dead Sea*, which was fertile but immoral and unstable (Genesis 13:1–13). He was rescued by Abraham from Kedorlaomer's attack (Genesis 14) and by *angels* from God's *judgment* on this wicked region, though his wife's hesitation led to disaster (Genesis 19:1–29). Having got their father drunk, his two daughters, fearing remaining unmarried and childless, became pregnant by him, and their sons became the founders of the *Moabites* and *Ammonites* (Genesis 19:30–38). pp. 24, 82

Love
Seen as one of the most fundamental aspects of God's nature in the *Bible*, so much so that *John* could write "God is love" (1 John 4:8). Despite common misconceptions God's love is seen as much in the *Old Testament* as in the New, though *Jesus* is shown to have expressed it clearer than anyone else ever had, and the *New Testament* sees his death for sinners as the ultimate expression of God's love (e.g. John 3:16; Romans 5:8). In the light of this *Christians* are called to love one another, reflecting the love of God himself (e.g. John 13:34–35; 15:9–14; 1 Corinthians 13; Galatians 5:22; 1 John 4:7–21). pp. 12, 16, 18, 27, 31, 39, 43, 47, 61–62, 73–74, 78, 81, 91, 97, 114, 119, 130–31, 141, 143, 153, 168, 170, 176–77, 179, 186

Luke
Doctor, friend, and companion of *Paul* (e.g. Colossians 4:14), author of Luke's *Gospel* and *Acts*, extremely careful historian, the only *Gentile* writer in the *Bible*. pp. 17, 19–21, 44, 46, 162–63, 189

Lydia
Businesswoman, dealer in expensive purple cloth, converted at *Philippi*, whose home became the base for the new church (Acts 16:13–15, 40).

Lystra
Roman colony in *Galatia*, *Timothy*'s hometown (Acts 16:1), where *Paul* healed a crippled man leading its citizens to think he and *Barnabas* were gods (Acts 14:8–20).

M

Maccabees
Followers of *Judas Maccabeus* who led the revolt begun by his father, the *high priest* Mattathias, against the *Hellenization* programme of *Antiochus IV Epiphanes* and his desecration of the *Temple* in 168 BC. After a period of guerrilla warfare, Judas marched on *Jerusalem*, reclaiming it and purifying the Temple in 165 BC, an event commemorated in the Festival of *Hanukkah*. pp. 16–17, 79, 152, 154

Macedonia
One of the four nations into which *Alexander the Great*'s empire disintegrated after his death. By *New Testament* times it was a Roman province in northern Greece whose capital was *Philippi*, to which *Paul* sailed from Asia after seeing a *vision* of a Macedonian man asking for his help (Acts 16:6–12). pp. 40, 76

Machaerus
One of Herod's fortresses, east of the *Dead Sea*, where *John the Baptist* was beheaded.

Machpelah
Cave in which *Sarah*, *Abraham*, *Isaac*, *Rebekah*, *Leah*, and *Jacob* were all buried (Genesis 23:19; 25:9; 49:31; 50:13). p. 160

Magi
Visitors at *Jesus'* birth from *Arabia*, whose role involved being *priests*, astronomers, and royal advisers (Matthew 2:1–12). Their gifts symbolized Jesus' future: gold to represent his kingship; *frankincense*, his priestly role; *myrrh*, his death for all. pp. 43, 54–55, 77, 144, 167

Magic
The attempt to influence people and events through supernatural means such as charms, spells, *amulets*, and potions, forbidden in the *Bible*. pp. 21, 67, 71, 91, 125, 145

Magnificat
Mary's song of praise on discovering her barren relative *Elizabeth* was indeed pregnant, as the *angel* had said, a *sign* of the significance of her own pregnancy (Luke 1:39–55). p. 164

Malachi
Prophet whose name means "My messenger", contemporary of *Nehemiah*, who challenged people's lifestyle in post-exilic *Jerusalem* and *Judah* (1:6 – 2:16), calling for *repentance* in the light of God's coming messenger (3:1–5), for only the faithful would survive the *Day of the* LORD (ch. 4). His reference to *Elijah* appearing as a forerunner is seen in the *New Testament* as a *prophecy* of *John the Baptist* (Matthew 11:11–14; 17:12–13; Luke 1:17). pp. 14, 39–40, 77, 86, 117, 130, 150–51, 168

Malchus
High priest's servant whose ear *Peter* cut off when soldiers came to arrest *Jesus* and whom Jesus healed (Luke 22:49–51; John 18:10).

Malta
Mediterranean island where *Paul* was shipwrecked and spent three months on his way to *Rome* (Acts 27:39 – 28:11).

Man
See *Adam*

Manasseh
1. Joseph's elder son born in *Egypt* (Genesis 41:51), adopted by *Jacob* (Genesis 48), and the tribe that was descended from him. pp. 29, 52, 82, 84
2. Territory of the tribe of Manasseh, half of whom asked for land in *Transjordan* to the east of the *Jordan*, and half of whom took the hill country of *Samaria*. The tribe was therefore treated as two half-tribes.
3. Wicked king of *Judah* (697–642 BC), son of the godly *Hezekiah* with whom he initially co-ruled. He led Judah into *idolatry* (2 Kings 21:1–9), and his *sin* was seen as being largely responsible for their exile (2 Kings 21:10–15; Jeremiah 15:3–4). It was only in exile in *Assyria* that he repented (2 Chronicles 33:10–13). pp. 17, 33, 36, 154

Manna
Food of uncertain composition ("manna" in *Hebrew* means "what is it?") miraculously provided for the *Israelites* in the *wilderness* (Exodus 16), a jar of which was kept in the *tabernacle* (Exodus 16:33–34), and which continued

until they reached the *Promised Land* (Joshua 5:12). Often called "bread from heaven" (e.g. Exodus 16:4; Nehemiah 9:15; Psalm 105:40), *Jesus* picked up the imagery and used it of himself, seeing himself as food that, in contrast to manna, would satisfy forever (John 6:47–58). pp. 27–28, 99, 146

Mara ben Serapion
Syrian philosopher who, in a letter dated sometime after AD 73, refers to three wise men who were persecuted: Socrates by *Athens*, Pythagoras by Samos, and "their wise king" by the *Jews* shortly before *Judea*'s destruction. While not specifically naming *Jesus*, this is probably one of the earliest non-Christian references to Jesus' existence. p. 21

Marduk
Babylonian god of thunderstorms, seen as the one who defeated chaos, thereby becoming the supreme deity, and who created the world. He had some fifty titles but was chiefly known as Bel or Lord. pp. 23, 74–75

Mark
Also called *John* (Acts 12:12), cousin of *Barnabas* (Colossians 4:10), who wrote the *Gospel* bearing his name. He accompanied *Paul* and Barnabas on Paul's first *missionary* journey but left halfway through, so Paul refused to take him again (Acts 13:13; 15:36–40), though they were reconciled later (2 Timothy 4:11; Philemon v. 24). *Peter* describes him as "my son Mark" (1 Peter 5:13), and early church tradition closely associates the two, reflected in Mark's Gospel, which seems to be based around Peter's memoirs.

Market place pp. 103, 110, 122

Marriage
The *Bible*'s setting for intimate relationships between a man and a woman as the two "become one flesh" (Genesis 2:24; Malachi 2:15; Matthew 19:4–6). pp. 20, 39, 62, 81, 84–85, **86–87**, 89, 119, 156, 159, 164, 173, 176

Martha
Sister of *Mary* and *Lazarus* in whose home Jesus stayed (Luke 10:38; John 11). While renowned for her over-concern with practical affairs (Luke 10:38–42), she was in fact deeply spiritual, and it was she, rather than Mary, who affirmed her *faith* in *Jesus* as the *resurrection* and the life, leading to the raising of Lazarus (John 11:17–44). pp. 160, 182, 198

Martyr, martyrdom
Someone who suffers death for their beliefs, from the *Greek* "martys" meaning "witness". pp. 44–46, 81, 161, 163

Mary
1. Mary, mother of *Jesus*, husband of *Joseph* (Matthew 1:18–25; Luke 1:26–38). After the birth stories, which highlight her *faith*, there are few references to her in the *New Testament*, and those that do exist highlight her very real humanity: her anxiety at losing Jesus (Luke 2:41–51); her prompting Jesus to act when the *wine* ran out at a wedding, prompting Jesus' rebuke (John 2:1–11); her worrying about Jesus when she thought he was overworking (Mark 3:20–21, 31–35); her witnessing the *crucifixion* and being commended to *John*'s care (John 19:25–27); her praying with the *disciples* in the *upper room* (Acts 1:14). pp. 43, 81, 88, 103, 144, 164–66
2. Mary Magdalene, delivered from *demons* by Jesus (Luke 8:2), who was with the group of women at the *cross* (Matthew 27:55–56) and was the first to see the empty tomb and the risen Jesus (Matthew 28:1–9; John 20:10–18).
3. Mary, sister of *Martha* and brother of *Lazarus*, who sat at Jesus' feet and was commended for her devotion (Luke 10:38–42) and who anointed Jesus' feet (John 12:1–3).
4. Mary, mother of *Mark*, whose home was used by the *Jerusalem* church (Acts 12:12–17).
5. Mary, mother of *James* and wife of Clopas, known as "the other Mary", who was at the crucifixion and visited Jesus' tomb (Matthew 27:55–56, 61; 28:1–10).

Masada
Herod's fortress near the *Dead Sea*, location of the *Zealots*' stand against the Romans that ended in mass suicide in AD 73. pp. 47, 93, 95, 129, 153

Matthew
Tax collector who became one of *Jesus'* twelve *disciples* (Matthew 9:9; 10:3) and who wrote the *Gospel* bearing his name. pp. 19, 40, 111, 163, 167, 171–72, 176, 179

Matthias
Chosen after *Judas Iscariot*'s suicide to become the twelfth *apostle* by *casting lots* (Acts 1:15–26). p. 188

Meals pp. 27, 29, 54, 97–98, **99**, 132, 137–38, 141, 147, 177–78, 183

Meat pp. 54, 5–60, 80, 97, **99**, 124, 135–36, 170, 172

Medes, Media
People group in northwest *Mesopotamia* who came under *Assyrian* control but who, by allying with *Babylon*, overthrew them. Incorporated into the growing *Persian* empire in 550 BC by *Cyrus*. pp. 24, 35, 37, 72, 76–77, 83, 116

Mediator
Go-between who reconciles two parties. The *New Testament* sees *Jesus* as the one mediator between God and *man* (e.g. 1 Timothy 2:5).

Megiddo
City dominating the *Egyptian–Syrian* highway running through the *Carmel* hills, conquered by *Joshua*, allotted to *Manasseh* (Joshua 12:21; 17:11), and fortified by *Solomon* (1 Kings 9:15). Its strategic position meant it was the site of many battles, and so *Revelation* uses it as the setting for the final battle of *Armageddon* (Har-Magedon, "the Hill of Megiddo", a reference to the *tell* on which it stands). pp. 29, 32, 50, 52, 69, 103, 179

Melchizedek
"King of Salem [*Jerusalem*]... and priest of God Most High" (Genesis 14:18), who blessed *Abraham* and received his *tithe* (Genesis 14:17–24). Seen in the book of *Hebrews* as a "type" (foreshadowing) of *Jesus* (Hebrews 5:6, 10; 6:20; 7:1–17), something *David* foresaw (Psalm 110:4).

Memphis
Ancient capital of *Egypt* on the River *Nile*, mentioned by *prophets* who condemned *Israel*'s false trust in Egypt (Isaiah 9:13; Jeremiah 46:14, 19; Ezekiel 30:13–16; Hosea 9:6). pp. 27, 37, 40, 64, 112

Menorah
Seven-branched candlestick, constantly kept burning to give light in the *tabernacle* and *Temple*. p. 146

Mephibosheth
Son of *Jonathan*, crippled when dropped as a child (2 Samuel 4:4), to whom *David* showed kindness, despite his potential threat to the throne (2 Samuel 9).

Merchants pp. **110–111**, 114, 147, 152, 169, 183

Mercy
Common translation of the *Hebrew* word "chesed" which occurs almost 250 times in the *Old Testament* referring to God's loving-kindness and loving-patience, demonstrated in his readiness to forgive.

Mesopotamia
Name given by Greek historians to the region "between the rivers" (the literal meaning of Mesopotamia), the *Tigris* and *Euphrates*, home to several civilizations – *Sumerians*, *Arameans*, *Chaldeans*, *Assyrians*, *Babylonians*, and *Persians*. pp. 23–25, 34, 40, 48–51, **62–63**, 64, 66, 68, 71–73, 75–78, 82–83, 91, 95, 97, 104, 112–113, 154

Messiah
Messiah, from the *Hebrew* "mašiah", meaning "Anointed One"; translated in the *Septuagint* as "christos" (from which the word "Christ" comes): the deliverer-king expected by *Israel*. By *Jesus'* time there was widespread expectation that Messiah would soon appear, hence Jesus' reluctance to use the title lest it be understood in nationalistic terms. pp. 31, 40–41, **42**, 43, 49, 53, 124, 129, 133, 163–64, 166, 168–69, 174–75, 183–84, 192

Methuselah
Son of *Enoch*, grandfather of *Noah*, who lived to a proverbial old age (Genesis 5:21–27).

Mezuzah
Wooden or metal case containing *Scripture* affixed to the front doorpost of Jewish homes. p. 137

Micah
1. *Prophet* in eighth-century BC *Judah*, contemporary of *Isaiah*, who prophesied *judgment* on both *Samaria* and *Jerusalem*, yet who also saw the coming glory of Jerusalem and the day when all nations would go to it (Micah 4:1–5).
2. *Ephraimite* whose silver *idols* and *priest* were taken by migrating Danites, reflecting the lawlessness of those days (Judges 17–18).

Michael
Archangel (Jude 9) whose name means "Who is like God?". *Daniel*, like later Jewish writings, saw him as *Israel*'s guardian, "the great prince who protects your people" (12:10), who is resisted but prevails (10:12–14). In *Revelation* 12:7 he and his *angels* defeat *Satan* in heavenly warfare.

Michal
Saul's daughter who was married to *David* for a dowry of 100 *Philistine* foreskins (1 Samuel 18). While she protected David from Saul (1 Samuel 19), she despised his exuberant *worship*, for which she remained childless (2 Samuel 6).

Midian, Midianites
Land inhabited by the descendants of Midian, son of *Abraham*'s *concubine* Keturah (Genesis 25:1–4), east of the Gulf of Aqaba. *Moses* married a Midianite (Exodus 2:11–25). Midian resisted *Israel* on their way to *Canaan*, thereby becoming their enemy (Numbers 25:16–18). pp. 24, 26, 82

Miletus
Port where *Paul* met the elders from *Ephesus* when he didn't have time to visit them, giving them final exhortations about leading the *church* (Acts 20:17–38).

Millennium
One thousand-year reign of *Christ* during which *Satan* is bound (Revelation 20:1–7). p. 195

Mining p. 51

Miracles
Various *Hebrew* and *Greek* words are used of "miracles", but all express powerful action that is seen to be utterly God's doing and that carries significance beyond itself. They tend to be clustered at significant historical points, like the *exodus*, the entry to *Canaan*, the combat against *Baal* worship, and the coming of *Messiah*. pp. 21, 34, 43, 53, 125, 144–45, 162, 171–72, **174–75**, 182, 187

Miriam
Elder sister of *Moses* and *Aaron* who watched when Moses was hidden in the bulrushes and proposed their own mother as a nurse to *Pharaoh*'s daughter (Exodus 2:1–10). She led the dancing after crossing the *Red Sea* (Exodus 15:19–21) but experienced *judgment* when she later criticized Moses, acquiring *leprosy* for a time (Numbers 12).

Mission, missionary
The sending of people to convey God's message of *salvation*, through word and deed, expressed by *Jesus* through his life, death, and *resurrection*, and continued by his followers whom he sent into the *world* as his missionaries (e.g. Matthew 28:18–20). *Acts* is the account of the early Christian mission.

Moab, Moabites
Country between *Ammon* and *Edom* east of the *Jordan* which refused passage to *Israel* on their way to *Canaan* (Numbers 22–24) and which was in constant conflict with them thereafter. pp. 27, 29, 31–32, 34, 36, 82–83, 141

Money pp. 86, 111, **114–115**, 117, 124, 127, 147, 171–72, 177, 182–83

Moneychangers/-changing pp. 115, 147

Money-lenders/-lending p. 114

Monotheism
Belief there is only one God, a fundamental of *Judaism* and Christianity. pp. **63**, 130

Mordecai
Exile who raised the orphaned *Esther* (Esther 2:5–7). When she was chosen to marry *Xerxes I* (486–465 BC), he encouraged her to use her position to foil *Haman*'s plot to exterminate the *Jews* (chs 5–9), an event remembered in the Festival of *Purim*.

Moriah
Mountain where *Abraham* went to sacrifice *Isaac* (Genesis 22), claimed by the writer of *Chronicles* as the site in *Jerusalem* where *Solomon* later built the *Temple* (2 Chronicles 3:1), though this was disputed by the *Samaritans*, who believed the location was Mount *Gerizim*.

Moses
Born a *Hebrew*, raised as an *Egyptian*, chosen to lead God's people out of Egypt and to the *Promised Land*. At *Mount Sinai* God gave him the *Ten Commandments* and the *Law*, and he is seen traditionally as the author of the *Bible*'s first five books. pp. 14, 26–29, 36–37, 50–51, 57, 59, 61, 67, 74, 82, 87, 104, 109, 118–119, 121, 130–36, 138, 140–41, 143, 148, 151, 163

Mount of Olives
Hill overlooking *Jerusalem* from the east, one of *Jesus'* favourite spots (John 18:1–2), from where he entered Jerusalem on *Palm Sunday* (Matthew 21:1–17) and where he spent his final night (Matthew 26:36–56). Roman soldiers camped here during Jerusalem's siege in AD 70, destroying most of the olive trees, according to *Josephus*. Home to an ancient Jewish cemetery, there are some 150,000 graves on its hillside, for many devout *Jews* believe this is the spot to which *Messiah* will come. p. 182

Mount Sinai
See *Sinai*

Mourning
Expression of grief after bereavement, normally lasting seven days (Genesis 50:10; 1 Samuel 31:13), though longer for important people (e.g. Exodus 34:8). pp. 69, 155, 161

Murder
Seen as a heinous crime throughout the ancient world where, with few exceptions, it was punishable by death. But Jewish *Law* distinguished between murder and manslaughter (Exodus 21:12–14). pp. 22, **119**

Musical instruments pp. 56, 109, 123, **140**

Myrrh
Aromatic resin, often used for embalming or, mixed with *wine*, as a pain-killer; one of the gifts brought by the *Magi* to *Jesus*. pp. 54–55, 99, 111, 125, 167

Mystery, Mystery religions
Various eastern cults promoting personal devotion that became popular in Greece and *Rome*. Providing a more personal *faith*, in contrast to the great state religions, they involved initiation into secret societies which then revealed their secrets of spiritual enlightenment. *Paul* sometimes used mystery religion language to engage with his hearers, saying God too had a mystery, but one he has shared with everybody through *Jesus*. pp. 22, 43, 78, 80, 156–57, 165, 173

N

Naaman
Syrian army commander healed of *leprosy* by *Elisha* (2 Kings 5). pp. 34, 82

Nabateans p. 83

Naboth
Landowner whose *vineyard* was illegally taken by *Ahab*, for which he and *Jezebel* were condemned by *Elijah* (1 Kings 21).

Nadab
1. *Aaron*'s eldest son (Numbers 3:2) who, with his brother Abihu, offered "unauthorized fire" (literally, "unholy fire") to God, for which he was judged (Leviticus 10:1–5). The issue was perhaps offering fire or *incense* at the wrong place (i.e. not on the *altar*, Leviticus 16:12–13) or at the wrong time (Exodus 30:7–8).
2. King of *Israel* for just two years (909–908 BC) (1 Kings 5:25–32).

Nahum
Late-seventh-century BC *prophet* in *Judah* who prophesied God's impending *judgment* on *Nineveh*, and author of the book that bears his name. pp. 37, 72–73, 151, 169

Nain
Town in *Galilee* where *Jesus* restored a widow's son to life (Luke 7:11–16).

Names
Seen as very important, reflecting a person's history, character, or destiny. Changes of name at key moments were common in the *Bible*. p. **24**

Naomi
Mother-in-law of *Ruth*, whose problem (a lack of heirs) lies at the heart of the book of Ruth.

Naphtali
1. *Jacob*'s sixth son, whose name means "My struggle", born through *Rachel*'s servant, Bilhah (Genesis 30:7–8).
2. *Tribe* descended from him. Allotted land west of the *Sea of Galilee* (Joshua 19:32–39). Although conquered by *Assyria* prior to *Samaria*'s fall and its people deported in 732 BC (2 Kings 15:29), *Isaiah* prophesied future honour for the region (Isaiah 9:1–7), fulfilled in Jesus' ministry (Matthew 4:13–16).

Nathan
Prophet to King *David* who brought God's word that his descendants would always be on the throne (2 Samuel 7), yet rebuked his *sin* with *Bathsheba* (2 Samuel 12). Played a key role in ensuring a smooth transition of kingship to *Solomon* (1 Kings 1).

Nathanael
One of *Jesus'* twelve *disciples*, from *Cana* in *Galilee*; called Bartholomew in the *Synoptics*. p. 169

Nations, The
Used in the *Bible* of those who oppose God. pp. 23, 82–83

Nazareth
Hometown of *Jesus* in *Galilee* (Luke 2:39; 4:14). Jesus was often called "Jesus of Nazareth" (e.g. Mark 10:47), even though he left here when Nazareth rejected

him and relocated to *Capernaum* (Luke 4:24–31). pp. 43, 52, 103, 164, 166–69, 187

Nazareth Inscription p. 187

Nazirite
Someone who took a special *vow* of devotion to God, involving abstinence from *wine* or strong drink, not cutting the hair, and taking care to avoid defilement through touching dead bodies (Numbers 6:1–21). The vow was normally for a limited period, but *Samson* was subject to a lifelong vow (Judges 13:2–5), though he failed to keep it. Its origins are uncertain, but was still practised in *New Testament* times (Acts 18:8; 21:23–26).

Nebo
Mountain in *Moab* where *Moses* died after seeing the *Promised Land* (Deuteronomy 32:48–52; 34:1–8). p. 37

Nebuchadnezzar
King of *Babylon* (606–562 BC), frequently mentioned by *Jeremiah*, *Ezekiel*, and *Daniel*, and in the history of *Judah*'s closing days. Defeated *Assyria* in 605 BC leading to increased threat on Judah, culminating in a series of deportations and finally the destruction of *Jerusalem* in 586 BC. The exiled *Daniel* interpreted some of his *dreams*, courageously speaking of God's coming *judgment* (Daniel 2–4). pp. 37, 39, 74–75, 173

Neco
Egyptian *Pharaoh* (610–595 BC) who killed *Josiah* in battle at *Megiddo* and who replaced *Jehoahaz* with *Jehoiakim*, making him his vassal (2 Kings 23:29–35).

Negev
Desert and dry scrubland in the south of *Judah* which merges with the *Sinai* desert, described by *Isaiah* as "a land of hardship and distress, of lions and lionesses, of adders and darting snakes" (Isaiah 30:6). Used poetically of difficulties and hardship (Psalm 126:4). p. 82

Nehemiah
Cupbearer to *Artaxerxes I* who, in 445 BC, allowed him to return to *Jerusalem* to rebuild its walls (Nehemiah 1–6) and where he worked alongside *Ezra*. His *work* finished, he returned to *Persia* in 433 BC, though returned for a second term in 432 BC (Nehemiah 13:6–31). pp. 14, 17, 39, 57, 77, 90, 106, 110, 140, 142, 154, 161

Nero
Roman emperor (AD 54–68) whose authority *Paul* saw as God-given (Romans 13:1–7) and to whom he appealed (Acts 25:10–11), despite his growing opposition to and ultimately persecution of *Christians*, using them as the scapegoat for the Great Fire of *Rome* (AD 64). pp. 45, 81, 123, 192

New Testament
The twenty-seven books in the second half of the *Bible*, telling the story of *Jesus* and his followers. pp. **18–19**

Nicodemus
Pharisee, member of the *Sanhedrin*, who visited *Jesus* at night and whom Jesus challenged with the need to be "born again" (John 3:1–14). He argued against condemning Jesus without a fair trial (John 7:50–51) and, with *Joseph of Arimathea*, buried Jesus (John 19:38–42).

Nile
Egypt's great river, flowing 4,145 miles (6,670 km) from Uganda to the Mediterranean, on which its life depended through the annual flood which brought fertility to the land. pp. 26–27, 48–49, 55, 64–65, 82, 106, 113

Nineveh
Assyrian city on the banks of the *Tigris*, founded by Nimrod (Genesis 10:8–12), eventually becoming the nation's capital. Destroyed by *Babylon* in 612 BC, fulfilling *Nahum*'s prophecy, and bringing Assyria's empire to an end. pp. 20, 24, 35–37, 49, 72–74

Noah
Godly man saved from the *flood* that destroyed mankind through building an *ark* into which he gathered his *family* and pairs of all living creatures (Genesis 6–7). Here they remained for 150 days until the waters receded and the ark grounded on Mount *Ararat* in modern Turkey. God marked a new beginning for humanity by making a *covenant* with Noah. The sign of this covenant was a *rainbow* (Genesis 9:1–17). pp. 23, 56, 60, 67–68, 117, 133, 136

Nomads
People who lived in tents, constantly moving from place to place in search of pasture, the lifestyle of the biblical *patriarchs*. pp. 24, **25**, 58, 77, 82, 92, 102, 104, 128

Numbers
Fourth book of the *Law*, covering the thirty-eight year period of *Israel*'s desert wanderings after leaving *Mount Sinai*.

O

Obadiah
1. Official in charge of *Ahab*'s palace who hid 100 *prophets* from *Jezebel* (1 Kings 18:1–4).
2. Prophet from *Judah* whose name means "Servant of the LORD", who spoke *judgment* against *Edom* for gloating over *Israel*'s devastation and whose prophecies are recorded in the book that bears his name. pp. 82, 151

Obed-Edom
Man in whose house *David* temporarily placed the *ark of the covenant* after *Uzzah*'s disastrous death through touching it (2 Samuel 6:9–12).

Occult
From a *Latin* word meaning "knowledge of the hidden", referring to practices that try to use supernatural powers, like *magic*, spiritism, divination, and astrology, all of which the *Bible* forbids (e.g. Deuteronomy 18:9–13). p. 145

Og
King of *Bashan* east of the *Jordan*, whose territory was conquered by *Israel* and given to *Manasseh* (Numbers 21:32–35; Deuteronomy 3:1–20).

Old Testament
First part of the *Bible*, telling the origins and history of the Jewish people. pp. **14–15**

Olive pp. 34, 50–51, 57, 59–60, 88, 95–96, 98, 104, 154, 182

Olives, Mount of
See *Mount of Olives*

Omri
Israelite army commander who was made king after Zimri's *murder*. Ruling from 885 to 874 BC he established *Samaria* as Israel's new capital and was strong politically, though is denounced for corrupting Israel's *faith* (1 Kings 16:21–28). pp. 32–34, 52

Onesimus
Runaway slave from *Colossae* who became a *Christian* through *Paul*. Paul wrote to *Philemon*, his master, appealing to him to not only receive Onesimus but also to forgive him (Colossians 4:9; Philemon). p. 127

Ophir
Region famous for its high quality gold, of uncertain location (1 Kings 9:26–28).

Opposition pp. 103, 180, 184, 189, 192–93

Othniel
Judge in *Israel* who opposed *Canaanite* worship and subdued *Aram* (Judges 3:7–11).

P

Pacifism p. **129**

Palestine
Term used to describe the land between the Mediterranean and the River *Jordan*, from the word "*Philistines*" who inhabited its southwestern coastal strip. pp. 20, 40–41, 49, 55, 60–61, 64, 70, 80, 100–101, 104, 106, 109–114, 120, 129, 152

Palm Sunday
Term given by *Christians* to the Sunday before *Easter* when Jesus entered *Jerusalem* on a donkey (e.g. Matthew 21:1–17). pp. 56, 58

Pamphylia
Province on the southern coast of *Asia Minor* whose capital was Perga, the starting point of *Paul*'s mission in the region on his first missionary journey (Acts 13:13). *Jews* from this area were among the first to hear the *gospel* on the Day of *Pentecost* (Acts 2:8–12).

Paphos
Town in southwest *Cyprus* whose governor believed in *Jesus* when he saw his sorcerer blinded by *Paul* (Acts 13:4–12).

Papyrus
Writing material made from the pith of reeds, layered in alternate directions and pressed into sheets. pp. 13, 55, 101, 121

Parable
Fictitious story conveying a spiritual truth, one of *Jesus'* favourite ways of teaching since it provoked thought and demanded *faith*. pp. 12, 43, 55, 59, 86, 104–105, 109, 113, 115, 123, 136, 150, 161, 170–73, 179, 194

Paradise
Loan word from *Persian* meaning "walled garden" or "park", found in the *Old*

Testament only in Nehemiah 2:8, Ecclesiastes 2:5 and Song of Songs 4:13. Used in the *New Testament* by *Jesus* in his promise to the man crucified alongside him (Luke 23:43) as the place where the dead go after death, by *Paul* in his description of his heavenly experience (2 Corinthians 12:2–4), and in *Revelation* as God's gift to those who overcome (Revelation 2:7).

Parents pp. 84–86, 89–91, 128, 131, 157, 166

Passion
Christian term for the *sufferings* and death of Christ.

Passover
Annual festival recalling God's deliverance of *Israel* from slavery in *Egypt* (Exodus 12:1–30; Leviticus 23:5; Numbers 9:1–14; Deuteronomy 16:1–8). pp. 21, 27, 36, 54, 96, 99, 113, **138–39**, 141, 182–84

Patmos
Mediterranean island, a Roman penal colony in *New Testament* times where *John* received his *revelation* (Revelation 1:9). pp. 46–47, 127

Patriarchs
Israel's founding fathers: *Abraham*, *Isaac*, *Jacob*. pp. 20, **24–25**, 48, 82, 84–85, 92, 99, 118, 140, 146–47, 188

Paul (Saul)
Originally a persecutor of *Christians* (Acts 8:1–3; 9:1–3), Paul's life was dramatically changed through an encounter with the risen *Jesus* who called him to be an *apostle* to the *Gentiles* (Acts 9:1–18; 22:1–21; 26:1–23). After *preaching* in *Damascus* and a period of time in *Arabia* (Acts 9:20–25; Galatians 1:17), he went to *Jerusalem*, *Caesarea*, and *Tarsus* (Acts 9:26–30), before settling in *Antioch* (Acts 13:1–3), the base for his journeys described in *Acts*. Thirteen *New Testament* letters are attributed to him. He was *martyred* in *Rome* around AD 67/68, probably, as a Roman citizen, by being beheaded. pp. 18–19, 41, 44–47, 49, 52, 78–79, 81, 83–85, 87, 90–92, 101, 103, 112–113, 119, 123, 127, 129, 135–36, 140–41, 143, 145, 150, 158–59, 163, 185–87, 189, 190–92

Pavement
"The Stone Pavement", also called *Gabbatha*, where *Pilate* passed judgment on Jesus (John 19:13–16). p. 184

Pentateuch
Term used by Christian scholars for the first five books of the *Bible*, from the *Greek* "pentateuchos", "five-volumed [book]". Called *Torah* by *Jews*. p. 14

Pentecost
Jewish festival celebrating the wheat harvest, originally called the Feast of Harvest or the Feast of Weeks (e.g. Exodus 23:16; Leviticus 23:15–22). Because it was held fifty days after *Passover*, it later became known as Pentecost (*Greek* for "fiftieth"), becoming associated with God's gift of the *Law* to *Moses*. In Christian usage it refers to the day when the *Holy Spirit* was given in the distinctively Christian way (Acts 2:1–4). pp. 44–45, 96, 120, 138–39, 144, 150, 179, 181, 187, **188**, 189, 191–92

Pergamum
City in the Roman province of Asia, recipient of one of the Letters to the Seven Churches in *Revelation* (3:12–17), described as "where *Satan* has his throne" (v. 13), a reference to it being the official centre of emperor worship in Asia.

Persecution pp. 19, 45–46, 77, 80–81, 123, 157, 161, 187, 189, 192, 194–95

Persia, Persians
Nation in the southeast of *Mesopotamia* that grew into a huge empire stretching from India to the Aegean Sea and *Egypt*. *Daniel* prophesied its defeat of *Babylon*, and its ultimate own defeat by Greece. pp. 15, 37–41, 48–49, 62–64, 74, 76–78, 83, 114, 116, 139, 167

Peter
Also called Simon, Galilean fisherman, one of *Jesus'* twelve *apostles* (Matthew 4:18–20; John 1:35–42), renamed Cephas ("Rock"). The *Gospels* show his great *faith* – like acknowledging who Jesus was (Matthew 16:16) and attempting to walk on water (Matthew 14:25–33) – but also his weakness – like struggling with *forgiveness* (Matthew 18:21), having unrealistic views about himself (Matthew 26:33–35), and even denying Jesus (Mark 14:66–72). Transformed at *Pentecost*, he played a key role in the church's life in *Judea* and *Samaria*, eventually overcoming his old prejudices and taking the gospel to *Gentiles* (Acts 10). Later he travelled further, accompanied by his wife (1 Corinthians 9:5), working as "an apostle to the Jews", and ended up in *Rome* where he was *martyred* around AD 67/68. pp. 18–19, 44–47, 52, 55, 79, 81, 92–93, 97, 105–109, 113, 121, 127, 135–36, 144, 150, 157–58, 161, 163, 169, 179, 181–82, 184–89, 191–92, 194

Peter's Letters (1 & 2)
Letters in which the apostle *Peter* writes of *Christians* being the true inheritors of the *Old Testament*'s promises and giving lots of practical advice on how to live in difficult times.

Pets pp. 58–59

Pharaoh
Title of *Egypt*'s kings. pp. 25–27, 33, 61, 64–67, 70, 138, 144

Pharisees
Jewish laymen who lived in scrupulous obedience to the *Law* and the oral traditions based on it, as preparation for God coming to liberate his people. They were frequently in conflict with *Jesus*, who believed their traditions undermined God's original intentions (Matthew 5:21–48) and berated their *hypocrisy* (Matthew 23:1–39). pp. 46, 54, 61, 103, 135, 142, 152–53, 161, 163, 170, 176, 180

Philadelphia
City in the Roman province of Asia, whose name means "Brotherly love", to which one of the Letters to the Seven Churches was written (Revelation 3:7–13) encouraging them that there was "an open door" before them despite the work of "those who are the synagogue of Satan", a stark description of hostile *Jews*.

Philemon
Letter from *Paul* appealing to Philemon to not only take back his runaway slave *Onesimus* but also to forgive him, especially since he had become a *Christian*. While unable to change the cultural pattern of slavery, Paul certainly undermined it. pp. 18, 47, 127

Philip
1. One of *Jesus'* twelve *apostles* (Mark 3:18) who introduced *Nathanael* to Jesus (John 1:43–46) and who lived, like *Andrew* and *Simon*, in *Bethsaida*.
2. Philip the *evangelist*, one of "the Seven" chosen to serve the *Jerusalem* church in practical matters (Acts 6:1–6). When persecution arose after *Stephen*'s *martyrdom*, he went to *Samaria* where he very effectively preached the *gospel* (Acts 8:4–8) and was then led to an *Ethiopian* eunuch with whom he shared the gospel and whom he *baptized* (Acts 8:26–40). Spirited away to Azotus, he there conducted further effective *evangelistic* ministry (Acts 8:39–40) before moving to *Caesarea* where we find him twenty years later (Acts 21:8).

Philippi
Roman colony in *Macedonia*, which meant its residents had the same rights as those in *Rome*. *Paul* was directed here through a *vision* and found fruitful soil for the *gospel* (Acts 16:6–15). Their *preaching* led to imprisonment, though they were released when they explained they were Roman citizens, but only after an earthquake led to the jailer and his family being saved. (Acts 16:16–40). pp. 46, 119, 198

Philippians
Letter from *Paul* to the church in *Philippi*, probably written from *Rome* c. AD 60. pp. 18, 33, 47, 79, 101, 123, 141, 143, 158, 161, 165

Philistines
Part of "the Sea Peoples" who migrated from *Crete* and *Greece* in the fourteenth to thirteenth centuries BC, eventually settling along the coast of *Palestine*. They were a constant threat to *Israel*, prompting Israel to ask for a king (1 Samuel 8), and weren't subdued until *David*'s time. In the eighth century BC they were defeated by *Assyria*, and were swallowed up by *Babylon* in the sixth century BC. pp. 29–31, 36, 50, 52, 56, **70–71**, 73, 109, 118, 128–29

Philosophy pp. 12, 17, 21, 78–80, 90, 110, 156, 170, 172, 176, 193

Phoenicia, Phoenicians
Inhabitants of coastal city-states north of *Canaan* whose key ports were *Byblos*, *Tyre*, and *Sidon*; leading sea-traders who established colonies across the Mediterranean. *Solomon* used Phoenician products and expertise in constructing the *Temple* (1 Kings 5). pp. 12, 31–32, 34, 36, 50, 69, 82, 106, 109, 113–114, 120, 125, 147, 179

Phrygians
Inhabitants of west central *Asia Minor* (modern Turkey) after the collapse of *Hittite* power, who became great traders in copper and slaves.

Phylactery
Small black box containing texts from the *Law*, bound to the left arm and forehead by pious *Jews* in

literal obedience to Deuteronomy 6:8. p. 142

Pilate
Roman procurator of *Judea* who, fearing for his position, authorized Jesus' *crucifixion* in response to demands from the Jewish religious authorities. pp. 43, 80–81, 103, 115, 119, 122, 153, 180, 184

Plagues
Demonstrations of God's power and *judgment* when *Pharaoh* refused to free the *Israelites* from slavery. A series of ten plagues (Exodus 7:14 – 12:51), the first nine relating to natural phenomena in the *Nile* Valley, were challenges to *Egypt* and its gods, as God applied increasing pressure on Pharaoh. When he refused to yield, death came in a tenth plague and took their firstborn sons, leading to *freedom* for the slaves at last. pp. 26, 53, 74, 88, 94, 106, 129, 144

Plants pp. 54–55, 57, 100–101, 125, 172

Polygamy
Having more than one wife at a time, common in the early *Old Testament* period for economic reasons, but which disappeared as it became uneconomic. *Jesus* reaffirmed that God's plan for *marriage* was for one man to be with one woman for life (Matthew 19:4–6). pp. 22, 87

Poor
See *Poverty*

Potiphar
Egyptian master of *Joseph* who initially promoted him but then imprisoned him when his wife falsely accused him of attempted rape (Genesis 39).

Potsherd
Broken piece of pottery, often used for writing short notes. p. 121

Pottery pp. 48, 63, 71, 97, **108**, 121

Poverty
Though sometimes seen as the result of foolishness or laziness (e.g. Proverbs 6:9–11), more often the *Bible* sees poverty as the result of others' *greed* and lust for power, denouncing those who oppress the poor (e.g. Isaiah 3:13–15; Amos 4:1; 8:4). The *Law* commanded alms-giving and generous lending, and prevented the exploitation of the poor (e.g. Leviticus 25:37–43; Deuteronomy 15:1–3; 24:6). In the early church remembering the poor was a foundational apostolic principle (Galatians 2:9–10). pp. 45, 52, 91, 93, 112, 115, 126, 156, 177, 193

Praise pp. 28, 36, **141**

Prayer
Talking to God. pp. 16–17, 19, 31, 38, 72, 90, 93, 99, 101, 115, 122, 141, **142–43**, 147, 151, 153, 155, 163, 169, 172, 179, 183

Preaching
In the *New Testament*, the public proclamation of the *gospel* to non-Christians.

Priests
Descendants of *Aaron*, appointed to offer *sacrifices*, teach God's *Law*, act as *judges* and public health inspectors, and seek God's will. In the *New Testament* all believers are seen as "a royal priesthood" (1 Peter 2:9) and Jesus as their "high priest", especially in the book of *Hebrews*. pp. 32, 38, 40, 42, 54–55, 57, 67, 74, 77, 84–85, 88, 99, 101, 108, 119, 124–25, 127, 133, 136–38, 146–47, **148–49**, 151, 153, 164, 167, 180–81, 18–84, 192

Priscilla
See *Aquila*

Promised Land
Common term for the land promised to *Abraham* by God, *Canaan*. pp. 14, 26–27, **28–29**, 49, 51–53, 57, 69, 77, 112, 128, 132, 134–35, 139, 146, 167

Prophecy, prophet, prophetess
Words brought from God by his spokesmen, known by three terms in the *Old Testament*: "Man of God" ('ish 'elohim), underlining their relationship and closeness to God; "Seer" (ro'eh; hozeh), underlining their ability to "see" what God was doing; "prophet" (nabi), from a word meaning "to call": men and women called by God who called to others in his name. pp. 12, 38, 44, 58, 72–73, 81–82, **150–51**, 165, 169, 182

Prophets, the
Second section of the Hebrew *Scriptures*, between the *Law* and the *Writings*. pp. 37, 137, **150–51**, 155

Proselytes
Gentiles who, attracted by Jewish *monotheism* and high morality, converted to their *faith*, involving *circumcision*, *baptism*, and keeping the *Law* (Acts 13:26, 43).

Proverbs, Book of
Collection of short sayings providing wise ways for living.

Psalms
Israel's hymnbook, its *Hebrew* title "Tehillim" ("Songs of Praise") highlighting they were originally songs to be sung. The title "Psalms" comes from the *Greek* title, "Psalmos" ("music played on instruments"). pp. 14, 16–17, 21, 23, 31, 38, 43, 53–54, 56–57, 59, 67, 71, 88–90, 97, 104, 125, 130, 140–42, 144, 150, 154, 160

Pseudepigrapha
Term used to describe Jewish writings excluded from the Old Testament *canon* and which were not included in the *Apocrypha*, important for understanding Jewish life and beliefs in the inter-testamental period. Titles include: Psalms of Solomon, Testaments of the Twelve Patriarchs, The Martyrdom of Isaiah, the Book of *Enoch*, the Assumption of Moses, 3 and 4 *Maccabees*. Many were written under assumed names (pseudonyms).

Ptolemies
The Macedonian–Greek dynasty of fourteen kings that ruled *Egypt* after the death of *Alexander the Great* and the break-up of his empire from 323 to 30 BC. pp. 40, 64

Purim
Jewish festival celebrating the thwarting by *Esther* of attempts to exterminate the *Jews* in *Persia*. pp. 39, 122, **139**

Q

Quail
Small game birds, diverted from their migratory path by a strong wind, that provided the *Israelites* with food in the *wilderness* (Numbers 11:31–34). pp. 27, **61**, 98

Queen of Sheba
Ruler of a country in southwest *Arabia* who visited *Solomon* (1 Kings 10:1–13). Her country's wealth came from its location on trade routes, importing gold and spices from Africa and India, so she may have felt their economy was threatened by Solomon's new fleet (1 Kings 9:26–28). pp. 31, 111

Quirinius
Roman governor of *Syria* when *Jesus* was born (Luke 2:2).

Qumran
Home to the monastic *Essene* community, northwest of the *Dead Sea*. pp. 21, 91, **152–53**, 177

Quotations
There are some 250 direct quotations from the *Old Testament* in the *New Testament*. If partial quotations or allusions are included the number exceeds 1,000, reflecting the importance of the Old Testament to the early church and their conviction that it prepared the way for *Jesus*.

R

Rabbah
Capital of *Ammon*.

Rachel
Younger daughter of *Laban* who became *Jacob*'s second wife after Laban deceived him into marrying *Leah*, the elder daughter, first (Genesis 29:16–30). Mother of *Joseph* (Genesis 30:22–24) and *Benjamin*, during whose delivery she died (Genesis 35:16–18). pp. 25, 53, 84, 86–87, 89, 125

Rahab
1. *Jericho* prostitute who sheltered *Israelite* spies and helped them escape from the city (Joshua 2) and so was spared when Jericho was attacked (Joshua 6:20–25). Cited as an example of *faith* in the *New Testament* (Hebrews 11:31; James 2:24–25). p. 102
2. Monster of pre-creation chaos in ancient mythology, used in poetic parts of the *Bible* to show God can overcome everything (e.g. Job 26:12; Psalm 89:10) and applied to God's *redemption* of *Israel* when he mastered the waters by dividing the *Red Sea* (e.g. Isaiah 51:9–10).

Rainbow
Sign of God's *covenant* with *Noah* (Genesis 9:8–17). pp. 23, 133

Rainfall
Crucial to survival in *Canaan* (which had no great rivers like *Egypt* and *Mesopotamia*), reflected in the many different *Hebrew* words for "rain". pp. 50, 94

Rameses
Store city in the *Nile* built by *Israelite* slaves for *Pharaoh* (Exodus 1:11) in the region where *Joseph* had settled his *family* (Genesis 47:11).

Ramoth-Gilead
City of refuge in *Gilead*, east of the *Jordan* (Deuteronomy 4:43), assigned to the *Levites* (Joshua 21:38), where *Ahab* was killed in battle despite his ruse (1 Kings 22:29–38) and *Jehu* was anointed king (2 Kings 9:1–13).

Rebekah
Wife of *Isaac* who bore him *Esau* and *Jacob* (Genesis 25:21–26).

Reconciliation
Restoration of relationship between two estranged parties, a central *New Testament* image of what Christ's *crucifixion* achieved, the bringing together of God and humans by removing the barrier of *sin* (e.g. Romans 5:10–11; Ephesians 2:11–22; Colossians 1:19–22). *Christians* are now called to be ambassadors of reconciliation in the *world* (2 Corinthians 5:18–21). pp. 158, 190

Red Sea
Stretch of water separating *Egypt* and *Arabia* that, traditionally, was parted to allow the *Israelites* to escape from *Pharaoh*'s pursuing army (Exodus 14). However, the *Hebrew* text calls this not the Red Sea, as wrongly translated in the *Septuagint* and perpetuated by tradition, but the "Reed Sea" (Hebrew "Yam Suph", "Sea of Reeds"), probably a marshy area in the *Nile* delta where a strong wind could easily drive back the water. pp. 27, 40, 46, 48, 82, 99, 112

Redemption
Buying back something lost, used to describe God's releasing *Israel* from slavery in *Egypt* (e.g. Exodus 6:6–7; Deuteronomy 7:7–8; 1 Chronicles 17:21; Isaiah 43:1–7). So that Israel never forgot this redemption, God wrote reminders of it into the *Law* (e.g. Exodus 13:11–15; Leviticus 25:25–34, 47–55). *Jesus* used the concept to describe what his death on the *cross* would achieve, saying he had come to "give his life as a ransom [redemption] for many" (Matthew 20:28). It is one of the key explanations of his death in the *New Testament* (e.g. Romans 3:23–25; Ephesians 1:7–8; 1 Peter 1:18–19). pp. 88, 190

Rehoboam
Solomon's son whose lack of *wisdom* split the kingdom (1 Kings 12). pp. 32–33, 35–37, 53

Religious year, Jewish p. 138

Remnant
Small surviving group of God's people, evidence of his *faithfulness*. p. 39

Repentance
Radical turning from *sin* and selfishness to wholehearted following of God. In both *Hebrew* and *Greek* the underlying idea of the main words for repentance is "turning" – turning from sinful ways, and turning to God in *love* and obedience. The Greek word "metanoia" implies a complete reorientation of thinking and life. pp. 17, **35**, 37, 42, 73, 75, 155, 168, 191

Reptiles p. 61

Rest
Seen as essential to the human condition and life's routine, modelled by God who himself rested on the seventh day of *creation* (Genesis 2:1–3), not because he was tired but because his *work* was finished. The word "rested" (v. 2) comes from the *Hebrew* root for "sabbath", thus establishing the divine pattern for healthy living: six days of work, followed by one day of rest. pp. 22, 59, 122–23, 138, 139, 182, 185

Resurrection
God's action in raising *Jesus* from death to life, the heart of the Christian *faith* without which it falls (1 Corinthians 15:14–20). The *New Testament* sees it not as a spiritual experience on the part of the *disciples*, but as a real physical event on the part of Jesus, who could be touched (John 20:27), hold conversations (Luke 24:13–35), and eat (Luke 24:30). It sees his resurrection as confirmation that he is truly the Son of God (Romans 1:4) and that he has conquered death for all who believe in him (Romans 6:4–10; 1 Corinthians 15). pp. 18–19, 21, 43–45, 106, 139, 144–45, 153, 158, 160–61, 169, 175, 178, 180, 183–88, 190–91, 194–95

Resurrection body
Body given to believers by God at the *return of Jesus*, suited to life in God's new *creation*. pp. 187

Return from exile
Return of the *Jews* to the *Promised Land* from their *exile* in *Babylon*, in three main stages: a main group returning with *Zerubbabel* (538/537 BC), a group returning with *Ezra* (458 BC), and a group returning with *Nehemiah* (445 BC). pp. 52, 38–39, 141

Return of Jesus
The return of Jesus at the end of the age, just as he promised, through which God will finally defeat *Satan*, destroy *evil*, judge sinners, save his people, and establish his new creation.

Reuben
1. *Jacob*'s firstborn son, born through *Leah* (Genesis 29:31–32). 2. *Tribe* descended from him, given land east of the *Jordan* (Numbers 32; Joshua 13:8, 15–23).

Revelation
1. What God chooses to show to people of his character, ways, and purposes, revealed through nature (e.g. Romans 1:20), history (e.g. 2 Kings 24:20), *prophecy* (e.g. 2 Peter 1:21), *Scripture* (e.g. 2 Timothy 3:16), and above all through *Jesus Christ* his Son (e.g. Hebrews 1:1–2). *Christians* regard the *Bible* as the record of God's revelation. pp. 12–14, 130–32, 146
2. Final book of the Bible in which Jesus shows the *apostle John* "what must soon take place" (Revelation 1:1), showing him events from God's perspective to help him make sense of the *persecution* that was happening. Through a series of panoramic *visions*, John is taken from the church in his time through to the return of *Jesus*, the overcoming of *Satan* and *evil*, and God's new creation. pp. 19, 22, 46, 50, 52–53, 55–56, 60, 75, 79, 81, 83–84, 87, 95, 103, 109–110, 113, 121, 125, 127, 131, 140, 145, 151, 155–57, 161, 163, 187, 192, 194–95

Rewards
Jesus taught that God rewards right behaviour (Matthew 6:4) and punishes bad behaviour (Matthew 25:41). The ultimate rewards lie in the future life "when we must all appear before the judgment seat of Christ, so that each of us may receive what is due us for the things done while in the body, whether good or bad" (2 Corinthians 5:10). p. 177

Righteousness
From a root *Hebrew* word meaning "straightness", that aspect of God's character that means he always is right and always does right. God wants his people to be "straight" or "righteous", but the *New Testament* stresses this isn't something that can be earned but only received through *faith* as a gift from Christ (e.g. Romans 1:16–17; 3:21–31; 1 Corinthians 1:30; 2 Corinthians 5:21; Philippians 3:7–9).

Ritual cleansing p. 136

Roads pp. 10, 41, 49–50, **112–113**, 160

Romans, Letter to the
Letter written by *Paul* to the church in *Rome* in AD 57 laying out the *gospel* he preached, particularly as it concerned God's *righteousness* (1:16–17), how sinful people could become righteous (chs 3–8), and where the *Jews* still fitted into God's plan (chs 9–11) in preparation for his anticipated visit (15:23–24).

Rome
Capital of the Roman empire. *Jews* from Rome were in *Jerusalem* at *Pentecost* (Acts 2:10), and it was probably converts who took the *gospel* back with them. In AD 49 Claudius expelled Jews for causing disturbances "at the instigation of Chrestus" (*Suetonius*, "Life of Claudius"), almost certainly a reference to Christ, and *Aquila* and *Priscilla* were among those expelled (Acts 18:2). *Paul* was a Roman citizen (Acts 16:37) and was determined to preach in Rome (e.g. Acts 19:21), something that happened through his appeal to *Caesar* during his trial (Acts 25:11). Rome's fall was prophesied in *Revelation*, where it is cryptically described as "Babylon" (Revelation 17–18). pp. 17, 21, 41, 45–47, 49, 52, 64, 78, 80–81, 83, 87, 94–95, 103, 106, 110–113, 119, 123, 127, 136, 147, 153, 163, 166, 180–81, 183, 187, 192, 194

Rosetta Stone p. 120

Ruth
Moabite woman in the *Judges* period whose commitment to her mother-in-law took her to *Bethlehem* where she played a key role in *Naomi*'s redemption and became the wife of *Boaz* and future great-grandmother of King *David*.

S

Sabbath
Jewish day of *rest*, reckoned from Friday sunset to Saturday sunset, based on the pattern God set at *creation* (Genesis 2:2–3; Exodus 20:8–11). pp. 22–23, 38, 40, 59, 117, 122–23, **137–38**, 152, 169, 179–80, 182, 184–85

Sabbath day's journey
The distance *Jews* could travel on the *sabbath*, 2,000 cubits (about 2/3 mile/1 km).

Sacrament
"An outward and visible sign of

an inward and spiritual grace" (St Augustine). Two sacraments come from the *Gospels* – *baptism* and the *Lord's Supper* (Communion, Mass) – while some church traditions have added five others: confirmation, holy orders, *confession*, *anointing* the sick, and *marriage*. p. 159

Sacrifice pp. 18, 25, 34, 36, 40, 47, 53–54, 58–60, 68–69, 77, 88–89, 105, 128, 132, 136, 138–43, 146, **148–49**, 158, 162, 187, 190

Sadducees
First-century AD Jewish religious group controlling the *high priesthood* and *Temple* who feared *Jesus* might upset the political status quo and lead them to lose influence. They therefore joined the *Pharisees* in opposing him, and it was their man *Caiaphas*, the high priest, who pressed for Jesus' execution (John 18:14). pp. 153, 161, 180

Sailing p. 113

Salt Sea
Old Testament name for the *Dead Sea*. pp. 28, 50

Salvation
God's rescue of mankind, his "bringing them into a spacious place" (the literal meaning of the *Hebrew*) in every aspect of life. The major act of salvation in the *Old Testament* was God's rescuing the *Israelites* from slavery in *Egypt*, while in the *New Testament* it is *Jesus*' rescuing people from the slavery to *sin* (e.g. Matthew 1:21; Luke 19:9–10; Romans 10:13; Ephesians 2:8–9). pp. 37, 52, 88, 125, 159, 167, **191**

Samaria
1. City built by King *Omri* as the new capital of the northern kingdom of *Israel* (1 Kings 16:24). His son *Ahab* built a palace (1 Kings 22:39) and temple to *Baal* here (1 Kings 16:32). Besieged and captured by *Assyria* in 721 BC (2 Kings 17). Rebuilt by Herod the Great and renamed Sebaste.
2. The name of the surrounding region after the fall of its capital (2 Kings 17:24). A Roman province by *New Testament* times. pp. 32, 34–35, 37, 39–40, 52, 72–73, 103, 109, 119, 167

Samaritans
Descendants of the mixed *Israelite/Assyrian* population of the northern kingdom of *Israel* after *Samaria*'s fall in 721 BC, and therefore despised by orthodox *Jews* by *Jesus*' time because of their racial impurity. Jesus happily mixed with Samaritans, however (e.g. John 4), crossing their territory while pious Jews made detours around it, and commanding his *disciples* to include them when *preaching* the *gospel* (Acts 1:8). The early church found considerable *evangelistic* success here (e.g. Acts 8:4–25).

Samson
Judge in ancient *Israel*, dedicated by his parents as a lifelong *Nazirite* (1 Samuel 13), whose weakness for women undermined his God-given strength and led to his death (1 Samuel 16). pp. 29, 61, 71, 122

Samuel
Judge and *prophet* who played a significant role in *Israel*'s transition from *theocracy* to monarchy. pp. 14, 29, 30, 118, 121, 137

Sanballat
Samaritan governor who tried to stop *Nehemiah* rebuilding *Jerusalem*'s walls (Nehemiah 2:10, 19; 4:1–23; 6:1–14).

Sanctification
The process of becoming more holy through the inner work of the *Holy Spirit*. Whereas *justification* marks the beginning of the Christian life, sanctification characterizes it throughout (John 17:15–19; Romans 12:1–2; Ephesians 4:22–24; Philippians 3:12–16; 1 Thessalonians 4:3–4; 2 Peter 1:3–11).

Sanctuary
Place set apart for worshipping God. *Israel*'s earliest sanctuary was a tent, the *tabernacle*, replaced by the *Temple* by *Solomon*. pp. 33, 126, 139, **147–48**

Sanhedrin
Jewish ruling council in *New Testament* times, comprising chief *priests*, elders, and *scribes* (Mark 15:1), *Judaism*'s high court, granted certain powers by *Rome*, but not the ability to impose the death penalty, hence their need to win over *Pilate* if *Jesus* were to be executed (e.g. Luke 20:20). pp. 21, 90, 119, 152, 184

Sanitation pp. **93–95**, 103, 125, 149

Sapphira
See *Ananias* (1)

Sarah (Sarai)
Wife of *Abraham*, who was barren (Genesis 11:3). Discouraged she couldn't give Abraham the child God had promised, she encouraged him to father a child through *Hagar* her maid, the fruit of which was *Ishmael*, whose birth was the beginning of many problems (Genesis 16). She finally conceived, around the age of ninety (Genesis 17:17), giving birth to *Isaac* (Genesis 21:1–7), which produced further tensions with Hagar and Ishmael (Genesis 21:8–20). pp. 24, 67, 87, 160, 196

Sardis
Ancient capital of the Lydians, enriched by gold deposits, and city in the Roman province of Asia, located at the junction of two trade routes and where a thriving woollen and dyeing industry was established. One of the Letters to the Seven Churches was sent to the church here (Revelation 3:1–6) accusing it, like the city itself, of relying on past reputation, but promising new white garments if they would wake up and repent. pp. 40, 46, 82

Sargon
King of *Assyria* (722–705 BC), named in the *Bible* only in Isaiah 20:1. Claimed the capture of *Samaria*, which had been besieged by his predecessor *Shalmaneser V* for three years, and deported its citizens, leading to the end of the northern nation of *Israel* (2 Kings 17:3–6). pp. 35, 63, 72

Satan
Leader of spiritual forces opposed to God whose name means "the accuser" (Job 1:1–11; Revelation 12:10). Also called the devil and the tempter (Matthew 4:1–11) and the *serpent* (Revelation 20:2; see also Genesis 3). Traditionally believed to be a fallen *angel* (Isaiah 14:12–15; Ezekiel 28:12–19), he is never seen as an "opposite equal" of God but merely a created being, overcome by Christ at the *cross* (e.g. Colossians 2:15) and destined to eternal torment (Revelation 20:7–10). pp. 42, 68, 81, 143, 145, 156–57, 181, 195

Saul
1. *Israel*'s first king, initially humble (1 Samuel 9:21) and successful (1 Samuel 11:1–15) but who forgot that he was subject to God's *covenant* and called to be obedient. Twice over-ruling *Samuel*'s instructions, and then blaming others (1 Samuel 13:1–15; 15:1–35), he was rejected as king and replaced (1 Samuel 13:13–14). He unwittingly brought his replacement, *David*, to the court (1 Samuel 16:14–23), but soon turned against him causing David to flee. He was finally killed in battle against the *Philistines* on *Mount Gilboa* (1 Samuel 31). pp. 30–31, 46, 53, 57, 70–71, 82, 128
2. Also called Paul, an *apostle*. See *Paul*

Saviour
Title given to *Jesus*, initially describing his work of saving people (e.g. Acts 5:31; 13:23; Philippians 3:20) but soon becoming part of his title (e.g. 2 Timothy 1:10; Titus 1:4; 2 Peter 1:11). Jesus, his personal name, underlined the same message, meaning "Yahweh saves". In the *Old Testament* God was often described as *Israel*'s saviour (e.g. Deuteronomy 32:15; 2 Samuel 22:3; Psalm 51:14; Isaiah 43:3, 11; Micah 7:7). pp. 81, 107, 158, 164, **167**, 185

Schools pp. **90–91**

Scribes
Copiers of the *Law* who, during the *exile*, began to interpret that Law for the new situation *Jews* found themselves in. By *New Testament* times their interpretations were seen to be as important as the Law itself, which often brought them into conflict with *Jesus*. pp. **14–15**, 20–21, 38, 52–53, 60–61, 90, 119, 121, 153, 170, 180, 195

Scripture, the Scriptures
Common Christian term for the *Bible*, found fifty-three times in the *New Testament* (referring there to the *Old Testament*). Its root meaning is "that which is written". pp. 13–16, 18–19, 21, 40–41, 91, 111, 121, 130–31, 133, 141–43, 147, 153, 169

Scrolls
Made from sheets of *papyrus* glued together, though for *Scripture* leather was preferred. Handles at both ends, to which the scrolls were attached, enabled readers to unroll and roll the scroll as they read, the text being written in vertical columns. pp. 12–13, 21, 121, 152, 163

Sea of Galilee
See *Galilee*

Sea People
Migrants from the Aegean who settled along the coasts of *Syria* and *Canaan* in the twelfth century BC, of whom the *Philistines* were a part. p. 70

Seal
Emblem used as a means of authentication, impressed into wax dripped onto a document.

Second Coming
See *Return of Jesus*

Selah
Found in the *psalms*, probably indicating a pause or musical interlude giving the worshipper time to reflect.

Seleucids
Dynasty of Greek kings that ruled *Palestine* and *Syria* after the death of *Alexander the Great* and the break-up of his empire. It was one of these kings, *Antiochus IV Epiphanes*, whose anti-Jewish actions provoked the *Maccabean revolt*. pp. 40–41

Self-denial p. 177

Semites, Semitic
People group and their languages descended from *Noah*'s son, *Shem* (Genesis 5:32; 10:21–32), including *Akkadians*, *Canaanites*, *Hebrews*, *Phoenicians*, *Ethiopian* Semites, and Arabs. The biblical classifications of Semitic, Hamitic, and Japhethite peoples does not correspond to classifications by language.

Sennacherib
Assyrian king whose army besieged *Jerusalem* in *Hezekiah*'s reign (2 Kings 18–19). pp. 20, 36–37, 53, 73, 129

Septuagint
Greek translation of the Hebrew *Scriptures*. pp. **15**, 16–19, 27, 41, 131, 133, 147, 196

Seraphim
Heavenly beings around God's throne (Isaiah 6:1–4).

Sermon on the Mount
Name given by St Augustine (AD 354–430) to *Jesus*' teaching on a hillside by the *Sea of Galilee* (Matthew 5:1 – 7:29; Luke 6:17–49) in which he challenged traditional interpretations of the *Law* and outlined the ethics of *God's kingdom*. It begins with the *Beatitudes*. pp. **171**, 176–77, 198

Serpent
1. See *Snakes*
2. The creature of Genesis 3 who tempted *Adam* and *Eve* to disobey God, thereafter symbolizing deceit (e.g. Matthew 23:33) and the ultimate deceiver, *Satan* himself (Revelation 12:9, 15; 20:1–2).

Servant Songs
Prophecies of *Isaiah* (Isaiah 42:1–4; 49:1–6; 50:4–9; 52:13 – 53:12) foretelling one who would come as God's servant to bring *God's kingdom*, not through military might but humble servanthood and *suffering*. *Jesus* and the *Gospels* referred to these "Servant Songs" (Matthew 8:17; Mark 9:12).

Servanthood p. 33

Seven-branched candlestick
See *Menorah*

Shalmaneser V
Assyrian king who besieged *Israel*'s capital, *Samaria*, leading to its fall in 722/721 BC, bringing an end to the history of the northern tribes (2 Kings 17:3–6; 18:9–12). pp. 35, 72

Shamgar
Judge in *Israel* (Judges 3:31; 5:6) about whom nothing is known other than his killing 600 *Philistines* with an ox-goad.

Sharon
Israel's northern coastal plain. p. 50

Shechem
Town in the hill country of *Ephraim* where God promised *Abraham* the land of *Canaan* and where he built an *altar* (Genesis 12:6–7), leading to it becoming an important religious centre. Here *Jacob* built an altar (Genesis 33:18–20), *Joshua* renewed the *covenant* (Joshua 24), and *Rehoboam* was crowned but then rejected, leading to *Jeroboam* becoming king of the northern tribes and establishing Shechem as his capital (1 Kings 12). It survived *Israel*'s fall to *Assyria* and in post-exilic times became the chief city of the *Samaritans*. It may be *Sychar* where *Jesus* met the woman at the well (John 4:4–42).

Sheep pp. 30, **59**, 60, 96, 100, 105, 136, 172

Shem
Eldest of *Noah*'s three sons, ancestor of several *Semitic* nations, including the *Hebrews* (Genesis 9:18–19; 10:21–31).

Sheol
Old Testament term for the place of the dead, called "Hades" in *Greek*. Initially seen as the destiny of good and bad alike, it gradually developed into the destiny of the wicked, though without any connotations of punishment. pp. 160–61

Shepherds pp. 43, 60, 76, 105, 119, 122, 166–67, 190

Shiloh
City in the hill country of *Ephraim* where *Joshua* set up the *tabernacle* (Joshua 18:1), *Eli* was *priest*, *Hannah* made her *vow* (1 Samuel 1:9–17), and *Samuel* began his ministry (1 Samuel 3:21). It was destroyed c. 1050 BC by the *Philistines*, an event *Jeremiah* recalled many years later as a warning to *Jerusalem* (Jeremiah 7:12–15). pp. 29, 32, 52, 71, 140

Ships pp. 103, 113, 150

Shishak
Egyptian *pharaoh* (ruled 945–924 BC) who gave *sanctuary* to *Jeroboam* when he fled from *Solomon* (1 Kings 11:26–40). Invaded *Palestine* in 925 BC, subduing *Judah* and taking treasure from the *Temple* and palace, including Solomon's gold shields (1 Kings 14:25–26; 2 Chronicles 12:1–11). pp. 20, 33

Sickness pp. 124–25

Sidon
Phoenician port whose name was often used for the surrounding area. *Jezebel*, *Ahab*'s wife, was a Sidonian princess who promoted Sidon's form of *Baal* worship in *Israel* (1 Kings 16:31–33). In *New Testament* times Sidonians went to hear *Jesus* preach (Mark 3:8), and he himself visited there and marvelled at a *Gentile* woman's *faith* (Matthew 15:21–28). *Paul* stayed with friends here on his way to *Rome* (Acts 27:3).

Siege warfare p. 129

Sign
Spectacular proof, often demanded by *Jesus*' opponents (e.g. Matthew 12:38–40; Mark 8:10–12; Luke 11:16), but constantly refused by him. *John*'s Gospel, however, uses the word to describe Jesus' *miracles*, and especially their significance (e.g. John 2:11). pp. 132–33, 137–39, 159, 167

Silas
Leader in the *church* at *Jerusalem* entrusted with the letter from the *Council of Jerusalem* to the church in *Antioch* (Acts 15:22). Accompanied *Paul* on his second *missionary* journey (Acts 15:36 – 17:15). Associated with two of Paul's letters (1 Thessalonians 1:1; 2 Thessalonians 1:1) and one of *Peter*'s (1 Peter 5:12). pp. 46, 141

Siloam
Pool in *Jerusalem*, linked to the Gihon Spring outside the city via *Hezekiah*'s tunnel, where *Jesus* sent a blind man to be healed (John 9:1–5). pp. 37, 94, 154, 185

Simeon
1. *Jacob*'s second son, born through *Leah* (Genesis 29:33), whose name means "One who hears". Left as a hostage in *Egypt* to ensure the *family*'s return (Genesis 42–43).
2. *Tribe* descended from Simeon, allotted territory in the *Negev* (Joshua 19:1–9).
3. Devout man in the *Temple* who, having been told he would see *Messiah* before dying, blessed the infant *Jesus*, prophesying his future and *Mary*'s pain (Luke 2:25–35). His *prayer*, called the "Nunc Dimittis" from its opening words in *Latin*, is still used in *worship* by some *churches*.

Simon Peter
See *Peter*

Sin
Used to translate several words in the *Bible* describing disobedience to God. In the *Old Testament* key *Hebrew* words literally mean: missing the mark or deviating from a norm, rebellion, twisting or perverting, and straying from the correct path. In the *New Testament* the *Greek* words mean: missing a target or taking a wrong road, a blunder or misdeed, transgression or going beyond the norm, ungodliness, lawlessness, *evil*, and wickedness. pp. 22, 24, 28, 32, 37, 43, 69, 74, 77, 84, 103, 125, 127–28, 139, 148–49, 157, 165, 170, 180, 185, 190–91, 194

Sin, Desert of
Wilderness area in the *Sinai* Peninsula where the *Israelites* grumbled but were provided with *quail* and *manna* (Exodus 16). p. 27

Sinai
Mountain in the Sinai Peninsula, also known as Mount *Horeb*, probably modern Jebel Musa, where God made his *covenant* with *Israel* and gave them the *Ten Commandments* and the *Law* (Exodus 19ff.). pp. 13, 19, 26–27, 34, 49, 56, 82, 112, 117–118, 130, 132, 134, 136, 146, 168

Singleness p. 87

Slavery, slaves pp. 20, 26, 29, 47, 54, 82, 87, 89, 106, 119, 123, **126–27**, 129, 134, 138, 144, 155, 159, 178, 183, 190, 193

Smyrna
City in western Asia (modern Izmir), at the forefront of emperor

worship and with a large Jewish community that opposed the *church*, which received one of the Letters to the Seven Churches in *Revelation* (2:8–11). Polycarp, bishop of Smyrna, was an early Christian *martyr* (AD 155).

Snakes pp. 59, 61, 125

Social justice p. 193

Sodom
See *Gomorrah*

Solomon
Israel's third king (970–930 BC), *David*'s son, renowned for his *wisdom* (1 Kings 3:5–15; 4:29–34), building of the *Temple* (1 Kings 6, 8), and strengthening of the nation (1 Kings 9:15–28). However, his many foreign wives, married to forge alliances, turned his heart from God (1 Kings 11:1–8) and contributed to the kingdom's division after his death (11:9–13), though taxation and conscripted labour also played a significant part (1 Kings 12). pp. 16, 20, 31–34, 39, 52–54, 56–59, 64, 68–69, 82, 93, 103, 109–111, 113, 118, 128, 146–47, 153–54, 185

Son of Man
Jesus' favourite title for himself, used instead of *Messiah*, which carried too many nationalistic overtones. Its background is the *Old Testament* where "son of man" speaks of humanity in its frailty (Psalm 8:3–4; Ezekiel 2:1), yet also of a heavenly figure given "authority, glory and sovereign power... an everlasting dominion that will not pass away... a kingdom... that will never be destroyed" (Daniel 7:13–14). These two aspects – human yet heavenly – summed up perfectly who Jesus believed he was: God's eternal Son who had come humbly as a man to serve even to the point of death. pp. 42, 163, 187

Song of Songs
Old Testament wisdom book, showing how *love* is to be enjoyed as God's gift, though many have interpreted it allegorically of the love between God and *Israel* or Christ and the *church*. Its *Hebrew* title, "Solomon's Song of Songs", is a Hebrew way of saying *Solomon*'s "greatest of songs". pp. 14, 31, 55–56, 60, 97, 156

Soul
Used in the *Bible* to mean "our whole being", in contrast to Greek philosophy where it meant the immortal aspect locked within the body (an idea carried over, erroneously, into some Christian thinking). People are not separate "bits" (body, soul, mind, spirit) but physical–psychological–spiritual entities. When *Jesus* spoke of loving God "with all your heart and with all your soul and with all your mind and with all your strength" (Mark 12:30), he meant "with all your being". When *Paul* prayed, "May your whole spirit, soul and body be kept blameless" (1 Thessalonians 5:23), he wasn't identifying different aspects of humanity, but meant "your whole life".

Sovereignty
God's complete over-ruling of circumstances to further his purposes. p. **41**

Spirit
See *Holy Spirit*

Spiritual gifts
Gifts given by the *Holy Spirit*, some heightening natural abilities, some more clearly supernatural, a hallmark of early *church* life and *evangelism*. p. 189

Sport pp. 40, 54, **79**, 106, 122–23

Star of Bethlehem p. 166

Stephen
Greek-speaking *Jew*, one of the seven men chosen to take responsibility for practical matters in the *Jerusalem* church (Acts 6:1–7). Though practical, he was "full of *faith* and the *Holy Spirit*" (6:5) and his *preaching* and *miracles* (6:8) provoked such opposition that he became the first Christian *martyr* (Acts 6:8 – 7:60).

Submission pp. 32, 85, 129, **183**

Suetonius
Roman historian (c. AD 70–130) who noted in one of his works that Claudius expelled the *Jews* from *Rome* for causing disturbances "at the instigation of Chrestus", probably a reference to Christ. He also blamed *Nero* for starting the Great Fire of *Rome*.

Suffering
Generally seen as the natural consequence of life in a fallen *world* rather than the result of personal *sin* (e.g. John 9:1–3). *Job* discovered the solution to suffering lies not in asking "why?" but in finding God afresh. The *cross* is shown as demonstrating God's ability to turn suffering into good, and it was here that Christ broke *Satan*'s power, making possible the end-time new creation where there will be no more death, *mourning*, or pain (Revelation 21:4).

Sumer, Sumerians
Southern part of *Mesopotamia* and its inhabitants, whose settlements go back to the seventh millennium BC. City-states developed in the fourth millennium BC alongside the *Tigris* and *Euphrates*, reaching the height of their power in the third millennium BC. It was here that writing, art, architecture, and technology developed. pp. 22, 49, **62–63**, 120, 125, 127–28

Supernatural pp. 124, 143, **144–45**, 151, 175

Susa
Winter residence of *Persian* kings, where *Nehemiah* served (Nehemiah 1:1), where *Esther*'s story unfolds (Esther 1:2), and where one of *Daniel*'s visions was set (Daniel 8:2). pp. 24, 35, 37, 39–40, 76, 83

Sychar
Town in *Samaria* where *Jesus* talked with a *Samaritan* woman at *Jacob*'s well (John 4). Probably Old Testament *Shechem*.

Synagogue
Greek for "gathering", the gathering place of *Jews*, established during the *exile* when they were far from the *Temple*, a venue for reading the *Law*, hearing sermons, *prayer*, and friendship. pp. 38–39, 41, 46, 90–91, 102, 141, 147, 169

Synoptics, the
Name given by scholars to *Matthew*'s, *Mark*'s, and *Luke*'s *Gospels*, which all have a similar content and order of material. The word means "same viewpoint". p. 165

Syria
Old Testament name for *Aram*, nation to the north of *Israel*. pp. 15, 20–21, 29, 34, 40–41, 46, 49, 52, 60, 62, 64, 66–68, 70, 73, 80, 82, 112, 119–120, 166

T

Tabernacle
Tent used as a meeting place with God during Israel's *wilderness* journey and during the early monarchy. pp. 26–27, 29, 52, 54–55, 67, 95–96, 122, 134, 138–40, 146, 148–49

Tabernacles, Feast of
Festival celebrating harvest, when the *Israelites* lived in shelters to remember their journey to the *Promised Land* and God's provision during it (Exodus 23:16; Leviticus 23:33–43; Numbers 29:12–40; Deuteronomy 16:13–15). pp. 95, 122, 139

Tacitus
Roman historian (c. AD 56–117) who noted that *Nero* blamed *Christians* for the Great Fire of *Rome*, and that their founder, "Christus", was executed under Pontius *Pilate*, which prompted an outbreak of "mischievous superstition". p. 21

Talmud
Collection of Jewish writings, including "Mishnah" (the oral law, completed by AD 200) and "Gemara" (rabbinic comments on the Mishnah dating from AD 200 to 500), considered binding for Orthodox *Jews*. Helpful in seeing how Jews interpreted the *Old Testament*. p. 21

Targum
Aramaic translation or paraphrase of part of the *Old Testament* to facilitate understanding and study. Rabbinic tradition believes this was what happened when *Ezra* read the *Law* and the *Levites* had responsibility for "making it clear" (Nehemiah 8:8), though no evidence exists for targums at such an early date.

Tarshish
City in the western Mediterranean, possibly in Spain, to which *Jonah* tried to flee when God sent him to preach in *Nineveh* (Jonah 1:3).

Tarsus
Principal city of Cilicia in *Asia Minor*, home of the apostle *Paul* (Acts 21:39), an important commercial centre and university city. Hair from the region's goats was used for tent-making, which became a specialized occupation in Cilicia, one that Paul himself learned (Acts 18:3). pp. 24, 40, 46, 92

Tax collectors pp. 103, 111, 115, 169, 178

Taxes pp. 103, **111**, 115, 153, 169, 178

Tekoa
Town in *Judean* hills, home of *Amos* (Amos 1:1).

Tell
Archaeological mound. pp. **48**, 71

Temple
Focal point of Jewish *worship*, built in *Jerusalem* by *Solomon*, destroyed by *Babylon*, rebuilt on a smaller scale by returning exiles, and massively developed by Herod the Great. pp. 16–17, 20, 31–33, 36–40, 44, 47, 49, 53, 56–57, 65, 69, 75–76, 79–82, 94–95, 109–110, 114–116, 122, 136, 138–43, **146–47**, 153–55, 169, 180–85, 188, 194

Temple, Cleansing of p. 183

Temptation
Seen in the *Bible* as *Satan*'s attempts to lead God's people into wrongdoing, as he tried with *Jesus* at the start of his ministry (Luke 4:1–13). Jesus taught his *disciples* to pray, "Lead us not into temptation, but deliver us from the evil one" (Matthew 6:13), and the *New Testament* warns *Christians* to be constantly on their guard against temptation (1 Corinthians 10:12–13; Ephesians 6:10–18; James 1:12–16; 1 Peter 1:8–9), encouraging them that Jesus is always at hand (Hebrews 2:18; 4:15–16).

Ten Commandments
The heart of the *Law* given on *Mount Sinai*. pp. 13, 26, 37, 69, 121–22, 126, 130–33, **134**, 135, 138, 143, 146, 157

Tents p. 92

Testimony p. 163

Thebes
Ancient capital of *Egypt*, modern Karnak. Despite its remoteness down the *Nile*, it fell to *Assyria* in 663 BC.

Theocracy
Government under the direct rule of God or through his appointed intermediary. From the *Greek* "theokratia", meaning "rule of God".

Theophilus
Roman official to whom *Luke* dedicated his two works (Luke 1:3; Acts 1:1), possibly his patron.

Thessalonica
Chief city of *Macedonia* where *Paul* planted a *church* on his second *missionary* journey (Acts 17:1–10) and to which he wrote two letters (1 & 2 Thessalonians) in AD 50/51. pp. 20, 46

Thomas
One of *Jesus*' twelve *apostles* (Matthew 10:3), also called Didymus ("the twin") (John 11:16), renowned for doubting the *resurrection*, but who quickly acknowledged Jesus as "my Lord and my God" once he saw him (John 20:24–29).

Thyatira
City in the Roman province of Asia, important for the production of dye, clothes, pottery, and brass-work, home of *Lydia* who became a *Christian* in *Philippi* (Acts 16:11–15). The *church* here received one of the Letters to the Seven Churches (Revelation 2:18–29), warning them to beware of teaching that was leading them astray.

Tiberias
Spa town on the western shore of Lake *Galilee*, which is sometimes referred to as the Sea of Tiberias (John 6:1; 21:1).

Tiglath-Pileser III
King of *Assyria* (745–727 BC) whose expansionist policies included invading *Israel* (2 Kings 15:29). pp. 20, 35, 72–73

Tigris
Second of *Mesopotamia*'s two great rivers, 1,150 miles (1,850 km) long, whose name ("the Tiger") reflects its faster flowing nature than the more leisurely *Euphrates*. The great *Assyrian* cities of *Nineveh*, Calah, and Ashur arose along its banks. pp. 38, 48–49, 62, 72, 83

Time p. **117**

Timothy
Christian from *Lystra*, *Paul*'s spiritual son (1 Timothy 1:2,18) who accompanied him on his second *missionary* journey (Acts 16:1–5). Sent as Paul's representative to *Thessalonica* (1 Timothy 3:1–3, 6), *Macedonia* (Acts 19:22) and *Corinth* (1 Corinthians 4:17), and to lead the *church* in *Ephesus* (1 Timothy 1:3). Lacking confidence, he often needed *Paul*'s encouragement (1 Timothy 4:12; 2 Timothy 2:1–7).

Tithes, tithing
Giving one-tenth of your income to God (Leviticus 27:30–33; Deuteronomy 14:22–29). Although commanded in the *Law*, the *patriarchs* tithed before the Law was given (Genesis 14:18–20; 28:20–22). While *Jesus* never referred to tithing, it is likely he did so as a practising Jew, and he never abolished it, simply insisting it be done with the right attitude (Matthew 23:23–24). But he also went way beyond tithing, commending the widow who gave all that she had (Luke 21:1–4). pp. 52, 54, **115**, 135, 152, 180

Titus
Gentile convert, whom *Paul* described as "my true son" (Titus 1:4) and "my partner and fellow-worker" (2 Corinthians 8:23). Accompanied Paul and *Barnabas* to *Jerusalem* (Galatians 2:1–3) and sent by Paul to *Corinth* to deal with difficulties in the *church*, returning with good news (2 Corinthians 7:5–16). Returned to Corinth to organize the offering for Jerusalem (2 Corinthians 8:16 – 9:15) and left by Paul to *work* with the church in *Crete* (Titus 1:5). Recipient of the letter bearing his name.

Tobiah
Ammonite opponent of *Nehemiah* who tried to stop him rebuilding *Jerusalem*'s walls (Nehemiah 2:10; 4:1–23).

Toilets pp. 93, 95, 120

Tongues, speaking in
pp. 44, **189**

Topheth
Area in the *Hinnom Valley* outside *Jerusalem* where *altars* were erected for child sacrifice, something forbidden in the *Law* (Leviticus 18:21; Deuteronomy 18:10). Destroyed during *Josiah*'s reforms (2 Kings 23:10; Jeremiah 7:30–32).

Torah
See *Law*

Trachonitis
District in Herod Philip's tetrarchy to the northeast of *Galilee*. p. 119

Trade pp. 20, 24–25, 27, 31–32, 46, 50, 62–63, 68, 78, 82, 85, 90, 96, 103, 107–108, **110–111**, **114–115**, 117, 160, 182, 189

Transfiguration
God's glory manifested in *Jesus* on *Mount Hermon* (Matthew 17:1–13; Mark 9:2–13; Luke 9:28–36) when *Moses* and *Elijah* appeared, representing the *Law* and the *prophets*' witness to him, and when God confirmed he was his Son.

Transjordan
Land to the east of the *Jordan* occupied by *Reuben*, *Gad*, and half of *Manasseh*. pp. **50–51**, 82

Travel pp. 24, 43, 45–47, 63, 70, 80–81, 97, 100, 107, 110–111, **112–113**, 121, 141, 160, 173, 187

Trees and shrubs pp. **55–57**

Tribes of Israel
Descendants of the twelve sons of *Jacob* whose name was changed to *Israel*. pp. 25, 29, 32, 52, 84, 108, 149, 178

Tribute
Payment made by one nation to another as a mark of subjugation. pp. 35–36, 73

Trinity
Christian doctrine that the one God exists simultaneously in three persons, Father, Son, and *Holy Spirit*, such is his complexity. pp. 84, 158, **165**

Troas
Port 10 miles (16 km) from Troy in northwest Turkey where *Paul* had a *vision* of a *Macedonian* man calling for help, leading to the *gospel* going into Europe (Acts 16:8–12).

Trophimus
Christian from *Ephesus* who accompanied *Paul* to *Jerusalem* (Acts 20:4; 21:29), and who was left in *Corinth* when he got sick (2 Timothy 4:20).

Twelve, the
Expression used of *Jesus*' group of twelve *apostles* (e.g. Matthew 20:17; 26:20; Mark 4:10; 9:35; Luke 8:1; 22:3; John 6:67–70; 1 Corinthians 15:5; Revelation 21:14).

Tyre
Phoenician seaport with two harbours, one on the mainland, one on an offshore island, making it virtually impregnable, as *Babylon* discovered when it took thirteen years to conquer it. Its fall was foretold by the *prophets* because of its pride (e.g. Isaiah 23; Ezekiel 26–28). pp. 24, 32, 35, 37, 39–40, 45, 48, 68–69, 82, 106, 109–110, 112, 145, 189

U

Upper room
Setting for the *Last Supper* and, traditionally, the giving of the *Holy Spirit* at *Pentecost*, though the latter is more likely to have happened in the *Temple* courtyard. pp. 154, 183, 188

Ur
City of southern *Mesopotamia*,

home of *Abraham*'s family (Genesis 11:31), from where God took him to the *Promised Land*. pp. 24, 62–63

Uriah
Hittite officer in *David*'s army whom David conspired to have killed to hide his adultery with his wife *Bathsheba* (2 Samuel 11). p. 31

Urim and Thummim
Two stones carried in a pouch in the *high priest*'s *breastpiece* (Exodus 28:30) that were manipulated to seek God's *guidance*. One theory is that one side of both stones was the "yes" side, while the other side was the "no" side. Two same sides gave you an answer, while different sides meant "no answer". References to people "enquiring of the Lord" almost certainly refer to using Urim and Thummim (e.g. Judges 1:1–2; 1 Samuel 14:36–37; 23:1–2; 2 Samuel 2:1). Their use didn't guarantee an answer, however (e.g. 1 Samuel 28:6). For some reason, their use seems to have disappeared after the early monarchy, not reappearing until the *return from exile* (Ezra 2:63; Nehemiah 7:65). p. 148

Uzzah
Man who touched the *ark of the covenant* and was struck dead for doing so (2 Samuel 6).

Uzziah
See *Azariah*

V

Valley of Aijalon
Place where the sun is said to have stood still while *Joshua* fought the *Amorites* (Joshua 10).

Valley of Dry Bones
Vision of *Ezekiel* in which dry bones came to life and became an army, symbolic of how God would restore his people (Ezekiel 37).

Vashti
Queen of *Persia*, deposed by her husband *Xerxes* for refusing to appear at a banquet, and replaced by *Esther* (Esther 1–2).

Vegetables pp. 54, 95, **98**, 125

Vegetarianism p. **99**

Via Maris
See *Way of the Sea*

Vine, vineyard
Shrub producing clusters of green or black grapes, planted in rows on sunny slopes in vineyards. The vine became a national emblem of *Israel*, and *Jesus* spoke of himself as the True Vine, the New Israel (John 15:1). pp. 34, 50, 52, 54, 57, 59, 92, 99, 104, 170, 173, 178

Virgin Birth
Mary's conception of *Jesus* while still a virgin through the intervention of the *Holy Spirit*, essential for the *incarnation*. pp. 42, 165

Visions
Something seen by the recipient while asleep, in a dream, or in a trance, through which God brings *revelation* (e.g. Genesis 15:1; Isaiah 1:1; Ezekiel 1:1; Luke 1:22; Acts 10:9–23; 16:9–10). *Joel* said visions would be common in the Messianic Age (Joel 2:28, quoted by *Peter*, Acts 2:17).

Visitors pp. 24, 31, 72, 84, 92, **97**, 113, 123, 164, 167

Vow
A pledge to do something (e.g. Genesis 28:20–22; Numbers 21:1–3) or refrain from doing something (e.g. Psalm 132:2–5) in return for God's favour or as an expression of devotion. Vows were binding (Deuteronomy 23:23) so weren't to be made rashly (Proverbs 20:25).

Vulgate
Latin translation of the *Bible* by Jerome in the fourth century AD. pp. 15–17, 145

W

Warfare pp. 26, 40–41, 47, 50, 58, 68, 71–74, 76, 80, 84, 126, 128–29, 193

Watchtower
Built in *vineyards* for watchmen to look out for thieves or foxes (e.g. Isaiah 5:1–2; Mark 12:1). More complex towers were built into the walls of larger cities to look out for enemies (e.g. 2 Kings 9:17). The *prophets* were meant to be spiritual watchmen, looking out for threats to *Israel*'s life (Ezekiel 3:17; Hosea 9:8). pp. 34, 104

Water pp. 20, 23, 27–28, 30, 34, 36–37, 41, 48, 51, 56, 58–60, 72, 92–93, **94–95**, 96, 98–99, 102–104, 107–108, 112, 121, 124–25, 138, 143, 154, 164, 173–74, 184–85

Water supplies pp. 27, 37, 72, **94**, 99, 102, 129

Way of the Sea
Also called the Via Maris, the coastal road running from *Memphis* in *Egypt* through *Canaan* to *Tyre* and *Sidon*, before turning east to Aleppo in *Syria*.

Wedding at Cana pp. 86, 174

Weddings pp. 86–87, 122, 169, 172, 174, 177–79, 194

Weights and Measures
pp. 63, **116–117**

Well
See *Water supplies*

Wholeness
Hebrew "shalom" (meaning "peace"), including health, prosperity, security, friendship, and *salvation*. pp. **124–25**

Widows
The object of special care in the *Bible* (e.g. Deuteronomy 24:17–21; 1 Timothy 5:3–16), especially those who were childless (e.g. Genesis 38; Deuteronomy 25:5–10), and the focus of God's particular attention (e.g. Psalm 68:5). The early *church* stressed the importance of caring for widows (e.g. Acts 6:1–7; James 1:27). pp. 16, 34, 87–88, 115, 174

Wilderness
The *Hebrew* words translated "wilderness" or "desert" include not only desolate wastes of sand and rock but also steppe land suitable for grazing. Often used to refer to the *Judean* wilderness west of the *Dead Sea* and the *Sinai* peninsula crossed by the *Israelites* on their way from *Egypt* to *Canaan*. See map, pp. 27–28, 61, 94, 99, 124, 134, 168, 173

Wildlife pp. 60, 98

Wine
Most common drink in Bible times, reflected in the many *Hebrew* words for it, made from the fermented juice of grapes. pp. 51, 54–55, 57, 78, 81, 86, 99, 104, 111, 116, 125, 132, 139, 141, 159, 174, 183

Wisdom
Pursuit of success through God-centred living, letting God shape every aspect: intellectual (understanding the truth), ethical (living the truth) and practical (using the truth). *Solomon*'s reign saw huge interest in wisdom and it was around this time that the Wisdom books (*Job, Proverbs, Ecclesiastes, Song of Songs*) were written. pp. 12, 14, 16–17, 31, 78, 81, 90–91, 119, 156–57

Witness
See *Testimony*

Wool
Basic clothing fabric in Bible times, its value reflected in its inclusion in the annual *tribute* paid to *Israel* by *Moab* (2 Kings 3:4). Its whiteness after washing was used to symbolize purity (e.g. Isaiah 1:18). pp. 59, 93, 100–101, 105

Word of God
1. God's message or *revelation* delivered through *prophets* or the *Law*, which carries God's authority and therefore demands obedience. Because it is God's word, adding to it or taking from it is seen as dangerous (e.g. Revelation 22:18–19).
2. Title used by *John* for *Jesus* (John 1:1, 14; 1 John 1:1). Readers from a Jewish background understood the Word as a dynamic reality that carried out God's will (Psalm 107:20), even personifying it (Proverbs 8:22–31); readers from a Greek background understood the Word ("Logos") as a philosophical term, first used by Heraclitus to designate what held an ever-changing world together and gave it order. To both *Jews* and Greeks, John was saying: this Logos that you believe in is Jesus. He is the one who created everything, holds everything together, brings God's word, carries out God's will, and alone makes sense of life. pp. 12–14, 75, 89–90, 146, 150–51, 153, 168, 171

Work
Gift of God to humanity at *creation* (Genesis 2:15), part of being made in God's image, for he too works (Genesis 2:2; John 14:10). The *fall* didn't curse work, but rather led to it being characterized by hardship rather than pleasure (Genesis 3:17). pp. 22, 71, 87, 92, 105, 109, 122, 138, 156–57, 166

Works
1. The works of God, his activity in *creation* and history (e.g. Job 26:13–14; Psalm 8).
2. The works of *faith*, doing good deeds as the natural expression of faith (e.g. Matthew 5:16; James 2:14–26).
3. The works of the *Law*, attempts to get right with God or win his favour by what we do, which the *New Testament* says can save no

one (e.g. Romans 3:20; Galatians 2:15–16; Ephesians 2:8–9).

World
1. The created universe (e.g. Psalm 24:1; John 1:9).
2. People (Psalm 9:8; John 3: 16–17).
3. The world system in rebellion against God (e.g. James 4:4; 1 John 2:15–17).

Worship
Expression of devotion to God. pp. 17 24, 31, 34, 36, 46, 52, 59, 65, 67–69, 71, 73–74, 77, 81, 88, 118, 122, 127, 130, **140–41**, 142–47, 154, 159, 164, 167, 183, 185, 189, 190

Worship, Places of pp. 141, **146–47**

Writing pp. 13–15, 18–19, 26, 33, 41, 44, 62–63, 73, 79, 82, 89, 91, 108, 116, **120–21**, 124, 157, 163, 170, 193

X

Xerxes I
Also called Ahasuerus, king of *Persia* 486–465 BC, who assembled a huge army to conquer Greece but failed (480–479 BC). He married *Esther* (c. 460 BC) who foiled an attempt to exterminate the *Jews* (Esther 3:1 – 9:17). pp. 39, 76

Y

Yahweh
God's personal name, revealed to *Moses* (Exodus 3:14), comprising in *Hebrew* just four consonants: YHWH – sometimes called by scholars the Tetragrammaton (*Greek* for "four letters") – whose vowels today we can only guess, but which was probably read as Yahweh. Historically translated "Jehovah" or, in many English Bibles, "the LORD" in lower case capitals. pp. 26, 34, 38, 51, 68–69, 71, 88, 118, 130–31

Yoke
1. Wooden frame between two oxen enabling them to pull loads or a plough. Used metaphorically of describing someone's subjection to another (e.g. Exodus 6:7, 1 Kings 12:4) or alignment with another, for good or bad (2 Corinthians 6:14; Philippians 4:3).
2. The area ploughed by a yoke of oxen in one day, about an acre, called a "jugerum" by the Romans. p. 117

Z

Zacchaeus
Tax collector in *Jericho* who climbed a tree to see *Jesus* and to whose home Jesus invited himself (Luke 19:1–10). pp. 53, 57, 111

Zadok
Priest at *David*'s court (2 Samuel 8:17) who was entrusted with the *ark of the covenant* when David fled *Jerusalem* (2 Samuel 15:23–29) and who anointed *Solomon* as king (1 Kings 1:32–48). His descendants served as *high priests* until 171 BC, when *Antiochus IV Epiphanes* transferred the role to Menelaus, though *Qumran* stayed loyal to the Zadokite priesthood.

Zarephath
Phoenician town between *Tyre* and *Sidon* where *Elijah* stayed with a widow during a drought, for whom he performed a miracle of provision and whose son he restored from the dead (1 Kings 17:7–24).

Zealots
Guerrilla fighters who believed *Israel*'s only king was God, so strongly opposed *Rome*'s rule. Responsible for several revolts, one of which led to *Jerusalem*'s destruction in AD 70. One of *Jesus*' *disciples*, Simon, had been a Zealot (Mark 3:17–18). pp. 47, **153**, 169

Zebulun
1. *Jacob*'s tenth son, born through *Leah*, whose name means "Honour" (Genesis 30:19–20).
2. *Tribe* named after him that settled in southern *Galilee* between land occupied by *Asher* and *Naphtali* (Joshua 19:10–16). Although one of the smaller tribal areas, it was very fertile. p. 84

Zechariah
1. King of *Israel* who reigned for just six months before being assassinated in 753 BC (2 Kings 15:8–12).
2. *Prophet* who, with *Haggai*, encouraged God's people to complete the rebuilding of the *Temple* after the *return from exile* (Ezra 5:1–2; 6:14) and whose prophecies are recorded in the book of his name.
3. *Priest*, father of *John the Baptist*, who was struck dumb for his unbelief at the *angel*'s message until John's birth (Luke 1:5–25, 57–66). His song of praise on naming John, called the Benedictus ("Praise be"), is still used by some Christian traditions.

Zedekiah
1. Last king of *Judah* (597–586 BC), who rebelled against *Nebuchadnezzar* who appointed him (2 Kings 24:15–17; Jeremiah 37:1), leading to *Jerusalem*'s destruction and *Judah*'s *exile* (2 Kings 25). pp. 33, 37, 75
2. Leader of false prophets at *Ahab*'s court (1 Kings 22).

Zephaniah
Prophet in *Judah* during the reign of *Josiah*, whose prophecies are recorded in the book of his name. pp. 37, 73

Zerubbabel
Grandson of *Jehoiachin*, one of the leaders of the first group of returning exiles in 537 BC (Ezra 2:1–2), who instigated rebuilding the *Temple* (Ezra 3). The work was hindered until 520 BC, when Zerubbabel once again took a lead (Ezra 5–6; Haggai 1–2).

Zeus
Chief god of the Greeks (called Jupiter by the Romans). *Barnabas* was mistaken for Zeus and *Paul* for Hermes in *Lystra* after healing a lame man (Acts 14:8–18). pp. 40, 78, 80–81, 97

Zilpah
Servant of *Leah*, *Jacob*'s wife, who bore Jacob two of his sons, *Gad* and *Asher*.

Zion
Name of the southernmost hill of a *Jebusite* city, located on the boundary of *Judah* and *Israel*, captured by *David* and made the capital of his united kingdom (2 Samuel 5:6–10), also known as *Jerusalem*. As the city expanded, Zion was applied to the whole city, especially in prophetic and poetic descriptions. pp. 27, 30, 38, 53, 110, 113, 154, 185

Photographs

Cover and title page: Getty Images, Shutterstock and Mike Beaumont

b = bottom
bkg = background
c = centre
l = left
r = right
t = top

AdobeStock/Violeta 5br

AKG images 13tl, 17tl; /Erich Lessing 112br, 120c

Alamy Stock Photo/Anthony Briselden 118; /Art Directors & TRIP 191; / ASAP 138; /Danita Delimont 110; /dpa picture alliance 193tr; /Duby Tal/ Albatross 32,177tr; /gameover 27; /Glyn Thomas Photography 11; /Hanan Isachar 148; /Haydn Hansell 149br; /Hoberman Publishing 127cr; /Horizons WWP 84bkg, 84; /Jon Arnold Images Ltd 18; /Jurijus Dukinas 8b, 146tr; / Kevin Foy 157b; /Magica 28; /PhotoStock-Israel 150; /Prisma Archivo 5tr, 26c; /robertharding 23cr, 178; /The Picture Art Collection 91t; /The Print Collector 85; /Tim Graham 177tl; /Werner Otto 123; /World History Archive 26br; /World Religions Photo Library 107tc; /Zev Radovan 35, 124, 126

Bible Land Pictures Zev Radovan 13br, 15tl, 19, 20, 21, 24, 33, 37c, 40, 48cl, 63t, 66, 67, 68b, 71t, 73t, 86, 100 bkg, 100b, 108bc, 109bl, 115t, 140t, 140b, 187

Bridgeman Images/Alfredo Dagli Orti 151; /© Cameraphoto Arte Venezia 4–5bc, 22–23t; /© Godong 132; /Granger 131; /© Jean Bernard. All rights reserved 2025 / Collection fondation regards de Provence, Marseille 25; /© Israel Museum, Jerusalem /purchased and donated by The Feuchtwanfer Collection 87; /© Look and Learn 175b; /© Luisa Ricciarini 121tl; /©NPL - DeA Picture Library / G. Nimatallah 116c; /© Trinity College Library Dublin 162; /© Vicky Alhadeff. All rights reserved 2025 89t; /© Zev Radovan 145br

British Museum © The Trustees of the British Museum 7cr, 51cr, 77tr, 116bl

David Alexander 22, 70br

Gettyimages/35007 189; /brunette 130; /by-studio 157t; /clamon 184cl; /dislentev 144; /Dorling Kindersley 146b; /edelmar 15cr; /Ekaterina Chuyko 195; /GlobalP 6cl , 58tr, 58cr, 59tl, 59cr; /Grafissimo 17cr, 111cr; / HomoCosmicos 38b, 63b; /Hulton Archive 41b; /Instants 170; /iStock 59bl; /jacquesvandinteren 7b; /kavram 9; KevinHolt 145tl; /lilly3 114b; LiorFil 175t; /Luso 114t; /Mindaugas Dulinskas 47; /pawopa3336 105b; /Petershort 58bl; Photos.com 120br; /pixelfusion3d 194bl; /RnDmS 190; /RobertoDavid 75; /sodapix sodapix 158; /tupungato 107tr; /whitemay 194br; /Yehoshua Halevi 137br

Hanan Isachar 45

Mike Beaumont 3, 6cr, 6b, 8cr, 14, 29, 30br, 36, 37l, 41t, 42, 43tl, 43cr, 44, 48c, 48b, 51t, 52, 65tl, 65tr, 65bc, 68t, 69t, 71b, 79tl, 79tr, 79b, 81, 90, 91bl, 92, 93b, 94, 95tl, 95b, 97t, 98cr, 99, 101tr, 101bl, 103tl, 103c, 104, 105tr, 106, 107b, 108cr, 109tr, 111tl, 112tr, 113, 116tr, 121cr, 122t, 122b, 125t, 129t, 137tl, 139b, 141, 142, 143, 152, 155t, 155b, 159t; 160; 161b, 164, 165, 166, 167tl, 167tr, 168t, 168b, 173b, 174, 176, 179, 183cl, 183b, 184b, 185, 186, 188, 192b

Photolibrary.com 50bkg

rawpixel 98bl

Robert Harding/Duby Tal 171

Shutterstock/Borna_Mirahmadian 77bl; /Dan Shachar 97bl; /David Leshem 7cl; /Delpixel 161t; /Dima Moroz 74; /Dmitriy Feldman svarshik 153; / FooTToo 125c; /Kamira 128–129b; /Luis Roco 173t; /Marcin Kadziolka 159b; /Offthecouchexperience 34; /Peng Heng Lim 133; /Teo K 181; / ZoranOrcik 136

Sonia Halliday Photographs 69b, 88 bkg, 89br, 102

The Schøyen Collection, Oslo and London MS2064 8l, 135; MS3032 127tl

Topfoto 88br

Wikimedia Commons 134, 156, 193cl; /cjh1452000 192t; /Joyofmuseums 38tr; /Ppja 95tr; /Robert Griffin, London 73b

Maps

Cosmographics 78

NASA, MODIS Rapid Response Team at GSPC (satellite image), Andy Rous and HL Studios (artwork) 82–83

Oxford Designers and Illustrators 72

Richard Watts 27, 64, 80, 119, 169, 182

Simon Emery 24, 58, 31, 32, 35, 37, 39, 40, 46, 48, 49, 50, 53, 62, 66, 70, 74, 76, 96, 154, 185, 188

Artwork

Lion 112

Mark Stewart 60–61

Martin Sanders 149

Rex Nicholls 54–55

Roger Kent 56–57

Simon Emery 30, 51

Steve Conlin 147b

Steve Noon 147t